Radical Traditions

REIMAGINING CULTURE IN
BALINESE CONTEMPORARY MUSIC

Andrew Clay McGraw

Oxford University Press is a department of the University of Oxford.
It furthers the University's objective of excellence in research, scholarship,
and education by publishing worldwide.

Oxford New York
Auckland Cape Town Dar es Salaam Hong Kong Karachi
Kuala Lumpur Madrid Melbourne Mexico City Nairobi
New Delhi Shanghai Taipei Toronto

With offices in
Argentina Austria Brazil Chile Czech Republic France Greece
Guatemala Hungary Italy Japan Poland Portugal Singapore
South Korea Switzerland Thailand Turkey Ukraine Vietnam

Oxford is a registered trademark of Oxford University Press
in the UK and certain other countries.

Published in the United States of America by
Oxford University Press
198 Madison Avenue, New York, NY 10016

© Oxford University Press 2013

All rights reserved. No part of this publication may be reproduced, stored in a
retrieval system, or transmitted, in any form or by any means, without the prior
permission in writing of Oxford University Press, or as expressly permitted by law,
by license, or under terms agreed with the appropriate reproduction rights organization.
Inquiries concerning reproduction outside the scope of the above should be sent to the Rights
Department, Oxford University Press, at the address above.

You must not circulate this work in any other form
and you must impose this same condition on any acquirer.

Library of Congress Cataloging-in-Publication Data
McGraw, Andrew Clay.
Radical traditions : reimagining culture in Balinese contemporary music / Andrew Clay Mcgraw.
pages cm
Includes bibliographical references and index.
ISBN 978-0-19-994140-7 (hardback : alk. paper)—ISBN 978-0-19-994142-1 (pbk. : alk.
paper) 1. Music—Indonesia—Bali Island—History and criticism. 2. Music—Social aspects—
Indonesia—Bali Island. I. Title.
ML345.I5M25 2013
780.9598—dc23
2013001810

9 8 7 6 5 4 3 2 1
Printed in the United States of America
on acid-free paper

For N.W.M.
In memory of W.S. and M.N.
Siang malem berpikir sendiri, menjadi orang jaman sekarang...
(thinking day and night, how to become a man of today...)
—Geguritan Nengah Jimbaran, 1903

Contents

Acknowledgments ix
About the Companion Website xi
Musical Examples xv
Technical Notes xvii
Map of Bali xix
Preface: Encounter xxi
Prelude: The Scene xxv

1 Introduction 1

2 Placing Bali in the Global Aesthetic Network 14

3 *Kosong*: Developing Culture in the Empty New Order (1966–98) 47

4 *Moha*: Aesthetic and Social Dissensus in the Reformation (1998–) 82

5 *Téori* and the *Komposer* 109

6 The Materials and Technologies of *Musik Kontemporer* 138

7 *Ombak*: Time, Energy, and Homology in the Analysis of Balinese Music 165

8 The Semiotics of *Musik Kontemporer* 193

9 *Musik Kontemporer* and Intercultural Performance 215

10 Conclusion: Reimagining Balinese Culture 236

Glossary 241
Bibliography 245
Index 263

Acknowledgments

THE IDEAS REPRESENTED in this text began percolating nearly fifteen years ago while studying the *gamelan semara dana* in Banjar Kaliungu Kaja in Denpasar under the mentorship of I Ketut Gede Asnawa. I am indebted to his rigorously critical perspective on both Balinese music and society. Since that time I have passed through numerous institutions both as student and teacher and have benefited from innumerable conversations on Balinese music with a wide range of scholars, only some of whom I have space to thank here. I beg forgiveness from those whose names are not listed.

At Wesleyan my advisors Sumarsam, Mark Slobin, and Marc Perlman, and my classmate Christopher J. Miller helped shape my thinking on contemporary *gamelan* music and its relationship to global aesthetic networks. My participation in a number of *gamelan* ensembles on the American east coast allowed me to develop my performance skills while in the states and were often crucibles of conversation on the topics covered in this text. These ensembles include *Gamelan Galak Tika* and *The Boston Village Gamelan* in Boston, *Gamelan Dharma Swara* in New York City, and *Gamelan Raga Kusuma* in Richmond, Virginia. I am deeply grateful to the directors, guest artists, and members of these ensembles for the social, intellectual, and aesthetic harbor they provide.

Any project of this sort is in fact a collaboration between many thinkers. Several members of the global *gamelan* community inspired and helped to develop the ideas presented in this text through their conversation and critiques, these include: I. M. Harjito, Nicole Reisnour, Kate Wakeling, Peter Steele, Wayne Vitale, Evan Ziporyn, Leslie Tilley, Kitsie Emerson, Bethany Collier, Marty Hatch, Nezia Azmi, Laura Noszlopy, Mari Nabeshima, Matthew Isaac Cohen, Ed Herbst, Jody Diamond, Yasuko

Takei, Danis Otnayigus, Aloysius Suwardi, Kendra Stepputat, Lisa Gold, Michael Bakan, Suka Hardjana, Emiko Susilo, David Harnish, Dieter Mack, Peni Candrarini, Sarah Weiss, and Sonja Downing, among others.

I was fortunate to receive a fellowship from the Cornell Society for the Humanities in 2010-2011, when the bulk of this text was written and where I was inspired by the lively conversation among the fellows. This project has been assisted as well at various points by support from the Fulbright-Hayes foundation, the Dharmasiswa program, Arts International, the MidAtlantic Arts Council, the VFIC Foundation, and faculty grants from the University of Richmond. Indonesian institutions including AMINEF, LIPI, and conservatories in Solo, Yogyakarta, Jakarta, and Bali graciously supported my research and residencies.

Special thanks is due to Michael Tenzer both for his inspiring scholarship and for being a model of professionalism and collegiality. I am grateful to Oxford University Press and its editors for their careful attention and gracious willingness to accommodate the many figures, charts, and hours of online ethnographic documentation that accompany this text. I thank Lee Wall for designing and producing the figures in chapters 8 and 10. Two anonymous reviewers provided invaluable comments and suggestions on an inchoate draft. The faults that remain are entirely my own.

This text would not exist if not for the bottomless patience and love of my wife Jessica Zike, my son Noel, and my family in Kansas City, all of whom have for years endured loud practicing at home in alternation with long, silent absences spent abroad.

Finally, I thank the many Balinese composers and performers whose work is the subject of this text. Their generosity and patience in discussing the topics presented here are profoundly humbling. I cannot possibly name each in the space available but those who have had the most direct influence on the present work include: I Ketut Gede Asnawa, I Komang Astita I Wayan Gede Yudane, I Wayan Sadra, Sang Nyoman Arsawijaya, I Madé Subandi, I Gusti Putu Sudarta, I Wayan Beratha, I Dewa Beratha, I Dewa Ketut Alit, Ida Bagus Gede Widnyana, Dr. I Nyoman Catra, Ni Desak Madé Suarti Laksmi, Ni Ketut Suryatini, I Wayan Konolan, I Wayan Loceng, Dr. I Madé Bandem, Dr. I Wayan Dibia, Dr. I Wayan Rai, I Gusti Komin Darta, Dr. Ida Bagus Granoka, I Nyoman Saptanyana, I Nyoman Suadin, I Madé Arnawa, I Nyoman Windha, Pande Madé Sukerta, I Wayan Sinti, Agus Teja, Ni Kadek Dewi Aryani, I Wayan Gede Arsana, I Kadek Suardana, I Madé Sidia, Dr. I Nyoman Sedana, and Dr. I Wayan Sudirana.

About the Companion Website

THROUGHOUT THIS BOOK two different sets of recordings are indicated in the margins. The first of these, *Balinese Voices,* is taken from ethnographic interviews with composers and performers. The symbol ⓔ indicates these. The second of these, *Musik Kontemporer,* is a collection of recordings of performances discussed in this text. The symbol ⓜ indicates these. Those interested may listen to these recordings at www.oup.com/us/radicaltraditions.

Balinese Voices

Track BV-P/1. Arsawijaya discusses his process of composing and performing *Geräusch* (July 2007).
Track BV-P/2. Arsawijaya discusses the dynamic relationship between *kreasi baru* and *musik kontemporer* (July 2007).
Track BV-P/3. Yudane discusses his musical education and early compositions (August 2001).
Track BV-1/1. Arsawijaya discusses tensions between conservatory conservatism and the experimentalism of young composers (July 2009).
Track BV-1/2. Subandi discusses *tradisi radikal* and *ceraken* (July 2011).
Track BV-1/3. Arsana discusses global aesthetic links in *musik kontemporer* (September 2001).
Track BV-2/1. Yudane discusses the intercultural origins of Balinese culture (August 2001).
Track BV-2/2. Sukerta discusses his composition *Asanawali* (December 2002).
Track BV-2/3. Darta and Alit discuss the transformation to a cash economy in the Balinese arts (July 2008, March 2012).
Track BV-3/1. Asnawa discusses composing and performing *Kosong* (August 2001).
Track BV-3/2. Sudarta discusses the aesthetic consequences of the erasure of the PKI (July 2008).

Track BV-3/3. Bandem discusses the relationship between sacred and profane arts in Bali (July 2001).
Track BV-3/4. Astita discusses composing *Eka Dasa Rudra* (September 2001).
Track BV-3/5. Alit discusses tourism and its relationship to music (July 2008).
Track BV-3/6. Yudane critiques the appeal to *tradisi* in the development of new compositions (August 2001).
Track BV-3/7. Prawasari discusses restrictions on the female dancing body (July 2009).
Track BV-3/8. Sudarta discusses the cash economy of contemporary ritual (July 2008).
Track BV-3/9. Bandem discusses the influence of scientific paradigms on conservatory curriculum (September 2002).
Track BV-3/10. Widnyana discusses the conservatory's role in homogenization (March 2012).
Track BV-3/11. Hardjana discusses the history of the PKM (August 2003).
Track BV-3/12. Alit discusses the differing aesthetic atmospheres of Solo and Bali (July 2008).
Track BV-4/1. Arsana discusses composing *Moha* (August 2002).
Track BV-4/2. Arsawijaya discusses definitions of *musik kontemporer* (July 2008).
Track BV-4/3. Arsawijaya discusses popular and serious forms of *musik kontemporer* in Bali (July 2009).
Track BV-4/4. Sadra discusses *musik dialektis* (October 2003).
Track BV-4/5. Sudarta discusses *reformasi* religious reformism (July 2008).
Track BV-4/6. Windha discusses composing *Lekesan* (April 2001).
Track BV-4/7. Sudarta discusses the social impact of migration (July 2008).
Track BV-4/8. Arsawijaya discusses the spread of *slonding* as a medium for *musik kontemporer* (July 2008).
Track BV-5/1. Alit discusses the relationship between composition and *téori* (July 2008).
Track BV-5/2. Arsawijaya discusses rejecting traditional compositional ethics (July 2008).
Track BV-5/3. Arsawijaya and Yudane discuss the role of *tema* and *konsep* in *musik kontemporer* (July 2007, August 2001).
Track BV-5/4. Widnyana discusses *pangus* (July 2010).
Track BV-5/5. Widnyana discusses the tension between individualism and communalism (March 2012).
Track BV-5/6. Hardjana discusses the emergence of the Balinese *komposer* (August 2003).
Track BV-5/7. Suanda discusses his comic compositions (December 2001).
Track BV-5/8. Sukerta discusses his naughty compositions (December 2002).
Track BV-5/9. Subandi discusses the relationship between work and performance (July 2011).
Track BV-5/10. Widnyana discusses authorship and ownership (July 2010).

Track BV-5/11. Asnawa discusses copyright in *reformasi*-era Bali (August 2001).
Track BV-5/12. Sinti discusses the relationship between composer and audience (December 2002).
Track BV-6/1. Arsawijaya discusses computers as a compositional tool (July 2009).
Track BV-6/2. Hendrawan discusses intonation and *diatonis* tunings (July 2009).
Track BV-6/3. Teja and Sudarta discuss Indian viruses (March 2012).
Track BV-6/4. Sadra discusses *transmedium* composition (July 2008).
Track BV-6/5. Sinti critiques festival compositions (December 2002).
Track BV-7/1. Alit and Yudane discuss *ombak* (April 2004, September 2001).
Track BV-8/1. Yudane discusses his broken *gong* form and audience response (March 2012).
Track BV-8/2. Widnyana discusses mode and affect (March 2012).
Track BV-8/3. Widnyana discusses hearing and arranging *Santa Claus Is Coming to Town* (March 2012).
Track BV-8/4. Arsawijaya discusses *kanon* (July 2009).
Track BV-9/1. Aryani discusses intercultural collaboration (July 2009).

Musik Kontemporer

Track MK-S/1. Sang Nyoman Arsawijaya. *Geräusch.*
Track MK-1/1. Madé Subandi. *Ceraken*, excerpt
Track MK-2/1. Wayan Sadra. *Beringin Kurung.*
Track MK-2/2. Pande Madé Sukerta. *Asanawali.*
Track MK-2/3. Ida Bagus Gede Widnyana. *Dadu.*
Track MK-3/1. Ketut Gede Asnawa. *Kosong*, excerpt. From Tenzer (2000), used with permission of the University of Chicago Press.
Track MK-4/1. Wayan Gede Arsana. *Moha.*
Track MK-4/2. Wayan Sudirana. *Kreasi 45.*
Track MK-4/3. Gusti Putu Sudarta. *Kidung Mpu Tantular*, excerpt
Track MK-4/4. Nyoman Windha. *Lekesan.*
Track MK-4/5. Sang Nyoman Arsawijaya. *Slonding Baru*, excerpt
Track MK-5/1. Agus Teja. *Senggama.*
Track MK-6/1. Sang Nyoman Arsawijaya. *Pinara Tunggah*. Sequenced composition.
Track MK-6/2. Sang Nyoman Arsawijaya. *Pinara Tunggah*. Live performance.
Track MK-6/3. Gusti Komin Darta. *Aptiningulun.*
Track MK-6/4. Ida Bagus Gede Widnyana. *Trimbat.*
Track MK-6/5. Wayan Gede Yudane. *Entering the Stream*, excerpt.
Track MK-6/6. Dwiki Dharmawan, Nyoman Windha. *Soul of Indonesia*, excerpt.
Track MK-6/7. Madé Subandi. *Gender Romantis*, excerpt.
Track MK-7/1. *Tabuh Gari*, excerpt (Bali Stereo B761).
Track MK-7/2. Sang Nyoman Arsawijaya. *Pamoksa.*
Track MK-7/3. Dewa Ketut Alit. *Mecaru*, excerpt.
Track MK-7/4. *Lengker*, excerpt (Bali Stereo B706).

Track MK-7/5. *Tabuh Pat Jagul,* excerpt 1 (Vital Records VR 401).
Track MK-7/6. *Pengastung Kara,* excerpt (Vital Records VR 440).
Track MK-7/7. *Tabuh Pat Jagul,* excerpt 2 (Vital Records VR 401).
Track MK-7/8. *Legong Keraton,* excerpt 1 (Maharani RCD-10).
Track MK-7/9. *Legong Keraton,* excerpt 2 (Maharani RCD-10).
Track MK-7/10. *Kebyar Duduk,* excerpt (Vital Records VR 401).
Track MK-7/11. Dewa Ketut Alit. *Salju* (fourth movement).
Track MK-7/12. Sang Nyoman Arsawijaya. *Ambisi.*
Track MK-7/13. Dewa Ketut Alit. *Salju* (first movement).
Track MK-7/14. *Luang,* excerpt.
Track MK-7/15. *Panji Marga,* excerpt (King Records KICC 5127).
Track MK-8/1. Wayan Gede Yudane. *Lebur Seketi,* excerpt (Bali Stereo B918).
Track MK-8/2. *DyDeDi,* excerpt.
Track MK-8/3. Ida Bagus Gede Widnyana. *Santa Claus Is Coming to Town,* excerpt.
Track MK-10/1. Madé Karmawan. *Tajen,* excerpt.

Musical Examples

Ex. 6.1. Sang Nyoman Arsawijaya's double gong structure. 140
Ex. 6.2. Sang Nyoman Arsawijaya's prescriptive notation. 141
Ex. 6.3. Gusti Komin Darta. *Aptiningulun*, excerpt. 142
Ex. 6.4. Ida Bagus Gede Widnyana. *Trimbat* polyrhythm excerpt. 143
Ex. 6.5. Wayan Gede Yudane. *Entering the Stream*, excerpt. 144
Ex. 6.6. Komang Astita. Gema *Eka Dasa Rudra*, pengawak. 153
Ex. 6.7. Leluangan topic. 154
Ex. 6.8. Sang Nyoman Arsawijaya. *Geräusch*, improvisasi excerpt. 156
Ex. 6.9. Sang Nyoman Arsawijaya. *Pinara Tunggah*, konterpoin excerpt. 157
Ex. 6.10. Ida Bagus Gede Widnyana. *Trimbat*, kromatis excerpt. 160
Ex. 6.11. Madé Subandi. *Gender Romantis*, jugalbandi and pohon excerpt. 160
Ex. 6.12. Agus Teja. *Senggama*, excerpt. 161
Ex. 6.13. Gusti Putu Sudarta, *Kidung Mpu Tantular*, qawwali excerpt. 162
Ex. 6.14. Wayan Gede Arsana. *Moha, Cina* excerpt. 163
Ex. 6.15. Nyoman Windha. *Lekesan*, Sasak melody excerpt. 163
Ex. 8.1. Wayan Sadra. *Beringin Kurung*, excerpt. 201
Ex. 8.2. Wayan Gede Yudane. *Lebur Seketi*, excerpt. 200
Ex. 8.3. Sang Nyoman Arsawijaya. *Ambisi*, excerpt. 201

Technical Notes

LANGUAGES: I AVOID extensive use of diacritics in this text, generally following written Indonesian, which uses the Roman alphabet with few modifications. Throughout this book I refer to text translated from various languages. I use the following abbreviations:

B: Balinese
I: Indonesian
J: Javanese
D: Dutch

Translations: All translations, unless otherwise noted, are by the author.

Names: Most Balinese names begin with an honorific: I for men and Ni for women. Because this is rather awkward in English I generally avoid honorifics in this text. This should in no way suggest a lack of respect. Generally, after the first appearance of a full name, I use the last name only. Javanese names are typically singular.

Musical notation and transcription: Following standard practice in the ethnomusicology of Balinese *gamelan* music, I notate the Balinese *pélog* scale in the following manner:

Western Pitch	Balinese Pitch Number	Balinese Pitch Name
C#	1	Ding
D	2	Dong
E	3	Deng
F#	4	Deung
G#	5	Dung
A	6	Dang
B	7	Daing

While actual intonations may vary, this is the generally accepted closest Western equivalent for the most common versions of *pélog* in Bali. I notate the common *selisir* mode as: C#, D, E, G#, A, and the common *tembung* mode as: C#, D, F#, G#, A.

Following the widespread Javanese *kepatihan* form of cipher notation, which is used in adapted forms in Bali, I notate colotomic points thusly:

Gong: O
Kempur: U
Kemong: +

Map of Bali

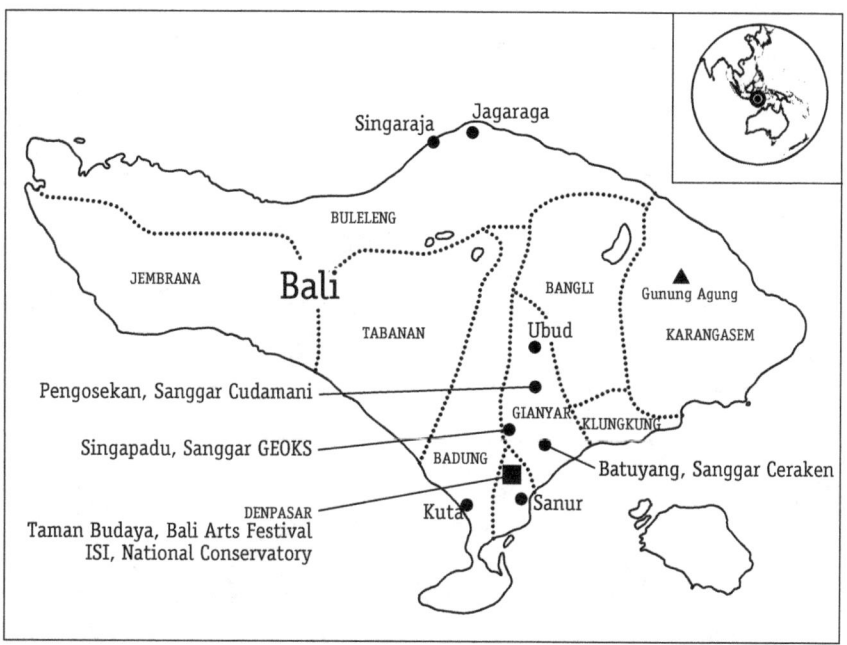

Preface: Encounter

I WAS BORN at the bottom of a primeval ocean. Independence, Missouri, sits upon an ancient seafloor—waves hardened into crumbly limestone. The flat, landlocked middle of America is a homogenous expanse of wheat fields and strip malls extending panoramically to the horizon. Bali floats upon a living sea, and its inhabitants, celebrated in anthropological romances for their communal cultural expressions, orient themselves geocentrically to the peak of an active volcano rising steeply from the small island's center. Many Balinese describe their land as the world's navel, a button riding on the earth's pregnant belly.

A McGraw family bible, a utilitarian 1896 printing sold by Sears Roebuck, includes in its yellowed back pages a map of Noah's posterity, a post-diluvian world ending upon the eastern shore of Java in the Extra Gangem. Just beyond the margin of the page, to the east, is where Bali lies. Posted as a bombardier in Papua during the Second World War, my grandfather made Bali (and the Dutch East Indies) present through hyperbolic war stories. Over time the island's silence beyond the margin grew louder. When the opportunity arose to travel there in 1996, its music (almost unknown to me) was already loud in my imagination.

The ethnographic accounts I discovered in the local library prior to my departure conjured difference with an undeniable precision, assuring me that this place would be the opposite of mine. Jane Belo's *Traditional Balinese Culture* (1970) provided the first tantalizing images.

> To a Westerner, the most striking characteristic in the ordinary behavior of a Balinese is the absolute poise and balance of his bearing, noticeable in his posture, his walk, his slightest gesture. All mature men and women have this poise, and even the small children develop it with remarkable rapidity. Almost never does one see a stooped or curving back even among the old people, and clumsiness and lack of coordination are rare. The impression is that of a nation favored with an unusually fine physique, with natural dignity and ease in every motion.

But together with the impression of ease, one remarks a sort of carefulness in the bearing, as if each foot were placed in its appointed place, each turn of the head or flick of the wrist calculated not to disturb an equilibrium set up, and hanging somewhere unseen within the individual. One learns that the Balinese is never unconscious of his position in space, in relation to *kaja*, north, which is the direction of the mountains, and *kelod*, south, the direction of the sea; and in relation to his position above the ground, which should not be higher than that of his social superior. It would seem that a great deal of the "carefulness" in the manner of the Balinese springs from his habit of adjusting his position according to the laws of his cosmology and his social group.... The individual Balinese moves slowly, with deliberation. Westerners, seeing for the first time films representing the Balinese at their daily tasks, are immediately struck by the slow tempo of their actions. If a man seated in one pavilion of his house-court suddenly wished to show something which is in another pavilion, he will rise to his feet and saunter across the intervening space, quite as if he were going for a casual stroll. He will never hurry, as we would, eager to grasp the object which has come to mind. There is plenty of time, and to hurry would be unusual, unnecessary, and stupid—a waste of energy. Walking along the roads, each individual progresses with an even, measured step. The custom is to walk in a single file.... Rarely does one individual walking in the single file pass another, for all go at the same rhythmic pace. The idea is not to get there more quickly.

The celebratory evocation of community, timelessness, and ceremony I encountered in both the touristic and academic literature (occasionally difficult to differentiate) was repeated to me by many of the Balinese I first encountered. Romantic images accreted in me such that, against overwhelming evidence of a more complex world, my first experience of Bali in 1996 jibed neatly with Belo's account, which was based on fieldwork from the 1930s.

A second trip two years later was spent studying the music of the newly invented *gamelan semara dana* ensemble in the neighborhood of Kaliungu in Denpasar, Bali's densely populated capital. This urban, tightly knit community was known for producing daring composers; the foremost at that time was Wayan Yudane, who accused me of being stupidly naive (I: *naif*), poisoned (I: *diracuni*) by the images of Bali produced by my culture's anthropologists. He sped me off on his motorcycle to see Bali's trash island, an enormous, poorly managed landfill near the resort town of Sanur. Here was a distorted miniature of Gunung Agung, the island's holy volcano, where the collected effluence of Bali's overdeveloped tourist industry was picked over by a population of desperately poor Balinese and Javanese living in caverns dug into the pile. Yudane's point was simple: I'm not going to tell you that Geertz, Belo, McPhee, Mead, Bateson, and all the rest are *wrong*, but this is *also* Bali. Writing in my diary that evening, I toyed with Belo's images, recording in the peculiarly aloof style of the ethnographic present my own experiences of quotidian behavior in contemporary Bali.

To a Westerner, the most striking characteristic in the ordinary behavior of a Balinese is the absolutely frenetic daring of his driving, noticeable in his speed, maneuvers, and seeming total disregard for his own safety and that of all others. The impression is of a nation cursed with an omnipresent death wish, each citizen awkwardly hurling himself ever closer each day to inevitable traction if not death. A foreign observer is struck by the unnatural chaos of this behavior. But together with the impression of unease, one notes a sort of recklessness in the overall bearing of the Balinese, as if each turn, passing, and advance was meant to disrupt the possibility of calm pace and equilibrium within the individual. Lore suggests that the Balinese of yesteryear were always conscious of their relative positions in space and that a great carefulness apparent in their temperament sprang from a habit of adjusting their positions according to the laws of their cosmology and respective social groups. But this carefulness now seems replaced by impulsive and epileptic movements as if bodily stasis might disturb some vital Balinese life force. Westerners experiencing for the first time the Balinese going about their daily commute are immediately struck by the seemingly wasteful bursts of unreasonable speed and the dangerously close proximity with which each driver passes and overtakes another. If a man at home suddenly wishes to take his supper at some traditional café only 100 meters away he will jump upon his motorbike rather than walk. He will fly, unhelmeted and at top speed, towards the café, burning off twice the fuel than he would were he to saunter along in third gear. He will always hurry, as we would only if we were in danger of missing our own wedding or the birth of our children. For the Balinese there is never enough time, and to move slowly, deliberately, and safely would be unusual and annoying—the sign of a slow mind. The idea is to always get there as quickly as possible, an approach most Westerners find highly ironic considering the famously lax attitude the Balinese have towards the actual time of arrival, so-called *jam karet* or rubber time.

Riffing on ethnographic styles reminds us that any account—this one as much as any other—is a highly mediated representation. Describing contemporary activities in the style used to construct the classical anthropological image of the Balinese sounds strange to us for its generalizing allochronism. We know things must be more complicated, more particular than this. But Belo's account cannot simply be exploded as just more Western bourgeois nostalgia; it conforms to an image that many Balinese hold of themselves, a story endlessly recounted to tourists and ethnographers, and so in some ways must be partly true. Many of the composers discussed in the following pages described Belo's account as an image of *tradisi*, traditional Balinese culture, whereas my playful parody was for them a representation of the *moderen*, Balinese experiences of modernity. Both representations perform ethnographic othering. Both emic *and* etic representations of Bali have tended to flatten the reality of lived experience by subsuming the individual into a generic, ethnonational character or ethos and categorizing behavior and expressive culture as either *tradisi* or *moderen*, infrequently recognizing their complex interpenetrations.

For the composers with whom I worked, that there was such a thing as Balinese culture was unquestionable; it was their bread and butter. As represented by much ethnographic and touristic discourse, that culture was synonymous with *tradisi*. As lived in the everyday it seemed very much more *moderen*. Balinese contemporary music—*musik kontemporer*—embodies the apparent tensions between culture as represented and lived, between the idea of Balinese culture and the experience of living it. Its composers capture the feeling of existing within both the actual and the representational, the material-phenomenological and the ethnographic, in all of their apparent incommensuration. The most radical among them figured *musik kontemporer* as a reimagining of Balinese culture itself, one that attempted to nullify the insidious opposition of *tradisi* and *moderen*, perpetuated by Western ethnography, state cultural policy, and regional polemics, as a pointless friction that retarded the natural flow of change.[1]

---

[1] The contemporary Balinese artist A. A. G. Kusumawardana captures this sentiment in a canvas depicting a Balinese painter, his arms and legs chained to the ground, as he paints a traditional *legong* dancer alongside a modern sports car. This painting hung in the private contemporary arts club (I: *sanggar*) Kusumawardana sponsored in Denpasar where several *kontemporer* ensembles rehearsed.

Prelude: The Scene

AUGUST 2005. *The rehearsal was held at a family compound on the northern outskirts of Denpasar. I arrived late, stopping to pick up a few bottles of* bintang *beer at a Circle K on my way from a lesson in Sukawati, a forty-five-minute motorbike ride from the North. I parked my grimy Yamaha in the narrow lane outside the compound and entered yelling a Balinese greeting to no one in particular and that was answered only by a group of children happily surprised by the opportunity to cheer* turis! *(I), tourist. A toothless, topless grandmother, ostensibly monitoring the children, took no notice of me, focusing instead on the Mexican telenovella beamed down from the enormous TVRI*[1] *antennas looming over the compound. Like many of the homes in this part of town, it combined modern and traditional architecture and was organized along the cosmological* kaja-kelod *axis. The rehearsal itself was held near a small courtyard in the far* kaja *corner nearest the holy mountain. This was the family's* sangah, *in which several elaborately carved offering pedestals hosted ancestors and gods. A flock of pigeons wheeled above. The buzzing of the tiny Aeolian harps tied to their feet mixed with the children's squeals and the static of two televisions, a radio, and the humming traffic of the nearby bypass. Incense burned in the* sangah, *commingling with the acrid smell of plastic trash burning in the lane and the shit from the several cocks encaged in wicker baskets set alongside the compound wall, a sharp stench that stirred nostalgia for the family farm in Boonville, Missouri. A young mother, deep circles under her eyes, walked over, dropped an infant in my lap and slipped away.*

The five musicians, young men between nineteen and twenty-five years old, were students at the local government conservatory. Two of them dragged instruments into the rehearsal space while the others compared with detached sobriety pornographic images they had downloaded onto their smartphones. The composer, Sang Nyoman Arsawijaya, was on his hands and knees looking around for electrical outlets. His "ensemble" included two sets of found industrial pipe (apparently scrap from the TVRI aerial) struck with metal hammers, a set of gamelan *keys amplified and distorted using guitar pedals and performed on by hacking*

---

[1] *Televisi Republik Indonesia.* The state-owned national station.

at them with small handsaws, and a gong, *the sacrosanct spiritual center of the traditional gamelan* ensemble, *on which the composer performed with an electric grinder. I thought of the Italian futurists demanding a "music of noises" composed of backfiring motors, the howl of saws, the noises of city life. Sparks from the* gong *shot dangerously close to the child in my lap whose oblivion was only disturbed by the sudden silence after the fuses blew.*

> Noise only produces order if it can concentrate a new sacrificial crisis at a singular point, in a *catastrophe*, in order to transcend the old violence and recreate a system of differences on another level of organization. (Attali 1985:34)

I had returned to America to resume teaching by the time the work, later entitled *Geräusch,* was performed as a final graduation recital (I: *ujian*) at the conservatory, as seen in Plate S.1. Email and threads on social networking sites allowed me to follow the controversies the performance stirred. It appeared that few faculty at the conservatory appreciated Arsawijaya's daring. Several members of the jury had arrived wearing earplugs, a section of the audience had walked out, and the piece had generated a lengthy discussion among faculty on the structure of departmental curriculum and advising. Subsequent graduating students were restricted in their final recital options. In conversation, one faculty member referred to Arsawijaya's "gang" as "sound terrorists" (I: *teroris bunyi*), a highly charged phrase following the devastating terrorist bombings in Bali in 2002 and 2005. However rebarbative observers may have found it, *Geräusch* got people talking [Track MK-S/1].

Through *Geräusch*, Arsawijaya unambiguously pricked the assumptions of institutional power. For some young Balinese composers and musicians the composition

PLATE S.1 Sang Nyoman Arsawijaya performing *Geräusch*. 2006. Photographer unknown.

embodied the *agon* between the state conservatory (and broader government) and the experimentalism natural to youth. In a jarring aesthetic break, Arsawijaya eschewed the Aesopian language of standard Indonesian critique perfected among *dalang* (I), puppeteers, during Suharto's totalitarian New Order (1966–98) as a maneuver to protect oneself from political harassment. In Balinese traditional contexts the *gong* is a revered symbol of one's ancestors, elders, or teachers; it is an abode of spirits given special offerings and prayers. By apparently defiling the instrument, Arsawijaya sought simultaneously a social and aesthetic effect: the exploration of new sound qualities aligned with a provocative statement of protest against a faculty and administration that, in his estimation, did not fulfill their roles as thoughtful, open-minded composers or mentors.[2]

No *perruque*, Arsawijaya's was a direct counter-statement against the preciosity of conservatory works designed to sate touristic imaginations. As the voicing of a political entity (rebellious youth) and an artifact of modern technology, *Geräusch* embodied aspects of Balineseness rarely found in touristic imagery. If the classic ethnography of Bali proposed the image of a continuous culture, *Geräusch* was a rupture intended to remind observers that Balinese culture as lived was not seamless with Balinese culture as represented. In written descriptions of his work Arsawijaya appealed to French *musique concrete*, German noise, and American performance art. John Cage abounds in his thesis (cf. Arsawijaya 2005). In interviews Arsawijaya described the work as avant-garde (I: *garde depan*), as an experiment (I: *eksperimen*), and as pure art (I: *seni murni*), relating it to an aesthetic of *ketidakindahan* (I), un-beautiful-ness or ugliness (p.c. July 2006). *Geräusch* represented a new skepticism towards the aestheticized new creations (I: *kreasi baru*) fostered at the national conservatories and regional government-sponsored contests [Track BV-P/1].

During my research, *kontemporer* expressions in music, dance, and the visual arts symbolized for many artists the contours of reform- (I: *reformasi*) era democracy that emerged following Suharto's ouster in 1998. Many *kontemporer* artists understood democracy not as a homogenous, harmonious state, but one in which antagonisms constantly emerge to be drawn into debate, a world in which conflict is sustained, not erased through the imposed consensus of authoritarianism or official aesthetics. In the hands of its most radical composers, *musik kontemporer* functioned like a funhouse mirror, reflecting and distorting the musical elements of the *kreasi baru* and older *gong kebyar* repertoires while simultaneously being those forms' crystal ball, foretelling their future.

Arsawijaya was the youngest of a community of composers to emerge in the Kaliungu neighborhood of Denpasar where he was preceded by Wayan Sadra (1953–2011), Komang Astita (1952–), Ketut Gede Asnawa (1955–), and Wayan Yudane (1964–), each of whom helped to lay the foundations for a wider community of Indonesian

---

[2] Fearful of karmic repercussions, Arsawijaya removed the iconic boss from the center of the iron *gong* prior to the final performance, thus transforming it, in his mind if not in the minds of others, into a metal plate (I: *plat besi*).

contemporary composers linked to global aesthetic networks. Each of these composers, born into working-class, casteless families in a rapidly urbanizing area of Bali, would go on to earn degrees, teach, or compose within Western universities. During my preliminary research (yearly trips between 1998 and 2001) I lived and studied traditional music with Asnawa while participating in ritual (and sometimes tourist) performances with the Kaliungu Kaja neighborhood ensemble he directed. By the late 1990s the marmoreal Asnawa and his brother Astita were in their mid-forties and had, according to both, outgrown their earlier days of energetic and occasionally experimental composition.

I would later meet Yudane, Asnawa's younger cousin, a figure the elders of the Kaliungu community had not lost the opportunity to warn me about. Rebellious, hot-tempered, and tattooed, Yudane was as likely to be found hanging out with the punk crowd in Denpasar as with *gamelan* musicians. He would upend my newly gained knowledge of Bali, gleaned from older members of the community, with a simple: "Are you *sure*...?" More often than not he found an excuse to avoid the ritual requirements to which the other Kaliungu men seemed endlessly committed. In his small compound Yudane, pictured in Plate S.1, held court for the small community of radical (I: *radikal*) or naughty (I: *nakal*) composers in the Denpasar area, drinking strong Balinese *arak* while animatedly discussing composition and politics. If some composers' works tickled the belly of tradition, Yudane's put it in a headlock, jabbing it sharply in the ribs. His composition fed on the death of tradition's codes [Track BV-P/3].

PLATE S.2 Wayan Gede Yudane. Photo by Michael Norris.

Casting a long shadow over this new music community was Wayan Sadra, a composer raised around the corner from Yudane but who had, in the early 1970s, suddenly left home for a job offer in Jakarta and who, after the job fell through before he had even arrived, supported himself by improvising music for "naked snake dancer burlesque" shows before eventually settling in the dynamic arts scene in Solo, Central Java (p.c. October 2003). There he studied new composition at the local conservatory, blooming under the mentorship of the energetic dancer and administrator Gendhon Humardani who had studied under Martha Graham in New York in the 1960s. Sadra would eventually accept a position on the faculty at the conservatory in Solo. Later, in 2003, I moved there to study Javanese *gamelan* and perform and tour with Sadra's Sono Seni *musik kontemporer* ensemble.

Balinese *musik kontemporer* developed in tandem with broader social changes during the middle to late New Order. Increased investment in tourism beginning in the mid-1980s raised per capita income on the island from below average to one of the highest in the nation, expanding the Balinese awareness of their culture as an institution and commodity. A growing, urbanizing middle class began to develop new popular and self-consciously artistic forms of expression. The standard of living for some highly credentialed composers rose dramatically during the 1990s. Flush with funds from teaching foreign students, several of my teachers moved their nuclear families from traditional, cramped family compounds to modern, multi-floor homes with several bedrooms, Western bathrooms, and lush gardens.

My research in Bali began just as the death knell for the New Order rang. Artists, often denied access to direct political discourse during the New Order, once again entered the fray during the subsequent era of reform. Economic and governmental reforms were thrown into flux following the first Bali bombing in the resort town of Kuta in 2002, attributed to Javanese Islamic fundamentalists. The bombing, which sent Bali's economy into a temporary tailspin, led to strained relations between the minority Hindu Balinese and the hegemonic Islamic Javanese. As a partial response to the rise of Islamic fundamentalism in Java, Balinese cultural commentators and politicians developed their own conservative rhetoric known as *Ajeg Bali*, or Balinese uprightness. Many contemporary artists became embroiled in extended debates over cultural purity and experimental composers were occasionally accused of breaking tradition (I: *merusak tradisi*) by *Ajeg* commentators.[3] By the end of the decade tourism had recovered, surpassing pre-bombing levels, and Indonesia had become Asia's third-largest economy after China and India. But the disruptions of the *reformasi* era appeared to have opened a cultural and political Pandora's box from which there could be no return to the predictable authoritarian rule of the New Order. Seemingly loosened from the grip of state conservatory aesthetics and the New Order sponsorship of depoliticized *tradisi*, music during the *reformasi* became an active site in the control over meaning.

---

[3] See newspaper clippings in Sadra (1986) for earlier examples of the "*merusak tradisi*" polemic.

I spent four years in Bali and Java over the course of several research trips between 1998 and 2012 during which time I studied and performed both traditional and new music. The composers of the latter were all expert performers of the former. Many of these composers did not embody the ethnographic image of the Balinese which anthropology has overwhelmingly associated with a rather narrow set of cultural and religious practices observed by the Hindu Balinese of the central southern plains: those Balinese who live within the main tourist corridor and who trace their genealogy to fourteenth- to sixteenth-century migrations from Majapahit Java. My research brought me into contact with individuals who considered themselves fully Balinese but who are not represented in the classic anthropological image.

The physical trappings of the *kontemporer* scene differed from the traditional artistic community in which I was also engaged. While my older music teachers almost all lived in traditional Balinese homes closely associated with ancestral temples, village (I: *desa adat*) and neighborhood (B: *banjar*) associations, composers engaged in *musik kontemporer* were more likely to live in modern homes in the peri-urban or urban space of the *perumahan* (I), new housing development, alongside not their own extended families but newcomers from all parts of the island and nation. These were often ethnically and architecturally heterogeneous spaces from which families would regularly return to their ancestral agrarian home *kampung* (I), country village, to observe traditional ceremonies. Experimental composers often spoke of living in multiple temporal frames: the speed of the city versus the languorous pace of the home village; and multiple social spaces: the protective but potentially suffocating extended family compound versus the anonymity and privacy of urban life.

Conversing cross-legged on the floor in a traditional raised pavilion at an elderly teacher's home during my morning lessons was often replaced in the afternoon by conversations at a table with composers engaged in *musik kontemporer*. The table would often display the telltale signs of a college-educated, contemporary artist: a laptop, CDs, a personal recording device, beer, clove cigarettes (more so in Java), a bottle of *arak* (*ciu* in Java), books (again, more so in Java), Western sodas, pads of musical notation, a passport. More often than not there would be a car, not a motorbike, in the garage, and often a Western or Japanese, rather than Balinese, wife or girlfriend would join in the conversation, behavior that might be considered forward from a Balinese spouse.

Musik kontemporer was a scene in which individuals self-consciously expressed new ideas about authorship, originality, time, space, transnational experience, politics, sexuality, tradition, and modernity. Whereas *tradisi* and *klasik* (I), classic, genres were often just as political as *musik kontemporer*, they pretended to be only forms of historical evidence, concealing their politics behind common sense and taste. In contradistinction to *kreasi baru*, a form of expression perfected under New Order governmentality in which overt political expression was subsumed under virtuosic brilliance, *musik kontemporer* often embodied a more explicit politics mediating culture as lived and represented.[4] Through its very title (meaning noise in German), Arsawijaya's *Geräusch* posed a blunt question: *What is music in Bali?* Sounds deemed noise are often associated with the disempowered, the marginal, and the threatening, whereas music is the sanctioned domain of those in power.[5] In the hands of composers such as Arsawijaya, *musik kontemporer* eroded the categorical boundaries between *gamelan,* music, and noise, and questioned the authority of those who named them as such.

---

[4] Although, as anyone who has closely observed the composition, performance, and adjudication of Balinese *kreasi baru* can attest, few forms are surrounded by as intense politicking.
[5] Following the Bali bombing, many of the Balinese I knew began to refer to the sounds of the Islamic call to prayer as noise (I: *bunyi*) rather than voice/sound (I: *suara*) as was their prior habit.

RADICAL TRADITIONS

1 Introduction

RADICAL TRADITIONS ADDRESSES a simple question: How are culture and change thought in Bali? My approach to this question has been guided by the thesis that imagining and enacting cultural change is a complex contest between variously positioned social actors. My central assertion is that *musik kontemporer* emerged as a form to express new ideas that could not be articulated through pre-existing genres and that it, better than these other forms, works to reconcile for its creators and audiences the discursive paradox between contemporary Balinese culture as lived and Balinese culture as represented.

To keep Balinese voices in the mix, I regularly refer to passages from my recorded interviews, which are available on this text's website and are indicated by the ❶ sign in the margin. These are extended passages in which composers elaborate upon topics most important to them, sometimes providing alternate interpretations from my own. Each section of this text begins with a vignette, a particular entry from my field notes that struck me as heavy with meaning and through which I present profiles of the composer-characters of the *musik kontemporer* story in order to describe their discourse and social space. Beginning discussions with vignettes is a conceit that I hope will temper the totalizing potential of theory. Abstract theorization has historically characterized Balinese Culture as a complete and all-encompassing framework that ostensibly tells individual Balinese what to do in every situation. My experience was often of a contested, contradictory, and indeterminate space. Culture was not an overdetermined, hermetically sealed structure, but something more like a jungle gym: more gap than structure. This is not to say that there are not strong discourses, shaped by forces of production, that restrict individual choice and which individuals breezily sidestep through their creative play, but that such forces do not completely determine experience or action.

Interactions with foreign cultures have long catalyzed change in Balinese culture. As described in Chapter 2, I understand Bali as a node within intercultural aesthetic networks that stretch far back in time and that today expand to encircle the globe. *Musik kontemporer* emerges partially as a consequence of global cold war cultural interactions. In Chapter 3 I discuss the form's emergence in the New Order state conservatory, analyzing it as an example of the regime's efforts to develop the arts on a national scale. During the subsequent era of reformation, *musik kontemporer* became a form through which many composers distanced themselves from and sometimes openly critiqued state aesthetics, as described in Chapter 4. As a form in which institutions, administrators, performers, and composers dispute aesthetics and identity, the social meanings of *musik kontemporer* remain multiple and in motion. During the *reformasi*, the form voiced many composers' need to behold themselves and their expressions as distinct from the state and its aesthetics.

Chapter 5 concerns the relationship between the theory (I: *téori*) of composition and the identity of the composer (I: *komposer*), an emergent figure characterized by changing notions of authorship and ownership who communicated to new audiences within novel contexts. Here I ask why Balinese compositions have over the past fifty years come to be increasingly associated with singular, named authors rather than ensembles. In Chapter 6 I differentiate the technologies and materials of *musik kontemporer* from earlier genres, asking what it was possible to say in *musik kontemporer* that was not, or not so easily, expressed through other genres. In Chapter 7 I present novel forms of musical analysis, focusing upon temporality and dynamics, followed by a consideration of ethnomusicology's preoccupation with the identification of homologies between musical and extra-musical phenomena. I consider the problems of intercultural meaning and its potential for driving cultural change in Chapter 8. More than any other Balinese form, *musik kontemporer* is marked by intercultural semiosis. The intercultural aesthetic interactions that catalyze much *musik kontemporer* today are conditioned by complex relationships between the Balinese and their others, relationships that, in one way or another, connect us all. Chapter 9 is an analysis of intercultural collaborative performance between the Balinese and their others (primarily Americans) as a process that, ironically, often re-inscribes allochronism.

While not intending to essentialize or flatten the image of *musik kontemporer* as ipso facto a mode of dissensus, my analysis naturally reflects the era in which I worked and the composers with whom I studied. If, in the following pages, my tone seems sometimes provocative and politicized, it is in following the spirit of composers' aesthetic aims to question the assumptions of prior representations and styles. I follow Wayan Sadra's materialist analysis of Balinese culture, asking, who pays for, who benefits, and what is at stake in any work of art (cf. Sadra 1986:5)? If the political appears stressed in my account, it is in direct proportion to its relative absence in many prior studies of the Balinese performing arts. Despite the shift of focus, this work is the beneficiary of several excellent prior studies of Balinese *kreasi baru* and introductions to Balinese *musik kontemporer* by authors such as Tenzer (2000), Bakan (1999), Sandino (2008), Mack (2004), and Wakeling (2010). My account of *musik kontemporer* as a broader, national phenomenon builds upon the groundbreaking work by Roth (1986), Notosudirdjo (2001), and Miller (2011).

Like the riptide that pulls against the inertia of the tide or the waft of incense flowing against the prevailing wind, we can identify countercurrents in any culture and in any era. My analysis of change in Balinese culture takes its cue from the work of Picard (1996, 2003), Vickers (1989, 2005), Baulch (2007), Hobart (1997), and Schulte Nordholt (1994, 2000), among others, each of whom has provided nuanced descriptions of aesthetic, political, and cultural plurality in Bali. In *Radical Traditions* I am interested in examining the contradictions in the thought of an age. *Musik kontemporer* reminds us that the culturally marginal can be symbolically central; we cannot fully understand dominant forms of expression without also understanding their inversions, alternatives, and negations. *Musik kontemporer* plays a role in Balinese society out of proportion to its comparatively small oeuvre.

And yet to refer unproblematically to an ostensibly unified field of production called *musik kontemporer* introduces its own distortions. The term does not retain a consistent meaning across its history or across Indonesia's various regional cultures; even among Balinese composers it has no enduring, core identity but is instead an evolving, contested, and sometimes contradictory expressive field. The various musics called *musik kontemporer* are not logical or natural outgrowths of one another but represent competing world views often manifesting as the tension between cosmopolitan and nativist impulses. To portray the form as neatly unitary would be to ignore composers' particularity and agency. (The same could be said for both *kreasi baru* and *tradisi* expressions.) As described in Chapter 4, the many flavors of *musik kontemporer*—which in Bali divide roughly into popular and serious forms—have each developed in rather different contexts and bear different messages for different audiences.

Similarly, my inability to straightforwardly refer to *musik kontemporer* composers suggests a wide variety of approaches and subjectivities and reveals the complex interpenetrations of discourses, representations, and lifestyles termed *tradisi* and *moderen*. Few of the composers with whom I worked were dedicated solely to the production of *musik kontemporer*.[1] While Madé Subandi and Gede Arsana, for instance, are expert composers of neotraditional and traditional forms, their daring *musik kontemporer* works invert the rules of those very genres.

What does my inability to point directly at either *musik kontemporer,* or *musik kontemporer* composers imply for the reality of Balinese culture? The practice of *musik kontemporer* often revealed in stark terms the aporias of Balinese culture through the celebration of mixed forms and interculturalisms, suggesting that all origins may in fact be borrowed and that culture may be too porous a thing to stand up on its own. Nevertheless, just as their identities were transforming, nearly all of my informants represented themselves and their art first and foremost as Balinese and they invested in the culture concept almost as steadfastly as did the classic ethnography of their island. The resultant paradoxes often emerged as long, heavy silences in my recorded interviews.

This work is primarily an ethnography. We write ethnographies—highly detailed descriptions—because we recognize that no algorithm, however rigorously complex, and no framework, however elegantly reductive, can generate again our experience in the field. In the game of the singly authored book, there is no way around representation, no matter how dialogic we attempt to be. Yet it is key that ethnographic

---

[1] It is perhaps telling that the only two composers involved exclusively with *musik kontemporer,* Wayan Sadra and Pande Madé Sukerta, lived in Central Java.

understanding be built upon a bedrock of intersubjective knowledge that can only come into being when the self and other share the same space-time. Fabian (1983) famously critiqued anthropology's conflation of spatial with temporal distance. In this framework time is rendered harmless, as it were, by postulating that it is plural, that each society is encapsulated in its own representations of time (198). This is the pernicious face of cultural relativism, for which Bali remains a beast of burden. While such allochronism is old news in contemporary anthropology, the denial of coevalness continues nonetheless in representations of Bali; it is why tourists and ethnographers alike fall over and again for the gag of the Balinese *legong* dancer wearing shades and driving a motorbike, and it is why *musik kontemporer* seems so surprising to so many observers.

Tradisi Radikal/Radical Traditions

July 2002. Madé Subandi (1966–) and I arrived at the gongsmith's in Blahbatuh shortly after eleven in the morning. The drive from his home in Batubulan, halfway between Ubud and Denpasar, took nearly an hour. It would have taken only twenty minutes on our motorbikes. The gongsmith was a sharply dressed businessman; a clove cigarette dangled below his John Waters mustache. Below him on the floor nearly naked lackeys sweated over hot metal. As Subandi negotiated the price of a new set of instruments, the gongsmith interrupted him midsentence to dryly ask why Subandi was wearing his pants inside out. The composer pretended not to notice the question and continued probing the gongsmith as to whether or not he could forge a new tuning that sounded antique.

Subandi had returned home the previous morning at 4:00 a.m. after directing rehearsals of his music in three different villages. Eight ensembles had commissioned him to compose original works for their upcoming arts festival performances. The works, each roughly twelve minutes long and totaling over an hour and a half of material, were highly complex, dense arrangements for full *gamelan* orchestras of up to thirty performers. Subandi composed and taught each of the parts without the use of notation and to me it seemed remarkable that he was functional enough to get his pants on at all.

We rode back to Batubulan in the used Toyota jeep Subandi had recently purchased with funds earned teaching *gamelan* in San Francisco. He had invested in an enormous sound system that never seemed to work and we filled the silence by discussing how he planned to use the funds recently awarded to him by the Indonesian Kelola Foundation to found his own *sanggar* (I), *privately owned neighborhood arts foundation*. Flush with a bit of cash, busy with numerous commissions, and inspired by recent collaborations with foreign artists, Subandi was bursting with ideas for new works. Raised in a renowned family of musicians and dancers, he was a famously virtuosic performer of many forms, had graduated from the national conservatory, and was now teaching music at the local arts high school. But this pedigree did not always immunize him from occasional accusations of overstepping by more senior artists and administrators at the conservatory. Questions of cultural change, the relationship between *tradisi* and *moderen*, and the nexus between aesthetics and power were, at this time, foremost in his thoughts.

We drove alongside green sawah *paddies interspersed with new housing complexes and the occasional crumbling, half-built warehouses abandoned after the 1997 crash. I mentioned an idea that a mutual friend, the ethnomusicologist Christopher Miller, had proposed to describe new musics in East Asia. Miller characterized the use of traditional instruments by Japanese and Korean modernist composers as a kind of "radical traditionalism." But Subandi seemed to have drifted away from the conversation, driving with one hand while attempting to rewire his sound system with the other, swerving repeatedly into oncoming traffic.*

When I returned to Bali the following spring after several months studying in Central Java I found Subandi's new sanggar *thriving. Classes in traditional music were being offered to neighborhood children, boys* and *girls. The club's centerpiece was an active new music ensemble composed of Subandi's leading students from the arts high school and national conservatory. Rehearsals were held on a new plot of land around the corner from his home in a quickly expanding housing development. A bungalow was constructed on the space to host his foreign (primarily American) students who often studied and collaborated with the ensembles in the* sanggar*. During their weekly rehearsals, all members of the club wore the black (pink for the girls) T-shirts Subandi (Plate 1.1) had printed and that featured an abstract logo (Plate 1.2) framed by the* sanggar's *name:* Ceraken, *and its motto,* Tradisi Radikal: *Radical Tradition.*

PLATE 1.1 Madé Subandi. Photo by Peter Steele.

PLATE 1.2 *Ceraken* logo designed by Nyoman Erawan.

The *Ceraken*

Ceraken is a distinctly odd name for a Balinese arts club, most of which adopt vaguely ancient, puffed-up religious appellations such as *Dharma Swara* (Voice of the True Path) or *Gunung Sari* (Essence of the Mountain). A *ceraken,* by contrast, is a completely unremarkable utilitarian object of Balinese daily life. Often a roughly hewn wooden box made of several open containers, it holds a collection of heterogeneous things. Fancier versions are carved to hold the betel kit, herbal medicines, or spices. The box is not sealed, hermetic, or locked; each container is open to the air. It might be a box of curios collected from where- and whenever. The kitchen in my childhood home included a similar space we called the "stuff drawer," which was filled with a collection of objects that didn't make sense anywhere else.

Ceraken works well to describe both the heterogeneous materials of *musik kontemporer* compositions and the highly divergent musical styles described as such, helping us to see the ambiguity and dissensus at the center of its production. The term also encapsulates the ways in which many composers engaged in *musik kontemporer* imagine their culture more generally. If early Western (and later Balinese) anthropologists tended to describe Bali in bounded, organismic, structuralist, and ahistorical terms, the *ceraken* offers an alternative model of Balinese culture, one open to difference and through which Balinese composers can imagine traveling an unbounded sonic (if not literal) space. The logic of *ceraken* blurs the division between what is ours and what is theirs, as does its history. Before the installation of policies segregating colonial from local society in the late-eighteenth century, most Dutch living in the colony took betel and used local spices and medicines, stored in their own *ceraken* which were prominently displayed in paintings of the era and which stood as symbols of the cultural and racial mixture that so bothered administrators in the Netherlands (Taylor 2009:41).

As a facet of both Western and Balinese aesthetics, organismic metaphor suggests self-contained wholes defined by their relations of interiority in which components are characterized and constituted by their connection to other parts. When detached, components lose their meaning and identity. Against the totalitarian potential of organismic thinking, the *ceraken* embodies a philosophy of external relations and the internally differentiated singularity. In this scheme components may be broken off and inserted into other works in which their functions and interactions are transformed. Between 2003 and 2006 Subandi applied the title *Ceraken* to a constantly morphing composition, or set of compositions, which combined ancient *slonding* instruments with gongs, chimes, and other non-Balinese percussion he had amassed during various performance tours through Asia. The work(s) combined local musical topics from the *slonding, gender wayang,* and *gong kebyar* repertoire with musical ideas borrowed, stolen, and half-digested from Indian, Japanese, and Western repertoires [Track MK-1/1].

As described in Chapter 4, if the national conservatory tended to territorialize the boundaries between compositional forms, bringing their edges into focus through homogenization and explicit rules, composers engaged in *musik kontemporer* during the *reformasi* often deterritorialized conservatory aesthetics through the combination of diverse historical forms and by breaking cardinal rules of composition. If the conservatory attempted, through its development of *téori* (I), theory, to apply organismic metaphors of form to historical genres such as *gong kebyar* and *kreasi baru*, *musik kontemporer* increasingly pointed to the internal inconsistencies in *téori's* logic and the overwhelming evidence that these musics were instead composed as strings of hooks: the *and...and...and...* juxtapositional logic of the assemblage in which, as in the *ceraken,* components could be added and removed without a work necessarily losing its identity

Many composers engaged with *musik kontemporer* responded with ambivalence to the conservatory's arborescent logic in which musical structure was predetermined, genres were neatly bound, and historical eras unequivocally delineated. The polyglossia of official performances, in which multiple languages (literal and stylistic) were rule-bound, socially segregated, and distinct (to facilitate didactic instruction), was answered in *kontemporer* forms through a heteroglossic, eclectic, and unregulated mix of languages and styles. In the *reformasi*, *musik kontemporer* embodied a nominally bounded space of possibilities rather than the ready-made body-plans and properties of conventional conservatory composition [Track BV-1/1].

The Space-Time of *Musik Kontemporer*

Transformations in the Balinese music scene during my research reflected changing conceptions of space and time, two themes that appear throughout *Radical Traditions* not as a framework, but a refrain. *Musik kontemporer* was a chronotope, symbolizing in both its forms and processes of production the transforming spatial and temporal imaginations of its composers, performers, and audiences.[2]

Time

The English word "time" is a notorious patch of intellectual quicksand; it means too many things, and it means even more to most musicians.[3] Time is a recurrent, sometimes implicit, theme in the ethnography of Bali. As described in Chapter 2, the Balinese are often conflated with their history and their personhood is linked to their supposed experience of motionless time while the structure of timing in their music is linked homologically to their cosmology, as discussed in Chapter 7. Composers often spoke of the texture of time and timing in musical performance and composition. They described the persistent pressure of the past (I: *zaman dulu*) and expressed anxious sentiments of belatedness in regard to the West. I use the phrase *temporal imagination* to highlight the mutable aspects of experienced temporality as against metaphysical and biological explanations and counter to the top-down forms of social time presumably determined by modes of production either modern (Durkheim) or ecological (Evans-Pritchard).

Many composers suggested that Balinese temporal imaginations had undergone several transformations over the past century. The precolonial era, prior to notions of *tradisi* and *moderen*, was focused, they suggested, on the present. Reification of traditional culture during colonization and through the effects of tourism oriented temporal imaginations towards the past. The contemporary era represents then a simultaneous juxtaposition of past, present, and future temporal imaginations which many musicians mapped respectively upon musical forms designated *tradisi, kreasi baru*, and *musik kontemporer*.[4] Recent anthropologies of time have similarly suggested that many contemporary populations live in a plurality of time regimes.[5] The homogenous slices

---

[2] "In the literary artistic chronotope, spatial and temporal indicators are fused into one carefully thought-out, concrete whole. Time, as it were, thickens, takes on flesh, becomes artistically visible; likewise, space becomes charged and responsive to the movements of time, plot, and history. This intersection of axes and fusion of indicators characterizes the artistic chronotope" (Bakhtin 1981:84).

[3] At least three different discourses concerning temporality can be identified: social (ethnographic), empirical (scientific/cognitive), and metaphysical (philosophical), each regularly speaking past or overlapping the other and too infrequently connected to actual, explicit statements uttered by actors themselves. I steer clear of speculative metaphysics and am concerned only with how ethnographers have categorized time in Bali and the ways in which composers and musicians characterized time in both its mundane and musical manifestations. Nevertheless, it is my hunch that it is a category mistake to speak of calendars, musical tempos, grooves, work schedules, and the Hindu *yugas* (epochs) using the same terminology and in the same breath. I encountered little evidence to suggest that the Balinese experience of musical time was connected, or similar to, their experience of calendar or cosmological time, for example. However much confusion it has caused, the English term "temporality" catches up all of these distinct phenomena.

[4] This scheme is synthesized from separate conversations in 2003 with the composers Ketut Gede Asnawa, Wayan Sadra, and Gede Arsana.

[5] See for instance Schulte Nordholt and van Schendel (2001).

of globalized time interact in Bali with variable ceremonial calendars; metronomic musics live alongside the sinuous tempos of *kebyar*. As described in Chapter 7, Balinese composers used the metaphor of the wave (I: *ombak*) to describe transformations in musical temporalities.

Subandi's notion of *tradisi radikal* faced head-on the apparent temporal incommensurability of past-oriented *tradisi*, in which destruction and forgetting are taboo, and the forward-facing *radikal*, a strategy for change and thought for the future. Brought together, they suggest an active present that attempts to resuscitate the inherently dynamic contents of tradition from being instrumentalized as a means of internal subjugation by state and neocolonial power structures. *Tradisi radikal* represented a response to the state conservatory's rhetoric of "continuities in change," meant to encourage smooth, incremental, and officially sanctioned adjustments as opposed to the sudden ruptures of unbridled experimentalism. As I demonstrate in Chapter 3, the conservatory's careful regulation of aesthetic change accommodated broader New Order cultural policies that sought to aestheticize politics and depoliticize culture. Not sharing the state's obsessions with origins, *tradisi radikal* suggested an attempt to recapture the dynamism and open possibilities of *tradisi* by revealing, if only for a moment, the outlines of the Balinese archive (in Foucault's sense), exposing in fits and starts the means by which imagining change itself was circumscribed [Track BV-1/2].

Space

As the consideration of the historical record introduced in Chapter 2 quickly demonstrates, Balinese culture has always been connected to a larger world: from Dongsonian migrations, to spiritual links to a distant Indic holy land, to trade links within the *pasisir* world of insular Southeast Asian coastal trade itself integrated into a global economy.[6] Bali has long functioned as a node in various far-flung aesthetic networks. During the twentieth century, colonial policy and the exigencies of tourism encouraged the Balinese to enfold their spatial imaginations inward while inviting the Western world to imagine Bali as a geocultural extreme, so impossibly distant that it must be in the past, as if looking towards Bali was the same as gazing into the night sky.

As described in Chapter 3, the transformations initiated by modernization and nationalism encouraged the concept of Balinese society as a space in which the individual could move *through* and *up*. The advent of tourism initiated a series of power struggles over the control and meaning of space in Bali. Tourist spaces—sites of leisure and nostalgia—were mapped along areas of the island deemed real Balinese spaces (e.g., Ubud) versus deteriorations (e.g., Kuta). If Balinese music is anything, it is *Balinese*, always and already tied to a place, irrespective of where it is performed. *Musik kontemporer* suggested a virtual heterotopia, a space in which norms may be transgressed

---

[6] Vickers describes the *pasisir* as the "maritime world bordered by the ports of mainland Southeast Asia and encompassing what is now Malaysia, the southern Philippines, and Indonesia, [that] were important for centuries before Europeans made their presence felt in the area" (1993:56).

and social order shifted. In *musik kontemporer*, spatial imaginations are outlined by virtual cartographies of musical topics and forms. As outlined in Chapter 6, Western, Japanese, Indian, African, and other topical elements populate *kontemporer* musical forms to suggest their relative placement and interconnection within the contemporary Balinese spatial imagination.

Space is increasingly theorized as multiple.[7] Lefebvre warns us not to think of space as an empty, a priori ether, but as a social phenomenon constantly recreated and linked inexorably to power. He suggests a hypercomplex flow of interpenetrating spaces against a simplistic model of spatial frames subsuming each other: the global over the national over the local (1991:87). This model, in which spatial frames neatly nest like matryoshka dolls, is seductive to Indonesianists because the locals are so obviously bounded (often by water), the nation has appeared so overbearingly total, and the global (i.e., the West) is as far away as it could be. But this framework has often led us to ignore what we know to be the case, that "no place dominates enough to be global and no place is self-contained enough to be local" (Latour 2005:204). As notions such as translocal and glocalization suggest, the global and the local are not mutually exclusive. Neither is the nation state somehow now irrelevant. As illustrated in Chapter 9, the global is often experienced at the local level through a variety of processes initiated by the nation state as in the state conservatory's efforts to internationalize its curriculum.

As compared to the primarily nationalist aspirations of Indonesian musical experimentalism from independence through the New Order, the cultural geography of Balinese *musik kontemporer* in the beginning of the twenty-first century was marked by a global cosmopolitanism mediated by digital networks. My research period coincided with the introduction of both cell phone technology and the Internet in Indonesia. By 2010 Indonesia represented the second largest Facebook community after the United States. All of the composers with whom I worked owned smartphones through which they accessed their Facebook accounts, often by the hour. The *musik kontemporer* network, although small, was extremely high density; everyone was linked to everyone else and new ideas (and gossip) spread quickly. Beyond the dense network of strong links between the Balinese, each composer was connected by a broader network of social and digital links to transitory foreign music students and artists from whom novel information diffused. While many Balinese historically imagined space as outlined by a constellation of specific but distant vectors relative to nonegocentric points of reference—Gunung Agung, Java, India, Mount Meru—it is now also experienced as a pattern of interlocking global networks in which the individual is a node represented by a personalized profile, the vast expanse of this space folded into the smartphone. Like the composition of *musik kontemporer* itself, Balinese space is increasingly egocentric [Track BV-1/3].

---

7 Jameson refers to "hallucinogenic depth planes in a space of many dimensions" (1991:372). Appadurai sees a former Euclidean world fracturing into fractals (1996:46). Soja (1989) identifies nested locales.

Radical Traditions Globally

Balinese *musik kontemporer* is one of many forms of contemporary music around the world not dependent upon Western modernism, the avant-garde, or experimentalism as its primary aesthetic referent. Considering their unique and divergent histories, independent development, and dissimilar sonic structures, it may make little sense, indeed it may represent epistemological violence, to attempt to trap the variety of these musics within the Procrustean bed of a single term, the bounty hunter ethos of academic theory shooting us in our ethnographic feet. But if understood as a logic or a mode, rather than as a thing, genre, or language, Subandi's *tradisi radikal* gives us a provisional name to talk about expressions linked through similar conceptions of and relationships to tradition, modernity, postcoloniality, global aesthetic networks, the past, and the future. Here I will outline the similarities between these various local expressions and Subandi's notion of *tradisi radikal* rather than attempt to broaden the boundaries of the avant-garde to invite previously ignored musicians into the club.

These musics are often produced by small pockets of composers and performers who are chimerical in their styles and whose bands may quickly dissolve.[8] They may be condemned by traditionalists for being too experimental while critiqued by Western-trained sporadic composers for being too popular. But their experiments, while stop-and-go and frequently small-scale, often represent what Bateson called the "difference that makes a difference" (2000:459), offering alternatives that may influence the evolution of larger scenes. Wary of the corrosive effects of canonization upon creativity and seeking to control their histories, these composers may appeal to a variety of sometimes conflicting genre terms: avant-garde, experimental, popular, traditional, neotraditional, classical, world music, rock, jazz, noise.

Radical traditions often reside in the slippery space between the local—often valorized as inherently authentic—and the global, typically portrayed, in an inverse figuration, as always already artificial and inauthentic (Biddle and Knights 2007:3). They are valorized by the state when they can play the role of an ultramodern national art music for an international clientele, but are decried as corruptions when they transgress or resist the state's control. Composers working in this mode increasingly engage with Western musics through the mediascape of digital aesthetic networks, but they do not neatly epitomize Appadurai's (1996) model of the localization of globalized media as a way of bypassing identities imposed by

---

[8] My direct interaction with such musics includes ensembles from Thailand (Changsaton), the Philippines (Grace Nono), Ghana (the Pan-African Orchestra), and Kazakhstan (Roksonaki), among others. See also discussions of local contemporary musics in West Africa (Euba 1975), Finland (Austerlitz 2000), and Brazil (Neto 2000). We may also consider the development of Japanese experimentalism in the 1960s by performers such as Takayanagi Masayuki, apparently working independently of the models provided by Western counterparts such as Derek Baily (Atkins 2001:232). Of course there are many instances in which an individual composer's output straddles the divide between local experimentalism and Western modernism. Tenzer's (2003) work on the Philippine composer Jose Maceda's corpus is especially relevant here.

the nation state. Radical traditions have a kind of authenticity, but one that might be described using Graham's concept of ironic authenticity (1999). That is, to local audiences they can represent national identity as something other than a given essence or unchanging character while appearing traditionally authentic to outside audiences.

Artists in this field work within the fluid, ill-defined junctures between revivalist, avant-garde, popular, and world music forms and are often involved in intercultural performance projects sponsored by academic, festival, and granting institutions centered in the West. Radical tradition describes a strategy of composition that can accommodate a range of stages from the local to BAM, WOMAD, and the Smithsonian Folklife Festival. They are often a venue for individualistic expression in music cultures that have historically maintained more anonymizing modes of composition. Affinity intercultures (Slobin 1992) often play an important role here; many composers seek out and maintain links beyond their shores, sometimes with Western composers, but the knowledges exchanged sometimes enter through improvisation or willful misunderstanding rather than through structured, continuous study of foreign traditions. These composers often seek catalysts for their new creations rather than specific knowledges.

The array of musical topics in forms such as Balinese *musik kontemporer* suggest new networks of global cultural exchange that look beyond the north-south colonial axis, forging alternate cartographies of cultural interaction and internationalisms independent of those traveled by Euro-American modernism. Play in a multidimensional spatial/temporal imaginary lies at the heart of radical traditions in which the ahistorical tendencies of the Western avant-garde are rarely adopted, especially within Indonesia where cultural memory and specificity are essential in the effort to maintain local cultural identity within a context of nationalization, globalization, and cultural tourism. The choice to turn one's back on tradition is a privilege given to those whose traditions are not otherwise at risk. While the Euro-American avant-garde embodies myths of the frontier where "that which lies before us must take precedence over the 'past'" (Lewis 1996:109), for postcolonial artists living in the era of global capital an insistence on moving beyond this past might be held in some suspicion (ibid.).

If the avant-garde figures itself as being in the forefront of time and space, composers of radical traditions might imagine themselves in a middle ground, a position from which every time and every place is readily accessible. From this perspective the artist may imagine his creative palette as infinitely wider and less discriminatory than that of the most radical avant-gardist. Composers working in this mode often aim to subvert or step around the homogenizing forces of the Western avant-garde, ironically recalling the historical avant-garde's effort to marginalize itself in order to resist bourgeois commodification (Bürger 1984). These artists may interpret the labels "experimental," "avant-garde," and contemporary as "avatars of assimilation" (Harney 2004:xxv) within a structure of cultural imperialism. They may resist their worlding in ways that conform to the Western politics of representation and interpretation in which the radically new is valued and conflated with an authorial image of genius, lunatic, and otherness. The recurrent association by outside observers of *musik kontemporer* with the avant-garde occasions a discussion of Bali's placement within global aesthetic networks, the question of influence, and the representation of cultural change, and carries us to the next chapter.

> [The Balinese Conservatory] organized an "avant-garde" festival...strong-arming various...faculty members into throwing something together that would be "avant-garde," [telling us] all this would be concluded with a "really crazy" jam session...The concert was preceded by long speeches...about the meaning and history of the avant-garde in the west, and about [the conservatory's] commitment to being on the cutting edge. There followed the forced-march of the pieces themselves, admittedly of varying quality, and then the "jam session"...[with] about seventy-five people standing around looking embarrassed, and finally [a dancer] throwing himself into a water fountain and dancing around for about forty-five seconds, after which everyone applauded...to my knowledge, there isn't much "new" music happening in Bali right now...This is difficult to write about because it concerns people I care about and artists I respect.
>
> —message posted to the gamelan@listserv.darthmouth.edu listserv, February 3, 1996

2 Placing Bali in the Global Aesthetic Network

MANY OF THE composers and musicians with whom I worked repeatedly cited the *Festival Musik Masa Kini* (Festival of Contemporary Music) described above as a historic event that introduced novel notions of performance and composition and that marked for them a new era in meaningful collaborations between Balinese and foreign composers and performers. The divergence between Balinese and Western perceptions of the event leads us to ask: How can we characterize aesthetic innovation in Bali? How can outsiders recognize it? What is the relationship between Balinese contemporary music and the Western avant-garde?

The passage above neatly summarizes a common sentiment regarding the apparent mimetic quality (symbolized by quotation marks, e.g., "avant-garde") of Balinese experimentation that I frequently heard expressed by Western observers and which I sometimes expressed myself. In this chapter I assert that foreign observers are repeatedly blinded from fully recognizing and understanding aesthetic innovation in Bali due to persistent romanticizations of Balinese culture as the historic artifact of a self-enclosed society so that apparent breaks with the past are often interpreted as mimetic, inauthentic, and embarrassingly kitsch. As I demonstrate in this chapter, anthropological romanticizations that portray Balinese society as spatially bounded and characterized by temporal stasis neglect the historical record of precolonial, colonial, and modern interactions.

Both colonization and nationalist modernity expanded Balinese spatial and temporal imaginations. Western artists carrying the technologies of an ostensibly global modernism resided in Bali during the interwar period, establishing the island as a node in global aesthetic networks despite their own and colonial administrative efforts to encourage the Balinese to look inward. Although musical modernism was deeply domesticated in other areas of Asia, Indonesian (and especially Balinese) composers were only tangentially linked to the movement during the first half of the twentieth century and remain marginalized in modernist organizations such as the Asian Composers League. Since independence, most Indonesian composers have experienced only discontinuous, brief, and second-hand encounters with the Western avant-garde.

During the second half of the twentieth century Indonesian artists' experience of Western radical aesthetics was partly determined by the exigencies of national development and the Cold War cultural imperatives of the United States as mediated by foundations such as Rockefeller and Ford. While continuing to view Bali through the aestheticizing gaze of earlier ethnography, these foundations also—although sometimes indirectly—catalyzed local innovations through the support and guidance of Indonesian artists. Following the violent emergence of the New Order, in which thousands of artists were slaughtered, the Indonesian government and American foundations stepped in to energetically revive symbols of traditional cultural particularity. It is in this highly charged and contradictory context that *musik kontemporer* first emerged.

In considering the status of art as an autonomous institution in Bali—a precondition for the emergence of the avant-garde—I argue that neither the ethnographic description of a unified praxis nor a model of autonomous bourgeois art fit the bill. I conclude this chapter by revisiting the questions of influence and mimesis alluded to in the passage above. Eschewing a straightforward model of influence or diffusion, I suggest that Sperber's concept of the "epidemiology of representations" (1996), with its focus upon mutation through the constructive cognitive processes of the individual, captures well the incorporation and transformation of foreign materials in *musik kontemporer*, aligns closely with emic terminology, and leads to a nuanced understanding of cultural change.

Anthropological Romances

Bali is a fool's paradise; it requires a peculiar suspension of disbelief to understand it as anything other than a modern, paradoxical topos as complex as any other in today's world.[1] Yet Bali, and Indonesia more generally, have long been regarded as a kind of Eden, an anthropological playground teeming with a seemingly inexhaustible supply

---

[1] The title of this section is borrowed from Boon's (1977) important critique of anthropological representations of Bali.

of Culture. To the anthropologist each island appears to offer up for study unique ethnic groups tidily bounded by the sea. Partly due to this idealized perspective, Indonesia has served as one of the central sites for the study of cultures as self-contained and internally coherent systems: cultural islands floating on an apparently rising sea of Western imperialism. Anthropology and ethnomusicology grew in tandem with decolonization, their favored cases providing examples of what was left of premodern culture to remind the West of what it feared it had destroyed. Western interpretations of Balinese culture are often partly autobiographical; the unease with apparent cultural mimesis alluded to in the passage above reveals a concern for the maintenance of cultural particularity to counter images of Westernization.

In the 1930s, ethnographers of Bali, including Mead, Bateson, Belo, Spies, and McPhee, worked in an environment apparently depoliticized through colonial intervention. In the 1970s a second generation of researchers experienced a state-sponsored explosion of ceremonial spectacle embodied in the enormous Eka Dasa Rudra ceremony of 1979. Similarly awed by Balinese orthopraxy, foreign researchers again turned their attention primarily to the performative aspects of forms designated *tradisi*. As ethnographers, musicologists, and performers, we often remain concerned to demonstrate the internal coherence of Balinese society, ceremony, and musical structure. As Heider has demonstrated: "A romantic commitment to harmonious functionalism can lead to overemphasis on the harmonious aspects of a culture" (Heider 1988:76).[2] In the following I explore what might be concealed through a disciplinary bias that prioritizes internal structure over the external relations of power that determine the ethnographic encounter itself.

Romantic images of Bali and the Balinese have been deconstructed in numerous recent studies that have done much to provide a more nuanced, dynamic, politicized, and agent-based perspective.[3] To deconstruct again the anthropological romance of Bali is to break down an open door; contemporary anthropologists and ethnographers are aware of these problematic issues and representations. But the paradisiacal image reappears with routine regularity in touristic literature and with parasitic persistence in academia and intercultural performance projects fulfilling Said's prognostication that, despite its deconstruction, orientalism would only creep with electronic media; critical analysis does not make it disappear.[4] For the composers and musicians that

---

[2] See also: Rohner, DeWalt, and Ness (1973); Carroll (1974).
[3] See especially: Schulte Nordholt (1994), Robinson (1995), Hobart (1997), Picard (1996), Vickers (1989), Reuter (2003), Harnish (2005). Boon (1977) is the primary early reference.
[4] Grimshaw (2009) and Ornstein (2010), to name two recent examples, are excellent studies that, nevertheless, see Bali through the lens of ceremonial practice and musical form to the exclusion of a consideration of ideological and political structures. Consider also recent major exhibitions on Balinese culture at the San Francisco Asian Art Museum (2011) and the Horniman Museum in London (2011) both focusing narrowly on Balinese art prior to World War II. The frequent appearance since 2010 of both *gamelan* ensembles and robotic *gamelan* at American raves, "burns" (i.e. Burning Man) and installations suggests that signs of Bali continue to satisfy primitivist fantasies of the other. Since 2008 no less than six robotic *gamelan* projects have emerged in America and Europe, the most active being the *Gamelatron*, based in New York.

are the subject of this study the aestheticizing gaze of both tourism and ethnography was a theme to be riffed upon either with an ironic wink or outright hostility. Many composers mobilized it, if pragmatically rather than unquestionably, to reach larger audiences. Throughout this text I will refer to the legacy of the early ethnography of Bali, risking the potential for it to appear as the straw man against which I counterpose the world of *musik kontemporer*. However, to understand its continued power, one need only observe that its classic texts still do brisk business in bookstores in Ubud and that the classic tourist imagery of the island reappears in contemporary forms such as *Eat, Pray, Love*.

Historic romanticizations of the island oscillated between positive images—natural overabundance, an intriguing culture of performance, proper kingship—against images of degeneracy—nakedness, disorder, lost greatness, and anarchic slaughter. Bali was two-dimensional; its Edenic face was understood as a "functionally integrative mechanism" of its wicked obverse (Robinson 1998:6). I am concerned here not to fall into the same formulaic commonplaces by viewing the sometimes transgressive and restive sounds of *musik kontemporer* as the logical counterpoint to the persistent image of the exotic *legong* dancer.

However, *musik kontemporer*'s marginality both in the ethnographic account and in Balinese culture is explained partly by persistent representations of idyllic cultural stasis painted in the face of contrary evidence. Early Dutch observers recorded images of stability during an era of extended civil war. As Balinese society was undergoing massive changes brought about through colonization during the first decade of the twentieth century, colonial scholars described an island of artists and their culture in which life and art were still a "beautiful totality" (Rouffaer in Boon 1977:41), representing a mirror of premodern Europe.

The persistent tendency to see stasis over change was due partly to prior theorizations of the island as a kind of time capsule. In his 1817 *History of Java*, Raffles established the image of Bali as a timeless museum of Java's Hindu golden age, by then seen to have deteriorated under Muslim and European influence.[5] A museum is populated with objects that can be lost, stolen, or broken; by the beginning of the twentieth century some ethnographers had begun to portray Bali as already despoiled, its authenticity shattered by the modernity thought to be brought by colonization and tourism (Pollmann 1992:13). Indeed, Western observers have, since the Enlightenment, held it as axiomatic that contact with Europeans ensured cultural loss in the Orient (Fabian 1991:195).

The recurrent trope, found in both emic and etic discourse, of *tradisi* and *moderen* as co-present but incommensurable in contemporary Balinese life was prefigured in Margaret Mead and Gregory Bateson's framing of the Balinese character as schizophrenic, a condition they theorized was produced by Balinese society rather than

---

[5] This discourse survives in Western academia and has become prevalent in Balinese discourse. See Stephen (2005) for an image of Bali as a museum of Saivite Tantrism and Burhanuddin (2008) for an example of the museum image in local discourse.

biology.[6] Their study polished the then-hackneyed colonial concept of cultural Bali, as opposed to an image of political Bali, economic Bali, or theoretical Bali. For the majority of its modern history, art and culture have been the dominant topics through which to discuss the island. In his *Bali: The Value System of a Steady State* (1949), Bateson suggested that Balinese culture embodies stasis—a series of "a thousand plateaus"—and that the continually active nature of Balinese culture was not an expression of development or change (schismogenesis), but the embodiment of an ultimately undevelopable static state maintained by continuous ceremonial and artistic tasks neither economically nor competitively determined. This model falls apart when confronted with the mass killings of 1965–66, the intense and sometimes violent rivalries between *gamelan* ensembles, and the mutual inspirations flowing between Western and Balinese composers. It is deeply ironic that Bateson's homeostatic vision of Bali persisted in its influence despite his later pioneering work in the fields of cybernetics and reflexivity in which he attempted to account for the role of the observer in observed systems.

Time lies at the heart of the anthropological romance. In the classic anthropological image the Balinese are denied a sense of either personal or communal history, thus proving their radical distance from Western temporalities.[7] As Hobart (1997) points out, such a perspective, blind to plentiful counter-evidence, conflated the Balinese with the transcendental agent of their timeless cultural essence. Bali stands as a model of what Lévi-Strauss called "cold societies" in that their internal environment neighbors on the zero of historical temperature (1967:46–47).[8] Lacking kinetic heat, cold societies such as Bali's are characterized by so-called motionless time (what Lévi-Strauss called synchronic time) in that history is denied by the very imperviousness of the cultural system to change. Within otherwise cold societies, the individual may experience the qualitative time identified by Durkheim (following Bergson's notion of inner *durée*), in which time is felt as an alternation of intensities and qualities (as in Geertz's 1973 description of the Balinese calendar) or various rhythms of social life as opposed to the homogenized, rational, Western time regime. Balinese *gamelan* music, from its supposed lack of development as described by McPhee (1966), to the commonplace characterization of its forms as cyclical as opposed to Western linear musical temporality (Kramer 1988), is a manifestation of the anthropological romance of Balinese temporality more generally.[9]

---

[6] Their work in Bali (published in 1942) was partly funded by a foundation focused upon schizophrenia. Suryani and Jensen (1992) question many of Mead and Bateson's conclusions, biases and methods.
[7] This convoluted debate snakes through Geertz (1973b), Bloch (1977), Howe (1981), Duff-Cooper (1990), Hobart (1997). See also Gell (1992).
[8] Possibly reacting to the suggestion of universal modes of time consciousness proposed by Husserl, Heidegger, and empirical psychology, Lévi-Strauss appeared interested in the sociological potential for annulling time as an example of cultural relativism.
[9] For a recent (1997) example of persistent exotifications, consider Levine's characterization: "The Balinese, for example, have been labeled right-hemisphere people [sic], while Anglo-Americans in the United States lean more toward the characteristics of L-mode thinking. These differences are plainly reflected in attitudes toward time. It is telling that the Balinese—whose daily activities are entwined with religious, musical, dramatic, and artistic ritual—often refer to the hour on the clock as 'rubber time' (*jam keret* [sic])" (1997:58).

Following Parsons, the ethnography of time has been bifurcated. On the one hand, universal (real) time is left to the physicists and cognitive psychologists, whereas ethnographic time is relativized to as many flavors as there are (premodern) cultures. As Fabian (1983) and Hobart (1997) point out, this originary bifurcation has lead to more than one epistemological dead end. The absurd logic of the anthropological romance conflates the Balinese with a past which, it is postulated, they do not have a truly historical consciousness of.

June 2007. Gusti Putu Sudarta and I sat on the front steps of his new home built in the rice fields that sloped down towards the coast in the village of Bona, Gianyar. His wife Jenny (Chen Ni Ma) brewed the green tea she had just brought back from Taiwan. The caldera atop Gunung Agung appeared over the clouds to the east as the sun set towards the west. We took long pauses in our listless conversation to listen to a rehearsal being held at Madé Sidia's compound to the west. Sidia, a colleague of Sudarta's at the conservatory, was rehearsing a new massive performance intended for the Bali Safari Park's Tuesday evening tourist show. Sudarta, a rather shy personality who nevertheless stirred awe (if not fear) among other performers through his calm virtuosity, began to animatedly describe a project he had clearly been hatching for some time. He would apply for funds to support the recreation of an ensemble based upon the iconography of the Borobudor, the ninth-century Buddhist monument in Central Java. The ancient mandala, the largest Buddhist structure in the world, illustrates in its three miles of bas-reliefs several episodes featuring musicians and dancers. Rather than gamelan, the scenes depict musical instruments and ensembles now extinct in Indonesia. I played the devil's advocate: he had no access to the music itself; he did not even know if these were correct representations of the instruments of the era.[10] *Sudarta, pictured in Plate 2.1, performing with Madé Subandi, shot me a sly glance: "Of course! But because we don't know anything about it, I could compose* musik kontemporer *for it. Being even older than* gamelan, *I'm sure I could get funding, probably from Ford, and my performance would automatically become* tradisi!*"*

Sudarta's comments reflect off the patina of authority that anthropologists, ethnomusicologists, and Indonesian policymakers have invested in premodern cultural artifacts and representations. Most of the composers and musicians I worked with believed that foreign researchers and funding institutions were primarily interested in *tradisi* rather than *kontemporer* expressions. Sudarta's hypothetical project would leverage the fetishizing of ancient cultural forms, in which historic origins can only tenuously be suggested, to catalyze the creation of *new* music.

The ethnomusicological investment in the anthropological romance of Bali is revealed in the recurrent interest in *gamelan*'s origins. The dubious suggestion of

---

[10] I remembered a sculpture of Saraswati recently erected at the conservatory in which she performs on an impossible instrument: a plucked (rather than bowed) *rebab* fiddle featuring four rather than the normal two strings, six pegs in the box, and a body recalling McCartney's Höofner semi-acoustic bass I imagined some ethnoarchaeologist of the future frantically trying to reconstruct the instrument.

PLATE 2.1 Gusti Sudarta (left) and Madé Subandi (right) play Subandi's *gender romantis*. Photo by Christopher Romero.

extremely early origins shares with the anthropological romance the conflation of age and authenticity in which those expressions that emerged even before contact would be best, being immune from accusations of hybridity and mimesis. It is de rigueur in texts on *gamelan* to suggest their origin as an evolution of the ancient Dongsonian bronze drum.[11] Spreading from the mainland to maritime Southeast Asia beginning around 1500 BCE, cast-bronze drums of many types share a common morphology and a repertoire of animist iconography (Bernet-Kempers 1988). The largest known example, the *bulan Pejeng* (I), moon of Pejeng, is housed in the Penataran temple in the central Balinese village of Pejeng. The enormous drum was made in Bali probably around the first century CE and incorporates both localized and intercultural iconography.[12] But there is no concrete evidence connecting *gamelan* with the Dongsonian drums.[13]

---

[11] For examples see: Gold (2004), Spiller (2008), Kunst (1973), Pickvance (2005), McPhee (1966), Basset (1993), Bandem (1986), Siagian (2005). The most elaborate statement of the case is made in Hood (1984).

[12] The leading Balinese archaeologist, Wayan Ardika, associates the drums in Bali with burial ceremony rather than music (Hobart et al. 1996).

[13] While certainly possible, there is no evidence to support the hypothesis of gradual concatenation and morphological transformations of Dongsonian bronze drums leading to the development of large *gamelan* ensembles. The metallurgy involved in casting bronze drums is significantly different from that of forging bossed *gongs* and chimes.

My informants expressed little or no interest in the object aside from its spiritual aura; it represented to them the lost cultures of Bali's dark ages and embodied one of many phases of cultural transformation and loss over a span of several millennia.

Precolonial Intercultural Interaction

The anthropological romance simultaneously elided Bali with a premodern past, denied the Balinese a historical sense of that past, and cultivated an image of Balinese culture as a hothouse flower, sealed off from external networks. In this section I contextualize Bali's place within historical aesthetic networks in order to counter the preoccupations of the anthropological romance and to historicize the interculturalisms of *musik kontemporer*. If we understand globalization as something more than the economic rise of the West during the age of empire and industrial revolution, we can better recognize the networks established by non-Europeans prior to the modern era and the role of knowledge and aesthetics (as much as money) in the establishment of global connections.

Southeast Asian trading networks, the Sanskritic cosmopolis (Pollack 2000), the Buddhist *sangah*, and the Islamic *umma* had, by the twelfth century, linked the entirety of Asia and beyond through shared languages, scripts, religious beliefs, and aesthetic forms. Kant's notion of the aesthetic community—groups of people formed on the basis of taste over other social categories—evokes the evolving expressive forms that emerged in the multicultural flux of the ancient Southeast Asian entrepôt. Contemporary Balinese represent a combination of successive, complex in-migrations likely beginning around 1000 BCE (Hobart et al. 1996) in which each settling community encountered an earlier "original people." Balinese society appears to have maintained multiple categories for peoples with different origins (Reuter 2003) and multicultural trading communities lived alongside and occasionally merged with otherwise indigenous Balinese since at least the first century (Hauser-Schäublin 2004).[14]

If the archaeological horizons of first-century Bali suggest a world in which Balinese, Javanese, Malay, Chinese, and Indian (and other) peoples and their material cultures interacted in complex ways, must not have also their sounds? It is only through the interaction of disparate, mobile peoples between whom new aesthetic technologies and ideas would flow, that new art worlds (Becker 1982) could be forged in which aesthetically syncretic objects such as the *bulan Pejeng* could emerge.[15] In these worlds, as in *musik kontemporer*, foreign cultural signs symbolized sophistication for an elite whose power lay in controlling the trade and transformation of aesthetic style and material culture (Bérénice 2003).

---

[14] Ardika has identified the largest collections of early Indian trade pottery in Indonesia around the northern Balinese port of Singaraja (Hauser-Schäublin 2004). Direct trade with China, primarily through intermarriage with Hokien traders, was established by at least 400 CE (Sulistyawati 2008).

[15] As Lansing (2007) suggests, intercultural interaction is quite literally built into the material of the *bulan Pejeng;* neither tin nor copper are found in Bali.

The earliest Javanese inscriptions of the fifth and sixth centuries describe the important social roles of musicians in local courts. As depicted on the reliefs of the ninth-century Borobudor, these musicians performed instruments classically associated with the Sanskritic cosmopolis (Kunst 1973:111–12). Bossed *gongs*, the iconic instruments of the *gamelan*, appear to have emerged through complex Southeast Asian trade networks during the thirteenth century. Analyzing the cargo of several premodern shipwrecks, Nicolas (2009) has concluded that the first bossed *gongs* appeared in mainland Southeast Asia, probably Thailand, to replace earlier Chinese and Vietnamese bells and flat *gongs*. Emerging contemporaneously with the Yuan Dynasty, the Mongol invasions into Java, Thai maritime expansionism, and the Singhasari–early Majapahit period (late-thirteenth to early fourteenth centuries CE), the bossed *gong* was a symbol of cultural sophistication among a cosmopolitan elite during an intensely dynamic era of intercultural interaction. Similar to the earlier transformation of Dongsonian bronze drum technology, Balinese and Javanese smiths indigenized the imported object, enlarging the diminutive mainland *gongs* to an enormous scale and thereby modulating their acoustic properties and musical functions. By the fourteenth century the large bossed *gong* appears as a central symbol of Javanese and Balinese culture.

The emergence of the large Indonesian *gong*, as if symbolically ushering in the nascent power of Javanese empire, coincided with the rise of the Majapahit Kingdom and its colonial rule of Bali beginning in 1343.[16] Although Javanese colonial accounts suggested that at this time "all Balinese customs were [made] consistent with [those in] Java" (quoted in Hobart et al. 1996:34), a highly syncretic performance culture appears to have emerged and flourished during the sixteenth century in Gelgel (Karangasem) under the leadership of Waturrenggong who sponsored massive performances for large commoner audiences outside the walled palace grounds (ibid. 40).[17] While many contemporary Balinese trace their genealogies to aristocratic Javanese who abandoned the dissolving Majapahit courts for an already densely populated Bali in the mid-sixteenth century, it is important to remember that this origin emerges after Islamic and Chinese cultures were well established in Bali and just before European contact.

The Balinese of the precolonial era were linked to the complex *pasisir* trading network of maritime Southeast Asia dominated by Islamic Malay mariners. Arab trade with the islands was established by the ninth century, and the *subandars*, a Persian term usually referring to Chinese Muslim harbormasters, were the preferred coastal administrators of Balinese and Javanese rulers (Hauser-Schäublin 2004:40). Vickers (2005) describes the cosmopolitan milieu of the *pasisir* world as recorded in Balinese

---

[16] Javanese cultural forms were introduced earlier (in the eleventh century) by the Balinese ruler Udayana, his Javanese queen, and their sons. Udayana's son Airlangga controlled both Java and Bali from his palace in Central Java.

[17] Here we might speculate on the acoustic divergence between Javanese and Balinese *gamelan* ensembles over time: the former is a courtly symbol of refinement historically performed for small aristocratic audiences listening within the reverberant space of the Javanese *pendopo*; the latter is designed for maximum carrying power in an open space appealing to larger, and no doubt louder, lay audiences.

Malat epics composed between the end of the Majapahit Kingdom to the nineteenth century. These tales enlivened a Balinese spatial imagination extending throughout Southeast Asia and stretching to northern India, China, the Philippines, Byzantium, and the broader Middle East. The intercultural lineaments of the *pasisir* world fostered syncretic Hindu-Islamic religious practices still observable on Bali's North Coast.[18] Now iconic dance genres of the Hindu Balinese, including *baris, jauk, jangger*, and the *legong*, were reportedly first introduced to Bali by *pasisir* Malay and Sasak traders (ibid. 300 and Liem 2003:91). The image of an intensely insular, inward-looking, and culturally conservative precolonial Balinese, as portrayed in Geertz's *Negara* (1980), sits uncomfortably with the evidence of intercultural interaction.[19] As today, precolonial intercultural interactions likely encouraged communities on Bali to think through their culture in terms of local and foreign others, a semiotic hallmark of *musik kontemporer* [Track BV-2/1].

Colonial Interaction

European trade in Bali began at the end of the sixteenth century.[20] At first Europeans represented just another group in the multicultural mix trading on Bali's shores. Intensifying engagement with the Dutch eventually drew the Balinese into a global market economy. The Dutch slowly gained control of Bali after a series of halting battles beginning in the north at Jagaraga in 1845 and culminating in the concession of Bangli in 1910. During the early colonial era, European presence was largely limited to a small population in the north where the colonial administration leveraged the Balinese rajas' social conservatism and political hostility towards the Javanese in order to stem nascent nationalism. By 1875 the Dutch had opened schools accessible to *jaba* (B), casteless commoners, and had outlawed slave trade and corvée labor while instituting severe taxation regimes. Taxed beyond their ability to sustain many of the large ensembles they had once patronized, many rajas sold their *gamelan* to village cooperatives which began to more freely transform courtly genres. New social relations brought about through colonization initiated a series of aesthetic and

---

[18] Adherents of *slam* Hinduism, now primarily self-identified as Balinese Hindu but who trace their ancestry to Javanese or Madurese Muslims, host shrines to Mecca and Chinese gods and eschew pork within their temples (Vickers 2005:301).

[19] Liem's (2003) review of the evidence suggests that during periods of the sixteenth century and possibly before, the raja in Gelgel attempted to isolate the commoners of the interior from the influences of the Islamic Mataram and Makassarese kingdoms, and the Dutch East India Company (VOC, *Vereenigde Oost-Indische Compagnie*), consolidated in 1602. But this was only partly successful and the kings themselves fostered far-flung aesthetic and political networks. To a certain extent, foreign communities of Chinese, Malay, Indian, and Arab traders were segregated in port towns during the seventeenth and eighteenth centuries and may have remained distinctly non-Balinese. But by the twentieth century many of these groups were densely intermarried with Balinese communities (Liem 2003:49–57).

[20] Early accounts (including those of Lintgens of 1597, see Vickers, 1994) describe Portuguese explorers dumbfounded to encounter Portuguese-fluent Moluccan translators at inland Balinese courts where rajas enquired as to the realm's current foreign relations with England (Boon 1977:14–15).

epistemological crises catalyzing the creation of new forms of expression throughout the island (Vickers 2005:308).

By the 1910s newly composed court *malat* texts (the so-called *uug* or *rusak*, broken texts) documented the fragmentation of the courts and expressed reconfigurations in the Balinese spatial imagination. A world bound by *pasisir* trade and Majapahit legend transformed into one in which the Netherlands East Indies and Europe were principal horizons. The homogenous, even slices of the Mercator map, based upon the totalizing classification of a geometrical grid, impinged upon an older Balinese conceptualization of space which, like traditional temporal regimes, is a nonhomogenous scheme of shifting intensities and qualities oriented around the central pivot of holy mountains (Agung, Meru). The Balinese Hindu notion of the recapitulation of the universe, the *buana agung*, within the human body, the *buana alit*, was overlain with astronomical theories of the universe introduced through public education.[21]

The establishment of purely secular spaces in Balinese society, apparently independent of divine or royal jurisdiction, suggested to a large underclass that it might be possible to create a city of man in an entirely human space (Geertz 1980), the dream Marx saw in a global loosening of religion. But the sense of a dialectical relationship between a manifest world of experience (*sekala*) and its complex entanglement with the unmanifest world of disembodied souls, ghouls, and the divine (*niskala*) expanded to encapsulate the entire globe as it became known to the Balinese, rather than retreating in the face of a secularizing world.

The experience of colonization suggested to the Balinese that their society, ostensibly past its monumental golden age, was simply a precursor to the modern West. Colonial control over time and history served political needs; the Western time regime functioned as a mode of governance. In the effort to codify (and thereby control) Balinese traditional practice, the Dutch attempted to standardize the ritual calendar. Whereas holidays such as *nyepi* had previously occurred on various dates throughout the island, the Dutch enforced an island-wide scheme. In 1908 the Dutch installed an enormous clock in the central crossroads of Denpasar, its alarm ringing in measured, precise continuity to mark school and work hours (Schulte Nordholt and van Schendel 2001). Like the ringing of premodern European village bells (Corbin 1998), the striking of the temple *kulkul* slit drum, marking the irregular intensities of the ceremonial calendar, came to coexist, but was not wholly supplanted by, the clock whose obstinate regularity stood as a permanent reminder of the profane world.

But the rational, metronomic slices of the clock apparently did not produce a similar musical effect. Instead, an evidently contradictory process occurred; as Western time regimes were introduced, Balinese musical temporality became increasingly a-metric,

---

[21] Although, according to Liem, under the Dutch Balinization policy (described below) the Balinese were taught their own culture at colonial schools. They were taught, for instance, to go to traditional healers (I: *dukun*) instead of a polyclinic. The lunar eclipse was explained through Balinese myth rather than modern astronomy (2003:80). This was not the case prior to or after the Balinization policy, nor at the nationalist Budi Otomo schools, first opened in Bali in 1919.

fluid, and smooth through the advent of *kebyar*. Nevertheless, we might wonder how newly available mundane temporalities became a heuristic for novel modes of experiencing sound; did Balinese music feel different while wearing a wristwatch? How was clock time experienced *through* the sound of *lelambatan*? Considering such questions reminds us that the new musical temporalities of *kreasi baru* and *musik kontemporer* are only the most recent in a history of transforming temporal imaginations.

The introduction of a time regime and a notion of historical progress (as deleterious as its effects may have been), common to both Balinese and their others, fed the universalizing and revolutionary thought of the socially progressive *pergerakan* (I), movement, throughout the East Indies between c. 1912 and 1926 (extending later in Bali) which brought Asians, Eurasians, and Europeans into close intellectual and aesthetic contact.[22] The intercultural interactions of the *pergerakan* were embodied in *stambul* (*stamboel*), a colonial-era theater form performed throughout the East Indies by mixed troupes of Chinese, Dutch, Mestizo, Arabs, Javanese, Balinese, and Indians for audiences of all classes, religions, and races. *Stambul* featured a complex, heteroglossic mix of languages employing Arabic, Indonesian, Chinese, and European tales (Cohen 2006). Marxist *pergerakan* literature envisioned a synthesis of Eastern and Western culture that did not efface local identity (Foulcher 2009), foreshadowing the ethos of *kontemporer* projects of the *reformasi* as described in Chapter 4.

Musicians and dancers from the Dardanella *stambul* troupe interacted with performers from throughout Asia during the 1930s, working especially closely with Indian artists. The troupe's lead dancer, Devi Dja, studied closely with the Indian dancer Rukmini Devi, in return teaching her both Javanese and Balinese dance (Cohen 2010:186). In the late 1920s and 1930s many Indian artists and intellectuals associated with the Greater Indian Society, including Rabindranath Tagore, visited and studied in Bali and Java, establishing a lateral channel of interculturalism that largely sidestepped Western imperialism. During this time Tagore also hosted artists from the Indies at his Sangit Bhavan College of Music and Dance, founded in 1921. Later, Uday Shankar (elder brother of Ravi Shankar) collaborated with Indies artists to develop his 1941 dance drama *Rama Lila*, modeled upon *wayang kulit* (ibid. 169).

During the 1930s a community of Western painters, novelists, composers, anthropologists, and elite tourists resided, sometimes for years, in Bali to weather the storm of interwar modernity brewing in the West. Attracted by the charismatic German painter and musician Walter Spies, many settled in the arts community of Ubud, forging aesthetic networks with Balinese artists.[23] Spies collaborated with Balinese artists to create the modern *kecak* monkey chant and with the Dutch painter Rudolph Bonnet catalyzed a

---

[22] The notion of a progressive social body moving towards an ideal through homogenous time foreshadows the temporal imagination of the nation and counters older beliefs in the cyclical Hindu *yugas*, a recurrent sequence of ages defined by a list of qualities rather than contents and ordered by increasing distance from the divine.

[23] Walter Spies (1895–1942), the German painter, musician, and scholar, arrived in Bali in 1927 after leaving his conducting duties at the orchestra in the court of the Sultan of Yogyakarta.

modern school of Balinese painting.[24] These interactions have often been characterized as a fortuitous and apolitical contact zone of cross-cultural stimulation.[25]

Although the composer and musicologist Colin McPhee resided for several years on the island, it appears his presence provided little in the way of concrete information about Western musical practices to Balinese composers or musicians and he initiated no known collaborative compositions.[26] Aside from Spies's early experiments with the Dresden avant-garde, many of the Western artists residing in Bali during the 1930s were rather conservative. Preoccupied with an orientalized image of Bali, they did not set out to intentionally shake up local notions of culture, art, modernity, or tradition. Nevertheless, their very presence functioned to transform Balinese arts in permanent, if sometimes subtle, ways. Despite colonial efforts to ghettoize tradition under the so-called Balinization policies of the 1930s, many innovative cultural representations, while often appearing completely indigenous, were in fact novel blendings of Balinese and Western aesthetics (H. Geertz 1994).[27]

Precolonial Balinese painting forms incorporated a flat spatial perspective and a seemingly random scatter of temporal events.[28] Bonnet and Spies trained Balinese painters (almost all high caste) in proper Western perspective, left to right temporal flow, and modern anatomy. They collaborated with the local aristocracy to promote Balinese painting abroad, linking Balinese artists to regional and global aesthetic networks.[29] In his publications and conversations with Balinese artists, Bonnet appeared concerned to keep the Balinese free from Western influence, encouraging them to develop their own globally intelligible styles influenced only by Asian cultures.[30] He often argued, sometimes violently, with the artist Ketut Ngendon over his experimental portraits in which Western styles such as cubism were boldly transformed (Hill 2006).

Spies's and Bonnet's considerable interventions in Balinese painting far overshadows any impact Western musical modernism had upon *gamelan* during the colonial era but prefigures the intense interactions between Balinese and Western composers that emerged during the late New Order (ca. 1990). Both scenes involved Balinese artists often working closely with, if not directly studying under, older, more powerful Western patrons concerned both to educate the Balinese while simultaneously fretting

---

[24] The Javanese choreographer Sardono Kusomo maintains that Spies "partly modeled the choreography of his *kecak* on Swan Lake" (p.c. September 2003).

[25] See Holt (1967:177), Harnish (2001), Oja (1990). See Wakeling (2010) for a critique of these representations.

[26] Harnish (2001) suggests that McPhee's mere presence stimulated the strategic cultivation of composition as a career for Balinese artists.

[27] Yamashita has called the same representations an expression of a "creole culture" (2003:37).

[28] Ida Bagus Madé Tibah's *The Tale of the Two Sisters Bawang and Kesuna* (in H. Geertz 1994:51), provides a good example. The temporal structure of the painting only makes sense if one already understands the narrative.

[29] Sponsored by Bonnet, Ida Bagus Kembeng's painting, *Ardja Performance in the Desa*, won the silver medal at the 1937 Paris exhibition (Hill 2006:20).

[30] The colonial scholar Hooykaas similarly argued against the use of Malay among Balinese authors of the era, suggesting that they should develop a modern literature exclusively in the local language (in Liem 2003:79).

over the dangers of Western influence. In both instances, those Balinese artists willing to align their aesthetics to Western interests were more likely to gain access to lucrative global aesthetic networks. In both contexts the expressions that emerged were neither a result of completely Balinese cultural processes nor a wholesale accommodation to Westernization but instead represented expressions in between.

GLOBAL MODERNISM

In this section I consider the relationship between Balinese performing arts and modernism. I first describe the development of modernism generally, its peregrinations through colonization, and the shape of local responses. I then consider musical modernism and its intersections with Indonesian *musik kontemporer*.

Modernism refers generally to an interdisciplinary constellation of aesthetic movements from the late-nineteenth to early twentieth centuries—symbolism, expressionism, cubism, constructivism, and so on—bound by a shared interest in technology and a future-progress-oriented ethos marked by a negation of older romanticism and classicism. In the West, modernism has been analyzed as a reaction to the frenzy and vertigo of modernity itself and as a form of protest against incomplete modernization (Jameson 1991:366, Born 1995:40); modernism was sometimes critiqued in the colony and post-colony as the "armed version" of modernity (Nandy 1983:iv).

Modernism spread asexually (Mitter 2007:13) around the globe, seeking to reproduce artists in its image without intimately engaging local histories. The illusion of a wholly voluntaristic, equitable global modernism was furthered by the subtle nature of postwar American imperialism, founded less on direct territorial domination than on interlocking forms of indirect economic, political, and cultural control (McQuire and Papastergiadis 2006:3). By the middle of the twentieth century, the newly global economy, while not solely controlled in the West, nevertheless functioned to extend western economic and political domination through an agenda of deregulation, privatization, and submission to Western market imperatives (ibid.). Within this context, non-Western modernists became caught in the minefield of authenticity: on the one hand encouraged to take part in increasingly globalized styles, while on the other risking accusations of colonial mimicry if their contributions did not fulfill Western primitivist fantasies. Double consciousness became the "poisoned gift" for all non-Western artists who would be modern (Gaonkar 2001:3).

Some local artists rejected global modernism's negation of the past by bearing witness to particular histories. In his 1928 *Cannibalist Manifesto*, the Brazilian writer Oswald de Andrade confronted the distortion of the exotic by Picasso and other European artists by asserting that through "cultural cannibalism" a unique Brazilian modernism could be developed that engaged meaningfully with local culture. In the early 1940s the Indonesian cultural critic Ki Hadjar Dewantara similarly articulated a vision of a new Indonesian form of high art based upon the *puncak-puncak* (I), peaks, of local cultures (Sumarsam 1995:9). Both Dewantara and de Andrade illustrate the strategies local cultural elites forged to respond to modernism's claims of universality.

Musical modernism spread with empire, emerging first in those locations where Western classical music was domesticated through colonial education. Its appearance in East and Southeast Asia was aided by the domestication of Western music in Japan during the Meiji Restoration (1868–1912). Japan's later occupation of China, Korea, and Indonesia (1942–45) furthered the spread of Western music throughout the region. By the 1960s a musical language combining late romanticism, atonality, dodecaphonic composition, and serialism had spread throughout the major cosmopolitan centers of the world, creating an imagined community of global musical modernism linked through performances and scores.

Musical modernism constituted a sprawling, sometimes conflicting body of aesthetics and techniques. Twelve-tone composition and serialism espoused a stringent philosophy of autarchy, appealing to universalism through a rationality that denied reference to other musical systems. Appearing as a response to the antiseptic, brainy praxis of Adornian high modernism, a group of composers working in the 1930s to 1950s, including Cowell, Britten, and McPhee, sought to enrich their compositional palettes through the new resources provided by non-Western cultures (see Lechner 2005:3). These composers appealed to universalism not through the slash-and-burn ethos of serialism and its Germanic obsession with personal, expressive self-revelation, but in the digestion of the world's musics. This "counter-movement, full-blooded and vital" (Cowell 1933:150) instead constituted the "impersonal and non-expressive" aesthetic symbolized in the functional craftsmanship of Balinese music, which retained a "rhythmic vitality both primitive and joyous" (McPhee 1935:163).

MUSICAL MODERNISM IN INDONESIA

Although Western musical genres—primarily Christian liturgical and colonial military musics—had slowly diffused throughout the archipelago beginning in the late-fifteenth century, Western classical music was not widely domesticated in the Dutch East Indies colony, being primarily limited to upper-class Dutch and mestizo communities in Batavia (Jakarta), Central Java, and Surabaya, East Java. In the early twentieth century these communities overwhelmingly preferred light classical song (I: *seriosa*) over modernist styles, which have never found a welcome home in the archipelago. The case of the Sumatran composer Amir Pasaribu (1915–2010) serves as perhaps the most illuminating example of the difficult career of musical modernism in Independence-era Indonesia.

Having studied organ with his father, Pasaribu was later introduced to Western classical music by the Dutch friars at his high school in North Sumatra from whom he began to study both violin and piano, continuing his studies at a teacher-training college in West Java. He later studied in Batavia with the Russian cellist Nicolai Varvolomeyev. Apparently the first Indonesian to study music abroad, Pasaribu enrolled in 1936 in the Musashino School of Music in Tokyo, studying for three years before returning to join the Dutch Radio Orchestra as a cellist in Batavia where he later studied composition with the Dutch composer James Zwart (Miller 2011:67). After independence, Pasaribu became the director of the music department of the national radio system (RRI) at its headquarters in Jakarta.

Adornian in his disdain for light Western and popular music (and especially antagonistic towards jazz), Pasaribu's modernist aesthetics aligned with other independence-era cultural elites, including the critics Dungga and Manik. Like these colleagues, Pasaribu had little experience of Indonesian regional traditional musics and he strongly advocated for the adoption of Western modernism as the language of Indonesia's emergent national music, citing the case of Turkey as a non-Western society that had taken the adoption of serious music to heart (Pasaribu 1986). Pasaribu's lasting influence upon the musical development of the nation would be dampened, however, by his need to flee the nation in 1968 for his long association with the Indonesian communist party, after which his music was banned from performance (Notosudirdjo 2001). Nevertheless, Pasaribu's example reminds us that musical modernism in Indonesia was not an aesthetic regime imposed upon the colony and postcolony by a top-down Western imperialism, but was actively adopted by a section of the population, albeit miniscule, genuinely enraptured by the style.

During the New Order, the question posed by the Philippine composer and European-trained pianist José Maceda encapsulated for many Indonesian artists working in the elite language of modernism the paradox of their situation: "What has all of *this* got to do with coconuts and rice?" (quoted in Tenzer 2003:94). Maceda's question leads ultimately to a different kind of political and aesthetic imagination, one in which the universality proclaimed in the musics and rhetoric of Schoenberg, Varese, Xenakis, and Boulez would be provincialized as a canvas upon which Philippine, Indonesian, or Thai values could be drawn (ibid. 100). The handful of contemporary Indonesian composers directly engaged with modernist approaches—principally Suka Hardjana, Slamet Abdul Sjukur, Franki Raden and (later) Michael Asmara, Wayan Yudane, and Tony Prabowo—appear to have shared Maceda's interest in provincializing the ostensibly universal aesthetics of musical modernism, an approach that seems to have placed them in an ambivalent relationship to the Asian Composers League (ACL), founded in 1973.

While the ACL's putative mission has been to foster a pan-Asian modernism, its membership has historically been dominated by East Asians trained in the West working in the style of Western modernism. The 1999 ACL meeting in Central Java highlighted the schisms between Indonesian composers and their Asian counterparts. When the steering committee singled Indonesians out for having a "completely different approach towards the development of New Music as compared to other Asian composers," Suka Hardjana, in his shocked response, noted that nearly all of his non-Indonesian ACL colleagues composed in the modern style of serial or dodecaphonic composition (Hardjana 2004:46). He asked if the members of the steering committee were not exhibiting "... an odd prejudice that betrayed their own self-alienation and cultural loss." Adding that: "In this situation, we are lucky that Indonesian composers do not fully understand the history and culture of Western music, including those of us who teach Western music!" (ibid.).

Rather than being consistently and directly trained in the materials, history, and techniques of Western modernism, many composers engaged with *musik kontemporer* have internalized and transformed a complex of decontextualized Western notions about the nature and role of art and experimentation introduced through a long, halting, and sometimes second-hand interaction with Western aesthetic modernism. Cold War cultural diplomacy established the most influential conduits of these complex aesthetic linkages.

Cold War Culture

February 2003. Wayan Sadra invited me to his rehearsals in Kemlayan, Solo (Central Java) after hearing I had spent time in his old neighborhood in Denpasar. Soon I was performing and touring throughout Java with his Sono Seni musik kontemporer ensemble. Rehearsals were held at Sardono's studio in the heart of old Solo near the palace, a dense honeycomb of narrow streets snaking between high-walled family compounds and batik factories.[31] *A rehearsal in Bali was open to the world, held in a public meeting hall or in one of the many small open pavilions in a Balinese home. A lesson, and each of your mistakes, was open for public viewing, comment, and ridicule with no escape from the heat and the bustle of Balinese everyday life. In Solo, by contrast, all of the sound, swelter, and confused flurry of the city was sealed off by the tall wooden gate at Sardono's compound, a dark garden interspersed with grottos, an antique* pendopo, *library, and a soundproof, deliciously air-conditioned, music studio.*

Sadra was the high priest of a rambunctious, multiethnic gang of young musicians—Gondrong, Zoel, Danis, Agus, Gombloh, and Peni. Each was conservatory-educated and fluent in a number of musical forms. Sadra spoke mainly in rough low Javanese with only a slight Balinese accent. And he spoke at length; our rehearsals ran from 7:00 to 10:00 p.m., but only half of this time might be engaged in music-making, the balance being animated bull sessions on music, composition, and politics. If more music was learned in a typical rehearsal in Bali, few fostered the kind of animated conversation had at Sono Seni. Sadra told war stories of a life in musik kontemporer, *all too good to fact-check: a composition for amplified defecating water buffalo; works for rotten eggs; an "electro-acoustic" improvisation for unsuspecting female dancer and prerecorded orgasms; lean times of busking behind "naked snake dancers" in Jakarta.*

In conversation following a rehearsal of his Beringin Kurung, I asked Sadra, pictured in Plate 2.2, what it was about. "What does it mean?" He eyed me suspiciously. In Bali, I had become accustomed to composers explaining their tema *or composition theme to me whether for annual arts festival works or the yearly performance of final recitals at the conservatory. Every composition seemed to have a theme, based upon religious motifs, Balinese philosophy, a nationalistic slogan, or, minimally, a* rasa *or emotional state. "What is it about, what's the* tema?" *I asked. He responded brusquely: "It has no tema. It is abstract (J: tan wadeg);*

---

[31] Sardono Kusumo, a dancer famous for his boldly experimental works, was by then the director of the Arts Institute in Jakarta (*Institut Kesenian Jakarta*).

PLATE 2.2 Wayan Sadra. Photo by Sukhmana Rucira Adhi.

music should be abstract." While denigrating those composers who resorted to themes, he appealed to abstract expressionism, to the meaning of music as synonymous with its structure. If I wanted to know what the work meant, he suggested I listen to it again, recalling Beethoven's legendary response when asked about the meaning of a sonata (de Certeau 1984:80) [Track MK-2/1].

Indonesia hosted emerging postcolonial states attempting to blaze a third way independent of both Soviet and US influence at its 1955 Bandung Conference. But while it remained officially unaligned, by the end of the Old Order in 1965, Indonesia—an enormous new nation with considerable natural resources—was home to the third-largest communist party after the USSR and China. Prior to and following the violent entrance of the US-aligned New Order in 1966, Indonesia was a major battlefield of the cultural Cold War, one in which both US and Soviet imperia struggled for artists' imaginations. Sadra, his colleagues, and mentors were trained in Central Java during the late Old Order and early New Order, a highly politicized era deeply crosscut by the cultural imperatives of Cold War conflict—one in which making the wrong aesthetic decisions could have profound, even life-threatening, consequences.

Following World War II, the American government coordinated its foreign cultural relations through an extensive and unprecedented state–private network of official governmental agencies and private foundations (Kennedy and Lucas 2005). This network combined State Department programs including the Voice of America radio system, the United States Information Service (USIS), the Fulbright education and cultural exchanges, and organizations such as the Rockefeller Foundation, the Ford Foundation, and the Asia Society, among others. Asia held the attention of this network following the loss of China to Mao's communists, North Korea to Stalin's proxies, and Vietnam to Ho Chi Minh. The Soviet Union appeared on the edge of snatching up Asia along with its global population majority and strategic resources.

In the 1950s the USIS established libraries around the world and hosted a string of lecture series, art exhibitions, and performances intended to symbolize American political and aesthetic freedom. Pollock canvases went up throughout US embassy halls and when conservative members of Congress vigorously contested the use of modernism as subversive, the government leveraged its private partners to present examples of abstract expressionism, avant-garde dance, and modernist music abroad and supported like-minded foreign artists through exchange programs (von Eschen 2004:23). The State Department initiated an energetic program of goodwill jazz tours, sending Dizzy Gillespie to the Middle East, Benny Goodman to Southeast Asia, and Dave Brubeck to Eastern Europe. Jazz musicians found themselves performing in exotic locales rich with coveted Cold War commodities such as oil and uranium. American performers, including Duke Ellington, Martha Graham, and the Alvin Ailey dance company, performed in Indonesia with State Department support.

American Cold War policy towards Indonesia was myopically binary, blind to the complex entanglements of aesthetics, cosmopolitanism, communism, nationalism, and ethnicity. By 1955 the Dulles brothers had rejected neutrality as subversive and, realizing that the Russians had a head start in Indonesia, turned their attention to the nation.[32] Sukarno thought himself a socialist rather than a communist and worked to domesticate the Indonesian Communist Party (*Partai Komunis Indonesia*, PKI), which he understood as independent of Soviet or Chinese control, within his government. Washington's machinations during Indonesia's fight for independence (declared in 1945 but not recognized until 1949) left the nation saddled with debt. When the Americans rejected Indonesian requests for economic assistance in 1956, the Soviets gladly obliged. Unhinged by Sukarno's acceptance of Soviet assistance, Washington began a program of CIA harassment of Sukarno and his government. Following Washington's recognition of Malaysia on the UN Security Council, an infuriated Sukarno rejected US economic assistance, recognized the Hanoi government, pulled out of the UN, and seized American oil company facilities.

With or without the CIA's help, Sukarno was ousted from power on September 30, 1965 in an abortive coup in which his army general Suharto took control of the capital. Suharto promptly alleged PKI responsibility for the murder of six top generals and inaugurated a pogrom against all communists, their trade unions, and village organizations. American-made weapons flowed freely between the army and village youths

---

[32] The Senayan stadium, Hotel Indonesia, and other Jakartan monuments had been constructed with Soviet funds.

precipitating one of the bloodiest massacres of the twentieth century (Roosa 2006). Six hundred thousand to one million Indonesians were killed within less than five months, including up to fifteen percent of the population in Bali.[33]

Against this backdrop, well-funded American foundations—Rockefeller prior to the 1965 regime change and Ford following it—handled many of the interactions between Indonesian and American artists and governments. In the following I consider the history of this intervention and its implications for the development of *musik kontemporer*. Although the intercultural character of much contemporary Indonesian experimentalism may appear novel—a manifestation of the intensely interconnected new millennium—the development of radical aesthetics in postcolonial Indonesia has long been associated with foreign patronage. In this section I am less concerned with these institutions' humanitarian goals and proven achievements, or the well-meaning intentions of their officers, than with the cultural effects of their policies.

Rockefeller was centrally concerned with updating the Indonesian arts and instilling a sense of experimental, abstract expressionism in response to the perceived influence of Soviet realism. Beginning in 1949 the foundation sponsored the avant-garde artists they associated with the nationalistic *angkatan'45* (I), generation of 1945, literary circle as well as experimental theater groups, painters, filmmakers, composers, and choreographers aligned against LEKRA, the cultural wing of Indonesia's communist party.[34] Rockefeller supported numerous Indonesian artists for study at top universities in Europe, Asia, and America, often providing generous per diems. In Indonesia the Foundation stocked local university libraries, provided materials to painters, and recording equipment and recordings to musicians.[35] Unable to find abstract painting in Indonesia, Rockefeller officers investigating developments in 1957 suggested that local artists were far behind the West in technique but could take the next logical step with Foundation support:

> [Indonesian] painting has great vigor and there is much natural talent but the reliance on [realism] is too strong and no real emancipation can occur until these artists have completely absorbed everything the West has to offer, whereupon they can begin to develop their own styles with more sureness and independence.[36]

---

[33] For the most recent account of the killings, see the Komnas HAM report presented to the Indonesian parliament in 2012. For more on the killings in Bali, see Robinson (1998). For more on the connections between artists, the massacre, and its aftermath, see Larasati (2013).

[34] Indonesian artists often played the Soviets against the Americans to consolidate their financial base. According to a Rockefeller interview with Carl Anton Wirth, a composer supported by the American State Department to work with the Indonesian State Radio Station (RRI) in 1961: "Despite vigorous opposition and sniping by the Communists in the radio station and orchestra, I was able to weld the musicians into an effective group which gave a series of well received concerts in Djakarta, the final one being in the [Senayan] Sports Pavilion constructed by the Russians for the Asian Games. The [Rockefeller] instruments have arrived and are being well used except for the harp which was seized by [LEKRA] as a symbol of Capitalism. No one would learn to play it." BRC [Boyd Compton] interview with Anton Wirth, September 27, 1963, folder 54, box 4, Record Group [RG] 1.2, Rockefeller Foundation Archives, Rockefeller Archive Center, Sleepy Hollow, New York [hereafter designated RAC].

[35] See, for instance, Fahs to Agung, September 11, 1957, folder 448, box 68, series 600, RG 1.2, RAC.

[36] Robert W. July, diary excerpt, May 24, 1957, folder 453, box 68, series 600, RG 1.2, RAC.

Rockefeller officers characterized the Western avant-garde as required reading and the basis upon which local experiments should occur. Similar rhetoric surrounds the Foundation's notes regarding its sponsorship of the Javanese choreographers Bagong Kussudiardjo and Wisnu Surjodiningrat whose study in America and Europe in 1957 was understood by Rockefeller to "improve their leftist views," and to "set free their imaginations," meaning to align them towards the right.[37] Kussudiardjo's foundation would later help lay the foundations of *kontemporer* dance and music in Java. Aesthetic valuation and guidance by American foundations continued a tradition of cultural arbitration in which the colonial power was invested with more authority than the colony was to comment upon its own cultural practices, an asymmetry that had been internalized by many Indonesians. Rockefeller officers reported in 1957 that, "being interested in understanding her own people, Mrs. Gusti Bagoes Oka would like to get a copy of Margaret Mead's *Study of Balinese Character*."[38] The foundation happily obliged.

Responding in 1957 to a request from the Balinese composer Tjokorda Agung Mas for support to study Western music in the US, Rockefeller sought advice from a former grantee, the Philippine composer José Maceda. "What would the effects of such a visit be; would it be constructive for the subsequent development of Balinese music, or might it actually detract from [Mas's] ability to contribute further to musical development in his indigenous situation?"[39] After pointing out that Mas played guitar and had a working understanding of Western music theory, Maceda responded:

> I feel that his formal education in Western music would enhance rather than detract from the development of Balinese music. Anyway, Balinese music has changed since the recordings of Hornbostel many years ago, and...Western influence is bound to seep in. Perhaps, after more studies of Eastern and Western music are made by musicians from both hemispheres, a new universal musical expression may evolve from the music of Schoenberg, Debussy and other contemporaries. (ibid.)

Mas was eventually brought by Rockefeller to UCLA's newly established Ethnomusicology Institute, but to teach Balinese traditional music rather than study modern Western music. With a $39,900 grant in 1958, Rockefeller supported the Institute's hosting of several Indonesian musicians and its purchase of a new *gamelan*.

While Rockefeller consistently claimed to allow artists to follow their own direction, in practice it encouraged the active alignment of aesthetics towards a specifically Western notion of abstract expressionism.[40] The case of the Javanese dancer Gendhon Humardani, Rockefeller grantee of 1961, provides the most salient example for the historicization of *musik kontemporer*. From an aristocratic Solonese family, educated

---

37 BRC diary excerpt, June 26 and October 3, 1958, folder 62, box 5, series 652, RG 1.2, RAC.
38 CBF (Charles Burton Fahs), diary excerpt, May 21, 1957, folder 448, box 68, series 600, RG 1.2, RAC.
39 Maceda to Fahs, August 25, 1957, folder 449, box 88, series 600, RG 1.2, RAC.
40 See Fahs's address to the President's Music Committee of the People to People Program, October 6, 1959, folder 48, box 5, series 600, RG 3.1, RAC.

in Dutch schools and trained in London as an anatomist, Humardani was granted Rockefeller support to study dance in New York under Martha Graham, continuing his studies in modern dance at UCLA during the 1962–63 academic year. Humardani was chosen over other candidates partly based upon his interest in developing Indonesian national forms and his sponsorship of performances in Java that competed for audiences with leftist forms of theater.[41] Upon his return to Central Java in 1971, Humardani became actively involved in new and experimental arts at the influential Center for Javanese Arts in Solo (*Pusat Kesenian Jawa Tengah,* PKJT), eventually becoming the head of the conservatory there in 1975 where he shifted its focus from preservation to bold experimentation.[42]

The opposition of abstract versus representational expression, the central polemic of the cultural Cold War, increasingly dominated Indonesian cultural policies and rhetoric under Humardani's influence and he railed against the representational (I: *representatip*), explanatory methods of dance movement in national *sendratari* theater as opposed to the classic Javanese arts which he idealized as nonrepresentational (I: *tidak representatip*) or, in Javanese, *tan wadag*. Humardani denigrated representational pantomime in dance (characterized by him as "idiotic kitsch") and realistic sound effects and themes in music (quoted in Roth 1986:258–9). Although Humardani appears to have adopted the philosophy of Western abstraction, he did not convey its specific contents to his students. Circumscribing the degree of direct exposure to foreign cultures, primarily Western modernism, appears to have been partly self-consciously engineered by administrators such as Humardani who argued that knowledge of such forms was "hardly necessary" for the healthy development of local culture (quoted in Sadra 1986:7).

Humardani instead conveyed to his students (including the young Balinese composers Wayan Sadra and Pande Madé Sukerta, among other *musik kontemporer* pioneers) a highly abstracted philosophy of expressionism and an ethic of cultural relativism. For Humardani, cultural values were not an immutable given, but changeable, learned, and at least partially artificial. The idea that Indonesian culture was malleable and could be made both more perfect and in tune with the needs of contemporary Indonesian society catalyzed his students' experiments. Humardani encouraged the Balinese composers he brought to his institutes to release their attachments to tradition and to forge an original voice more in accord with the modern Indonesian spirit (Rustopo 1990:83). Away from home and surrounded by musicians with little knowledge of their tradition, Balinese composers were less likely to feel bound to any specific regional traditional form and answered Humardani's call to the vanguard. Sadra and Sukerta were primed to respond to Humardani's challenges, having already taken part in Sardono's bold

---

[41] See Foundation correspondence regarding Humardani from 1961, folder 48, box 4, series 652, RG 1.2, RAC.

[42] His ascent to the post was delayed by several years of complex politicking during which time his rivals claimed Humardani had entertained tangential contact with the PKI prior to the 1965 attempted coup (Rustopo 1990).

experiments in the mid-1970s.[43] If Rockefeller sometimes encouraged Balinese artists to fulfill their classic ethnographic role as representatives of traditional culture—as in the case of Agung Mas—its activities in supporting Javanese experimentalists such as Humardani had the possibly unintended effect of helping to catalyze (albeit somewhat later) the emergence of Balinese experimentalism [Tracks BV-2/2 and MK-2/2].

While the Rockefeller Foundation, as an extension of America's Cold War cultural policy, encouraged many Indonesian artists towards American notions of experimentation, the Ford Foundation, an active sponsor of the Indonesian performing arts after the failed coup, sought to rein in the cultural forces its predecessor had helped to unleash. With the cultural war won and many communist performing artists in Bali and Java slaughtered, Ford invested heavily in cultural revitalization through its Traditional Arts Project, a $100,000 program conducted between 1973 and 1980—just as *musik kontemporer* began to emerge—in which traditional performing arts in several villages were revitalized and documented.[44] John Bresnan, director of the Ford office in Jakarta in the early 1970s, remarks that he "hesitated to step into a field that so deeply touched Indonesian's sense of their own identity, [instead proposing] an all-Indonesian committee to select [arts] projects we would support" (2006:175). The concern to avoid the appearance of direct Western management of Indonesian cultural identity is ironic considering the Foundation's profound and widely visible impact on the economic, governmental, and social organization of the nation and attests to the symbolic power of the performing arts in projecting Indonesia's image globally.

Between 1988 and 2005 the Foundation provided over $1,600,000 to several programs intended for the continued study and preservation of Indonesian performing arts while subsidizing programs at the national conservatories, occasionally hiring Americans to train local faculty in ethnomusicology. Ford rarely sponsored experimental projects.[45] Although cultural grants represented a small percentage of Rockefeller's and Ford's total activity in Indonesia, these programs were a significant form of patronage for the development of local arts which otherwise had few sources of capital support.

A peculiar catch-22 emerges when we consider the historic arc of these interactions: US institutions first encouraged experimentation to contest perceived Soviet competition in the cultural realm while Washington simultaneously encouraged regime change. With the fires of social strife stoked beyond control, the mass slaughter of the New Order's birth in 1965 endangered the very existence of symbols of cultural

---

[43] In collaboration with Sardono, both Sadra and Sukerta performed their works in Europe and took part in intercultural performance workshops held at Eugenio Barba's International School for Theater Anthropology. See Cohen (2010) for a discussion of earlier examples of intercultural performance involving Javanese and Balinese artists (most importantly Jodjana) in Europe.

[44] Considering that many large performance troupes were politically polarized and often performed for propagandistic events, it is likely that performing artists represented a disproportionate number of the victims of the killings in 1965–66.

[45] Ford underwrote costs for Sardono Kusumo's 1979 experimental choreography, *Meta-ekologi* ($1,213.88), as well as the seventh annual composers' week in Jakarta in 1987 ($3,500).

particularity needed to resist images of rampant Westernization in Indonesia during the subsequent era of intense economic globalization. Although Ford itself was an extension of American cultural, economic, and military influence, its cultural programming was intended to counteract the effects of both increasing Westernization and Javanization during the New Order (p.c. Philip Yampolsky, September 2011).[46] In resisting Suharto's privileging of Javanese traditional culture over regional expressions, Ford especially supported non-Javanese traditional arts and founded centers of ethnomusicology on other islands as part of a Foundation-wide initiative to support cultural diversity and pluralism in the late New Order and early *reformasi*. While it would be incorrect to suggest that the highly politicized actions of the Foundation in the 1970s guided its arts programming in the 1990s and beyond, it would nevertheless be naive to overlook the fact that the Foundation's consistent and overriding concern with preservation aligned with the pro-Western regime's own obsessions with origins and tradition (Pemberton 1994) and mollified Western anxieties about cultural loss globally at a time when American economic and military power was expanding its global reach.

Rockefeller hoped to inspire and upgrade Indonesian artists towards the freedoms ostensibly embodied in American culture. Ford was concerned that local cultures not be lost through a complete alignment with Western (popular or experimental) forms or through Javanized homogenization. As described in internal memos, Ford shared Rockefeller's nagging anxiety concerning cultural loss, and both foundations operated under the assumption that the young nation was unequipped to be the sole caretaker of its culture. Balinese artists appeared to need special protection in order to remain local in ways intelligible to Western observers. As the Dutch sought to limit modern influence by tightly limiting the number of Balinese allowed to attend secondary institutions in Java (Robinson 1998:36–42), Rockefeller and Ford similarly saw Bali through an aestheticizing lens focused upon *tradisi*, dissuading the introduction of foreign cultural influences that might catalyze radical change.

New Order preservation (I: *pelestarian*) policies in Bali aligned with the preservationist interests of Western institutions including Ford and Rockefeller. From the root *"lestari,"* meaning eternal or unchanging, the policy was articulated within the New Order's broader framework of recovered origins (Pemberton 1994:9). In Bali, long the object of anxious narratives of cultural loss, *pelestarian* itself became a tradition. The Dutch, seeking to highlight signs of traditional culture, supported the efforts of Spies and McPhee to revive *gambuh* dance drama (Vickers 2005:309).[47] Mobilized as

---

[46] Bresnan describes a 1953 annual report that outlines the pragmatic disbursement of aid by the Foundation, then the largest philanthropic organization in the world. It said publicly for the first time that its aid to alleviate poverty abroad was going to nations "whose welfare is of unusual significance to the Free World.... The Foundation supports undertakings only in those nations whose political philosophy and objectives, if sustained or achieved, are incompatible with Communism" (quoted in Bresnan 2006:29).

[47] Colonial-era preservation projects can be traced back to at least 1919 when Van Stenis arranged trade centers for Balinese arts and crafts hoping that business success would revitalize the interest of Balinese youth in their own traditions (Liem 2003:92).

propaganda by both nationalists and communists prior to the failed coup (ibid. 315), *gambuh* received emergency resuscitation by Ford and the conservatories following the slaughter of many of its practitioners in 1965 and 1966. These projects inspired young composers and dancers to invent new, *kontemporer* interpretations such as Asnawa and Suardana's *Gambuh Macbeth*. The point here is that although *pelestarian* appears concerned with the past and tradition it is in every instance entangled with innovation, if not in outward form, then in semiosis; a revived art is different from its progenitor. Cultural representations went in one end of the *pelestarian* machine, emerging out the other as art.

Balinese Art

> The Balinese say: "We have no art. We do everything as well as we can." (McCluhan 1967)
> The concept of art is located in a historically changing constellation of elements; it refuses definition. (Adorno 1997)

The Balinese case, as exemplified in the ubiquitous image repeated by McCluhan, is made to serve as an example of the integrated praxis dreamed of by the historical avant-garde.[48] Art, music, religion, and tradition, it is imagined, were once so seamlessly integrated into a holistic Balinese experience that they have no words of their own for such concepts, which have only become thinkable using borrowed Malay terms.[49] However, it seems unlikely that theological belief did not exist in Bali before the introduction of the Malay term *agama* (religion), nor that aesthetic pleasure was waiting in the wings for the Malay *seni* (art)[50] Nevertheless, we can legitimately ask at what point Balinese culture delimited and designated art and music as objects comparable to their English equivalents. It is possible that the increasing overlap between the Balinese use of the Malay "*seni*" and the English "art" emerged with the identification of the "Balinese arts" (I: *kesenian Bali*) in the tourist art market (as theorized by Yamashita, 2003) and colonial era ethnography, both of which invested in a wholesale aestheticization of the Balinese and their quotidian activity, an image in which everyone was an artist and they performed the most mundane activities with artistry (Covarrubias 1937). But if outsiders could continue to

---

[48] "What for Hegel means the end of art is its sublation in knowledge" (Bürger 1984:xlvi), that is, the word "art."
[49] Besides the legion touristic examples of this trope, see for instance Mead and Bateson (1942), Belo (1970), Harnish (2005), Picard (1999), Schulte Nordholt (2000), Stephen (2005), Ramseyer (2002). Contemporary ethnographic representations often continue to relegate Balinese art to a functional mode in which it either serves to bring the invisible world of the *niskala* into being (as in Stephen 2005) or is relegated to the sphere of ritual "work" (B: *karya*) (as in Ramseyer 2002:9).
[50] Considering Bali's historic position in Malay-speaking Southeast Asian *pasisir* coastal trading networks, concepts such as religion (*agama*) and art (*seni*) were likely available in Bali long before their formalized introduction into the Indonesian language in the mid-twentieth century. According to Liem (2003), Malay was used as a lingua franca across the archipelago since the eighth century, although it was likely not well known among commoners in the interior of the island until the nineteenth century.

imagine an integrated practice by seeing art everywhere, the introduction of the term enabled some Balinese to imagine certain forms of creative activity as a specialized, autonomous field.

If it might have once been absent, art (*seni*) is now a dominant category, institution, and discourse in contemporary Balinese life. In describing their activities, composers engaged with experimentalism today combine Indonesian, Balinese, and English terms. Artists and composers I interacted with distinguished between *seni*, referring to any expressive form, and *seni murni* (I), pure art. The latter category, which encapsulated all expressions also called experimental or avant-garde, referred to works that could not, it was imagined, be commodified and which appeared independent of the dictates and tastes of mass audiences. *Seni murni* maintained an ambiguous relationship to the Balinese concept of *ngayah*, or ritualistic, devotional performance. While *ngayah* performances may appear to be pure, they function to raise one's karmic stock and often provide, if only nominal, remuneration. *Seni murni* then reflects an increasingly autonomous institution of art in Balinese society as contrasted to the dutiful, workmanship resonance of the Balinese *karya*. Whereas *seni murni* may flow primarily within a manifest, *sekala*, economy, *karya* will increase revenue in the unmanifest, *niskala* realm.

August 2002. I had agreed to perform gender wayang, *the sacred music of the shadow play, for a friend's tooth-filing the next day. I routinely played in such ceremonies in Denpasar with my elderly teacher, Wayan Konolan. After our performances, the host would approach Konolan to covertly slip around* 200,000 *rupiah (twenty dollars) into his pocket. Konolan would laughingly push half of the money back into the host's palm. If there was greater social distance between he and the host, Konolan would push back less, or even pocket the full amount. But this time the host arrived at my home in a middle-class housing development in Denpasar a day before the ceremony to deliver an elaborate tray of Balinese saté and snacks, enough to tide me over for a couple of days. My neighbors, an extended family that had recently moved from Karangasem and were now running a very successful amphetamine ring, looked on nostalgically, taking pictures of the transaction with their camera phones. They often remarked on how my life seemed "more Balinese" than theirs. The next day, asking Konolan between pieces what it had meant, he answered excitedly, "Ah, they gave you a* pemanis *[B: sweetener]!? That's how we used to do things." His voice trailed off. "No money back then"* [Track BV-2/3].

The artist was born at the same time as his work went on sale. (Attali 1985)

Does the idea of art necessitate alienation? As compared to other areas in Indonesia, Bali did not experience the creation of a classic proletariat: a population cleared from ancestral lands, forced into crowded cities, and plunged into poverty through intensive labor for Western internationals. Until recently, most Balinese families had not experienced an alienation of the basic means of production; many maintained ties to the traditional *subak* rice irrigation system, *adat* traditional law, traditional *desa* village and *banjar* neighborhood administrative associations, and the shared devotional obligations related to the maintenance of village temples, the *khayangan tiga*.[51] However, during my research, inalienability, the idea that social relations could not be mediated with money, had become a site of nostalgia and there was a palpable sense that the alienation of social relations was an irresistible tide eroding remaining islands of community. It is still the case that within the sphere of traditional performance explicit reference to exchange value can be considered a vulgar form of social distancing, but this changed noticeably even over the course of my research. Tourism and the branding of cultural heritage have brought the Balinese the realization that their culture, indeed their own identity, is alienable property.

Conversations with Balinese composers concerning the status of their art and its relationship to economic relations reminded me of Kafka's last short story. In *The Mouse Folk* (1924), the mouse people understand themselves as proficient pipers, rather than singers. Piping is the real talent of the mouse people; they all pipe, but none dreams of making out that their piping is art. And so there is no genius, talent, or sublimity in their piping; every mouse in Kafka's tale is above average, begging comparison to Balinese women's intricate offerings or men's unremarkable virtuosity in temple performance. But Josephine, Kafka's mouse heroine, considers herself a singer—no mere piper—and she is nervous that her special status has never been quite recognized by her society. She rebels and is equated to an infant by mouse society. The emergent Balinese composer (I: *komposer*) is, like Josephine, partly alienated, sometimes viewed as a naughty child (I: *anak nakal*) by the folk (I: *masyarakat*).

A Balinese Avant-Garde?

> WY:(E) In watching and listening to Balinese art events over the last three years, I think I'm not wrong to say: bravo kitsch.
>
> AJ:(E) Avant-garde = vanguard, not kitsch or campy. The avant-garde is a means to resist the dumbing down of culture caused by consumerism. It arose in order to defend aesthetic standards from the decline of taste involved in consumer society.[52]
>
> GP:(I, B) [Festival] participants need to accept other [foreign] innovative concepts and be placed at their level.
>
> KS:(B) The world holds many different kinds of people, you have to look beyond yourself.[53]
>
> AJ:(B, I) Exactly, Thank You! We reach no conclusion on the cultural polemic. But at least it was a constant conversation in the papers when I was a kid [in the early

---

[51] Cultural tourism outstripped agriculture as the basic means of production on Bali in the early 1990s.
[52] This material is apparently quoted from Greenberg's essay of 1939.
[53] Loose translation of the common Balinese aphorism: *Clebingkah beten biyu, gumi linggah ajak liu.*

1960s]; art for art or art for people; now most of those involved in that conversation are long dead.

WY:(E,I,B) Kitsch is supported in Bali by the government, academics, and people who call themselves artists; but they do not know what art is. We need to think about this here; are we going to cut and paste or are we going to create something original?

AJ:(E, I) Kitsch is a bastard of the culture industry and produces uncertainty in all ranks of life. Victor Lebow's manifesto of consumerism is now seen in daily celebrations in Indonesia's shopping malls.

—Multilingual Facebook conversation between Balinese *musik kontemporer* composers regarding the Denpasar Arts Festival of December 2010. Posted December 28, 2010.

How is the avant-garde understood in Bali? Is it a relevant frame through which to understand *musik kontemporer*? Investigating these questions leads us to a broader consideration of influence and cultural change and links us again to the suggestions of mimicry contained in the quotation that opened this chapter.

The Western avant-garde emerged to critique the status of art as an institution in Western society, recognizing its tautological function as a "space of presentation by which the things of art are identified as such" (Ranciere 2009:23). The early European avant-gardists sought to expose institutionalized art as a foil for lives dehumanized through the instrumentalizing rationality of the Industrial Revolution. It was hoped that the shock of the new, as in the allegorical work of the Surrealists and Dadaists, would, through the withdrawal of meaning, shake the viewer/listener into a reconsideration of one's own life praxis. The torture instruments of shock were often foreign imports. Looking to the emerging field of anthropology for materials, the avant-gardists sought to mobilize the signs of their others to expose the constructedness of Western, indeed all, cultural institutions. The Surrealists were charmed by the non-Western cultures they encountered in colonial expositions, an obsession that would manifest itself in, for instance, Picasso's interest in African arts and Antonin Artaud's fascination with Balinese dance.

Identifying the failure of the early radical movements to bring either real or aesthetic revolution, the theoreticians of the Frankfurt School then argued for a radically self-conscious autonomy of art as a complete negation free of the means–end rationality of bourgeois culture, a kind of medium of "hibernation in bad times" (Bürger 1984:xvii). In this scenario the avant-gardists imagined themselves as rescuing art from capitalism and its kitschy commodity forms (Ray 2007). But such a detached position is vulnerable to a co-option that reaffirms the social conditions the original avant-garde sought to dismantle. This explains the complex entanglement between avant-garde and modernism, the latter now a mere ornament in Western life, hanging in boardrooms rather than causing chaos in the streets.

The ethnographic description of *musik kontemporer* as avant-garde suggests a direct historical-cultural link between Balinese and Western new music traditions, one of top-down, West-to-East cultural influence.[54] The reality is a significantly more complex history of indirect and discontinuous cultural connections. If *musik kontemporer* is not a straightforward avant-garde, it nevertheless displays a high level of what Anthony Braxton has termed "restructural potency," by which he means the potential of a new expressive form to radically reconfigure the social understanding of art and so act as a conduit for broader change (in Lock 1988:162).

The Indonesian term *avant-garde* (sometimes *garde depan*) may refer to anything new or out of the ordinary regardless of a creator's ideological intention. The Javanese composer Sapto Raharjo used the terms avant-garde and *musik kontemporer* interchangeably, suggesting that their aesthetic and ideological implications are aligned: "*musik kontemporer* is a movement concerned with change—an expression of struggle" (p.c. July 2003). This explicitly politicized view is not a widely held conception of *musik kontemporer* throughout Indonesia and Raharjo's characterization marks a philosophical and aesthetic division between various groups of *kontemporer* composers.[55] Balinese composers just as often characterized as avant-garde those projects that sought to reify art as an institution rather than question it.

If some composers did not explicitly proclaim a mission of questioning the first assumptions of Balinese aesthetics and cultural institutions, their iconoclasms nevertheless revealed the constructed nature of status quo composition. Through the quick juxtaposition of disparate elements of different cultural worlds—quotations of contemporary and ancient local musics alongside references to West African, Japanese, and Brazilian styles—*musik kontemporer* sometimes recalled the primitivisms of Surrealism and Dadaism by encouraging audiences to reflect upon cultural norms of beauty, truth, form, balance, reality, and so on, as possibly artificial arrangements.

The composer Ben Pasaribu's (1961–2010) description of *musik kontemporer* as "that which lay audiences find to be weird, unusual, confused, and...not entertaining" (Pasaribu 1990:12) was echoed in interviews by many composers working in Jakarta, recalling the antagonistic relationship between creators and audiences seen in the historical Western avant-garde. However, many Balinese composers of *musik kontemporer* were concerned to foster their audiences and to make their works intelligible to the public; they sought to maintain the large audiences that continue to patronize *gong kebyar* and *kreasi baru* genres. When presenting his sometimes highly experimental

---

54 For examples of *kontemporer* performances described as avant-garde, see for instance: Sutton (2006), Harnish (2000), McDermott (1986), Tenzer (2011), Ramstedt (1991), Wallach (2008), Benamou (2010). See also Seebass (1996:85) for a comparison of earlier forms of Balinese musical innovation (*gong kebyar*) to expressionism and the Italian avant-garde.

55 Raharjo is referring to the experimental, shocking, or absurd works of young performance artists in Yogyakarta, including Marzuki who composed a work for screams by having his body shocked by 100-volt electric cables. Notosudirdjo (2001) uses the term avant-garde regularly in his dissertation which focuses on *musik kontemporer* in Jakarta, theorizing it as a form of national music. The Sumatran composer Ben Pasaribu similarly aligned *musik kontemporer* with "experimental music in the United States or avant-garde music in Europe" (Pasaribu 1990:13).

kontemporer works, the composer Ketut Suanda, known more popularly as a clown, was sure to include comic monologues, dress in ludicrous costumes, and incorporate props. When staging his *kontemporer* compositions, the composer Ketut Lanus went to great personal expense to rent modern sound systems and arrange large lighting rigs and video projections to attract large audiences. In contrast, Balinese composers trained under Humardani often sought to shock audiences through unusual, if entertaining, means as in Sadra's use of live animals or Pande Madé Sukerta's use of musicians hidden among the audience.

Theorizing Change, Problematizing Influence

June 2008. While eating lunch at a burrito stand in Ubud I received a text message from Gusde (Ida Bagus Gede Widnyana) calling me to a rehearsal he had arranged at the Cudamani arts club just south of town. A couple of years younger than myself, Gusde and I had studied together at the conservatory and since graduating he had made a name for himself performing and composing with various clubs in Gianyar. Although from a village thirty minutes to the east, he and his brother were accepted into the tightly knit community of the Cudamani club in Pengosekan when it first formed in 1998 and had since taken part in numerous international tours and intercultural projects with the ensemble. His virtuosity was matched by a beaming, self-effacing optimism rather out of character for a Brahman of humble means. Gusde's ready smile could instantly lighten the mood of the most stuck-in-the-mud rehearsal.

Responding to a last-minute request for a musik kontemporer *work from organizers at the Bali Arts Festival, he breathlessly called friends together to the rehearsal space. I estimated that most gong kebyar ensembles rehearsed over 120 hours before their appearance at the festival. Gusde would have three hours to compose and rehearse his* musik kontemporer *work. He arranged five musicians in a circle, giving each a kajar (small gong-chime) and cueing them in an apparently random fashion to create an unpredictable texture. I mentioned that the work resembled Balinese gambling games. The following day Gusde distributed five comically oversized dice to the musicians. Rearranging our performance only minutes before we were to play, he instructed us to take turns rolling our die to initiate one of six prearranged musical options. After the performance I was thrilled to have witnessed, documented, and taken part in what I understood to be the first true example of indeterminacy in contemporary Balinese composition. Tickled to find that Gusde had never heard of John Cage, I mused at this example of independent genesis and was gratified to have captured an example of Balinese experimentalism that so clearly sidestepped accusations of Western influence.*

Later backstage an American gamelan student asked Gusde how he had developed this new, strange work. I was surprised when he smiled and pointed at me: Aku kena virusnya Andi *[I caught the bug (virus) from Andy]. I felt somehow guilty hearing this. I appeared to be tainting my scholarly object, polluting my informants, and exceeding the ethical limits of academic participant observation. I then felt embarrassed at being embarrassed, aware that I had fallen into the anthropological romance of Bali by imagining the island and its inhabitants to be somehow out of the wider world. I wondered if I had misremembered the rehearsal, if I had played a more direct role than I recalled* [Track MK-2/3].

Colonialism and imperial pillaging led to the unprecedented, rapid movement of cultural representations into new, foreign contexts—a Nigerian mask at the New York Metropolitan Museum, a disembodied Buddha's head at the Guimet in Paris, a Western orchestra in Central Java—to catalyze aesthetic transformations globally. In attempting to account for cultural change over the last century we are tempted to identify formal continuities, such as apparently similar sonic structures between the Western avant-garde and *musik kontemporer*, and to stop there, as if this was sufficient testimony to suggest direct historical continuity. But this method is premised upon a biased selection procedure requiring an ethnographic, historicizing response (Price 1980). As I have demonstrated in this chapter, *musik kontemporer* is not a wholly autochthonous phenomenon, but neither is it simply a result of straightforward descent from a single line of influence from the West. Its mutations have emerged from partial contact with foreign cultural forms rather than through sustained acculturation. While we could attempt to reconstruct the convoluted history of connections between Indonesian and other experimental and avant-garde forms—the degree of exposure Indonesian artists have had—this would not tell us anything about the *uses* to which Indonesians put them—the ways they are read, misread, reread, and transformed. Understanding the form and meaning of noise in *Geräusch*, for instance, cannot be achieved by attempting to dissolve it into the influence of its purported avant-garde sources.

As in the description of Widnyana's apparently Cageian work described above, many Balinese composers characterized new musical ideas as a *virus*. This recalls Sperber's (1996) notion of the "epidemiology of representations," useful in describing the transference and transformation of cultural materials and concepts and their role in catalyzing change. Sperber rejects the image of literal replication or synthesis found in the standard influence model and the (again popular) notion of the cultural meme as popularized by Dennett (1991). Like diffusion, the latter two models suggest the neat reproduction of information between persons and through generations. Sperber's model suggests that representations do not simply replicate but transform—or, as is sometimes the case with a virus, mutate—in transmission as a result of constructive cognitive processes (Sperber 1996:101). While evoking the image of genetic mutation, Sperber reminds us that there is much greater slack between descent and similarity in the case of cultural transmission than there is in the biological case (ibid. 108). The constructive cognitive processes Sperber refers to relate directly to my description of the adoption of foreign materials in *musik kontemporer* in Chapter 6 and the processes of intercultural semiotics in Chapter 8 in which

I am concerned with the mechanics of mutation that drive cultural change. Sperber's model draws upon cultural phylogenetics, the application of genetic descent models and their hallmark cladistic trees, to map the transfer and transformation of cultural information. Thinking in terms of the maximally connected networks of phylogenetics, rather than the straight, single arrow of influence allows us to recognize *musik kontemporer* as a polygenetic amalgam rather than as a poor imitation of the Western avant-garde.

PICASSO MANQUÉ

Sartre claimed that Surrealism had been stolen from Europe by "a black" (the poet Aimé Césaire) who used it brilliantly as a tool of the Universal Revolution (Mitter 2007:7). In his analysis of the Indian avant-garde, Mitter interprets Sartre's comment as encapsulating the knotted discourses of power, hierarchy, and authority in the complex relationship between non-Western artists and the Western avant-garde. Within this discourse, non-Western contemporary art is interpreted from an occidental perspective and is often described as derivative. Mitter terms this the Picasso manqué syndrome, based upon British critiques of Indian cubism as colonial mimicry. According to Mitter "Stylistic influence...has been the cornerstone of art historical discourse since the Renaissance..." (Mitter 2007:7). Indeed influence has been the key epistemic tool in studying the reception of Western art in the non-Western world: if the expression is too close to Western styles, it reflects slavish mentality; if on the other hand, the imitation is imperfect, it represents a failure (ibid. 7). In this model Euro-American artists may be celebrated for their informed borrowings of or affinity with a given non-Western form, whereas colonial and postcolonial artists imitate and are perceived to sacrifice their integrity.

In the 1930s, bold experiments by the Balinese painter Ketut Ngendon angered his Dutch mentor Bonnet who deemed his cubist work inauthentic and un-Balinese (H. Geertz 1994:17). Ngendon eventually learned to paint aestheticized temple dances, selling them to the Europeans who patronized the regular tourist performances he arranged at his local temple. In 1980, just as Balinese *musik kontemporer* was emerging, the Ford Foundation made official its stance towards innovation: "Contemporary arts have not been an area of Foundation interest nor are they likely to become one. Study tours for modern painters and musicians are more likely to result in imitation and art derivative of Western models than in creativity."[56] During a presentation on Sadra's *musik kontemporer* at the Society for Ethnomusicology's annual meeting in 1990 a scholar complained: "This sounds just like a performance piece from

---

[56] Sidney Jones. Ford Foundation Report: *Review of Foundation Programs in Culture and the Arts.* Bangkok, June 4, 1980.

New York! Isn't this just Western influence?" (Diamond 1990:14). Mimesis through influence has guided the perception, evaluation, and sponsorship of Balinese aesthetic innovation; it is why the term avant-garde appears in quotes in the passage that opened this chapter.

3 Kosong

DEVELOPING CULTURE IN THE EMPTY NEW ORDER (1966–98)

AUGUST 2003. SUKA Hardjana studied clarinet in the 1950s at the Western conservatory (AMI) in Yogyakarta and later in Germany and as a Fulbright scholar in America. He returned to Indonesia to settle with his family in what was then a sleepy rural suburb of Jakarta but by 2003 it was overrun with tenements and traffic. By the early 1970s Hardjana was the leading advocate of Indonesian contemporary music. A prolific author, music critic, music director, and composer, Hardjana hosted a series of composition festivals in Jakarta beginning in the late 1970s that linked experimental composers from around the nation. Conversing on his porch, he described Kosong, *a work by the Balinese composer Ketut Gede Asnawa that Hardjana had commissioned for the 1984 festival:*

> When I heard the works they were bringing each year I said: "God, you Balinese don't mess around! Everything you compose is good! Next year why don't you try just bringing rocks. Don't worry about all those heavy instruments. Try composing for *rocks*." They laughed, but the next year they arrived with only a small box, no instruments. I asked: "Was there a mix-up at the airport?!" They answered by opening the box. It was nothing but some bamboo, a few cymbals, and rocks.

Kosong (I), empty, caught up the maneuvers of culture at the height of the New Order when the arts appeared depoliticized, politics aestheticized, and the government's heavy hand emptied the public sphere of civic society. In *Kosong* musicians dance in circles, strike stones, and blow bamboo culms, enacting the rituals of *nyepi*, the Balinese new year, when demons must be scared off before the Balinese quarantine themselves for a day of silence. *Kosong* was about ceremony but not of it. Asnawa's bare-bones approach avoided explicit reference to the many *tradisi* forms of music that were *kebyar*'s bread and butter. Working with musicians at the conservatory, he crafted an ingenious cultural *trompe l'oeil*. Performed for Balinese lay audiences, Jakartan cosmopolitans, and Western *gamelan* enthusiasts, *Kosong*'s apparent emptiness invited observers to pour in their own meanings.[1] With musicians in rustic dress performing

---

[1] The work was taken on tour to the 1986 Festival of Indonesia in Vancouver.

primitive instruments to re-enact ancient ceremony, the work's foreground might appear as an exotic representation of Balinese traditional culture. But close your eyes and squint your ears and a *moderen* composition channeling American minimalism seems to emerge. By complexly mixing signs of *tradisi* and *moderen*, by eschewing direct critique (either political or aesthetic), and by aestheticizing ceremony, *Kosong* encapsulated perfectly its place, time, and context (B: *desa, kala, patra*): Bali at the height of the New Order [Tracks BV-3/1 and MK-3/1].

In this chapter I describe the intellectual history and the implementation of cultural policy during the New Order (1966–98), considering the consequences of the regime's violent birth upon those policies and their continued impact on reformation-era Indonesia. Although the traditional and the modern are often represented as an antagonistic battle between the past and the future, in Indonesia they emerged together as a consequence of the evolutionist assumptions of development (I: *pembangunan*).

The outlines of tradition and modernity were articulated in a series of discourses among Indonesian nationalist thinkers who argued that civil society and aesthetics should be developed in tandem to be in tune with the broader, modern world. Their conversations opposed nativist thinkers, influenced by such syncretic movements as theosophy and local mystical and aesthetic practices, against more austerely cosmopolitan intellectuals attracted to universal ideas such as Western aesthetic modernism. Dominated by a conservative high-caste elite and guided by Dutch Balinizing policies, Balinese artists generally fell into the former camp.

As I demonstrate below, cultural policies in early New Order Bali represented a reaction to the violent emergence of the regime itself. These policies, favoring feudal aspects of Balinese culture that had been challenged by the Old Order, ensured that ostensibly traditional Balinese values, rooted in religious principles, would be unchallenged for years. The New Order's vigorous investment in tourism heightened the awareness of the Balinese of their own ethnicity as a resource and posed special problems for the development of culture. Ultimately, tourism has become an internal process of Balinese society rather than an external, impinging force. The New Order developed *tradisi* as the prime commodity of tourism and by the 1980s the term had become the keyword of the regime's cultural policy. By the *reformasi* era many innovative artists recognized *tradisi* as a hardened form of ideology that served state imperatives over those of local communities.

New Order development policies led to rapid urbanization and class transformation. Economic developments raised living standards for many Balinese and underwrote the expansion of the state conservatory system. The conservatory replicated the form of other national development projects, producing artist-bureaucrats to manage the production of arts safe for general and touristic consumption. Although birthed in the New Order conservatory, *musik kontemporer* required policing lest it overstep the bounds of good taste and proper (a)politics. For all its flaws, the New Order improved the material conditions of many Balinese, offering to artists unprecedented access to higher education and links to global aesthetic networks. My concern in this chapter is to investigate the aesthetic and social implications of the regime's tendency to grant thing-like status to ideas such as tradition and culture.

The Development of Tradition and Modernity in Indonesia

In the early decades of the twentieth century many nationalist intellectuals and artists in the Indies colony adopted the European notion that both the nation state and its culture could be engineered. In their journals and public conversations they advocated for the development of a new, national Indonesian culture and debated the roles that cultural manifestations, newly termed traditional (*tradisi*) and modern (*moderen*), should have in the culture to come.

The traditional and the modern, while often imagined as antagonistic opposites, became, in the Indonesian case, the obverse and reverse faces of the same coin: development (*pembangunan*). In both colonial and postcolonial Indonesia, development has been figured as an effort to achieve modernity, a state partly characterized by the engineering of art as an apparently autonomous institution.

Cultural activities and artifacts identified as traditional are associated with a specific array of spatial and temporal attributes: local, rural, past. The traditional and the modern emerge as twins; the second term completes the dichotomies implied by the first. The modern becomes global, cosmopolitan, urban, and future-oriented by default. Both *tradisi* and *moderen* represent what Bakhtin called a chronotope: a concept linking space, time, and value. Whether denigrated or celebrated, *tradisi* is consistently associated with a comparative sense of stasis, even if discourse allows it some degree of flexibility and change; *moderen* then embodies positive dynamism, even if cultural conservatives identify it as threatening.

The idea of tradition served colonial and national exigencies during the twentieth century. Sometimes this represented the resuscitation (and inevitable reconfiguration of meaning) of actual historical forms. In other contexts it took the form of more original inventions that claimed continuity with state-sanctioned pasts, as in the invented traditions theorized by Hobsbawm and Ranger (1983). Despite its limitations, the notion of invented traditions points importantly to the role tradition plays in legitimizing power, its institutions, and authority, eventually becoming so inextricably linked with national identity that to question its pedigree is to risk being labeled unpatriotic. A state may encourage its subjects to complain about the loss of tradition, and then offer up tradition as a cure, but one in which an internally dissonant, contradictory, and fragmented folklore is replaced with more homogenized and managed representations, as was often the case during the New Order.

COLONIAL TRADITION

Following the communist revolts of the mid-1920s, the Dutch sought to turn Balinese attention inward by traditionalizing culture through a reinvestment in the symbolic capital of the courts and a codification of customary law (I: *adat*), religious practice, and caste. Arriving in Bali following a period of intense scholarly and colonial investment in India, colonial ethnographers saw the South Asian cultural forms they were more familiar with over Austronesian aspects of Balinese culture. Colonial policy resuscitated local traditions and aligned Balinese with South Asian Hinduism. Balinization (D: *Baliseering*) projects sponsored the performing arts, temple reconstruction, and the publication of conservative cultural magazines. Under its banner, foreign missionary activity was banned and arrogant policies regarding behavior, language (Balinese should be used rather than Malay), and dress fostered an environment in which even the wearing of Western pants by Balinese men could become a subversive act (Vickers 1989:104).

Balinization was a facet of the Dutch Ethical Policy that grew out of the Delft Academy for colonial officers in the Netherlands. According to Taylor, the academy encouraged aspiring Indies officers to look upon Indonesians as children needing protection rather than as subjects with rights and duties (2009:118). Through these policies the Dutch portrayed themselves as benevolently protecting the colony from the harsh modern world while uplifting local societies by encouraging the aestheticization and homogenization of local culture, an attitude later adopted by both the Old and New Order.

While the first Dutch schools[2] of the late-nineteenth century boosted literacy rates and fostered the development of new aesthetic expressions, traditional schools established as part of the Balinization policy precipitated sharp declines in literacy (Robinson 1998:49).[3] In 1930 illiteracy levels in Bali were by far the worst in the archipelago: 3.07% as compared to much higher levels in Java. Finding neither land appropriate for plantation crops or extractable commodities, the Dutch encouraged the museumification of Balinese culture to satisfy the colonial investment in tourism rather than invest in education or modernization. The Dutch trained only a tiny percentage of the indigenous middle class, haunting the development of Indonesian self-governance after independence (Kahin 1995:27). Literacy rates only began to rise again with the opening of Taman Siswa schools in 1933 in Singaraja, Tejakula, Karangasem, and Negara (Liem 2003:89). The national Taman Siswa system was first developed in 1922 by the Javanese nationalist Dewantara (1889–1959) and was modeled upon both the pedagogy of the modern Montessori schools and Rabindranath Tagore's educational philosophy (Cohen 2010:82)

Although the idea of tradition was cultivated primarily for the aims of colonial administration, local artists quickly mobilized it for their own purposes. Touring the

---

[2] The first formal school in Bali was a Christian missionary opened in 1870. The first Dutch school was opened in Singaraja in 1874; a second school was shortly thereafter added in Jembrana. In 1910, fourteen public schools were opened, but it was not until the 1920s that attendance levels began to become significant (Liem 2003:87).

[3] Seramasara associates the development of *gong kebyar* with both the introduction of rational thought and secular performance through Dutch education and administration and the later investment in the performing arts under *Baliseering* (1997:68). See Seebass (1996) for a more nuanced account.

archipelago in the 1930s, the Dardanella *stambul* troupe presented medleys of repertoire drawn from all over the colony. Although publicizing the great antiquity of these "traditional" expressions, the troupe had significantly modified them—cutting them down, quickening their tempos, and emphasizing sensuality and humor (ibid. 184). In 1935 Dardanella presented these expressions as the authentic, ancient tradition of the East Indies in a self-produced world tour that took them throughout Asia, the Middle East, Europe, and America.

COLONIAL MODERNITY

In Chapter 2 I outlined Bali's relationship to aesthetic modernism. In order to fully understand the cultural policies of the New Order, we must first understand Indonesia's historic relationship to modernity. In Indonesia modernity is sometimes parachronistically identified as emerging in the Old Order.[4] But beginning as early as the late-nineteenth century the use of Malay, rather than Balinese, among Balinese authors stood as a sign of cosmopolitan modernity. The *Kakawin Atlas Bhumi* (Poem of the World Atlas) was composed in Malay in southern Bali at the end of the nineteenth century and revealed a broad knowledge of global geography (Liem 2003:113). The *Geguritan Nengah Jimbaran* (1903) was composed in Malay by the Cokorda Ngurah Made Agung of Badung and expressed strikingly modern notions of statehood, time, and space.

By the 1920s the Malay/Indonesian term *moderen* regularly appeared in the pages of the Balinese commoner, anti-caste periodical *Surya Kanta* (1925–27) (Robinson 1998:34). Its contributors, who referred to themselves alternately as the *Surya Kanta* (B), beautiful sunrise, or the *kaum terpeledjar* (I: learned group), represented a loose network of young nationalist Balinese many of whom had been educated in Dutch schools in Bali and Java. Their discourse appeared preoccupied by time, which could now be seen as moving either forward or backward (I: *madjoe* vs. *moendoer kebelekang*) and they felt the simultaneity of both new time and old time (I: *zaman baroe dan zaman dahoeloe*) (Liem 2003:149). *Tradisi* was now felt to be behind them, as they faced forward to the *moderen*. Within the pages of *Surya Kanta*, culture was characterized by a number of binary oppositions, including *asli* versus *moderen* (authentic versus modern) and *asli* versus *asing* (authentic versus foreign). In this context "authentic" is conflated with the local and traditional, "modern" with the inauthentic and alien.

This self-consciously radical group (ibid. 138) of Balinese teachers and civil servants of common origins prefigures the later community of Balinese *musik kontemporer* composers through the shared vision that civil society and Balinese aesthetics could be, indeed needed to be, developed to be in tune with the broader, modern world. While the *Surya Kanta* movement aspired to a national civil society that embraced universal

---

[4] See for instance Supanggah (2003a) who identifies modernity as a direct import from the West to Indonesia following Independence.

humanism, many *reformasi*-era composers aspired towards a post-authoritarian, democratic society with a cosmopolitan outlook.[5]

Many authors of the *Surya Kanta* movement and their counterparts in other areas of the colony associated themselves with the Netherlands East Indies branch of the Theosophical Society, founded in New York in 1875. The society provided to colonial nationalists a critique of Western materialism and the rationalistic ethos of colonial administration. During the first decades of the twentieth century the society's activities in the colony linked intellectuals of Chinese, Javanese, Balinese, and Dutch descent (Foulcher 2009:39) and encouraged nativist nationalists in their belief that local traditional cultures held the potential to, in the words of Soetatmo, "overcome...the crisis of the modern age" (1918, quoted in Miller 2011:51). The society's belief that human perfection emerged from the interaction of Eastern and Western cultures remained a core value of many of the composers with whom I worked, many of whose ancestors had established connections to the colonial era Theosophical Society.

Explicit politicking being illegal under colonialism, the indigenous intelligensia of the early twentieth century expressed itself primarily in the realm of culture. The dynamic music of the *gamelan gong kebyar* emerged alongside the *Surya Kanta* movement to symbolize the potential society to come. Comparatively free of feudal or caste associations, the *kebyar* ensemble was a collaborative organization based upon meritocratic principles; a group's leaders were as likely to be casteless farmers as members of the *triwangsa*. Describing *kebyar* in an article entitled "Decline of the East" (1939), Colin McPhee complained of the form being "melodramatic" and "feverish....carrying with it all the germs of decay. Tradition has been thrown overboard, and law and order discarded for innovations which, at times beautiful in themselves, can only lead to empty, aimless forms of expression." McPhee suggested that *kebyar* symbolized Balinese youth's "unsettled mentality...vague discontent...and inferiority complex" that had emerged from a Bali increasingly conscious of the outside world (McPhee 1939:160–4). Decades before Zorn's mash-ups, *kebyar* composers spliced together all of those expressions the Dutch were busy identifying as detachable, alienable, and consumable elements of *tradisi*. Driven by the volcanic energy of young men, the competitive, if not militaristic, spirit of *kebyar* foreshadowed the struggles of the coming revolution.

The emergence of *kebyar* coincided with similar democratizations of the Javanese court arts. In 1918 Tejokusumo and Suryodiningrat, sons of the Sultan of Yogyakarta, founded the Kridha Beksa Wirama dance school, which they understood to be "an important step in modernising the court arts, and modernising not in a way which involved exposing the arts to the threat of Western infiltration, but through making the dance and music of the court more generally accessible, hence less 'feudal' and more 'democratic'" (Lindsay 1985:16). The Javanese national society Budi Utomo

---

[5] Aesthetic linkages connect the *Surya Kanta* movement with the *reformasi* composers as well. Prefiguring Gusti Sudarta's *kontemporer* arrangement, discussed in Chapter 4, the Sutasoma tale was a favorite of the *Surya Kanta* intellectuals.

(J: Beautiful Endeavor) was founded in 1908 by the journalist Wahidin Sudirohusodo primarily to revive Javanese culture in order to resist Westernization. Within the context of nascent nationalism-under-colonialism, expressive forms that appeared continuous with prior practice—*geguritan, gamelan, wayang,* and court dance, for instance—achieved a valence of modernity both through novel content and new contexts of use.

The *Polemik Kebudayaan*

The *Surya Kanta* movement was eventually shut down by conservative colonial policies. Many of the authors of the first *pergerakan* nationalist movement of the 1920s were silenced through detention or disciplined through the colonial publishing body, the *Balai Pustaka*. But in the 1930s the *moderen* re-emerged in a resurgence of nationalist, modernizing thought expressed most forcefully in the pages of *Poedjangga Baroe* (1935–42)—a journal dominated by Javanese and Sumatran authors—and the Balinese journal *Djatajoe* (1936–41). The latter journal was edited by the aristocratic Anak Agung Panji Tisna of Buleleng, a leading *pergerakan* author who had renounced his feudal roots to embrace the movement's *moderen* ideals. Writing almost exclusively in Malay, Tisna's novels figured Bali as part of a larger world, receptive to foreign cultures. As a trained violinist, Tisna also formed Bali's leading intercultural *stambul* troupe for which he composed new works.

Founded by the Bali Darma Laksana, an organization dedicated to the advancement of Balinese culture (Robinson 1998:48), *Djatajoe* featured debates on music education, cultural preservation, and Western musical pedagogies by authors including Wayan Djirne and Wayan Roeme (Ruma) who would later publish the first collection of Balinese vocal music using a hybrid Balinese–Western notation (Wakeling 2010:45). The journal maintained an intellectual exchange with *Poedjangga Baroe* (Schulte Nordholt 2000:104), in which nationalist authors forged a new discourse on cultural development and modernity. Taken as a whole these wide-ranging conversations became known as the *polemik kebudayaan*, or cultural polemic.

The primary fault line of the *polemik kebudayaan* divided nativist thinkers such as Dewantara, Soetomo, and others associated with the Taman Siswa schools and the theosophical movement, against more stridently cosmopolitan intellectuals, including Alisjahbana, Dungga, Manik, Pasaribu, and Balinese authors including Wirjasutha who appealed for the adoption of universal and modern cultural attitudes and modes of expression. In 1935 Alisjahbana advocated a transformation from Indonesia's "static culture" to a "dynamic society" achieved through the adoption of Western attitudes and techniques. Alisjahbana pointed to foreign cultural influences in the past, such as those from South Asia and Arabia, which had enriched rather than impoverished the culture of the Indonesian islands. He declared: "And now the time has arrived...when we turn our eyes to the West" (quoted in Holt 1967:211).

Between the late 1930s and the mid-1950s two camps within the *polemik kebudayaan* emerged concerning the development of new Indonesian music.[6] One side argued for the use of a primarily non-Indonesian musical language (i.e., Western art music). This camp, dominated by composers including Amir Pasaribu and the critics J. A. Dungga and Liberty Manik, vigorously argued for the adoption of Western modernism. Development rhetoric suffuses their critique of Indonesian music, which they generally considered woefully underdeveloped. In 1952, Dungga and Manik complained that "there are few works of Indonesian composers at present that have value as art" (quoted in Miller 2011:75–76). They forcefully rejected native musics as a model for a future national culture:

> We have studied how to think quickly and how to feel no fear, as is demanded by our situation and world nowadays, which is full of dynamism, turbulence, conflict, etc. We are familiar with the problems of life and their solutions, familiar with technical progress, scientific knowledge, etc. In music this spirit is no longer accommodated by any kind of native music, from Javanese gamelan to that from Sumatra or other islands.... This spirit demands music that can portray the turbulence of the soul, the contrasts of life and thought, feelings of ecstasy, etc., not only relaxation [*verpozing*], entertainment [*hiburan*] while chatting and snacking on fried peanuts, as is common with our native music. If Jaap Kunst says that most of our music has a magic/religious character that is loved and praised, we say that we are no longer fond of primitive magical music, and that our religious feelings have also changed. (ibid.)

The opposing nativist camp argued for the combination of regional traditional forms with selected foreign elements. This approach would transform and nationalize regional elements such as the *pélog* tuning system. The cultural critic Dewantara inspired this group and, in an oft-quoted phrase incorporated into the revolutionary governmental proclamations of 1945, suggested that a new form of Indonesian music be created in national conservatories (which he described as "laboratories") that would combine the peaks (I: *puncak-puncak*) of Indonesia's various regional cultures (Sumarsam 1995:9). Neither the cosmopolitan nor nativist approach achieved complete cultural dominance and their sustained coexistence partly explains the wide-ranging forms of expression now referred to as *musik kontemporer*.

Cultural theorists working at the turn of the twenty-first century identified "multiple" or "alternative" modernities to provincialize the concept of an ostensibly universal, rational, Western modernity. This perspective holds that each nation, beginning from particular historical and cultural starting points, produces its own distinctive modernity (Gaonkar 2002:4), a position that assumes a dialectic of convergence and divergence between a local-particular modernity and a more generic

---

[6] Notosudirdjo identifies the first public discussion of national Indonesian music in an article published in 1918 by Dewantara (Notosudirdjo 2001:150).

(Western) form. The theorization of alternative modernities typically celebrates cultural resilience through terms like hybrid, baroque, carnivalesque, nonlinear, and so forth. Such ideas place local difference at the periphery of an unmarked Western modernity. Alternative modernities come to be local cultural resistances or riffs on a global theme.

Alternately, the discourse of both nativist and cosmopolitan thinkers within the Indonesian *polemik kebudayaan* suggests that modernity is in fact a universal phenomenon, if not a monolithic creeping Western force then a huge haywire of uneven and missed encounters, complexly and partially interconnected. Nativists such as Dewantara argued against the idea that modernity was essentially a Western phenomenon. The universalisms identified therein would not be tied to specifically Western notions of rationality and governmentality but to the universalist perspectives on humanity and spirituality suggested by the theosophical movement. Decades later, Humardani argued vigorously against the notion that aesthetic modernity was a necessarily Western phenomenon, suggesting that this modern line is also built with the "bricks and mortar of other cultures" (Humardani 1981:243–5). Mediated by complex interactions with colonialism and imperialism and, later, contemporary economic globalization, modernity becomes less a goal point on the straight arrow of progress than a field of contested possibilities bound by only a few basic features: the antagonistic relationship between super- and substructure, the sense of a partly lost premodern state, and transformations in spatial and temporal imaginations brought about by interactions with global capital.

INDEPENDENCE AND THE OLD ORDER

Indonesia's emergence as a nation was tumultuous; America continued to support the Dutch as they attempted to retake the colony from the Japanese following Sukarno's declaration of independence in 1945. At the 1949 Hague conference, sovereignty was transferred to the Indonesian republic only following two major concessions extracted by American mediators: that the new republic shoulder $1.3 billion of the Netherlands East Indies debt (to shore up the Dutch government against creeping communism), and that the Dutch retain control of West Irian. The previously wealthy Netherlands East Indies was suddenly transformed into the impoverished Indonesia, born fragmented and saddled with a substantial debt, roughly half of which had been incurred by Dutch military operations against it (Kahin 1995:32). The administrative vacuum created by the colony's refusal to foster an educated indigenous middle class inculcated a culture of corruption following independence that remained palpable at the state conservatory during my research.

The struggle for independence left Sukarno reasonably suspicious of both capitalism and the motives of Western nations, whose societies confirmed his suspicion that political democracy did not necessarily produce economic democracy. Sukarno articulated the nation's core values in his *Pancasila*, the five principles of nationalism, internationalism (humanitarianism), representative government, social justice, and a belief in God.[7] During colonialism, the Dutch leveraged ethnic, linguistic, and religious difference to foment political strife. In response, the Old Order crafted policies intended to Indonesianize regional populations through national language, curricula, and culture. Bali became a target in efforts to downplay feudal relics, possibly as a response to, or retaliation for, the collaborationist tendencies of the Dutch-sponsored Balinese raja during the revolution and their subsequent gambit to retain power by attempting to have Bali designated a Special District. Symbols of the previously politicized courts, such as *gambuh*, became merely custom which, now detached from power, could be celebrated as *national* cultural treasures. The more ostensibly democratic expressions that had developed outside of the courts were favored for support by the Sukarnoists. When the first government conservatory (KOKAR) was opened in Bali in 1959, popular and non-feudal forms such as *gong kebyar* and *gong gede* received the most attention.[8]

Sukarno's distaste for Western culture complicated its position as an aspect of national cultural identity as promoted by the cosmopolitan thinkers of the *polemik kebudayaan*. In the early 1950s Western interculturalists in Indonesia often became targets of anticolonial sentiment. The Dutch poet Jef Last, whose version of the Balinese legend Djayaprana was staged throughout Java, and the English impresario John Coast, who produced the 1952 American tour of the *gamelan* from Peliatan, Bali, were both stamped cultural imperialists. The Javanese critic Trisno Sumardjo captured the anticolonial ethos of the day:

> If they are to intervene in our affairs, the ideal attitude we wish from them is simply to provide a synthesis of East and West for the outside world. They can do that much, if it is seen as necessary. (quoted in Cohen 2010:217)

In response to political obstructions at the UN in 1957, Sukarno ordered the departure of some 46,000 Dutch still living in the nation, including most of those teaching music in local and national conservatories (Kahin 1995:111). The government subsequently combined conservatory curricula with nationalist ideology; students at AMI in Yogyakarta, suddenly denied qualified faculty, found themselves studying *pancasila* alongside Western classical music (p.c. Suka Hardjana, July 2003).

Beginning in the Old Order, nationalist composers experimented with forms intended to forge imaginary sonic communities through musical tours of the nation. Variously termed *kreasi baru* or *musik nusantara* (I), "music of the archipelago," these works gathered together the musics of various ethnic groups, sometimes to

---

[7] The Balinese found themselves in a delicate position regarding Sukarno's insistence on monotheism and Balinese religious leaders struggled to highlight a central deity. Sang Hyang Widi Wasa (Acintia) slowly emerges from a fog to be figured as a male god at the top of a hierarchy (which only represent avatars of him) in order not to humiliate his devotees in front of their Western and Muslim guests. Balinese religion was finally recognized by the government in 1962, nearly two decades after Sukarno's declaration.

[8] However, the institution's leading musician, Nyoman Rembang, was a strident anti-communist and an expert in *gambuh*. He fostered the incorporation of *gambuh* and other feudal forms within the curriculum.

be performed on hybrid orchestras. Experiments in the 1950s by Cokrowasito (in Yogyakarta) and Nartosabdho (in Semarang) combined various regional elements. *Musik nusantara* was prefigured by the medleys of traditional music and dance performed by *stambul* troupes touring throughout the archipelago beginning in the early twentieth century. Although *musik nusantara* was often the self-consciously nationalist expression of educated artists working in governmental conservatories, the decidedly more working-class presentations by *stambul* troupes were similarly championed by nationalist intellectuals and popular audiences who were able to see, for the first time, "moving and speaking images of constituent ethnicities of the imagined nation" (Cohen 2010:183).[9]

Although such interregional cross-pollination likely always occurred, their presence in the Old Order signified a novel and self-conscious understanding of national aesthetic identity. Sukarno personally sponsored workshops in which diverse groups of young regional musicians and dancers rehearsed at length at the presidential palace in Jakarta, learning to perform one another's music before heading out for extended, high-profile international tours (Lindsay and Liem 2012).[10]

REGIME CHANGE

Communism arrived in Bali in the 1920s via Javanese teachers working in the colonial schools and through the Soerapati organization which attracted Balinese followers through communist reinterpretations of the Ramayana, Sutasoma, and Bharatayudha legends. From the late 1950s to 1965 leftist theater and *gamelan* troupes, most prominently Sukanta's *Gong Kronik* ensemble, were sponsored by Bali's communist-dominated RRI national radio station and A. A. Bagus Sutedja, the island's left-leaning governor installed by Sukarno in 1949 (Putra 2003:49). By the early 1960s, commoners were suffering acutely from soaring food prices, agricultural plagues, and the redistribution of lands to well-positioned caste families. The Communist party's platform championing social equality and equitable land redistribution seemed a sensible stance to many (MacRae 2003).

LEKRA (I: *Lembaga Kebudayaan Rakyat*, Institute of People's Culture), the cultural arm of the PKI, opened its offices in Denpasar in 1961 and maintained a complex relationship with the LKN (I: *Lembaga Kebudayaan Nasional*, Institute of National Culture). While LEKRA was endorsed by Sukarno, the LKN received support primarily from the

---

[9] A similar impulse is demonstrated in Lotring's compositions inspired by Central Javanese music (e.g., *Gonteng Djawa*). Lotring's work predates independence, demonstrating the colonial-era interest in imagining the nation sonically through the medium of new music.

[10] During my research, works described as *musik nusantara* continued to be composed and performed, primarily at the conservatory, for state-sponsored multicultural celebrations. *Musik kontemporer* composers, Sadra most vocally, denigrated such forms as "kitschy pastiche" or "*musik mini*" rather than as fully integrated compositions. The latter term referred to the sorts of compositions performed at *Taman Mini*, a national recreation park in Jakarta designed by Suharto's wife and inspired by her experience of Disneyland (see Pemberton 1994). During the *reformasi* this model was imitated at the Bali Mini Park near Ubud.

army and the right-leaning PNI (*Partai Nasional Indonesia*, National Indonesian Party). In 1962, LEKRA held its national meeting in Bali where it hosted PKI party leaders and communist representatives from East Germany, the Soviet Union, China, and Algeria (Putra 2003:60). The choice to assemble in Bali represented an unambiguous statement against perceived Westernization through tourism—critiqued as neocolonialism—and the Western-sponsored tours of Balinese performers, decried as exploitation (ibid. 71). By the early 1960s both the PNI and the opposing PKI hired *kecak, gambuh, drama gong, arja, gong kebyar,* and *janger* ensembles to spread their propaganda. In 1963 a group of artists uneasy with LEKRA's explicit subordination of art and culture to politics voiced their opposition through a cultural manifesto (I: *Manifes Kebudayaan*) espousing a Western-oriented universal humanist approach. Leftists derided the group as the *Manikebu* (I: *manik kerbo*, water buffalo sperm), and it was subsequently outlawed by Sukarno, further agitating American Cold War observers anxious to spread Western cultural values within nonaligned states.

In Old Order Bali, cultural politics never approached a neat dichotomy between the left and right that would have been intelligible to American cold warriors. While in other areas of Indonesia LEKRA and the LKN both appeared to counter the *Manifes Kebudayaan*, in Bali they attacked each other. Both organizations fostered a people's culture that may have appeared social-realist to American Cold War observers. LKN dances, including *Tari Nelayan* (I), Fisherman's Dance and *Tari Gotong Royong* (I), Cooperation Dance, were celebrated by poets in the pages of the leading LKN/PNI daily *Suluh Indonesia,* now the *Bali Post*, as revolutionary expressions of the people's struggle (Putra 2003:75). While most evidence of LEKRA works seemed to have disappeared with their performers, Arsana suggested that the revival at the conservatory in the 1990s of Ngurah Wardana's *Tari Tenun* (I), Weavers' Dance, composed in the early 1960s, was resisted for Wardana's supposed association with the PKI (p.c. Arsana, September, 2001).

THE NEW ORDER

As described by the Balinese author Putu Wijaya through the thinly veiled allusions in his novel *Nyali* (1983), following the abortive coup of September 30, 1965, Suharto and his group incited the murder of up to one million Indonesians through a cynical propaganda campaign, murders for which no one was ever brought to trial. Following the official establishment of the New Order in 1967, Suharto assigned a cadre of officials (many trained in America with Ford funding) to direct military, economic, and labor organizations and the nation opened its economy and minerals to Western investment and extraction.

The murder of up to fifteen percent of the Balinese population allowed cultural conservatives, previously the target of communist critique, to ascend again to power (Ramstedt 1991:113). This disproportionately high-caste group took up positions in the provincial bureaucracy and became the administrators of local arts institutions. According to Robinson (1998), the violence was represented in the West as an anachronism—an attempt, it seemed, by the Balinese to break violently out of history. It didn't jibe with the contemporaneous touristic image of the Balinese as having a kind of feminine, minor politics in which play and indirection was central. But flip the coin of erotic exoticism and one often finds an equally inscrutable image of blood, chaos, and rites of spring; both images satisfied Western primitivist fantasies.

In 1965, Suharto banned the explicit association of cultural institutions with party politics and dissolved the LKN, prompting the Balinese provincial government to establish Listibiya (I: *Majelis Pertimbangan dan Pembinaan Kebudayaan*, Arts Evaluation and Cultivation Board), a conservative organization peopled by former LKN members. Listibiya focused on the resuscitation of endangered traditional arts (I: *kesenian langka*) and sponsored people's forms by establishing the annual *gong kebyar* festival in 1968. According to Halim (1999) the early New Order exacted intensive and strategic control on traditional artists and through the politics of performance permission pressured prominent *dalang* (I), puppeteers, to become members of organizations managed by GOLKAR Suharto's ruling party.[11]

During the early New Order the national Hindu organization, *Parisada Hindu Dharma*, strongly encouraged public demonstrations of piety by maintaining temple roll calls. Recalling the colonial Balinization policy, national and provincial governments encouraged and funded the building and reconstruction of temples and often the creation of ceremonies to occur within them. Now linked to the Old Order, KOKAR's status appeared to wane; it became an arts magnet high school to feed a newly established (1966) tertiary-level national conservatory, ASTI (later STSI/ISI). The latter institution resuscitated feudal forms, sanctioned the authority of performances and performers for a burgeoning ceremonial culture, and upgraded village expressions to be redistributed to communities throughout the island. For New Order subjectivities, the heightened role for religion and the arts became entangled with an exhausted and traumatized acceptance of apparently inevitable political and economic transformations.

Schulte Nordholt (2002) has described the genealogy of violence that has haunted the Balinese since 1965. Since that time, musicians with any, even tangential, link to the PKI have found themselves ostracized from the arts establishment. During my fieldwork otherwise qualified descendants of musicians associated with the PKI were still denied employment at the institutions. Most musicians who lived through the events will not, or cannot, speak of them, their role in them, or of those musicians who were lost.[12] The composer Gusti Sudarta interpreted the rise of *Ajeg* fundamentalism and inward-looking spiritualism during the *reformasi*, described in the next chapter, as the consequence of post-traumatic stress syndrome.

---

[11] Every traditional artist had to register with the Department of Education and Culture at the level of the village, district, regency, and province. Without a membership card a traditional artist could not officially perform in public (Halim 1999:298).

[12] See Larasati (2013) for more on the aesthetic implications of the violent erasure of the PKI.

Look, you will see that many of those most involved in the killing are strident supporters of *Ajeg Bali;* you see them trying to work out their *karma-pala* through this. The long-term social effects of the killing have almost been more dangerous, and ugly, than the killing itself. Now, don't think this doesn't all still reverberate until today, informing our actions and our relationships. Those killings were like a *gong.* Zirrrr....We are still hearing, and feeling, its reverberations. (p.c. July 2008)

The massacres ensured that ostensibly traditional Balinese values, rooted in a religion centered around ancient ideas of caste, would be maintained and unchallenged for years. A history of political-cultural violence explains why *musik kontemporer* works which stray from representing and serving traditional Balinese culture have often been dismissed as unmusical and without artistic merit [Track BV-3/2].

Rendering culture and custom into an apparatus of subjection has long been theorized as a New Order strategy for disarming particularistic loyalties (cf. Acciaioli 1985). If the Old Order tended to imagine a monolithic national identity, New Order administrators saw in the national motto "Unity in Diversity" (J: *Bhinneka Tunggal Ika*) an inherently pluralistic national cultural identity in which regional cultures would be revitalized and recast as the possession of all Indonesians rather than as the expression of particular groups with particular social grievances.[13] Towards this effort, additional regional conservatories were opened in East Java (Surabaya), West-Central Java (Banyumas), and Sumatra (Padang Panjang). Along with conservatories in Bali and Central Java, these regional institutions provided representatives for the performance of national celebrations of ethnic pluralism in New Order productions such as *sendratari*, a spectacular, massive combination of dance, music, and drama performed on large outdoor stages for tourists and televised to the nation. During the New Order, ethnicity was often reduced to a superficial parade of costumes and dances, only occasionally returning to signify backwardness if it interfered, as in the Papuans' ethnonationalism, with the exigencies of national development.

NEW ORDER DEVELOPMENT

> This storm is what we call progress. (Benjamin 1968:260)

As it was figured in the *polemik kebudayaan*, "development" (I: *pembangunan*) suggested growth from an internal source. The preferred organic metaphor, a budding flower expanding outward in all directions, linked *pembangunan* to *perkembangan* (I: from the root *kembang*, flower), foreshadowing Subandi's notion of the *ceraken* and the outward orientation of *musik kontemporer*. Development discourse transformed under the New

---

[13] As Schefold suggests, this move towards highlighting pluralism was partially a response to the rising threat of fundamentalist Islam at the national level. "As a counterweight, traditional Indonesian pluralism suddenly appeared in a new, more attractive light" (Schefold 1998:273).

Order which preferred hierarchic, static, and arborescent metaphors symbolized by the banyan at the heart of the ruling party's seal. The New Order defined and justified its continued rule through five-year development plans (I: *Replita: Rencana Pembangunan Lima Tahun*) through which *pembangunan* came to mean something closer to the English "development and modernization," and its associations with manmade engineering and cost-benefit analysis.

During the New Order the pervasive discourse of development represented a series of problems at the intersection of culture and rationality. New Order Indonesia was a classic development state where the omnipresent discourse of *pembangunan* was a part of quotidian experience. To engage in the activities and discourse of development was to be patriotic and progressive. Homogenous time is embedded within development discourse and its cyclical five-year plans, development decades, and building timetables. Although as old as colonization, development in Indonesia never appears to approach its completion. Development in the contemporary postcolony is a future-focused discourse, an incubator of new and imported ideas rather than the outcome of a completely internal processes; it is often figured as a global evolutionary trajectory carrying societies from tradition to modernity. Along this path, some societies may be characterized as laggard, beset by social and cultural obstacles. Similarly, an anxious rhetoric of belatedness pervaded many of the *musik kontemporer* workshops and rehearsals I attended in which there was a perceived need to catch up to the development of music in Europe and America.

Since the 1970s, anthropology has placed "development" within scare quotes, focusing increasingly on a critique that searches for grass-root responses, local empowerment, and a celebration of local genius—just as those geniuses internalize external discourses of development. Escobar urges a deconstruction of development as "disaster, a structure of propaganda, erasure, and amnesia orchestrated by science, government, and corporations" (1994:214). To Balinese postcolonial critics, including Kurnianingsih (2008), the New Order appeared as a hack magician, holding open the empty palm of aestheticized culture as a distraction, only to snatch the coin of development from behind the ear of the Balinese. Heryanto and Lutz (1988) critique the discourse of development in Indonesia as a sinister simulacrum, one that promises benefits but is little more than a form of wealth extraction and oppression: mountains, forests, valleys, rivers, oceans, air, cities, and villages are massively destroyed in the name of 'development.' "The form and content of conviction, honor, beauty, taste, and lifestyle, along with the systems of human relations, have been massively altered by a series of gigantic and purposeful programs which are called 'Development'" (1988:3). As Heryanto and Lutz suggests, development in Indonesia comes in both infrastructural-economic and cultural categories.

In New Order Bali hegemonic lowland Majapahit Balinese sought to develop marginal groups such as the Aga of the mountains and eastern shore through governmental and university upgrading projects (I: KKN, *kuliah kerja nyata*). By the late New Order, *pembangunan,* increasingly associated with environmental overdevelopment in the service of mass tourism, took on pejorative resonances. Many Balinese recognized the hypocrisy in its heart; development pretended to be rational but it was not; it served the interests of elites rather than modernity (Day 2002:169). Many musicians evinced a sense that the island had been plundered beyond repair to satisfy the overdevelopment projects of New Order cronies. The composer Gusti Sudarta was forced to regularly clear the trash that obstructed the traditional irrigation canals that encircled his home. The low walls that bounded the surrounding rice paddies appeared to be made as much of plastic bottles and bags as earth. Urban composers often waxed nostalgically on how lucky Sudarta was to have constructed a home in a spot still pure (I: *murni*) and not yet developed.

The apparent tensions in the New Order's simultaneous development of both *moderen* and *tradisi* expressions was embodied in contradictory reactions to *musik kontemporer* at the conservatory. On the one hand valorized for locating Indonesia within globalized, developed aesthetic networks, *musik kontemporer* was often simultaneously decried by those taught to fear the negative impacts of globalization as detrimental to an idealized Balinese tradition. During and after the New Order, scholarship at the conservatory represented a kind of development knowledge, a form of thought and discourse about culture that differed in many ways from the representations found in traditional, nongovernmental performance and educational contexts. Faculty at the national conservatories were often hired, sponsored, and promoted based upon competencies that may have had little to do with their ability to actually perform or compose. Conservatory scholarship entailed the generation of taxa, categorizations of genres, and the placement of tuning data, instrument inventories, and formal features into charts, tables, and summaries that resembled the official censuses and production tables of governmental development programs.

According to Becker, "the sweeping and rapid social changes of the early New Order occurred too quickly for the traditional arts to evolve evenly in accordance with oral traditions and that in a curious way [the traditional arts were increasingly] out of phase with the thrust of the culture as a whole" (Becker 1980:101). To attempt to close the gap, conservatory administrators led by Humardani suggested that the traditional arts should not simply be preserved but constantly be developed at least partially in reference to global forms (Rustopo 1990). In the New Order conservatory *kreasi baru* and *musik kontemporer* provided signs of a modernizing culture, developed in ways, it was hoped, that were increasingly intelligible to external observers. During the New Order, it was de rigueur for graduating students at the conservatory to appeal to development in the written defense (I: *skripsi*) of their recital compositions. Development of some sort was expected, and students would not receive a satisfactory grade if they completely adhered to the models provided by *tradisi*. They attempted to thread a needle of aesthetic paradox: to create new works that appeared unambiguously Balinese while simultaneously including innovative elements that could be read as demonstrations of development. Sticking with the conservatory's models of *kreasi baru* was a safer bet than potentially overstepping through *musik kontemporer*.

Tourism

July 2008. A sorry-looking group of farmers, eyes downcast, shuffled out of the Taman Safari Park and Resort as I entered. Their straw hats, shorts, torn Ts, and calves caked with dry mud were a stark contrast to the shiny park gate. I found Madé Sidia playing with a baby elephant backstage behind the amphitheater. He explained that the farmers had apparently returned to again urge the park owners to keep their lions quiet. Too poor to afford mechanical plows, they tended their nearby fields in the traditional way, riding plows dragged by water buffalo. But when the head of the newly imported pride let out his lazy afternoon roar, the buffalo screamed off in a panic across the fields, the dirt road, sometimes even down to the shore, dragging the traumatized farmers all the way. Absentmindedly kicking clods of elephant dung with his black American cowboy boots, Sidia wondered to himself that there wasn't a word in Balinese for the simultaneously sad and funny.

In his mid-forties, Sidia taught in the theater department at the conservatory and was the leading Balinese composer of kontemporer shadow-theater, often collaborating with European, American, and Australian artists. With a preternatural understanding of Balinese audiences, Sidia had perfected the art of large-scale spectacles of excess created for the Bali Arts Festival, wowing with a combination of extravagant costumes, lighting effects, smoke machines, and fireworks. Having long emulated Julie Taymor's work, he continued to hold a grudge after I failed to arrange tickets for him to see *The Lion King* while performing together in New York. Sidia's father, a renowned dalang known for his classic style, often sat in the corner during his son's rehearsals, raising an eyebrow if he felt Sidia overstepped the boundaries of good taste. While Sidia described his work as kontemporer and often collaborated with composers including Subandi, Sudarta, and others, more critical observers referred to his work as "kitsch." The epithet bounced off Sidia, for whom the audience remained the foremost element in any performance and who, to the core, was a Vegas man. The bigger, brighter, and more entertaining the performance, the better. Expats referred to him as Bali's Busby Berkeley.

Years earlier, gambling on the completion of a modern byway along the eastern shore, a joint venture between Chinese and Jakartan businessmen bought up cheap land near Saba. Hoping to stimulate their economy, the local community, peripheral to the main tourist corridor, approved the project and the relocation or destruction of homes and temples it entailed. By 2007 the Taman Safari Park and Resort was barely turning a profit, the local community was seeing little benefit, and the owners sought for ways to attract larger crowds. Sidia excitedly accepted the commission to produce a weekly tourist performance in their amphitheater. Arranging an episode of the Ramayana, he ensured a maximum number of dancers by using prerecorded kontemporer music composed for a gamelan and keyboard by the young composer Ari Hendrawan.

After Sidia and I watched his regular Tuesday evening performance he excitedly pulled me backstage, across the park and into what appeared to be a partially constructed airplane hangar. As my eyes adjusted to the dark I realized I was standing on the largest stage I had ever seen. The indoor, air-conditioned theater included two thousand plush seats, a stage with three enormous hydraulic lifts ("strong enough for elephants!"), a giant lighting rig, *and a fully functioning indoor "river." Sidia had helped convince the owners of the park that staging* kolosal *(I), colossal,* kontemporer *performances would prove to be a unique draw unavailable at any of the island's other tourist attractions. He hoped also to sway conservatory administrators to allow students to conduct their final recitals on the stage, encouraging them to explore the possibilities of staging and lighting unavailable elsewhere in Indonesia. By 2010 Sidia was helping to direct weekly performances of Balinese legends at the venue in collaboration with Australian and Chinese theater directors and producers. It was, for him, a successful synergy between artistic innovation and tourism.*

> Children of the Sun, mother of the living. Found and loved ferociously, with all the hypocrisy of nostalgia, by immigrants, slaves, and tourists. (de Andrade, 1991 [1928], *The Cannibalist Manifesto*)

Tourism is a search for authenticity based in the belief that, as Marx observed, living in modernity alienates subjects such that they cannot fully realize their own identity. The temporal framing of tourism recalls the anthropological notion of ritual time; the tourist steps temporarily out of mundane, profane time into a magical or sacred temporality, purchasing a unique experience of time as much as place. Accordingly, tourist pamphlets for Bali refer to its timelessness and magic time with predictable regularity (Yamashita 2003:73). The dense and rich literature on tourism in Bali presents a more nuanced representation of cultural change than the celebratory image reproduced in touristic literature or, for that matter, in much ethnography in which tourism is often figured a priori as a negative force against which contemporary Balinese culture exists despite, rather than because of. The narrative of loss that Boon had described by 1977 as Bali's "long swan song" persists as the Balinese continue to produce artifacts needed by tourists and ethnographers. Bali will endure as a site of desire as long as it appears to resist the implications of modernity by maintaining an aura of marginal survivance, regardless of the actual historical accuracy or academic authenticity of its representations.

The Dutch managed a consistent, if limited, flow of primarily Western, wealthy tourists until the Second World War. Following independence, tourism was re-established at slightly higher rates. The New Order aggressively invested in the industry, beginning with its first five-year development plan through the construction of a new airport south of Denpasar that could accommodate jumbo jets. The government then hired a French consultancy firm that, with assistance from the World Bank and United Nations, presented a tourism master plan. Responding to a 1971 World Bank report predicting that by 1983 Bali's "cultural manifestations would probably have disappeared" (quoted in Vickers 1989:268), the French firm sought to craft a program of cultural tourism, revenues from which, it was hoped, would be partly reinvested into further resuscitation and preservation projects. The provincial law regarding cultural tourism (passed in 1974 and re-ratified periodically until the present) equates Balinese culture with Hindu religion and regards it as a resource to be promoted and developed through a harmonious balance with tourism (in Yamashita 2003:55).

In 1971 the Balinese Department of Education and Culture (I: *Departmen Pendidikan dan Kebudayaan*) convened a meeting intended to segregate sacred from profane performing arts, identifying which would be appropriate for either touristic performance or protection from commercialization and development. The committee developed a tripartite taxonomy that distinguished between *wali, bebali,* and *balih-balihan* genres, corresponding to the inner, middle, and outer courtyards of the Balinese Hindu temple. In this taxonomy, further distance from the center of the temple indicated increasing profanity (quite often literally). The Balinese governor ratified the conference in 1973, subsequently prohibiting the commercialization or development of forms deemed sacred by the study. Nevertheless, today all forms, even those esoteric and sacred ensembles such as *slonding* and *gambang,* are developed in *musik kontemporer,* but are rarely performed in their traditional forms for tourists [Track BV-3/30].[14]

Tourism rates grew from less than 30,000 in 1970 to over 300,000 in 1980 while hotel capacity increased tenfold (Lansing 1983:110). By the late 1970s, as mass tourism attracted more hippies to Bali's beaches than wealthy tourists to its upscale hotels, Balinese cultural commentators began to worry again about the industry's deleterious impact on Balinese culture (Moerdowo 1977). To symbolize and foster spiritual and cultural regrowth, the provincial and national government sponsored the Eka Dasa Rudra festival at the Besakih mother temple in 1979. As no living Balinese had ever witnessed such a rare ceremony, it needed to be reconstructed from fragmentary manuscripts with contemporary ceremonial inventions filling in the gaps. Many understood the ceremony as an exorcism of the calamities that had befallen Bali since the end of the Old Order.

As an outgrowth of the resuscitation at the conservatory of then-rare seven-tone *gamelan* ensembles, the composer Komang Astita developed a *kontemporer* work inspired by the ceremony and entitled *Gema* (I), echo, *Eka Dasa Rudra*. Incorporating experimental staging and musical techniques, the work was performed both at the ceremony itself and as the Balinese offering for Hardjana's first composition festival in Jakarta in 1979. In Jakarta, the Balinese musicians enacted elements of the ceremony while performing, inaugurating Balinese *musik kontemporer* as a fusion of the Balinese past and future on a contemporary, international stage [Track BV-3/4].

Seeking to recoup lost revenue following a slump in oil prices in 1986, Indonesian plutocrats invested in the overdevelopment of tourism on Bali, leading local critics to characterize the island as a colony of Jakartan New Order cronies (Burhanuddin 2008:80). Lured by banking deregulation and investment backing by Jakarta conglomerates, international hotel chains initiated a series of mega-projects (I: *megaproyek*) that further degraded the local environment and alienated the Balinese from

---

[14] In 1976 Udayana University conducted a study asking leading dancers and musicians whether or not *bebali,* semi-sacred forms, should be touristified or not. The majority argued that they should not, but some suggested that the touristification of *bebali* forms represented a welcome opportunity for their urgent "restoration" (Picard 1996:147). Many of these dancers' and musicians' students later pioneered the use of sacred ensembles in *kontemporer* forms.

66 | Radical Traditions

their land (Picard 2003:110).¹⁵ The political transformations of the *reformasi* did little to curb overdevelopment. Annual rates of international and domestic tourists had increased to nearly two million by 2001, or.66 tourists for every Balinese, and tourism accounted for seventy-five percent of the workforce and two-thirds of provincial GDP (ibid.). In an interview in 2008, the *kontemporer* composer Dewa Ketut Alit reflected: "our thinking is now completely dominated by tourism, which seems to motivate all of our actions. Somehow, everything leads back to it" (p.c. July 2008).

Despite persistent fears of cultural loss, the demand for tourist performances and the influx of cash from the industry has underwritten the creation of an unprecedented number of performing ensembles and, while quality varies, it is not the case that tourism has greatly degraded the overall quality of performance. Nevertheless, there has been a movement within the Balinese *kontemporer* community to resist, if not tourism itself, at least the commodification of Balinese ethnicity. The Cudamani ensemble, directed by *kontemporer* composers and American collaborators, established at its founding its intention to avoid the industry.¹⁶ *Musik kontemporer* remains, along with Balinese ethnic pop music, one of the few forms largely independent of the industry. When it does appear before tourists, *musik kontemporer* is either camouflaged as *tradisi*, or it takes the form of a new-age celebration of breezy cosmopolitanism, which many composers deride as kitsch.

June 2002. As we passed around clear plastic bags of cheap, blinding Balinese arak, Yudane recounted his participation at the Musik Masa Kini *event years before. For his performance Yudane placed a large* gong *horizontally on a table, tilted by a book underneath it. He hung the* gong's *edge over a pile of* gamelan *keys arranged on the floor. Standing at a distance of a few feet and wearing heavy combat boots, he stomped on a sheet of corrugated metal while tossing small pebbles at the* gong. *The pebbles made a wonderfully unpredictable scraping noise as they traveled down the* gong *and bounced among the keys. (I thought of the "pachinko" game from* The Price Is Right). *Shortly thereafter Yudane was berated by government officials, not for his musical transgressions, but for wearing combat boots and jeans rather than the traditional temple costume customary for public performances of* gamelan. *After all, they complained, tourists were there! Yudane had stepped out of the image that Bali's cultural elites worked so carefully to craft* [Track BV-3/5].

The greatest fear of both tourism and anthropology is that the non-West may be a construction of the West. Now made hyperconscious of their being ethnic others, we fear that the Balinese may no longer be able to be true Balinese, but can only act at it, just

---

¹⁵ The most notorious among these being the Garuda Wisnu Kencana (GWK), the Bali Nirwana Resort (BNR), the Bali Turtle Island Development Project (BTIB), the Bali Pecatu Graha Resort (BPG), and beach reclamation at Padanggalak.
¹⁶ Instead, the ensemble performs primarily in *ngayah* devotional contexts and for tourists at home, as it were, through its numerous international tours.

as Nerval's peasant Sylvie can only pretend to be a peasant after reading Rousseau.[17] Knowing they are a sign, they may be content with being merely that. Composers expressed the suspicion that many Balinese were merely going through the motions of traditional ceremonies without understanding their underlying philosophy. Kurnianingsih similarly deconstructs Balinese culture as a simulacrum (I: *simulakram*), suggesting that, now distanced by a service mode of production from the agrarian roots of their ceremony, the Balinese play pretend to satisfy the tourist gaze (2008:ix) and in the process become only alienated administrators of their own exploitation. Kurnianingsih suggests that the government mobilizes culture to ratify its investment in tourism, with foreign scholars acting as willing rationalizers and consultants helping to authorize a stage on which the Balinese play (ibid. xvii). Contemporary Bali does adhere in many ways to Baudrillard's concept of the simulacra as the map that precedes, and overwrites, the territory; as tourists, we know in broad outline what we will see before we get there. Bali keeps up with its image, preparing, through specialized tour and spa packages, to appear like the isle of *Eat, Pray, Love* (Gilbert 2007) before its readers arrive.

July 2005. Dewi texted me from her village just north of Ubud as her family crammed a gamelan *and performers into a rented truck. I should come, she said, to see their new tourist performance in Ubud that evening; I could get in for free. I hadn't seen a tourist performance in years and while Dewi was a wonderful dancer and her younger brother Gus Teja was an influential* kontemporer *composer, I had little interest in seeing the same, abbreviated, traditional works I had seen countless times before. But she promised that their new instrumental overture, composed especially for them by Subandi, would make it worth my while. I darted into the back of the full hall just as the overture began, freezing when the ensemble turned on a dime to play a long section of music I had composed for Subandi's ensemble the previous year. I grabbed a program and saw that the work was attributed to "tradition."*

The Balinese have long known they are a brand. To the extent that they are active vendors of their ethnic authenticity as a commodity, tourism is not an external force but an internal process of Balinese culture, suggesting the failure of the 1971 cultural congress to forge hard lines between touristic and non-touristic representations and subjectivities. Culture becomes two things at once: a heritage that must be protected and developed, and a form of capital that may be exploited. The same representations may reside in multiple discursive formations and economies; they may be performed as authentic tradition for tourists while simultaneously satisfying an insider economy of musical innovation. The composer engaged with *musik kontemporer* is pulled between the effort to keep up representations of the Balinese as a people with ceremony while simultaneously giving voice to the dynamics of cultural change. Ultimately, the Balinese have become their own tourists (Picard 2003). A line of disembodied heads peeking over the wall segregating them from paying tourists, they consume the enactment of their own

---

[17] De Nerval (1999).

identity on the stage and laugh at the various *perruque* snuck in for secret enjoyment, such as labeling as tradition melodies composed *by* a tourist.

New Order *Tradisi*

Again the plastic bag of arak came around Yudane's table. I tried to pass it along; this did not feel like a normal drunkenness and stories had been circulating the past month of Balinese and tourists dying from the lethal mixture of cheap alcohol and methanol being produced in home stills in Karangasem. Not to worry, Madé told me, this was "traditional, medicinal arak." I sipped as little as I politely could. In the background a radio transmitted frequency 96.5, Radio Global Bali, and on a call-in discussion about Balinese dance, a long-time listener, first-time caller speaking in clear, urbanized Indonesian free of the usual peppering of Balinese complained that moderen *choreographies and compositions were threatening to "break tradition" (I:* merusak tradisi*). In the face of this obloquy Yudane launched into an energetic diatribe against the very categories* tradisi *and* moderen*. "There is no such thing! It's all an illusion. Worse, it has blocked our thinking for decades. It's just an intellectual constipation that serves power. We have to shit this whole mess out now. What do the tourists in Ubud say? 'Detoxify!'"*

> Society applies tradition systematically like an adhesive; in art, it is held out as a pacifier to soothe people's qualms about their atomization, including temporal atomization.... Manipulated and neutralized by the bourgeois principle, tradition eventually turns into a toxin. —Adorno, "On Tradition"

> "When the real is no longer what it used to be, nostalgia assumes its full meaning." (Baudrillard 2001:174)

The Balinese, it can be said, had no word that mapped neatly along the Dutch *traditie*, the closest equivalent being the Malay (Arabic) *adat*, meaning local law, convention, or custom.[18] The Dutch used *adat* and *traditie* interchangeably in their descriptions of local culture (Lindsay 1985:39). In early nationalist writing *traditie* was localized to *tradisi* to indicate a new semantic field describing an aestheticized understanding of culture as bounded by local values and law (*adat*). *Adat*, as it is lived today, intersects more obviously with power and class. The advent of *tradisi* coincided with fundamental shifts in the Balinese temporal imagination such that their culture's apogee was now imagined in the past tense. Materials from that past would be understood as a heritage against which innovations must justify themselves. In those fields of experience in which the *moderen* was felt as deleterious, the Balinese looked to *tradisi* for spiritual support and models for action. The roots of *tradisi* could be traced to the precolonial era, but they were not necessarily outmoded or archaic.

---

[18] Some Balinese offered *awig-awig* as a translation for tradition, although this means something more like rules and regulations. Previously, customs and styles now described as *tradisi* were simply referred to as the way of this or that place (e.g., *cara Sukawati*, as in Sukawati).

Beginning in the late New Order, the senior composer Wayan Sinti bemoaned the marginalization of ancient forms such as *gambang* and strongly advocated for its resuscitation. For Sinti, the sacralizing of time and space that *gambang* signified seemed to be falling away along with a range of sonic meaning which *moderen* attentions could no longer grasp. The increasing appearance during my research of musicians performing in rustic dress and the use of sepia film reel video filters on Balinese pop videos suggested a fading of memory into the ideology of *tradisi*. Many Balinese shared tourists' nostalgia for their own history, although for the latter it was a doubly odd "imagined nostalgia" (Appadurai 1996:77), a sense of loss for something that was never theirs.

Tradisi conforms to the theorization of heritage as culture named and "projected into the past" (Comaroff and Comaroff 2009:10), in which the past itself becomes culture. Heritage in this sense is objectified identity: traceable and alienable, only taking on its full potential once exhibited for and consumed by others. As it was used in the everyday, culture (I: *budaya*) referred not to an anthropological sense of the complex whole of life—thought, morals, representation, and action—but was restricted to its aesthetic meanings: those behaviors that could potentially be staged for tourists (Picard 1996:167). It was this notion of culture-as-art that was, in many ways, indistinguishable from *tradisi*. Just as culture was imagined as a bounded space, one could choose to step into or out of *tradisi* (*keluar dari tradisi*) when it fit one's aesthetic needs.

From whence did *tradisi* spring? The term was often associated with a vague reference to *zaman dulu* (I), prior era. When asked about the development of the *tradisi* repertoire for the shadow play in Sukawati, my teacher Wayan Loceng would only commit to its emerging from *zaman dulu*. Coming to associate *zaman dulu* with a misty Balinese prehistory, I was surprised to learn later that Loceng meant the early 1960s. *Tradisi* belongs to a contingent temporal frame ranging from a depth of thousands of years to merely decades, and thus represents a qualitative measure of experiential time rather than a quantitative, homogenous time. For Loceng, the cultural transformations that have occurred since the early 1960s have been so substantive as to represent a different epoch.

In its vague appeals to an indeterminate past filled with idealized *tradisi*, *zaman dulu* served the New Order's attempt to sweep time's mess under the rug. In 1987, the New Order government constructed an enormous monument—the *Bajra Sandhi*—in the center of its modern administrative district south of Denpasar. Built to appear already ancient and eternal, the structure recalled both the ancient Borobudur and the shape of the Hindu priest's prayer bell. Dioramas inside the structure represented the government's officially imposed periodizations of Bali's *zaman dulu* from prehistory to the present in which the violence of the New Order's emergence is predictably absent. Often and unpredictably closed, unpopular except as a place to hook up late at night, visually spectacular but largely empty, the monument symbolized the spatiality of the New Order state as an imposed, abstract center. *Tradisi* was its representational space, similarly centralized and managed.

The materials of *tradisi* sometimes emerged as artifacts recovered through New Order *penggalian* (I), excavation, projects. Referring to resuscitation rather than literal excavation, conservatory *penggalian* efforts often inspired *kontemporer* projects as in Astita's *Gema Eka Desa Rudra* described above and Wayan Rai's *Trompong Beruk*, based upon a *penggalian* study of folk instruments in Karangasem. After being identified, documented, and studied, these instruments were then combined with invented instruments and innovative techniques to be performed, again, for Hardjana's *kontemporer* composition festivals (PKM) in Jakarta in 1982. The idea of *tradisi* as a kind of ore that could be extracted for present day uses pervaded arts discourse during and following the New Order. Between 2002 and 2005 the national arts magazine, *Gong*, distributed bookmarks inserted between its pages picturing a shovel, the shaft of which was printed with the (English) phrase "Keep Digging for Traditional Art!," its blade plunging towards an image of Balinese women performing rice-pounding music (*lesung*).[19]

IDEOLOGY?

Is *tradisi* the opium of the Balinese and their admirers? Is the aestheticization of politics, the depoliticization of culture, and the staging of *tradisi* a cynical, purposeful maneuver by the state for control? Is *tradisi* ideology? Most plainly, ideology is the "nexus of discourse and power" (Eagleton 1983:183). The notion of false consciousness, absent in Marx, was proposed by later writers to suggest that subjects subconsciously internalize the relations between them and their conditions of existence for the profit of the ruling class. In this arrangement, ideology is not a heavy-handed, top-down mechanism but a subtly narrowed system of representations through which subjects can think—a limited framework of assumptions about reality and possibility that formulate subjects' understanding of their place in historically constituted social formations as inevitable and natural (Kavanagh 1995).

The image of the Balinese as living a form of false consciousness cultivated by the New Order state and its linked apparatus of tourism occasionally appears in Baliography.[20] However, false consciousness as an ideology deceiving the unwitting masses has been thoroughly critiqued; the German masses were not tricked by the Reich, most *wanted* a fascist regime (Spivak 2010:27). Many Balinese may have genuinely wanted to slaughter each other in 1965 and they may want, just as genuinely and without Machiavellian state manipulation, to forget their trauma through *tradisi*. If *tradisi* was ideology, it would attempt to prevent action that would promote social change; on this point composers were divided. If the Balinese aren't completely alienated in a way that satisfies the frames of Marxist theory—they still have meaningful communities and gift economies—then neither is their contemporary reality felt to be adequate. In Marxist thought, alienation means the "…splitting up of the real community…followed by a projection…of the social

---

[19] Beginning in the late New Order the Ford Foundation underwrote the publication of *Gong*, a national arts magazine featuring profiles on Indonesia's leading artists. The magazine promptly folded after Ford withdrew its support following the global economic downturn in 2010.

[20] See Picard (1996) and Vickers (2005) for occasional appearances of this image.

relation onto an external 'thing'..." (Balabar 1995:76). During the New Order that thing emerged as *tradisi*. It was simultaneously an abstraction that stood in for the (partially) fragmented community *and* a rhetoric mobilized by the state and tourism that functioned to (partly) alienate the Balinese from political action and thought. Through their sometimes implicit deconstruction of *tradisi*, experimental composers exposed the double, if not false, consciousness produced through the alienating effects of touristic subjectivity.

While conservatives argued that *tradisi* required protection from outside forces, composers often rejected the classic and persistent spatialization of *tradisi* with the local and particular versus the *moderen* and its associations with the universal and global.[21] Newness that outstripped the innovations of global avant-gardes could be found, it was thought, in one's own village, while ideas considered cutting-edge in Western modernism may sound like any old work performed in the temple. Subandi once described *gamelan angklung* as *"lebih minamalis daripada minamalis"* (I), "more minimalist than minimalism" (p.c. July 2011). This is not to say that the global was not sometimes figured as a hegemonic and silencing force, but that Balinese composers engaged in *musik kontemporer* largely rejected the prevalent discourse in which Balinese *tradisi* was feminized and threatened by the penetrations of a masculine global culture (as in Sulistyawati 2008, Burhanuddin 2008).

Female dance students at the conservatory understood, if only implicitly, that their bodies were the ultimate icons of Balinese *tradisi* upon which, it was imagined, Balinese culture depended for its survival. Since the New Order, threats to the nation, the island, and its culture have been consistently gendered; Bali was a maiden to be protected from the West's penetrations. While the dance department at the conservatory was a primarily female realm, men tended to direct developments in *tari kontemporer*, experimental dance.[22] Within the overwhelmingly male realm of *musik kontemporer*, the experiments by the female composers Ketut Suryatini, Desak Madé Suarti Laksmi, and Wayan Mudiari stood out [Track BV-3/7].

Arbiters at the conservatory tended to reject overly static images of *tradisi* by distinguishing between *klasik* (I), classic, which they designated as styles free of outside influence (i.e., *legong*), and *tradisi*, which many argued should develop in accordance with the people, as in the constant transformation of *gong kebyar* materials in the compositional commons of *kreasi baru* (Dibia in Gombloh 2000b).[23] As in English, *klasik* came to point to a specific moment in Balinese antiquity: the emergence of a new performance culture among the Majapahit Balinese of the sixteenth through

---

[21] For a recent repetition of this spatialization see Sayuti (2002).
[22] Experimental choreographies by Wayan Dibia, Dewa Nyoman Sura, Madé Sidia, and Madé Tegeh Okta Maheri led the field. During my research, Ni Kadek Dewi Aryani was the only Balinese woman to contribute in a sustained way to experimental dance. The Javanese dancer Sefi Indah Prawasari and the Japanese dancer Jasmine Okubo both contributed to the *kontemporer* dance scene in Bali during the *reformasi*.
[23] Humardani delineated between folk arts (I: *kesenian rakyat*) and traditional arts (I: *kesenian tradisi*), suggesting that the former was rural, rough, and sporadic while the latter was urban, courtly, and refined. Such a distinction has never quite held in Bali where the people have been the curators of *tradisi* as much as have the courts.

eighteenth centuries. *Klasik* forms were imagined to have attained perfection such that their transformation could only represent degradation. While conservatory fathers sought to retain *tradisi* as a conceptual frame, even if it entailed epistemological contortions, Yudane and his coterie argued that the term was forever corrupted by the uses to which it had been put both by the New Order state and the tourist industry. Presaging the postcolonial critiques of *tradisi* by Balinese authors including Kurnianingsih (2008) and Santikarma (2010), Yudane rejected the branding of everything that happened in Bali as *tradisi*, arguing that this encouraged viewing the entirety of Balinese culture as a thing (I: *benda*) rather than a process (p.c. August 2001). This rhetoric recalls the debates of the *polemik kebudayaan*, specifically the ideas of the iconoclastic Sumatran author Armijn Pané (1908–70), who had little patience for those of his colleagues who persisted in seeing tradition and modernity as opposites. For Pané these were not mutually exclusive categories (Frederick 1997) [Track BV-3/6].

Yudane's thoughts coincide with recent Western analyses of the tradition–modernity rupture in the ethnography of Indonesia. Lansing (2007) critiques the "characterization of 'traditional' societies [as] merely the baseline from which modernity began to emerge, while fully modern societies are [described as a] theater of continual change" (2007:10). Tony Day (2002) presents a more sustained critique of the dichotomy, which he traces to Weber's categories for analyzing the state, and questions whether or not the distinction can be meaningfully maintained. Day argues for a more subtle account of human agency and the interpenetration of modes and economies rather than the neat categories of traditional, modern, colonial, and postcolonial. His magisterial analysis of the Javanese epic poem *Serat Centhini* demonstrates just how much of the modern is to be found in the heart of tradition. Rather than being its backdrop, tradition is produced by the distinctions modernity draws.

The persistent opposition of tradition and modernity continues in Balinese discourse in which tradition has, as Gadamer put it, "a justification that is outside the arguments of reason" (Gadamer 1989:288). Recorded in *lontar*, official conservatory publications, and electronic media, *tradisi* is imagined to be housed in the archives of the *griya* (B), Brahman priest's home, the conservatory, and the collections at *Listibiya*, where its keepers are accorded special hermeneutic rights. But as an archive in the Foucauldian sense, *tradisi* is more, and more powerfully subtle, than these mere physical artifacts. It is the "law of what can be said ... [and which] defines at the outset the system of its enunciability" (Foucault 1972:129). *Tradisi* is what allows Balinese audiences to hear certain musics as such. The self-conscious borrowing in *musik kontemporer* of musical materials from outside *tradisi*'s boundaries revealed, if only for a moment, the traces of *tradisi*'s power. *Tradisi* as a self-evident phenomenon is the *doxa* described by the sociology of knowledge and it is this to which Yudane referred, seeking to expose the pieties through which Balinese cultural conservatives defended an unthinking notion of tradition. What Yudane, and indeed many composers, sought was a melting of modernity into tradition that would recognize the inherent flux described by Gadamer when he stated that tradition exists only in constantly becoming other than it is.[24]

Sadra spoke of the *kontemporer* arts as penetrating (I: *menembus*) the scar tissues that restricted culture, which he defined as an ever-changing process (p.c. September 2003). Scar tissues grow in response to perceived injuries, sealing off an organ to protect it from further damage. Tissues grow around an injured knee, restricting movement; adhesions bind a damaged womb, hampering the healthy growth of the fetus. The scar tissues to which Sadra referred were the state policies of arts preservation and management, enacted as a response to the historical injuries of colonialism and the perceived risks of globalization. Often instituted with the best intentions, these policies, Sadra argued, stunted the growth and restricted the free movement demanded by *budaya* (culture), transforming it into brittle *tradisi*.

New Order policies were never coherent or consistently enforced enough to completely determine aesthetic production or to drain out prior, local meanings. In valorizing the social meanings of Western-style popular musics in Indonesia, Luvaas overstates the effects of New Order aestheticization: "In the process, ethnic traditions often became a stale, hollow version of themselves, museumified, standardized, and frozen in time...hardly the kind of dynamic, living force that makes alternative definitions of self possible" (2009:263). Even as managed by the conservative administrators at the national conservatories, the New Order policies of *penggalian* (I), resuscitation, *pelestarian* (I), preservation, and *pengembangan* (I), development, have always stimulated (sometimes veiled) innovations and maintained an intimate relationship with challenging expressions such as *musik kontemporer*. Wary of giving any institution or policy too much agency, we should recognize that policy formation and its implementation do not, especially in Indonesia, form a seamless web. It was often in gaps between policy and practice that experimental composers played.

Urbanization and Class

In 1979 the committee of the newly created Bali Cultural Center (I: *Taman Budaya*), located catty-corner to the conservatory in Denpasar, began hosting the annual Bali Arts Festival (I: *Pesta Kesenian Bali*, PKB) primarily for the performance of *tradisi* forms. Emerging with the growth of regional conservatories during the middle New Order, regional arts centers were founded as secular venues to provide art to the masses. The PKB remains the most significant arts festival in the nation, hosting up to ten events daily from mid-June to mid-July, including many *kontemporer* performances. The extended parade that annually opens the festival establishes it as a formal state event. As the procession winds its way around the grand manner New Order architecture of the administrative district in Renon, presidents, cabinet members and cultural

---

[24] On rejections of the *tradisi-moderen* split see also Mistortoify (2002) and the discussion of Putu Wijaya's *Tradisi Baru* (New Tradition) theater ensemble in Hellman (2003).

administrators annually pontificate on the need for the simultaneous development and preservation of Indonesia's cultural heritage.

The Art Center's urban performance spaces, where strangers sit in fixed seats, are given grand Sanskritic names—Natya Mandala, Ksirarnawa, Ardha Chandra—imbuing a sacred, liturgical aura to compensate for the loss of traditional communal intimacy in New Order spaces. An oversized monumental *candi*, the split gate of the Balinese Hindu temple, is positioned at the back of the Ardha Chandra stage, the enormous outdoor amphitheater that hosts the popular *gong kebyar* contests. Here the state seeks to capture the religious resonance of the Balinese Hindu *odalan* temple ceremony in which performances are held in the outer (B: *jaba*) courtyard of the temple. The difference, of course, is that there is nothing inside this temple. Passing through its gate, one steps into an apparently endless stream of urban traffic and crowded housing developments.

In New Order Bali modernity revealed itself most obviously in the increasingly urban demographics of its population. The first colonial census of 1921 records a Balinese population of 859,400. By the late New Order it had more than tripled, being most dense in and around the urban capital of Denpasar. By 2005 more Indonesians were living in cities than in the countryside. The emergence of *musik kontemporer* coincided with rapid urbanization and a tripling of per capita income in Bali between the late 1970s and the late 1980s. While *tradisi* forms such as *gong kebyar* remained popular throughout the class hierarchy, *kontemporer* expressions tended to align with the middle class. The significant cosmopolitan cultural capital associated with the form attempted to make up for a lack of truly upper-class economic distinction.

To be fully *moderen* in the New Order, a Balinese must have lived in Denpasar or have moved from the rural village (I: *kampung*) to Denpasar. The realization of one's *moderen* Balinese-ness was achieved by maintaining a second home in the village (as did nearly all conservatory administrators and many faculty) to which one regularly returned to be re-energized by *tradisi*. The composer Nyoman Windha (1956–), who normally resided in his modern multi-story home just north of the main bypass in Denpasar, often referred to his need for *represing* (I), refreshing, trips to his *kampung*, a fifteen-minute drive to the north in Singapadu. Part of being *moderen* in Bali was in living the tension between the urban and the bucolic.

During the New Order, urbanization and development furthered the interpenetration of spaces previously arranged along the binaries: local/foreign, *aga-jaba* (indigenous, Majapahit), and *asli/turis* (native, tourist). The creeping expansion of tourist villages such as Ubud drew once unique and separate spaces closer together, homogenizing their performing arts. The increasing urbanization of Balinese society led to an inevitable homogenization of *adat* custom and law as members from distinct rural communities streamed into tightly packed *perumahan* housing projects. Within these new communities families often struggled with the advent of urban anonymity and its implications for traditional mores. Students at the conservatory sometimes left natal villages to live unsupervised in urban dormitories (I: *kos*) where sex did not necessarily lead to marriage (much less wait for it), but could be traded and possessed [Track BV-3/7].

New Order urbanization had profound impacts on the island's acoustic ecology. The loud, rich sounds of motorbikes conveyed a plethora of information to the listening Balinese. Motorbike noises were gendered; women more often drove the automatics that produced a distinct humming tone. The sound of a motorbike driving within the village differed greatly from city driving where the sharp acoustic reflections of asphalt and cement walls served as a constant reminder of one's actual (and often social) place. Class was signified in the always audible quality of an engine, the difference between a motorbike and a real, and much more expensive, motorcycle being obvious to all Balinese. In 2003 the Yogyanese *kontemporer* composer Jumbek caught up the social significance of the contemporary acoustic ecology of Indonesia by arranging an orchestra of motorbikes, creating a music of thickly layered, phasing drones.

As with Europe's first bourgeois class, the rising Balinese middle class of the New Order knew that status needed to be continually won and that their position could be lost through negligence. If it was not always a strict caste society in the classic Hindu sense, Balinese society of the New Order was indisputably hierarchical. Ostentatious displays of status increased during the New Order as more Balinese claimed the signs of ceremonial splendor once restricted to the feudal classes. Middle-class weddings, tooth filings, and family ceremonies became massive spectacles. Gusti Putu Sudarta was particularly fond of pointing out in his *topeng* mask performances that a contemporary Balinese proved his modernity by being traditional in paradoxical ways, primarily through the conspicuous production (often beyond one's means) of ceremony. Recalling Adorno's critique of the culture industry, Sudarta asked if contemporary Balinese were worshipping their gods or the money invested in their offerings to them [Track BV-3/8].[25]

The Conservatory

Transformed into *tradisi*, culture became a business that required administration. The Indonesian state conservatory replicates broader development projects in which technicians (in this case artists) are subordinated to administrators who manage the production of cultural products safe for general consumption. Founded during the Old Order, the national conservatories grew expansively through the New Order's development projects. The conservatory was caught between mediating local concerns while attempting to read the tea leaves of sometimes opaque or contradictory national cultural policies.[26] Although culture was a contested field, its assumed civilizing role in forging Indonesian subjectivities and national pride was enshrined from the first in Indonesia's constitution which directed the government and its agencies to advance national culture, thereby adopting the colonial understanding of the arts as a field requiring official governing.

---

[25] From a *topeng* monologue performed at a domestic ceremony in Batuan, November 2003.
[26] The rich literature on the Indonesian conservatories includes Weintraub (1993), Sutton (1991), Tenzer (2000), Perlman (2004), and Heimarck (2003).

The characterization of *tradisi* and *moderen* as two separate worlds, each with their own spatial and temporal imaginary, marks both the ethnographic account and conservatory discourse.[27] Faculty described their institution as a bridge (I: *jembatan*) forging the aesthetic symbiosis of the *tradisi* and the *moderen*, the sacred and profane, through phrases such as "continuities in change," a mantra of New Order aesthetic governmentality introduced in the late 1980s by Madé Bandem.[28] The slogan's unspoken assumption suggests that certain practices persevered in their ostensible stasis *despite* a storm of surrounding change rather than because of it.

Through its association with the state conservatory, "continuities in change" suggested to many composers a state bureaucratic arbitration of change. In interviews Bandem suggested that the concept assured that aesthetic production (I: *penciptaan*) in Bali would remain rooted (I: *berakar*) in Balinese culture so that the essence of Balinese culture would not be lost within the modern context (p.c. July 2001). This notion conflates *budaya* (I), culture, with *tradisi* and suggests that certain representations made by Balinese, in Bali, might not qualify as authentic examples of Balinese culture. Subandi's notion of *tradisi radikal* was an alternate vision, one in which the Balinese are not only changing, but increasingly *capable* of change. By 2006, "continuities in change" had become overemphasized to the point of exhaustion, a magical incantation in which obvious historical ruptures became difficult to account for. *Musik kontemporer* became a site for the symbolic negotiation of continuity and change, replication and mutation. If not advocating a wholesale negation of previous forms as in the classic Western avant-garde, *tradisi radikal* asked: What change is allowable?

KOKAR/ASTI/STSI/ISI

KOKAR (I: *konservatori karawitan*) was founded in Denpasar in 1959 as a branch of the first national conservatory in Solo, Central Java. Under the guidance of the Balinese theorist, composer, and performer Nyoman Rembang—an anti-communist LKN member trained at Solo—KOKAR was simultaneously focused upon preservation and the creation of Balinese artist-intellects fluent in the rationalizing languages of modernization and development (Hough 2000:118–119). In 1967, as a manifestation of the New Order's increasing investment in culture, ASTI (I: *Akademi Seni Tari Indonesia*, Indonesian Dance Academy) Denpasar was founded as a tertiary-level institution

---

[27] For strong versions of this in the ethnographic account see Ramseyer (2002) and Lansing (1983). Lansing characterizes *moderen* and *tradisi* as two different civilizations, so radically different that they manage to coexist (1983:71). For similar Balinese characterizations see Kurnianingsih (2008), Geriya (2000), and Burhanuddin (2008). This segregation recalls an older Balinese spatial imaginary: the profane, manifest *sekala* and the spiritual, unmanifest *niskala*.

[28] This phrase was repeated to me, always in English, in numerous interviews. The inspiration for the term in Bali seems to be the title of Clair Holt's (1967) study of Indonesian performing arts, *Continuities and Change*. The characterization of Balinese culture as uniquely able to creatively negotiate incoming influences (Harnish 2005:103) has long been a mainstay of the ethnographic account. See also Hobart et al. (1996), Mead and Bateson (1942), Boon (1977), Bandem and deBoer (1995), Suryani and Jensen (1992:124), Gold (2006), Dibia and Ballinger (2011).

distinct from KOKAR. By 1974 the institution had added departments of music (I: *karawitan*) and shadow theater (I: *pedalangan*) and under the energetic leadership of Bandem, newly returned from doctoral studies in America, was upgraded to a college (I: STSI, *Sekolah Tinggi Seni Indonesia*, Indonesian College of the Arts). Awarded the equivalent of a BA, its graduates were certified as civil servants, qualified to work at a wide range of government bureaucracies. Conservatory faculty members were ratified as bona fide moderns by gaining a university degree that guaranteed the possession of a class status proportional to the prestige of the degree. The Javanese critic and new music composer Suka Hardjana described state conservatory credentials as merely the new badge of an old feudal structure in Indonesia in which *raden, bupati*, and so forth is replaced by S1, S2, S3, and *Professor* (p.c. July 2003).[29]

Although his salary was officially limited to that of a mid-ranking civil servant, the conservatory rector wielded an enormous influence over the landscape of the Balinese arts. During my research, administrators strenuously jockeyed for the position, coveted for the visibility, control, and opportunities for graft it provided through the management of recording, performance, and tour contracts. The rector's opinion of a composer, personal or aesthetic, determined if he or she received commissions, foreign teaching and study opportunities, and whether or not his or her works were included in programs and touring set-lists. Strong composer–director alliances drove the island-wide dissemination of a new *kreasi* canon. From the late 1970s to the mid-1980s the composer Wayan Beratha fostered a strong alliance with rector Gusti Nyoman Pandji who included Beratha's works in KKN projects, performances for state events, and international tours. In the late 1980s, this dynamic continued through an alliance between Bandem, the composer Nyoman Windha, and Bandem's wife, the faculty member and choreographer Swasthi Bandem. Precipitating dramatic political and social dramas in which the *kontemporer* arts played a conspicuous role, the institute was upgraded in 2003 to an ISI (I: *Institut Seni Indonesia*, Indonesian Arts Institute), theoretically qualified to confer graduate degrees.

New Order cultural elites in Bali often associated Western art with moral decay and sought to curtail its "sexualized and aggressive tendencies, out of line with the refined nature of the Indonesian people" (Djelantik 1999:178). The conservatory's conservative stance was most sharply articulated in Djelantik's monographs on aesthetics, required texts for all conservatory students since the late New Order, in which he decried the influence of Western-styled experimentalism in the works of

> "artists" who would, for instance, cover themselves in paint or mud, rolling on a canvas as a form of supposed "expression." Unfortunately this kind of work has already influenced the Indonesian artist. This is clearly not art, but a sensation intended to attract attention. This kind of spectacle is dangerous for the young

---

[29] S1, S2, and S3 refer to bachelor's, master's, and doctoral equivalents.

artist who may incorrectly use it as a way to derive benefit from specific parties. Fortunately, this kind of extreme "art" has not overtaken Indonesia. (ibid.)[30]

The New Order conservatory was invested with the power to define who could legitimately be called a composer, a performer, and interpreter of works. The boundaries of art discourse—what art itself meant—were made public through the conservatory's theory and rhetoric. The structure of academic knowledge at the conservatory replicated tendencies of other governmental development projects in which Western-based empirical, explicit, rational knowledges can sometimes replace local knowledges and overnight turn previously talented, intelligent village artists into seemingly ignorant bumpkins. In order to assure governmental funding, the institute was obliged to imitate research programs and reporting rubrics developed for Indonesian institutes of science. Faculty and students became accustomed to the awkward contortions required to represent aesthetic exploration and inspiration within the format of regimented empirical experimentation [Track BV-3/9].

The institution relished in the definition of aesthetic taxonomies—religious: *wali, bebali, balih-balihan* (referring to forms deemed sacred, semi-sacred, profane); temporal: *kuno, madya, baru* (I), old, medium, new; and formal: *klasik, tradisi, kreasi, kontemporer*. Each taxon suggested particular performance contexts, social inflection, and formal rules: *klasik* was barred from philandering through hybridity, *kontemporer* was shooed away from the temple. The struggle over categories served as a proxy for real social boundaries. The most popular indigenous New Order working-class forms such as *Dangdut* and popular musics in the Western style were barred from campus, ex-nominated from inclusion in the creation of canons celebrated as a universally valued Balinese cultural inheritance.

Conservatory faculty and administrators hailed overwhelmingly from the central, southern districts of Gianyar and Badung and it was their village styles that became the de facto argot of the New Order conservatory. Through their pedagogy and domination of contest juries, conservatory faculty functioned to homogenize village forms towards Southern styles, excluding outlying regions from participating in legitimating practices. Although interregional borrowing and influence had long marked Balinese expressive culture,[31] during the New Order, the conservatory's role in homogenization became a point of contention for many composers who sought to rediscover regional variations as inspirations for their experiments. Many of Yudane's, Subandi's, and Sudarta's *kontemporer* and *kreasi baru* of the late New Order drew inspiration (if not

---

[30] Rolling in mud is indeed a popular form of experimentalism throughout Indonesia and seems to have its origin in Sardono's, *Meta-ekologi* composed in 1979. Djelantik's veiled reference to "specific parties" may have been an oblique reference to *kontemporer* forms of protest, usually pro *Partai Demokrasi Indonesia* (PDI, led by Megawati), leading to Suharto's ouster.

[31] Sadra (1991:43) counters the image of top-down homogenization by the conservatories through his discussion of the intense borrowing and continuous aesthetic interaction between, for instance, musicians and composers in Belaluan (Denpasar) and those in Jagaraga, in Buleleng, between the 1920s and 1960s.

directly adopting materials) from the marginalized *gender wayang* forms of isolated villages in Karangasem. Through the participation in mandatory KKN projects in the villages, students simultaneously disseminated official canons intended to upgrade local practice while encountering styles that contradicted the standardizing practices of the conservatory [Track BV-3/10].

In the New Order conservatory, *gamelan* represented a field of social management in which ethnicity, religion, gender, sexuality, class, and social order could be targeted, ordered, and mobilized in the hopes of producing certain social effects. By combining a practice-based pedagogy and an uncritical curriculum focused on state ideology, the conservatory, consciously or not, robbed young Balinese artists of the language necessary to explicitly interpret their world. Sudirana suggested that the younger generation was made inarticulate by mentors providing them with only a blunt set of evaluative tools: one either enjoyed a piece or could not hear it (I: *tidak bisa dengar*) (p.c. November 2010). Nyoman Windha, the lead composition faculty in the *karawitan* department since the early 1990s, had begun to part ways with the conservatory leadership by 2010, suggesting that musicians had been made stupid (I: *pembodohan*) by its curriculum (p.c. July 2010). During the *reformasi*, many composers, including many employed by the conservatory itself, increasingly denigrated institutional scholarship and theorizing for producing pamphlets intended merely to satisfy Jakartan publishing quotas, rather than producing a meaningful dialogue on the arts.

MUSIK KONTEMPORER AT THE CONSERVATORY

Although the conservatory's official policies and aesthetics may seem at odds with radical innovation, in Bali nearly all composers engaged with *musik kontemporer* are graduates of the institution, many its faculty. Through hosting workshops, providing unrivaled facilities, and linking its students and faculty to a broader national scene of composition, the conservatory has fostered the development of *musik kontemporer* from its emergence. A series of workshops in the early 1970s, hosted by Humardani, encouraged the creation of experimental works by Balinese composers working in Central Java.[32] TIM (*Taman Ismail Marzuki*), a modern performing center that includes an arts campus, was opened in Jakarta in 1968; by the mid-1970s TIM regularly hosted national composition seminars for delegates from the regional conservatories who were urged by conservatory administrators to form a new generation of male [I: *putra*] avant-garde composers who would be responsible for the future of Indonesian music and who would question the continued existence of *karawitan* (Rustopo 1991:17).[33]

---

[32] The foremost being Wayan Sadra and Pande Madé Sukerta.
[33] The most influential of these seminars included the 1972 Arts Seminar hosted by Humardani in Solo, the 1975 Symposium of Traditional Music (*karawitan*) hosted by Frans Haryadi and Humardani at TIM, and the 1979 Music Composition Meeting again at Solo. For the latter conference, the use of the term *musik*, rather than *karawitan*, suggested that the world of non-*gamelan* sound was to be discussed and included within new conceptions of music and musical creation.

Most significant for the development of Balinese *musik kontemporer* were the Young Composers' Weeks (I: *Pekan Komponis Muda*, PKM) hosted at TIM by Hardjana from the late 1970s to the early 1990s. Simultaneous with the PKM events, the national conservatories hosted a rotating series of arts festivals (I: *festival seni*) in which young Balinese composers presented new works and interacted in workshops with composers of other traditions. Through these interactions composers began to develop specific techniques to creatively appropriate and transform the music of their others. Sadra's so-called *transmedium* approach, described below, emerged from these workshops as an attempt to simultaneously incorporate and mutate foreign materials. The regular interaction of a coterie of young conservatory students and faculty interested in radical innovation led some, primarily those composers with Western training, to advocate the creation of a distinctly national form of *musik kontemporer*.[34] Many regional composers, and especially the Balinese, remained ambivalent in this effort [Track BV-3/11].

During the New Order, the Balinese conservatory sometimes found itself caught between the interests of innovative young composers inspired by the national composition seminars, and the perceived need to preserve *tradisi* and provide performances appropriate to the touristic and ethnographic image of the island. The rector acted as a kind of pressure valve, carefully regulating the relative mix of *tradisi* and *kontemporer* within Bali's arts atmosphere. Made too rich through an overabundance of innovation, it was feared that Balinese culture might become combustible. Envious of the comparatively open arts environment of the Solonese and Jakartan institutions, Yudane staged a rebellion in 1993. Instead of producing the predictably milquetoast dance accompaniments expected of final recitals, Yudane composed a radically innovative instrumental *musik kontemporer* for a small, idiosyncratic set of found instruments.[35] Inspired by Yudane's boldness, the following year the (now well-established) composers Subandi, Wayan Widia, Ketut Cater, and Wayan Darya appealed to the music department for their right to compose *musik kontemporer* instrumental works as well. These students, who older faculty had described at the time as "*anak nakal*" (literally, naughty children), were quickly "re-channeled" (I: *arahkan*) by then-rector Bandem to create more conservative dance accompaniments (p.c. Madé Subandi, July 2003) [Track BV-3/12].

As late as 2012, final recitals (I: *ujian*) continued to be evaluated through New Order criteria. Although students were ostensibly allowed to create any kind of performance—*kontemporer* forms were not theoretically judged unfavorably against *tradisi* or *kreasi baru* forms—the criteria, seen in Table 3.1, channeled students to create moderately innovative *kreasi baru* works and to hew close to the musical status quo. The assumption of a "theme" (I: *tema*) resulted in programmatic and often representational works, leading composers away from improvisation or chance. A focus upon musical

---

34 For a contrasting viewpoint, see the Sumatran composer Ben Pasaribu's discussion of *musik kontemporer* as a national form (in Gombloh 2000a).
35 Yudane composed his ensemble from the "left over bits" (I: *sisa-sisa*), the random instruments not used by his more conservative classmates using standard ensembles.

TABLE. 3.1
Work Assessment Criteria (I: *Kriteria Penilaian Karya Karawitan*) for the *Ujian Sarjana Seni*, final recital

Idea	Form	Presentation
Concept	Composition	Expression
Theme	- musical technique	Feeling of Togetherness
Narrative	- musical structure	Harmony
	Ornamentation	
	Creativity	

disjunctions and juxtapositions may violate the criteria of a feeling of "togetherness" or "harmony." The former category assumes a large ensemble of performers rather than solo works.[36] Dissonant, chaotic, or minimalist compositions would potentially be criticized as being out of harmony.

"Ornamentation" assumes the incorporation of the interlocking *kotekan* figuration typically employed in *kreasi baru* and *tradisi* works. While high levels of innovation might implicate high marks for creativity, this was not the case in practice. Extreme creativity in the *ujian* recital could backfire, and the safest way to ensure graduation (and to avoid paying extra fees to enter the process a second time) was to create works that gradually introduced new playing techniques, musical structures, and concepts to the existing performance practice, rather than to attempt a musical revolution through the introduction of obviously radical, experimental, or foreign musical approaches or concepts.

As the New Order progressed, *musik kontemporer* shifted from officially sanctioned expressions of Balinese modernity, as in Asnawa's *Kosong*, to more contrarian expressions of "naughty students" with Yudane as their pioneer. Through a more radical form of innovation, the latter group formulated an anti-discourse of new compositional forms that sometimes revealed the constructed nature of conservatory approaches and institutional aesthetics. The sounds they produced revealed New Order aesthetic criteria as an instrument for making people believe in the apparent harmony of society itself. New Order *kreasi baru* developed in the conservatory suggested an idealized, nonconflictual humanity that was both predictable and controllable. Administrators' distrust of new musical codes recalled the refusal of the abnormal in all oppressive societies, reminding us that sounds perceived as "noise" call into question all differences and in so doing suggest the frightening dissolution of the current social order (Attali 1985: 19).

---

[36] The first solo *kontemporer* work was composed in 2007 by Gus Teja.

4 Moha

AESTHETIC AND SOCIAL DISSENSUS IN THE REFORMATION (1998–)

NOVEMBER 2002. GEDE Arsana was intensively rehearsing his final recital composition at ISI. Alternately gregarious or shy, depending on the number of women present, Gede was a favorite among the children in his neighborhood and they eagerly joined any musical project he initiated at the banjar in Penatih, a village on the northernmost edge of Denpasar. The village, for it still retained the feeling of a village, marked the last urbanized settlement before the landscape transitioned into the rice paddies that stretched to Ubud. From there Gede frequently drove his motorbike twelve hours to East Java, where his family had connections to Hindu communities in the mountains.

While other, more self-consciously cosmopolitan composers might be censured for their brainy kontemporer-isms, Gede's self-deprecating sense of humor, playful theatricality, and plain courtesy often allowed him to introduce whip-smart experimentalisms within otherwise kreasi baru contexts. If some kontemporer composers cultivated a rebellious persona, Gede was simply one of the nicest guys you would ever meet. Because of his virtuosic musicianship and popularity he was often selected for conservatory and state touring programs. Between 1997 and 1998 he spent several months teaching gamelan in Taiwan, developing a deep affinity for Chinese culture and returning with a heightened interest in Chinese cultural syncretism in Bali.

As student protests against Suharto intensified in May 1998, the New Order fanned an inflammatory rhetoric pitting so-called pribumi (I), indigenous, populations against Sino-Indonesians who became a scapegoat for rising living costs and the deflating rupiah. On May 14 Chinese shops in several urban areas were razed; up to fifteen hundred Sino-Indonesians were killed; hundreds were gang-raped. A major aspect of the merchant class, Sino-Indonesian presence in the archipelago stretches to prehistory and has for centuries functioned to link the islands to broader Asian trade and cultural networks.

The 1998 riots inspired Gede's recital composition, which he entitled Moha, from the Sanskrit for confusion. Rehearsing in the newly built gamelan museum on the ISI campus, Gede combined the ancient and rare seven-tone luang ensemble, which he would not have access to otherwise, with a large set of suling, a keyboard, and several kendang drums arranged to imitate a drum set. In the final performance the suling imitated Chinese flutes while a keyboardist performed melodies using a Chinese zither patch, its tempered intonation clashing sharply with the gamelan luang. At the violent climax of the work the keyboardist performed loud samples of screaming women; the luang musicians ran in circles around their instruments while playing; the suling performers howled while setting off fireworks, sending sparks flying around the stage in the packed auditorium. In the chaos I instinctively began to back up towards the single exit.

Moha *was unlike anything I had ever heard in Bali. It reveled in an apotheosis of dissonance and disorder totally out of whack with both Gede's outward character and the strong-armed guidance of the conservatory faculty who generally encouraged works celebrating "harmony" and "beauty."* Moha *appeared as a complete freak-out, dissolving from rigid composition into something much more like downtown free jazz. As the composition reached its conclusion I became nervous for Gede; he would surely be rejected by the audience and fail his recital. But after the final explosion of dissonance the audience immediately jumped to their feet in wild approval. Despite apparently eschewing many of the dry "work assessment criteria" of the* ujian, *Gede received high marks for* Moha [Tracks BV-4/1 and MK-4/1].

In this chapter I describe the social and aesthetic transformations of the *reformasi*, an anxious era of seemingly endless transition and crisis following Suharto's ouster in 1998. In the face of social upheaval, many artists celebrated the potential for the decentralization of culture that *reformasi* policies offered. The *reformasi* made possible the forging of novel identities, associations, and civic participation that would no longer be guided by the orthodoxy of New Order development programs. As a result, identity tended to shift simultaneously toward the global and the local, with an ambivalent eye on the national.

During the *reformasi*, artists struggled over the definitions of forms and categories; these struggles often represented the real boundaries that separated groups and their differential access to rights, resources, and representation. In Bali, *musik kontemporer* of the *reformasi* was characterized by both a serious form, produced by academically trained composers (the primary focus of this study), and a more popular form, exemplified by composers such as the guitarist Wayan Balawan. Some academically trained *kontemporer* composers, including Sadra, attempted a reconciliation with broad audiences by borrowing the ideas of organizations such as LEKRA, reference to which would have been banned in the New Order. *Musik kontemporer* was a contested space between those attempting to define it as a formal genre defined by rules derived from approved exemplars, and those who argued that it was instead an open assemblage of topics, references, and genres.

I argue that the struggle over defining *musik kontemporer* was an allegorical reference to concurrent attempts by conservative social movements to define (and contain) Balinese culture generally. Composers maintained an ambivalent relationship to fundamentalist movements such as *Ajeg Bali*, rejecting its primordialist assumptions of identity. Cultural conservatism emerged as a response to demographic changes in Bali that included increased urbanization and the influx of non-Balinese internal migrants, or newcomers (I: *pendatang*). Politicians strove for social integration and harmony through multicultural policies, a discourse answered by composers through the use of ethnically diverse musical topics. *Etnik* (I), ethnic, emerged as a keyword of the *reformasi* to refer to the nonhierarchical self-identification of regional groups as opposed to the top-down, managerial aestheticization of identity that marked the New Order.

Although many artists had consistently critiqued the power of the New Order government, it was not until the *reformasi* that some would energetically engage in party politics and open dissent. The persistence of New Order bureaucratic management at the national conservatory in Bali inspired a series of protests featuring the *kontemporer* arts. Partly as a reaction against state aesthetic hegemony, private arts clubs (I: *sanggar*) flourished during the era, symbolizing the spirit of dissensus that marked the *reformasi* era generally.

Reformasi

As neatly as Asnawa's *Kosong* had captured the New Order, Arsana's *Moha* encapsulated the subsequent era of *reformasi*. Although ostensibly about the violence of 1998, *Moha* articulated the zeitgeist of Bali in 2002. Just two months prior to the performance, Javanese terrorists had bombed the resort town of Kuta, killing 202 people and precipitating a collapse in the tourism industry. Hotel occupancy dropped from eighty percent to ten percent in a matter of days. As unemployment skyrocketed, industry managers mounted an aggressive recovery campaign. Placards and T-shirts appeared everywhere emblazoned with the keywords of peace: *Bali Aman Turis Datang*, (I), A Safe Bali Brings Tourists, *Bali Cinta Damai* (I), Bali Loves Peace, and in English: Bali Island of Peace. A glitzy campaign by Jakartan investors, termed "Bali for the World," sponsored rock concerts on the island. President Megawati attended with great fanfare, but the festival drew local scorn as a self-serving campaign intended only to fill hotels owned by Jakartan cronies.

The Bali bombing was the latest in a string of crises. The West restricted investment in Indonesia following the Asian crash of 1997 and in the worsening economic crisis Indonesians were reminded of their oppression under the New Order (Florida 2008:499). Artists were in the vanguard questioning the regime's apparent order, arguing for democratic reform in arts administration and broader government, and seeking channels for political expression withheld during the New Order (Budiman and Hatley 1999:20). This movement was already well established by 1989 when the keywords of openness, democratization, and human rights had been embraced by artists and the intelligentsia to challenge the regime's focus upon development, *pancasila*, and the "latent danger of communism" (Heryanto 1995:35). After Suharto was toppled in 1998, the government initiated a series of putative reforms. The period represented an introspective shift in which Indonesians considered the violent birth of the New Order through the lens of its tumultuous collapse (Ida Bagus 2006:94). Positive developments in civil society were accompanied by a string of crises: SARS, the war on terror, the Iraq War and US travel bans to Indonesia, education crises (I: *krisis pendidikan*), tourism crises (I: *krisis pariwisataan*), and economic crises (I: *krismon, krisis moniter*), finally reaching a climax in the *kristal* (I: *KRISis totTAL;* total crisis) during the global economic downturn beginning in 2008.

Continued social and political uncertainty turned the *reformasi* into an era, one that appeared to continue through 2013. If life under the New Order gave the impression of stasis through the displacement of terror into the appearance of normal life (Pemberton 1994:8), *reformasi*, in its constant transformations and crises, represented a world in which too much happened, an intense emotional roller coaster alternating between hopeful possibility and disappointment. Although ostensibly a more democratic era in which personal expressive freedoms were expanded, by 2008 many Balinese evinced nostalgia for the New Order when life was at least simpler.[1] *Moha* summed up through apocalyptic bursts of dissonance and confused energy what many Balinese characterized as *kali yuga,* the Hindu age of disorder.

Public intellectual and artistic life appeared to expand during the *reformasi*. Previously banned books, including those of the left and the works of Marx, became available, although this prompted some backlash and it was clear that fears of communism still haunted older generations.[2] Aesthetic freedom became associated with direct rather than allegorical critique. These freedoms were tempered by the constantly tenuous position of the middle class, which perceived itself as inexorably thinning while former New Order cronies in Jakarta continued to enrich themselves through corruption. Artists worried about the hazy prospect of social mobility. The economic downturn following the temporary collapse of tourism after the 2002 bombing revealed once again the inequities of governmental land reform programs as the disenfranchised returned to native villages to farm, leading to renewed complaints over land inequality that had been muted since 1965 (MacRae 2003:162).[3]

Ethnic clashes during the early *reformasi* in Central Kalimantan, Sulawesi, the Moluccas, West Papua, and Aceh led Presidents Wahid and Megawati to increase regional autonomy (I: *otonomi daerah*) through a series of laws passed in 1999 (but not implemented until 2001) that represented a compromise between pro-democracy movements and federalism. *Otonomi daerah* devolved greater autonomy to the regency (I: *kabupaten* e.g., Gianyar) rather than the province (e.g., Bali), and discouraged ethnonational provincialism by opening channels between county leaders (I: *bupati*) and Jakarta. This expanded the *bupati*'s influence as arts patrons. Many artists referred to this as the "decentralization of culture" (I: *desentralisasi kebudayaan*) (Gombloh 1999b) and hoped that the move would encourage heterogeneity in regional arts that had previously suffered from the homogenizing tendencies of centralized arts institutions.

---

[1] See Heryanto (2010) for more on nostalgia for the New Order and "democracy fatigue" in *reformasi*-era Indonesia.

[2] The Indonesian government continues to ban foreign books that deal directly with the brutality of the New Order, including Roosa's *Pretext for Mass Murder* (2006).

[3] Soethama (2006:40–42) cites reports that suggest poverty on the island rose sharply between 1998 and 2002, numbering up to 145,000.

The sudden departure of Suharto freed Indonesians from the father figure who attempted to discipline his children by prohibiting acts and expressions that might inflame communal sentiment, a policy summarized as SARA (I: *suku, agama, ras dan antar golongan*; ethnicity, religion, race, and class). *Reformasi* opened the possibility for forging new identities and forms of belonging that would no longer be guided by the orthodoxy of New Order development programs. As a result, identity tended to shift simultaneously towards the global and the local, with an ambivalent relationship to the national. Balinese tourism managers attempted to work around Jakartan (national) interference by forging global business networks. Many composers engaged with *musik kontemporer* became the champions of the most esoteric local traditions while simultaneously celebrating their cosmopolitan credentials; they displayed little interest in the development of national forms, a preoccupation of the New Order.

Following the New Order, discourses of belonging and civil society were in constant tension between the perceived need to usher in a moral revival that would finally rid the nation of rampant corruption (I: KKN, *kolusi, korupsi, nepotism*; collusion, corruption, nepotism) and the seemingly inexorable dissolution of the people (I: *rakyat*) into the mob (I: *massa*). Composers alternately described Bali as slipping into the disorder of the *kali yuga* or as waking from a long slumber as the Balinese began to recognize the structures of power (I: *kurung kuasa*) that had obscured their vision during the New Order.[4]

Several composers evinced nostalgia for the fading relationship between space and the Balinese body. This change became noticeable in the New Order but appeared to accelerate during the *reformasi*. While an owner's unique hand measurements are used to determine the dimensions of a traditional Balinese house compound, *moderen* construction styles, spreading rapidly during *reformasi*, represented an erasure of the body in favor of homogenized, rational measures. The composer Ida Bagus Widnyana compared the homogenization of architectural space to the perceived homogenization of *gamelan* tunings, to which he responded in his *kontemporer* work *Trimbat*, described below.

Many composers referred to *reformasi* experimentalism as *postmoderen*, not so much as an indication of concrete links to Western postmodern expressions such as minimalism, but as a means of dissociating *reformasi* era experiments from the *moderen* expressions of the New Order and their attendant associations with state development, administration, and censorship. Within this context the *postmoderen* suggested pure freedom and was often used interchangeably with pure art (I: *seni murni*). *Reformasi postmoderen* theater and visual arts became associated with political dissent and forms of opposition to state authority. Between 2007 and 2009 *postmoderen* performance and art installation became a vehicle of student protests against alleged corruption and mismanagement at the conservatory in Denpasar, discussed below.

---

[4] This sentiment was most often expressed by Dewa Alit, Wayan Sadra, and Wayan Yudane.

Conflicting Definitions

July 2008. Wayan Dibia, former rector of the conservatory, invited the composers Wayan Sadra, Dewa Ketut Alit (1973–), Nyoman Windha, and Madé Arnawa (1960–) to convene a roundtable on musik kontemporer *at GEOKS, his private arts foundation (*sanggar*). The full audience included faculty, students, and graduates from both ISI and KOKAR, and foreign students involved in Indonesian experimentalism. As the ranking senior composer with extensive international experience, Sadra opened the panel by suggesting that the Balinese had not yet learned how to converse constructively about art, being made mute by the conservatory's obsessive focus on* tradisi *and a pedagogy that favored practical skills over critical thought. The hall hummed with murmured approval. What followed was an interminable discussion over what* musik kontemporer *was, a back and forth between panel and audience members over the definitions of* kontemporer, kreasi baru, klasik, *and* tradisi. Kontemporer *should: have or not have* kotekan *interlocking, incorporate or not foreign materials, use or not traditional ensembles, incorporate or not traditional structural forms, and so on. The conversation repeated the sentiments expressed at numerous similar panels I had attended in Bali and Java and I quickly grew weary, turning off my digital recorder. These debates never reached an end and seemed to provide little traction for the actual creation of new works. Why did such intelligent composers revel in such circular debates?*

Only later I realized that it was the very frisson of the conversation, the debate itself, that was the point. Having grown up within a cultural environment in which definitions, meanings, genres, and classifications had too often been decided for them, the spirit of reformasi *opened the very possibility of dissensus, debate, argument, and the potential of defining for oneself what music was and what it could mean. These debates symbolized the broader exploration of the contours of* reformasi-*era democracy, understood not as imposed consensus but a world made better through vigorous debate.*

Musik kontemporer resists definition because it is a field of defining. What is *musik kontemporer* for one musician, composer, or critic may be *kreasi baru* or simply *musik* to another. While Kadek Suardana, for example, claims that he is not a *musik kontemporer* composer, many other Balinese composers suggest that he is. The struggle over categories and terms stands for the real boundaries that separate groups and individuals and the differential access they have to rights, resources, and representation. Since the 1930s cultural critics and conservatory faculty have offered a hodge-podge of terms for new forms of music: *kreasi baru, musik baru* (I), new music, *musik, kolaborasi* (I), collaboration, *musik kontemporer, musik eksperimental, konser* (I), concert, *karawitan, konser musik*...the list continues.[5] Each term indicates varying levels of distance or freedom from both traditional forms of Indonesian regional music and foreign, primarily Western, forms. The term *musik kontemporer* appears to have been introduced

---

5 Rustopo also identifies *gamelan kontemporer*, new experimental works for *gamelan*, stating that they are a subcategory of *musik kontemporer* (Rustopo 1988:1). The debate on terminology extends back at least to the 1930s when the cultural critics Dungga and Manik developed their taxonomy of art music (I: *musik seni*), and new Indonesian music (I: *musik Indonesia baru*).

in the early 1970s by the composer Slamet Abdul Sjukur as a translation of the French *musique contemporaine* but has been used retroactively to describe music created before that time. As a form, *musik kontemporer*'s own specificity comes in and out of focus over time [Track BV-4/2].

What is behind the proliferation of terms? First, there was a perceived need to describe the expressions of a new geopolitical region (Indonesia) with labels that transcended ethnically specific terms such as *karawitan* and *gamelan*. The increased interaction of populations, concepts, and languages that came about through the creation of the Indonesian nation state led to apparently neutral terms such as *kreasi baru* over more politicized possibilities such as *musik baru, gamelan baru, karawitan baru,* or *gendhing baru*. It is possible that, for young composers in Java and Bali, *kreasi baru* was favored over other terms because the Dutch-derived *kreasi* (creation) hinted at modernity but did not smack so blatantly of Westernization as did *musik*. Later, the incorporation of the Indonesian state into a global system of politics and culture led to the effort to create expressions that could be intelligible in a global milieu. The colonial and postcolonial ideal of commensurability fostered the development of forms comparable to Western expressions, while retaining identifiable differences. *Musik kontemporer* emerges as a form more commensurable than previous genres such as *gong kebyar,* while retaining obvious cultural particularity. Finally, especially during the New Order, there was a perceived need to support so-called great traditions. By categorizing contemporary composition under a different terminology, pre-existing works were de facto defined as *tradisi*, and therefore worthy of preservation.

Kontemporer compositions were linked by their promiscuity; composers seemed ready to bring anything into their forms and apparently little could escape the *kontemporer*-signifying machine. Writing in 1986, Sadra defined creativity, within the context of new music, as: "the ability to connect things/situations [I: '*hal-hal*'] that have never yet been connected" (Sadra 1986:12), linking this to the "cultural intersections" (I: *persilangan budaya*) that have informed *musik kontemporer* from its emergence. Since the late 1970s the form has centered around the question of how deeply to engage with foreign (primarily Western) traditions and has maintained a conceptual tension with the engineered distance that administrators, including Humardani, advocated as healthy for the future development of the Indonesian arts.

Sadra argued that the term should not be used to describe a form, but rather an approach or attitude (p.c. August 2003). *Musik kontemporer* was distinguished from *kreasi baru* less by its contents than by the symbolic discourse surrounding it and its relationship to conversations about tradition and innovation. While they may have deconstructed or distorted *tradisi*, none of the composers I interviewed eschewed it completely, often retaining it, if only as a kind of musical straight man against which more absurd, even comic ideas entered into dialogue and appeared in sharper relief. When creating *musik kontemporer,* many composers used traditional materials skenningly, with a wink, hanging them askew within their compositions.[6]

---

[6] As in Gede Arsana's tendency to displace standard *gong* strokes by a half beat from their traditional placement.

Through *kreasi baru*, composers tended to expand the new *within* local styles. *Musik kontemporer* was more ex-centric; its creators often sought the new in the foreign. However, plentiful counter-examples could be produced and it would be wrongheaded to suggest that *musik kontemporer* deterritorializes while *kreasi baru* territorializes, or that one consistently represented a more schizmogenic process than the other. The *kontemporer* choreographer Kadek Dewi Aryani suggested that *kontemporer* forms have no frame, other than the "frame of one's own identity" (p.c. July 2009). While *gong kebyar* appeared as a narrative of origin for *kreasi baru*, experimental composers tended to represent their expressions as a space in-between various established genres. Rather ambivalent regarding repeat performances, many resisted efforts of canon formation imposed upon both classic *kebyar* and *kreasi baru*. *Kontemporer* composers retained greater creative control by avoiding the homogenizing forces of institutionally defined contest criteria; their expressions contested definitions but were not contested in contests.

Popular/Serious: Art and the Market

August 2010. Headphones on and stretching over a guitar to reach his computer keyboard, Balawan greeted me as I walked into his home studio in Denpasar. I observed from the corner while he recorded a fourth guitar track over a densely multitracked work that channeled the Mahavishnu Orchestra, Stanley Jordan, and Balinese ethnic pop. Balawan began teaching himself guitar as a child, only occasionally participating in the gamelan *performances in his local* banjar *in Batuan. After studying jazz performance intensively in Australia, he returned to Bali in 1997 to form an "ethnic fusion" ensemble by combining a jazz trio with six* gamelan *musicians. By 1999 they had released their first album, entitled GloBALIsm.*

In performance Balawan placed the gamelan *instruments on pedestals in order that they be "equally respected." While all performers were Balinese, only his* gamelan *musicians wore the traditional Balinese costume; Balawan consistently appeared in casual Western dress. The ensemble quickly gained a moderate level of celebrity at both the local and national level through performing at world music and jazz festivals. Balawan variously referred to his music as jazz, fusion, ethnic pop, and* musik kontemporer

By 2002, Batuan Ethnic Fusion had inspired a cadre of young musicians to form copycat ensembles performing music that they similarly referred to as musik kontemporer *in their appearances at regional festivals,* banjar *talent contests, and the Bali Arts Festival. The conservatory administration and many of the composers with whom I worked often distanced themselves from the "ethnic fusion" phenomenon, as if it exceeded some unseen threshold of commercialism beyond which one could no longer legitimately aspire to the mantle of "composer." But by 2010 several conservatory-trained composers and some faculty, most notably Nyoman Windha, had initiated new music projects that curiously resembled Balawan's proven model.*

Sadra differentiated between two species of learned composition termed *musik kontemporer*. The first was characterized by the creative use of existing materials that combined contrasting musical elements of *tradisi* and might include hybrid experiments with popular forms. The second type, emerging from the *Pekan Komponis* meetings begun in 1978, was characterized by a more experimental attitude and an "open and free orientation" (quoted in Miller 2011:196). During my research the term *musik kontemporer* expanded to include both an academic and a popular form. The former was an expression of college-educated, virtuosic performers of *tradisi* forms with extensive cosmopolitan experience, little experience of Western music, but a strong sense of themselves as composers working in an elite global aesthetic network. The latter was often performed by younger, more amateur performers interested in combining *gamelan* and band instruments. While the former group often disregarded the latter as producing light (I: *ringan*), commercial (I: *komersil*), or kitsch work, the porous division between popular and serious musics in Bali facilitated sometimes surprising transfers and overlaps between the two manifestations of *musik kontemporer*. While some composers rejected the market as an a priori deleterious sphere within which one could not create pure art, others, including the Javanese composer Djaduk Ferianto and the Balinese Nyoman Windha were more sanguine [Track BV-4/3].[7]

In the early *reformasi*, Sadra, infamous for an early string of shocking and absurdist works, attempted a reconciliation with lay audiences through a compositional philosophy he termed *musik dialektis*. According to Sadra:

> Djaduk [Ferianto] once asked me how my "strange and absurd" music has anything to do with the "ideology of the stomach," suggesting that I was not trying to satisfy or entertain a broad range of people (in order to make a real living at composing). I've received constant complaints and even threats about my works. But I was always somewhat at a loss as to why people believed I was trying to be anti-social. Of course, when the artist recoils from the world in order to create, he is anti-social, but when he reappears to express something, I believe there has to be a dialectic. I borrowed this concept from, and I'm sorry, LEKRA. The communists used this. They suggested that in healthy art there is a connection between individual artistic expression and the larger society. I'm sorry I was forced to borrow the concepts of a banned organization. But I wanted to know, how can I become closer to more people?[8] [Track BV-4/4]

Sadra's open reference to a previously banned communist cultural organization indicated the extent to which previously muted discourses had become viable options for public debate in the *reformasi*. In contrast to the theorization of popular music as a commodity and serious music as critical to society as it is (Adorno 2002:335), Balinese *musik kontemporer* sometimes dreamed of its realization as a commodity while Balinese

---

[7] Yudane, Raharjo, and Alit were especially critical of market forces. Djaduk Ferianto is a Yogyakarta-based visual artist, composer, and founder of the *Kua Etnika* art community in Yogyakarta. Ferianto composed light *musik kontemporer* primarily for popular film (*Sinetron*) and ethnic pop ensembles which some composers denigrated as poseurism of serious intellectual composition (see McGraw 2013c).

[8] Quoted from an open panel discussion on *musik kontemporer* held in Yogyakarta in September, 2003.

pop musicians were often the most vocal critics of power. In terms of the market and social distinction, *musik kontemporer* functioned more like jazz than Western art music. The term denoted both learned compositions intended for elite audiences *and* populist fusions combining pop aesthetics and local traditions.

In the New Order and *reformasi* conservatory, a high–low art segregation rather out of step with the broader culture's more generous taxonomies was signified by the absence of classes in popular music.[9] Suka Hardjana, the organizer of the PKM meetings, described Indonesia's classical music tradition as lightweight and sought to bolster the art credentials of Indonesian new music relative to Western composition. "We got the idea of the popular/serious divide from you [the West] and it produced the division we called *musik hiburan* and *musik seriosa*. But our *seriosa* wasn't as serious as your seriousness and we needed to do something about that" (p.c. July 2003).

Faculty at the conservatory alternately dismissed as kitsch or encouraged young students' attempts to combine band instruments with *gamelan*. The rules for the proper combination of the Western and Balinese instrumentarium was a work in progress. The more important gesture was that the music appear thoroughly and rigorously composed, meaning difficult and virtuosic, thus immunizing it from accusations of being commercial (I: *komersil*). But the conservatory of the *reformasi* was no IRCAM and it hosted an active dissensus among its students and faculty regarding what *musik kontemporer* should be.

Genre

Is *musik kontemporer* a genre? When creating *musik kontemporer* works, composers were concerned less with exemplifying the genres identified by the conservatory and ethnomusicologists than making individualized statements. Rather than appearing as bound by tightly regimented stylistic features, *musik kontemporer* embodied an interest among composers to test the power of naming as such. Genre combines the elements of a recipe and a semiotic code; it is both formal and expressive. Genre are not given, discretely defined categories but are socially constructed through discourse and are understood relativistically through their relationship with other forms; the redundancies of style and canon help to give genre a sense of fixity. Once defined, genres then begin to shape perception, suggesting a kind of top-down listening that situates a work within a particular field of meaning. Listening through genre, certain patterns and connections will be heard, even invented, to confirm a work's inclusion in it while contradictory information may be downplayed or ignored.

The gap between works that genre attempts to bridge is often a site of innovation. Many composers exploited the aporias within the genre of *gong kebyar* (e.g., examples that did not align to the tripartite form held up as axiomatic in the conservatory) to

---

[9] See Miller (2011:30–34) for a detailed description of the emergence of light or paraclassical musics in Independence-era Indonesia, much to the despair of cultural purists such as Pasaribu, Dungga, and Manik.

catalyze their experiments. Even in the presence of such homogenizing forces as conservatory pedagogy and contest criteria, genres are not necessarily consensual fields. The recent history of contest-oriented *kreasi baru* for *kebyar* orchestras presents a host of struggles over the boundaries of genre.[10]

The power to define genre both reflects and generates social prestige; genres survive only through social construction and are often ideological. Balinese composers and conservatory pedagogies attempted to define genre along formalistic lines through the identification of prototypical works or schematic formula. In this scenario, an exemplar is made to represent an entire category, making other members of the category appear as variations. Often these exemplars are imagined to represent a temporal horizon, a golden age in which everything made sense and works were maximally communicative to their audiences. *Klasik gong kebyar* served as a historical protagonist; the experimentalism of its emergence was sometimes flattened into a continuous ground against which the variations of *kreasi baru* and *musik kontemporer* were alternately feared as potential degradations or celebrated as daring modernisms. *Taruna Jaya* appeared as an exemplar of *klasik gong kebyar* of the early twentieth century while Wayan Beratha's *Tabuh Pisan Bangun Anyar* (1978) served as a model of *tabuh kreasi lelambatan*. The schema that these works provided functioned as an expectational set for subsequent compositions.

Composers and scholars often described local genres, both popular and traditional, using tree diagrams.[11] No such prototypical center or tree was ever suggested for *musik kontemporer*. While genre was often associated with ensemble type, *kontemporer* had no specific ensemble proper to it. If it did not represent a formal genre, *musik kontemporer* sometimes represented an expressive genre that cut across multiple forms; *kreasi lelambatan*, for instance, could appear as comparatively *klasik* or *kontemporer*. Often characterized as an approach or feeling (I: *rasa*), *kontemporer*-ness might appear in otherwise *kreasi baru* or even *tradisi* expressions.[12] *Kontemporer*-ness oriented interpretation towards new possibility. *Kontemporer* composers celebrated the nominalism of individual works and were ambivalent regarding genre, recognizing its potential to distract listeners from the direct, fresh experience of new works.[13]

Rather than a cohesive formalistic genre, *musik kontemporer* was an assemblage of topics, references, and forms. This sometimes manifested in the clashing combination of *slendro* and *pélog* ensembles, as in Wayan Sudirana's *Kreasi 45* (2009) in which a four-tone *gamelan angklung* and a five-tone *gamelan gong kebyar* maintain a tense

---

[10] Madé Sue's *kreasi baru Mangrove* (2000) challenged the accepted instrumentarium by including experimental instruments. Dewa Rai's *kreasi lelambatan* for the 2010 festival challenged accepted notions of *gong* form. Gede Arsana's *kreasi* of the same year stretched limits of form and technique beyond the accepted limits of many observers.

[11] See Weintraub (2010) for Indonesian descriptions of *dangdut* as a tree, Sukerta and Nugroho (2009) for "family trees" of *gong kebyar*.

[12] Many composers commented on the *kontemporer* feeling of many of Wayan Lotring's compositions from the 1930s.

[13] In describing his highly experimental *kreasi baru* for the 2010 festival, Gede Arsana said: "You can't hear my work if you think of it as '*kreasi baru*'" (p.c. July 2010).

equilibrium.[14] Like the *ceraken*, *musik kontemporer* assumes only a space of possibilities, not a series of required properties. Sadra referred to this as the "form of the whatever" (I: "*bentuk entah apa*") (2002:34). But neither was this space completely open-ended or amorphous; it was determined more by a set of rules concerning what it could *not* be. It could not be indistinguishable from its predecessors. In its academic form, it could not slip seamlessly into popular music. In contrast to contest-oriented *kreasi baru*, the threshold beyond which possibilities were excluded in *musik kontemporer* was determined primarily by individual composers rather than institutions. Nevertheless, many *kontemporer* works were linked through the coexistence of heterogeneous musical topics, apparently reflecting the social conditions of the *reformasi* itself [MK-4/2].

Ajeg Bali and Religious Reformism

May 2008. While most recitals were held on the proscenium stage at the conservatory, Sudarta lobbied the caretakers of the ancient Samuantiga temple to host his theatrical kontemporer *master's recital. It was here, one thousand years earlier, that King Udayana brought together the three warring Hindu-Buddhist factions of Bali to forge a new religious syncretism. Sudarta placed two large shadow screens between the temple's imposing stone* candi *gates. A combined set of Balinese and Javanese gamelan, supplemented with a chorus, was set to the side. The temple's courtyard was lit by torches whose smoke was augmented by two fog machines, loudly pumping out the mists of time. The chorus sang in Sanskrit in a style reminiscent of Javanese* gerong *and Pakistani* qawwali, *accompanied by Islamic* rebana *frame drums and a large* bedug *drum, traditionally used to call the faithful to the mosque. Musicians marked time on small hand cymbals, instruments unknown in traditional Indonesian musics but depicted on ancient temple reliefs in Java. By avoiding all obvious reference to twentieth-century musical styles such as* kebyar, *the overture evoked the era of Udayana himself.*

Following the overture, which became a favorite among many composers and musicians who for several months used it as their ringtone, the young female MC asked audience members to take their seats, reminding them to turn off their cellphones and to refrain from applauding until the end in order to facilitate "a positive synergy between the performers and the audience." That is, the audience was required to behave in ways totally out of character for Balinese audiences watching temple performances in which a lively, carnivalesque atmosphere is the norm. The elite audience of conservatory faculty and expatriates took their seats as the young MC presented the work's synopsis. Entitled Kidung Mpu Tantular, *the performance evoked the philosophy of the fourteenth-century poet Tantular to whom both the national motto* Bhinneka Tunggal Ika *(Unity in Diversity) and the* Sutasoma, *a Buddhist tale extolling religious tolerance, is attributed. The MC described the performance as a "Balinese visualization of world peace," intended as a response to "religious fanaticism*

---

[14] While some traditional forms, such as *arja*, include the combination of singing in *slendro* alongside accompaniment in *pélog*, works such as Sudirana's represent a fundamental shift in the conception of intonational interaction.

and intolerance incompatible with pancasila *and the soul of the* nusantara.*" By melding the ancient world of Udayana, Samuantiga, Tantular, and Sutasoma with revolutionary rhetoric, Sudarta provided an image intended to counter the increasing religious fundamentalism and inter-ethnic violence of the* reformasi.

Kidung Mpu Tantular *simultaneously evoked the pre- and ultra-modern. Performers appeared in modest, rustic costumes rather than the flashy modern costuming typical of the* reformasi *recital. Traditional* wayang *puppets fought between the frames of multiple screens, recalling the windows of a multitasking desktop, illumined by both fire and electric lighting. As the* wayang *screens faded to the red and white of the national flag and the performers assembled for the final bow, Sudarta proclaimed: "This performance is an offering for* nusantara! *Long Live Indonesia!"*

The effect of Sudarta's performance appeared to overwhelm several in the audience, many of whom seemed to have read the performance through an ethical and aesthetic frame simultaneously; it was an intelligibly modern artistic performance that conveyed its own righteousness by simultaneously cementing national, religious, and ethnic truths. Many audience members understood it as expressing both fundamentally Balinese and universal values. Capitalizing upon the positive response the performance generated, the conservatory provided substantial funds for further development of the work and repeat performances at the temple for larger audiences and media [Track MK-4/3].

Described by local media as a "multicultural performance," *Kidung Mpu Tantular* was critiqued by some within the conservative *Ajeg* movement for its incorporation of Islamic cultural elements (I: *muslim-muslim-an*) within a performance on the grounds of an ancient Hindu temple. In interviews, Sudarta described the piece as a direct response to the *Ajeg* movement. Its liberal humanist vision recalled both the colonial-era theosophy movement, with which Sudarta's ancestors were associated, and Vidyasagar's Hindu reformism in which the polyphony of interpretation and hermeneutic debate, perceived to be at the origin of Indian religious traditions, were celebrated against a totalizing, institutionally enforced dogma.[15] For Sudarta, the tolerant coexistence of multiple beliefs embodied at Samuantiga and in Tantular's writing was philosophically allied with the spirit of both the revolution and the democratic potential of the *reformasi*. According to Sudarta, the *Ajeg* movement, emerging partly as a response to rising Javanese fundamentalism, fell into the retrogressive thinking (I: *pemikiran terbalik*) of the New Order and all other fundamentalisms in which a totalizing and enforced ethical universe erases the potential for moral democratic dissensus (p.c. July 2008). *Kidung Mpu Tantular* functioned like a historical novel by employing historical inversion as a narrative device to suggest that what is seen to have taken place in the past must be realized in the future.

---

[15] Granoka, director of the *sanggar Bajra Sandhi*, similarly espoused a rhetoric of combining the best of Western and Eastern philosophy that evoked the spatial imagination of the theosophical movement.

Kidung Mpu Tantular intersected debates surrounding conservatism and multiculturalism that marked the 2008 gubernatorial election and the efforts of the tourist industry to market Bali as a symbol of peace following the 2002 and 2005 bombings. The work continued a hallowed Balinese tradition of subtly politicizing ritual. During the New Order, ritual acts and performances became a domain of indirect political expression in a context in which overt dissent was a losing game. Many Balinese realized the practice of ritual itself as a form of political dissent, as in the ritual protests against the attempts by New Order cronies to establish luxury hotels near the southern coastal temple of Tanah Lot (Picard 2003). In the early years of the *reformasi*, the artist Nyoman Erawan developed a series of *kontemporer* ritual performances. These were invented ceremonies that allegorically suggested the individualized and democratic exploration of Balinese Hindu identity independent of state institutional guidance.[16]

During the *reformasi* era many artists were caught between a critique of orthopraxy and a revitalization of internal conversion energized by the *Ajeg* movement. As part of the former discourse artists questioned the conspicuous production of ceremony beginning during the middle New Order in which Balinese displayed their upwardly mobile trajectory not only by what they owned but by how extravagantly they heralded their gods. However, artists also benefited from the focus upon performance by both the *Ajeg* movement and the national Parisada Hindu organization and its promotion of canonized *Agama Hindu* among urban elites. Novel elements of orthopraxy emerging in the New Order included the *tri sandya* prayer—explained in tourist pamphlets as a prayer recited thrice daily (recalling Islamic and Christian prayer)—and an increasing focus upon the book (such as the *vedas* and the *gita*) following the model of Semitic creeds. Many composers negotiated the tension between an interest in a pluralistic and individualized notion of Balinese Hinduism and the *Ajeg* movement's obsessive focus upon *tradisi* by displaying more-*tradisi*-than-thou credentials through fluency with esoteric philosophical concepts and sacred repertoires including *gambang, luang,* and *slonding* [Track BV-4/5].

The term *Ajeg* was popularized by Governor Dewa Madé Beratha in a 2002 speech following the Bali bombing and was quickly adopted by local conservatives and media, primarily the *Bali Post*, which began sponsoring *Ajeg* essay contests and devoting daily columns to the topic (Putra 2008:186). Within the year *Ajeg* had become a valuable political commodity, most energetically trumpeted by the former New Order GOLKAR party. By 2004 all major local politicians, including presidential candidates Megawati and Susilo Bambang Yudhoyono, had signed plaques (I: *prasasti*) sealing for eternity their commitment to *Ajeg Bali*. While the rhetoric recalled the focus upon *tradisi* and cultural origins reminiscent of the New Order, its persistent and sometimes militant focus upon ethnonational pride would not have been possible under the New Order's

---

[16] Like similar experiments conducted in Java during the late New Order, Erawan termed these performances *seni ritual*, rather than *seni upacara*, suggesting their cosmopolitan, universalist, rather than narrowly Hindu, orientation.

SARA regulations; *reformasi* policies of regional autonomy (I: *otonomi daerah*) allowed *Ajeg* to voice itself.

While the movement manifested in a sometimes contradictory rhetoric, the publication of several texts on *Ajeg*, principally Titib's Ajeg Bali Dialogue (I: *Dialog Ajeg Bali*), (2005) helped to stabilize its discourse. The text figures the Balinese as an inherently religious people following traditional social customs which are threatened by modernization and globalization. To safeguard Balinese culture and its Hindu soul, every good Balinese must stabilize (I: *mengajegkan*) refined (J: *adiluhung*) cultural aspects (Titib 2005:vi). This should be achieved through the restoration of *tradisi* arts such as *wayang wong* and *gambuh* (ibid. 37). The movement was often framed as a Bali-for-the-Balinese discourse and was hostile to outside influence, both Islamic and Western.

Titib's text paints a picture of the Balinese struggling for ethnic dominance on their own island; tables chart the increase by year of local mosques, Chinese temples, and churches. Many within the movement interpreted the 2002 bombing as a karmic repercussion for the Balinese having betrayed their own culture. The movement advocated a retrenchment into sentiment and policies almost indistinguishable from those of the New Order, with the noticeable difference that this time the Balinese were doing the work of aestheticization and cultural bureaucratization themselves, without significant pressure from the nation state. *Ajeg* appeared at once as a form of defiant cultural resistance *and* self-colonization.

To many composers, *Ajeg* was an embarrassingly regressive movement that one could scarcely afford to reject outright. If its talking heads sometimes criticized *kontemporer* arts as breaking tradition, their celebration of the traditional performing arts meant more gigs for those same performers. Sudarta's *Kidung Mpu Tantular* rejected it in all but name. The writer Soethama decried the movement's Bali-centrism, advocated by a generation "made stupid" by the New Order. To Soethama, *Ajeg* was a slap in the face to ancestors who struggled during the revolution and Old Order to create a critical generation and who would have made the most of the *reformasi*, if given the chance. Instead, these contemporary, "uncritical Balinese blindly accept all the exoticizing foreign worship of their culture as a compliment, seeking to satisfy them by becoming 'hyper-Balinese'" (Soethama 2006:98).[17] Arsawijaya described *Ajeg*-minded critics of *kontemporer* arts as frogs living under a shell (I: *katak dalam tempurung*). Habituated to living within a confined space, once the shell is lifted the frog is too overwhelmed to venture out. "Sometimes those frogs starve, only eating whatever they can find in that space. You have to be ready to digest what the world has to offer. You have to venture out" (p.c. July 2009).

---

[17] For more on *Ajeg* see Couteau (2003), Allen and Palermo (2005), and McGraw (2009). The composers Yudane, Sadra, and Arsawijaya expressed strident and vocal rejections of *Ajeg* as a movement. Others, including Arsana, Widnyana, and Subandi did not deny it outright but advocated its flexible and personalized interpretation.

Multiculturalism

September 2001. Nyoman Windha, the reigning master of Balinese composition during the transition from the New Order to the reformasi, *was intensively rehearsing a* kontemporer *work commissioned by the prestigious Jakarta Arts Summit, an annual event begun in 1995 that continued in the tradition of Hardjana's earlier Composers' Weeks. Entitled* Lekesan, *the work combined twelve* suling, *twelve* kendang, *and several* kempur *gongs—instruments light enough to be carried onto the flight to Jakarta. Twice a week for a month a group of students and faculty met in the evenings on campus to perfect the work. Later that year Windha arranged* Lekesan *for the* gamelan gong kebyar *and with it winning for Gianyar the annual* kebyar *contests. Windha once described* musik kontemporer *as the "future cars" of* kreasi baru; *it functioned as a laboratory for the free development of materials later domesticated within* kreasi baru.

Lekesan *featured a complex and intercultural array of topics, opening with an austere arrangement of* kendang *performing unison rhythms in a medium, stable tempo. Windha referred to this section as minimalist (I:* minimalis), *an ostensibly Western musical technique that established* Lekesan's kontemporer *credentials by eschewing the hallmark characteristics of* kreasi baru: payasan *ornamentation,* ombak *dynamic and temporal fluctuations, and the ametrical* kebyar *proper. These minimalisms set up a contrapuntal (I:* kontrapoin), suling *arrangement in three-part harmony which Windha taught using Western, rather than Balinese, solfège that he read from prepared notation. Modally, the combination of independent lines suggested neither* slendro *nor* pélog *but a Dorian scale which Windha referred to as* diatonis

Sasak *melodic topics in the final section provided an infectious hook and a rare celebration of Indonesian Islamic music in Balinese contemporary composition. The melodies quickly went viral following Gianyar's performance of the* kebyar *version at the Bali Arts Festival. Windha described* Lekesan, *in both its* kontemporer *and* kreasi baru *manifestations, as "about and for multicultural Denpasar." It was part of his broader "musical mission to foster cultural one-ness (I:* persatuan) *among Indonesians."*[18]

The word lekesan *itself refers to the betel nut arrangement included in Balinese offerings. The* ceraken *held its various components:* sirih *(betel nut),* gambir *leaf, and tobacco. In combination these elements represent the Hindu triumvirate understood as a symbol of oneness and strength. During the* reformasi, *Denpasar's demographics shifted with an influx of poor, migrant Muslim workers primarily from Java and Madura. Composers including Windha sought to mediate through sound the potential tensions between the Balinese and their internal others [Tracks BV-4/6 and MK-4/4].*

While in Bali I often socialized with Javanese conservatory faculty living in the sizable *kampung Jawa* (I), Javanese village, in southern Denpasar, a densely populated community of mostly lower-income migrant Javanese. Although my abilities performing Javanese *gamelan* were unremarkable in Solo, where I was surrounded by more

---

[18] Windha's appeal to nationalism emerged in several of his *kontemporer* works beginning with his 1986 *Palapa* in which he combined Balinese and Javanese *gamelan* into a single enormous orchestra.

serious foreign students of the tradition, I was a complete novelty in Bali's *kampung Jawa*, where I regularly accepted invitations to perform for weddings and other ceremonies. The precarious position of the Javanese in Balinese society, being local minoritarian representatives of a nationally hegemonic culture, served as a constant reminder of the complex intersections of *Ajeg*, ethnicity, and discourses of multiculturalism in *reformasi* Bali.

Although non-Hindu populations of Arab, Javanese, Sasak, Madurese, and Chinese (etc.) descent have lived on the island long before colonization, the ethnography of Bali has led us to look past this multiplicity to associate the Balinese with Central Plains Hindu populations who trace their origins to Majapahit Java. The *reformasi* era tensions between the Balinese and other populations suggested that discourses such as the *Ajeg* movement had taken their cue from the ethnographic account rather than Bali's complex history of multiculturalism.

While American multiculturalism often manifests as an activist appeal for official recognition on behalf of the marginalized and is to a certain extent in conflict with the homogenizing tendencies of the nation state, Indonesian multiculturalism was more often a tool of the state, especially under the New Order, which used it to depoliticize ethnic communal sentiment. The New Order state encouraged subjects to imagine trying on various regional cultures as a display of their Indonesianness. Since the 1960s, state conservatories have employed faculty from other regions (e.g., Balinese faculty at conservatories in Central Java and vice versa), and since the early 1980s a multicultural curriculum, originally called Indonesian togetherness (I: *keakraban Indonesia*) by its creator Humardani, has been an important focus in the programs of all tertiary-level arts institutions.

Following the 2002 bombing an increased tension emerged between Islamists and secular nationalists who sought to diffuse potential regional and religious tensions through an increased investment in multicultural curricula and publications, partly funded by the American Ford Foundation. The discourse suggested that the melting pot imagined by the Old Order never got hot enough to boil the various Indonesian ethnicities down into an alloyed subjectivity; individual groups remained congealed. Following the dissolution of the New Order, the move by some conservative Islamic leaders to advocate the "wise destruction" (I: *dibasmi secara arif*) of local non-Islamic traditional arts in an attempt to align society towards an Arabic model prompted organizations including LPSN (I: *Lembaga Pendidikan Seni Nusantara*, The Educational Institutional for Indonesian Arts) to publish curricular materials intended to introduce students to regional cultural diversity through the comparatively unthreatening medium of the arts (Asia Society 2010).[19]

During and after the New Order, *musik kontemporer* was occasionally mobilized as a demonstration of state multiculturalism. Local cultural expressions were sometimes presented in national arts events as aestheticized and updated *kontemporer*

---

[19] Ujan's *Multiculturalism: Studying How to Live in Difference* (I: *Multikulturalisme: Belejar Hidup Bersama Dalam Perbedaan*) (2009) is a good example of the secular nationalist approach.

expressions.[20] At ISI Denpasar during the late New Order and *reformasi*, faculty, including Sudarta and Windha, as well as non-Balinese students (primarily Sumatrans), composed *kontemporer* works combining Balinese, Sumatran, and Javanese elements as self-conscious celebrations of cultural plurality mediated through sound.[21]

One would have to return to the early twentieth century to find similar celebrations of cultural plurality in Bali. The progressive poetry of 1920s and 1930s Bali, printed in journals such as *Surya Kanta* and *Djatajoe*, fused and celebrated both Hindu and Islamic cultural themes as did the rhetoric of numerous social organizations (Putra 2008:138).[22] As Putra notes, prior to the advent of mass tourism Islamic communities in Bali were more often referred to as Islamic brothers (I: *nyama Islam*). Following 2002, the cooler term *jalma* often replaced *nyama*, suggesting cultural distanciation. Ida Bagus recounts that during the New Order, Hindu communities in Jembrana often banned the use of pork in their offerings when their ceremonies coincided with the holy days of neighboring Islamic communities, while Muslim families requested holy water from Brahmana priests for Muslim life-cycle ceremonies (Bagus 2006:111). Such tolerance was rare during my research.

In 1999 East Javanese street vendors were attacked in Kuta, some killed, and their stalls burned by the hundreds on the beach, a move rumored to have been organized by the local Intelligence Bureau (Vickers and Connor 2003:26). Following the 2002 bombing many expected a wholesale massacre of migrant communities, but although sporadic killings were reported, tourist managers and politicians managed to cool violent sentiment. Instead, local leaders and populations called for restrictions on migrants and the institution of internal visas (Burhanuddin 2008:96; Reuter 2009). By 2003 regional and local politicians seemed to have realized that the *Ajeg* rhetoric had become overheated and counterproductive. Nearly 70,000 Muslim residents lived in Denpasar alone and were a major force of the local economy. In speeches in 2003 A. A. Puspayoga, the mayor of Denpasar, suggested that Bali could become *Ajeg* "not despite the *pendatang* (I), migrants, but precisely *because* of them" (quoted in Allen and Palermo 2005:244), arguing that a Balinese identity was centrally marked by the universal values of peacefulness and tolerance and that the multicultural demographics of Denpasar reminded the Balinese of their historical plurality. In his successful bid for the governorship in 2008, Mangku Pastika, with Puspayoga as his running mate, curiously embraced both *Ajeg* and multicultural rhetoric; their ubiquitous campaign stickers juxtaposed images of Hindu Balinese, Sasak, and Javanese performing arts [Track BV-4/7].

As Picard (1996) illustrates, the identification "Balinese" is not straightforwardly associated with an unambiguous ethnic group (as are the designations "Dayak"

---

[20] See Bing (2004) for a discussion of the Central Sulawesi Vunja ceremony presented as *kontemporer* performance for audiences in Yogyakarta and Jakarta.
[21] See for instance Taryadin (1996), Syafruddin (1998).
[22] These organizations included: Setiti Bali, Catur Wangsa Derya, Agama Hindu Bali, Surya Kanta, Bali Dharma Laksana, Putri Bali Sadar.

or "Atoni"), "but with the authorized culture of Bali as a 'province' (*Daerah Tingkat I Propinsi Bali*) of Indonesia...Bali's situation is unique in Indonesia in that its name designates an entity that is at once geographic, ethnic and administrative" (Picard 1996:174). That is, "Balinese culture" may refer as much to a social as an ethnic grouping. When *reformasi* politicians spoke of protecting Bali, it was often in terms of the island-as-tourist-destination itself, rather than in the interest of maintaining ethnic blood purity. Politicians such as Pastika attempted to defuse potential social strife by shifting identification from primordial ethnicities to administrative provinces.

Following the New Order it seemed possible for groups with discrepant histories to eventually become Balinese. When confronted with the demand to choose among the five official state religions in the late Old Order, some Northern Balinese chose Buddhism, eventually forging religious, social, and aesthetic networks within the Indonesian Buddhist *sangah* and among Theravada Buddhists throughout Southeast Asia. This community later accommodated an influx of Mahayana-practicing Sino-Indonesians seeking refuge from attacks in Java during the dissolution of the New Order (Ramstedt 2012). During the *reformasi*, this community dynamically straddled the conceptual division between Balinese and *pendatang*, demonstrating the aporias of both "the Balinese" and "Balinese culture."

World Musik and Ethnicity

In August 2002 a glitzy advertising campaign hyped the "First Bali World Music Festival." The event, sponsored by national and international corporations—primarily tobacco companies and Coca Cola—was held at the Garuda Wisnu Kencana, an enormous, privately owned "cultural park" located in the southernmost Bukit area of the island. Hatched at the end of the New Order, the park was originally conceived to host the world's largest statue: an enormous Vishnu riding his eagle perched upon a giant shopping complex. Following protest, mismanagement, and corruption, the project was scaled back during the reformasi. By 2008 its sprawling mall had been abandoned and the size of the statue itself reduced, its half-finished pieces placed haphazardly throughout the park's grounds. Perpetually under construction and decay, the site hosted a steady stream of elite events, many out of the reach of middle-class Balinese audiences. The sold-out performance by the American metal band Iron Maiden in February 2011 to a crowd of seven thousand young fans represented a rare working-class exception.

The 2002 world music event was held at the venue's outdoor amphitheater for those able to pay rather exorbitant ticket prices. Stylish MCs in flowing gowns introduced in English the evening's roster of "ethnic performers", including Balawan and Batuan Etnis from Bali, Suarasama from Sumatra, and Wayan Sadra's Sono Seni ensemble from Java. Backstage, festival participants debated a series of questions: How is it that a concert featuring only Indonesian acts counted as a "world music" festival? How had Indonesians become ethnic to themselves? Did world musik count as musik kontemporer?

David Lewiston's recordings of Balinese *gamelan*, which he brought to Nonesuch in 1966, inaugurated the label's popular Explorer series. Recordings of Balinese music, filed alongside those of Java, the mysterious singing of Bulgaria, and African pygmy chants, became iconic representatives of the burgeoning world music category by appearing to be pure expressions of premodern cultures. But Western middle-class kids could not dance to these genres and so the world beats of Africa and Latin America became the headlining acts at events such as Peter Gabriel's WOMAD festival, begun in 1982. World music has eventually come to refer principally to a hybrid form of local musics engaged with the musical, technological (and often ideological) processes of Western popular music (Corona and Madrid 2008:16). The adoption of world music by musicians in Indonesia appeared to reflect a more heterodox self-imagining (Comaroff and Comaroff 2009:47), one that sought to set aside, if only for a moment, the nation state in order to symbolically link the local and the global.

Between 2001 and 2010 *kontemporer* composers writing in the arts magazine *Gong* alternately critiqued and celebrated the appearance of *world musik* in Indonesia. To some contributors, its ambiguous status between serious and popular was problematic.[23] For Suharyanto, Indonesian *world musik* involved *kontemporer* composers "blending local *etnik* melodies and rhythms with jazz, blues, and *juju* (etc.) styles... in order to express a new aesthetic" (Suharyanto 2004:32–33). *World musik*, as a form of *musik kontemporer*, appears as a kind of aesthetic time machine linking the past to the present, shuttling the *etnik* from the *tradisi* to the *moderen*.

ETNIK

Dutch colonial administrators were frustrated to find that local rulers had never carried out a census and that they lacked even the categories to facilitate such a task (Hauser-Schäublin 2004:57). The Dutch classified peoples in the colony by differential relations to law and the colonial economy. Native (D: *inlander*) referred to all non-European colonial subjects as distinct from foreign orientals (D: *vreemde oosterlingen*), primarily Chinese, Indian, and Arab. This distinction was maintained during the Old Order to empower indigenous Indonesians over their internal others (ibid. 52).

Indigeneity in Bali is marked by a distinction between the hegemonic lowland Majapahit populations and their imagined predecessors, the Aga, located primarily in mountainous and eastern coastal villages. The Majapahit-Balinese origin myth recounts the invasion of noble Hindu warriors from fourteenth-century Java into Bali to liberate the population from the Aga king Mayadanawa, described as a half-animal tyrant. In reality, Balinese culture had already been engaged in a continuous domestication

---

[23] The Javanese composer and critic Gombloh, a consummate Adornite, describes it as an "exploitative aspect of the culture industry that seeks to use the shy girl of local tradition" (Gombloh 2001b:3–6). Harahap contrastingly associates *world musik* with the ethnic folk forms performed in villages as distinct from the "culture of massive consumption of the global capitalistic industry with which Indonesian urban populations are engaged" (Harahap 2003:11).

of Javanese and Indic thought for at least six hundred years.[24] Under Javanese vassalage, the Aga became a second-class population, albeit one perceived as invested with ritual authority through their relationship to important mountain shrines, ancestor spirits, and agricultural gods. During the Old and New Orders the Aga were treated as a separate ethnicity, one distinctly backward—they don't bury their dead or recognize caste and so do not neatly fit into the Hindu rubric—and in need of both research and upgrading. University and conservatory fieldwork projects focused upon the Aga and their ceremonies while state agencies attempted to manage both religion and custom in Aga villages through organizations such as the BPPLA (I: *Badan Pelaksana Pembina Lembaga Adat*, Agency for the Implementation and Cultivation of Traditional Institutions) and the PHDI (I: *Parisada Hindu Dharma Indonesia*), the governmental institution representing all Indonesian Hindus (Reuter 2003:182).

Lowland Majapahit Balinese became increasingly ambivalent towards migrant Javanese following the New Order. Apparently exhausted from over half a century of hegemonic Javanese state control, the continued celebration of a Javanese origin seemed less palatable. Regional autonomy laws encouraged a shift of identity priority from first Indonesian, then Balinese to its inverse.[25] Lowland Balinese began to take a greater interest in Aga cultural expressions as evidenced by the adoption of the *slonding* ensemble, the purchase of Aga textiles, lowland attendance at Aga temple ceremonies, and the emergence of traditional culture magazines such as *Bali Aga* and *Sarad*. By 2012 composers including Balawan, Suardana, Arsawijaya, Subandi, Gus Teja, Sudirana, and others had purchased their own *slonding* sets to use in their *kontemporer* experiments [Tracks BV-4/8 and MK-4/5].

Thus lowland Balinese repeated their experience under the New Order by vaunting a vision of a multicultural society in which each citizen of the civilization has equal identity access to various local ethnicities; all Balinese could now be Aga. The 2002 bombing further energized this inward orientation of identity. If the Balinese were meant to stand as the ultimate ethnics for cultural tourists, the Aga, perceived as more remote, older, and less refined, were even more ethnic. As ethnopreneurialists (Comaroff and Comaroff 2009) trading ethnicity as a commodity, the lowland Balinese could recharge their stock, which the bomb blew to bits, through association with the Aga's detachable cultural expressions.

While ethnicity was treated as a thing by the Balinese during the *reformasi*, it behaved more like a loose process, articulating shifting group relations through a repertoire of signs, music among them. Groups distinguished themselves by their comparative focus upon ethnicity as either primordial and innate or instrumentalist and voluntary. The *Ajeg* movement spoke in primordialist terms, while many composers instrumentalized ethnicity as capital and as a form of self-fashioning within a cosmopolitan

---

[24] Hinzler notes that "Majapahit fever," the construction of genealogies connecting one's family to Javanese origins in order to establish caste credentials, did not begin until the eighteenth century, well after Majapahit migrations and colonial contact (in Schulte Nordholt 1992:36).

[25] See Antons (2009) for a broader discussion of indigeneity following the New Order.

milieu. With the New Order in the rearview mirror, ethnicity could be celebrated as an achieved, rather than imposed, collective.

Etnik increasingly referred to categories of production and consumption that intersected with cultural tourism and stood as markers of financial success and cosmopolitanism. Besides Indonesian handicrafts, many tourist shops in Bali sold Native American dreamcatchers, West African djembes and mbiras, Aboriginal didgeridoos, and steel drums, and were often situated next to salons offering reiki, henna, and Ayurvedic treatments. Bali served as a stage on which tourists (international and domestic) played out fantasies of the generic vanishing other; one *etnik* stood for the other. Partly as a result of these new markets, *etnik* came to signify commercial success and cosmopolitanism generally. The self-described Balinese "ethnic death metal" band Eternal Madness worked with Yudane to integrate *gamelan beleganjur* patterns into their arrangements (Wallach 2008:117). The term was sometimes co-opted in unexpected contexts; I regularly passed the Etnik Motorbike Repair Shop (I: *bengkel etnik*) on my way to lessons in Sukawati.

Etnik radio stations and recordings proliferated after the New Order.[26] World *musik* and *musik kontemporer*, unlike more iconically traditional Balinese genres such as *gong kebyar*, facilitated the interaction of multiple ethnic groups in multicultural urban spaces such as Solo, Jakarta, and Denpasar. The interaction of performers of different ethnic and religious backgrounds, as in Sudarta's *Kidung Mpu Tantular* and Sadra and Ferianto's ensembles, contrasted with the ethnically homogenous ensembles associated with *tradisi* forms. While researching in southern Bali, I was only able to identify a single Muslim performer of *gong kebyar*.[27]

Art and Politics

The Balinese, not only in court rituals but generally, cast their most comprehensive ideas of the way things ultimately are, and the way that men should therefore act, into immediately apprehended sensuous symbols—into a lexicon of carvings, flowers, dances, melodies, gestures, chants, ornaments, temples, postures, and masks—rather than into a discursively apprehended, ordered set of explicit "beliefs." (Geertz 1980:103)

---

[26] In Jakarta 98.8, 107.9 in Yogyakarta, and 101.25 in Solo were the principal stations. After 1998 the Ford Foundation increasingly funded the production of *etnik* television and radio programs, often working with the producer Fred Wibowo. The state radio station (RRI) in Bali increasingly referred to its regular broadcast of *tradisi* and *kebyar* forms as *musik etnik*.

[27] This young man lived in Pedungan, Denpasar but was born in Banyuwangi (East Java) and had moved to Bali when he was twelve. A very proficient *gangsa* and *suling* player, he often performed in devotional performances in Hindu temples and prayed along with his Hindu friends before performance. Ethnically Chinese-Indonesian performers were more common, the leading choreographer Yampung being the most obvious example. Balinese Christian groups have incorporated *gong kebyar* into their services for decades.

Demographic changes and new discourses of multiculturalism and ethnicity during the *reformasi* were related to new forms of political engagement, expression, and civil society. The Balinese are often represented as apolitical (MacRae 2003) and by focusing upon repertoires, ethnomusicology has portrayed the Balinese arts as a depoliticized arena.[28] Recently, the political lives of Balinese artists have attracted increased attention.[29] Arts and politics were conspicuous bedfellows during the *reformasi*; discussion of one often led to discussion of the other and absent was the façade of apoliticism—a capitulation by the Balinese to accommodate touristic (and anthropological) expectations of their culture-obsession—described by MacRae (2003).

While the New Order government sought to suppress political debate and dissent through the depoliticization of culture generally, it did not refrain from leveraging artists for its own, monolithic political aims. Performers regularly appeared at the ruling party's ritualized "democracy parties" (I: *pesta demokrasi*) beginning with the reintroduction of elections in 1971. During this era many artists risked their lives and livelihood by critiquing the regime's propagandistic mobilization of the arts. Visual artists associated with the New Art Movement (I: *Gerakan Seni Rupa Baru*) of the 1970s and 1980s were among the first to voice this critique (2013). The Sundanese *kontemporer* composer Harry Roesli created intensely politicized and controversial works (Gombloh 1999a:4–5) and the Balinese theater director Kadek Suardana was occasionally arrested for expressing pro-democratic party (*Partai Demokrasi Indonesia*, PDI) sentiments in theater and music performances. Suardana, who had collaborated in the 1970s with the American theater director Julie Taymor, returned to Bali in 1980 after living in Jakarta and Sumatra to found the influential *Sanggar Putih* (White Theater). The Denpasar-based group included up to 100 politicized actors, dancers, writers, and musicians with a distinctly experimental, cosmopolitan, and politicized orientation (Noszlopy 2007). Fomenting protest against the New Order, *kontemporer* composers and theater directors, including Suardana, Riantiarno, Djaduk Ferianto, Rendra, and Putu Wijaya, created unambiguous statements against the regime that often stirred anti-government protest (Sutton 2004:211); it was, nevertheless, a dangerous game to mix art and politics during the era.

In the 1990s, Wayan Sadra composed a string of overtly politicized works in which he dragged, beat, and otherwise abused *gongs*. Sadra identified the instrument as the most salient symbol of oppression in Indonesia (McGraw 2013a). By abusing the *gong*, Sadra was aiming at the very center of Indonesian cultural identity. The "shining mythology" (I: *mitos berpendar-pendar*) of the *gong*, he suggested, attaches to it

---

[28] For examples see: Bandem and deBoer (1981), Gold (2004), Tenzer (2000), Herbst (1997), Ballinger and Dibia (2011), McGraw (2000). Working with the *gamelan* ensemble of Peliatan in the early 1950s, the English producer John Coast was surprised to encounter politicized Balinese, after all: "Bali was last place on earth where one would have expected to be caught in a 'revolution'" (Coast 1953:25). Characterizations of the Balinese as pre-political infants were also produced by Sukarno and other Asian leaders, most famously by Nehru in his description of Bali as the "morning of the world." See Coast 1953:44–45.

[29] See Allen and Palermo (2005), Hough (2000), Noszlopy (2007), Warren (1998), McGraw (2009).

because it moves into powerful hands; "the aura of its myth is simply a function of its exchange value" (Sadra 1999:12). A critique of the *gong* as a symbol of class relations first appeared in Sadra's 1994 *Otot Kawat Balung Wesi* in which several musicians are instructed to hit *gongs* with their bare hands until they are in pain. In 1995 he presented his *Gong Seret* (Dragging Gongs) in which twelve *gongs* were dragged along the tiles of a traditional *pendopo*, producing a cacophony of screeching overtones. In 1998 he staged his *Bunyi Bagi Suara Yang Kala* (Sound for the Silenced), referencing the assault on the headquarters of the Indonesian Democratic Party in Jakarta on July 27, 1998. At the work's climax Sadra pulled a water buffalo—the mascot of the PDI—upon the stage. According to Sadra the buffalo defecated across the stage, distressed by the resonant low sounds of the many *gongs* Sadra's musicians continuously beat. During this period Sadra appeared as concerned with the networks of power made visible by his compositions as in their structural coherence.

During the late New Order and early *reformasi* Yudane similarly spoke of the perniciousness of Indonesia's "*gong* culture," which he appeared to critique through several works (variously entitled *Laya 1–12*) in which he threw small stones at an iron *gong*.[30]

We speak of this "high and refined" (*adi luhung*) symbol of the *gong*, but what do we see? Jakartan cronies bang it three times to inaugurate their mega-projects in which millions of dollars, thousands of lives, and hundreds of acres are wasted. To me the *gong* is simply an instrument, one that we have not yet fully explored. Let the old traditionalists and ethnomusicologists get offended and obsess over its supposed holiness. I have to think creatively. (p.c. March 2012)

While Yudane made allusions to the political potential of his work during interviews in 2001, by 2012 he disavowed direct politics, arguing that his music was pure (I: *musik murni*), based solely upon structural and aesthetic, rather than political, concepts.

Pak Sadra's works are political through and through. Mine aren't; I'm not political. My works can be *read* as political, but I don't intend it as that. I don't know if I completely understand the politics in my work; I never put it in there intentionally. But, really, in Bali arguing for the freedom of the composer is a political statement about resisting the ideology of *tradisi*. I guess you could say there is a political *consequence* to my work; but it doesn't begin with politics. (p.c. March 2012)

On March 5, 2008 Dr. Wayan Rai, the incumbent rector of ISI, was roundly defeated in a faculty election by Nyoman Catra, a popular lecturer supported by the institute's two prior rectors, Madé Bandem and Wayan Dibia. Surprised by the loss, Rai appealed to the Minister of National Education for a re-vote, provoking the faculty and student body to protest. Rai and

---

[30] This work was prefigured by Pande Madé Sukerta's *Mana 689* (1986) in which he threw stones at a large thundersheet, released on Lyrichord's *New Music of Indonesia 2* (1993).

his cronies were frequently accused of mismanagement and corruption, just as his predecessors had been. Through his connections with the central government, Rai was able to obtain a letter from the Minister of Education annulling the first election, disqualifying twelve out of twenty-three members of the faculty senate and calling for a new election in which he was re-elected to his post amid protests. Members of the local people's parliament (DPRD) denounced the second election, claiming it was illegal.

Campus protests during and following the re-vote included shadow puppet plays by Bali's most popular dalang, Cenk Blonk, numerous kontemporer performances and installations that directly and unambiguously attacked Rai. Nearly all academic activity ceased on the campus following the re-vote. In mid-September faculty and students marched into the administrative offices escorted by a gamelan beleganjur and nailed the rector's door shut. Students then cordoned off the entire campus in police tape.

In the early reformasi, regional autonomy laws lent a sense of increased control and ownership over local politics and an expectation that New Order cronyism and corruption could, and would, be stamped out. Such expectations partly explain the protests at the conservatory. The election to replace the rector represented a statement in favor of change that many students and faculty expected to be realized. The faculty senate only later became aware that it was not authorized to install or remove rectors; its voice amounted to merely a nonbinding vote of confidence.[31] Prior elections were not contested as previous rectors had carefully established their base of power beforehand. According to the Department of Education's bylaws, the rector serves at the pleasure of the Minister of Education, functioning as an extension of the national department. Similar to the relationship between the Indonesian president and his ministers, there is no legally binding adjudicating body between the rector and the minister. The senate functions as a democratic foil for what is in fact a closed system vulnerable to corruption and nepotism.

In 2008 the Balinese for the first time voted directly for members of local and national parliament and governor. Within this changing political landscape the rector's backing by distant, non-Balinese officials in Jakarta against the wishes of the local majority and as the result of a vigorous, secretive lobbying campaign was viewed by many artists as a throwback to the days of shadowy New Order politicking in which the bureaucracy, rather than the parliament or the electoral system, was the principle arena of politics. That is, politics took place in the apparatus itself rather than between the apparatus and the people. The ISI bureaucratic structure transferred official authority into personal power. This structure was self-consciously built in to the colonial- and independence-era Taman Siswa school system developed by the Yogyanese aristocrat Dewantara who proposed an alternative to colonial modernity, rationality, and bureaucracy based upon the Indonesian family and the authority of the father figure or bapak. This family-ism recalled the power of pre-colonial feudal and

---

[31] See http://www.dikti.go.id/Archive2007/sk316u1998.html for the bylaws of the national Department of Education.

kinship structures and was dominant in state organizations under both Sukarno and Suharto (Day 2002:196). For many students and faculty, their protest against the ISI rector and the New Order political structures which kept him in power was a nostalgic re-enactment of the anti-Suharto protests of 1998, with the arts playing a similarly conspicuous role, one in which direct and unambiguous relationship to its object were displayed.

The botched ISI elections of 2008 cost both the rector and his detractors thousands of dollars in lobbying and lawyers' fees, severed decades-old friendships, postponed the graduation of hundreds of students, paralyzed the island's only tertiary-level arts organization, and severely tarnished its reputation overseas. Why would vast resources be deployed in trying to capture the rectorship, a bureaucratic governmental position with a modest salary? Lucrative recording contracts, foreign and domestic tours, contracts with the government and tourist industry, international collaborations, and research projects all pass through the rector's office before being handed down to lower-level faculty. The rector has access to a myriad of creative and financial bonuses not available to other faculty and is the primary conduit for lucrative foreign visiting teaching positions and graduate study. The demand for Balinese talent within the international academic industry exacerbated the potential for corruption within ISI. A major point of conflict between Rai and his subordinates was grounded in the latter accepting temporary foreign research and teaching positions that circumvented his authority and approval.[32] The continued dysfunction of the state art institutions energized the growth of private arts organizations during the *reformasi*.

Rise of the *Sanggar*

Modern *sanggar*, privately owned arts clubs independent of local governmental or religious oversight, emerged in Denpasar in the 1970s among graduates of the conservatory.[33] In the 1990s groups including Semara Ratih and Cudamani emerged in Ubud while Perinting Mas and Suardana's Arti Foundation were active in Denpasar. *Sanggar* flourished during the *reformasi*, many becoming centers of *kontemporer* performance.[34] Their growth coincided with a rise of the Balinese middle class; private clubs required significant capital investment to acquire rehearsal space, costumes, and instruments. Most organizations raised funds through grant writing, membership and performance fees, and donations from wealthy and aristocratic sponsors. The emergence of influential arts organizations owned and directed by commoner musicians of humble means,

---

[32] For more on the ISI controversy, including contrasting viewpoints, refer to e-mails posted to the gamelan@dartmouth.listserv.edu list from April 14–15, 2012.
[33] Earlier manifestations of such organizations are seen in the Literary Enthusiasts' Club (I: *Himpunan Peminat Sastra*), founded in Denpasar in 1961 on the initiative of the Sundanese author Apip Mustapa. In 1966 Wayan Beratha founded his dance *sanggar* Kridaloka in Denpasar (Sadra 1991:68).
[34] The foremost included: Madé Subandi's Ceraken, Madé Sidia's Paripurna, Nyoman Windha's Jes, Madé Suanda's ensemble, Bona Alit's ensemble, Dewa Ketut Alit's Salukat, Wayan Dibia's GEOKS, Wrdhi Swaram in West Denpasar, Wayan Yudane's Buriswara, and Penggak Men Mersi.

such as Subandi's Ceraken, represented an unprecedented level of individualized artistic autonomy.

Penggak Men Mersi, located in Denpasar, encapsulated the anti-hegemonic ethos of many *reformasi sanggar*. Sponsored by the aristocratic artist A.A.G. Kusumawardana, the space hosted *kontemporer* rehearsals, performances, and roundtables, and actively supported marginalized groups, hosting performances by ethnically Chinese *keroncong* ensembles and Muslim *sandiwara* ensembles.[35] Members of the *sanggar* described it as "a space for social criticism in music, dance, painting, and debate" (p.c. Wayan Dita, July 2010), and their logo, a co-option of the Mercedes-Benz symbol, embodied their critique of global capitalism and served as a talisman for the tensions inherent in Balinese contemporary performance: "*Penggak* means a foundational tradition; *Mersi* is from Mercedes and symbolizes the *moderen*; combined they are the paradox that we express" (ibid.).

The rise of the *sanggar* following the New Order represented a statement against the conservatory's long-standing assumption of its monolithic authority over the Balinese performing arts, a position many conflated with the totalitarian, centralized ethos of the New Order itself. Most *sanggar* were founded by graduates of the institution interested in forging alternative aesthetic communities and reviving regional variations that had been homogenized by the conservatory's pedagogy. Their sometimes being described as *nakal*, or naughty young children, was often embraced as a special source of symbolic capital. The outlaw forms and practices forged at the more politicized *sanggar* represented a reclaiming of artistic space that embodied the hopeful spirit of the *reformasi* itself: a potential for productive dissensus and democratic debate that might eventually produce a more just existence.

---

[35] The palaces (I: *puri*) are not in fact as anachronistic as they might appear in contemporary Balinese culture. Kusumawardana was the primary force behind *Penggak Men Mersi*. The otherwise iconoclastic and socially critical artists associated with the *sanggar* referred to him as their king. Similarly, Kadek Suardana's activities have long been sponsored by the aristocratic A.A.G. Puspayoga. Both Puspayoga and Kusumawardana exuded the figure of fatherly patrons for the artists under their wing.

5   *Téori* and the *Komposer*

JULY 2011. YUDANE *was arguing violently with his neighbors as I pulled into the half-built compound. His new home's experimental design—a ring of small structures around a central node—seemed completely devoid of Balinese aesthetics. He had rather reluctantly returned to Bali after several years of studying, performing, and teaching in New Zealand. Robby, his Wellington wife, seemed to miss Bali more than he, and had returned to teach in the international school where their son attended class. Yudane hurled a final epithet over the compound wall and turned to me: "I'll show them my gun. That will shut them up!" They had bought the plot in Lodtunduh to be closer to the "Ubud scene" but were having a difficult time coexisting with their "provincial" neighbors. Tempers on both sides cooled when Yudane's young son returned from school, carrying a heavy bag of books. "He reads constantly! His head is full of concepts. Nothing like a Balinese!" Yudane beamed.*

Conversation quickly turned to the "sorry state" of the Balinese composer. He was, Yudane argued, too often merely a penata tabuh, *a music arranger, rather than a "true composer." The typical Balinese composer was little more than a craftsman, throwing together bits of* tradisi. *To be a real composer required clear concepts and a theoretical sense of structure, not the "pretty pictures" suggested by the themes (I:* tema*) trotted out for conservatory and festival compositions. "We need theory, but not the rules of* téori. *The concepts of theory need to be argued over, talked through. But we're not good at arguing in Bali."*

This chapter is divided into two sections. First I describe institutional theories of composition (I: *téori*) and composers' responses to them. Second, I sketch the Balinese composer (I: *komposer*), an emergent figure characterized by his/her relationship to *téori* and by changing notions of authorship and ownership.

During the New Order, institutional *téori* partially overwrote regional variations in Balinese compositional practice to posit an ideal order of things against which local practice increasingly appeared as an outlier. *Téori* represented both a mode of analysis and a means of managing compositional development through official templates. During the *reformasi*, *musik kontemporer* sometimes appeared as a venue for deconstructing institutional *téori*. The publication by the conservatory of theoretical/mystical texts, including the *Prakempa*, allowed composers to demonstrate academic credentials while authorizing radical experiments by evoking ostensibly ancient cultural symbols. As the *reformasi* wore on many artists reacted against the homogenizing effects of state-sanctioned aesthetics (I: *estetika*)—the normative values embodied in institutional *téori*—that highlighted unproblematic notions of beauty over experimentation and individual expression. Although I aim a critical eye at institutional theory in this chapter, I contend that to critically examine the genealogy of New Order–era aesthetics is not to deny their indisputable power and meaning for the majority of Balinese artists and audiences living through the era, many of whom felt enriched by the oftentimes brilliant performances produced by the New Order conservatory and other state-sponsored cultural institutions.

Composers fashioned their identity as *kontemporer* partly through their relationship to *téori*. Generally the more incredulous one was of institutional *téori's* sacred cows, the more *kontemporer* one could appear. Nevertheless, one could not be fully *kontemporer* without having an explicit theoretical tool kit. The *kontemporer* composer's theory often combined subjective and folk aesthetic concepts such as *rasa* (B), feeling, and *pangus* (B), fitting, with adopted (and transformed) elements of Western compositional theory.

The *komposer* represented a new kind of Balinese subject; he (and, rarely, she) appeared as a community of multitasking inner selves rather than the monolithic person portrayed by the early ethnography of Bali. Nevertheless, a self-conscious Balinese-ness was the most vital aspect of a *komposer*'s identity. Partly because of this regional affiliation, *musik kontemporer* composers displayed only a low level of group identity nationally but were sometimes linked through the image of the trickster, an ancient cultural type that helped to insulate composers from criticism.

The mantle of the *komposer* was a means through which to express the idiosyncrasies of the self as contrasted to prior forms of composition which many composers denigrated as craft. The *komposer* was an author, seen to have special rights over the work. The *komposer*-as-author increasingly appealed to notions of copyright and intellectual property that were strengthened through a series of laws passed during the *reformasi*. However, many composers engaged with *musik kontemporer* simultaneously eschewed classically Balinese notions of communal ownership *and* straightforward Western notions of copyright, seeing it as a foil for neocolonialism. The *komposer* was further characterized by new relationships to audiences and new technologies for communicating to them. The audience itself underwent significant transformations, becoming more heterogeneous and anonymous in new types of performances spaces.

The *Téori* of Composition

Balinese composers speak of compositions (I: *komposisi*) as if they have always existed. Prior to the emergence of the conservatories, *gamelan* works were known primarily by their form and function. The term *tabuh* designated works by their form—for example, *tabuh telu*, referring to the number of *kempur* strikes in a *gong gede* work—or by their placement and function within a larger performance—such as *tabuh petegak*, the overture to a *wayang kulit* performance. The term *komposisi*, borrowed from the Dutch *compositie*, did not become widespread until after the emergence of institutional theories of composition and compositional form. Emerging from *téori*'s forge, the ontology of the *komposisi* differed from earlier sonic phenomena termed *tabuh*.

The task conservatory fathers assigned to *téori* was massive. Overwriting the desultory reality of regional Balinese expressive culture, *téori* was imagined to posit an ideal order of things against which local practice increasingly appeared as derivation, deterioration, and contradiction. The knowledge of *téori* became temporally fixed, imagined as an unchanging object prior to practice, oftentimes ignoring the continued evolutions of its exemplars. Through inductive reasoning, limited cases (e.g., intonations and *gong* forms favored in Denpasar) were extrapolated to serve as fundamental principles underlying all Balinese practice. Institutional *téori* was an explicit and propositional form of "knowing that," as distinct from the practical and implicit forms of "knowing how" (Ryle 1945) embodied in village musicians' praxis. As conceived in the conservatories, *téori* recalled Leibniz's conceptualization of clear, distinct knowledge; it should enable practitioners to *consciously* recognize and define their objects. As was the case for its colonial predecessor—the Dutch *theorie*—Indonesian *téori* implied a conceptual distance between knower and known. Conservatory faculty could have theory without being expert performers.

The emergence of Balinese *téori* was partly a response to the geopolitical status of Western Theory, characterized as a priority, even a mission, of the West (Sakai 2010:13). In the colonial and postcolonial context, the Western humanities engaged in the production of theory, refining anthropological knowledge produced at its imagined boundaries, into a more universal "Theory" which then flowed to a Western and elite non-Western audience. While the West–Rest model for the production of Theory has to a certain extent eroded, it informed the emergence of Indonesian musical *téori* through the interaction of colonial and local scholars in Indonesia. As a Balinese mode of thought, *téori* maintains an anthropological, rather than universal status. That is, Balinese knowledge continues to function primarily as raw data for Western Theory. Indonesian *téori* is sometimes, like *musik kontemporer* itself, figured as poorly mimetic, aping the forms of Theory without producing meaningful results.[1] Balinese composers including Sadra anxiously observed the complex relationship between *téori* and Theory, noting many Indonesians' tendency to accept the latter as authoritative and superior (Sadra 1986:1).

However, while all forms of Theory (and *téori*) are linked by being, at their base, an exercise in power, *téori* is not simply a response to Western modernity. Similar kinds of totalizing activities and epistemologies predate Balinese modernity, even if they were not as successful in homogenizing practice as was conservatory *téori*. Esoteric and infallible religious and musical knowledges have long been guarded within the *griya*, the archives of the Brahman caste. Institutional *téori* as an expression of national development ideology emerges in the 1930s among figures such as Dewantara, who advocated the founding of progressive schools based partly on Western pedagogical methods.

---

[1] Consider the description of the analyses printed in the conservatory's journal, *Mudra*, as not analytical in a "Western sense" (in Roeder and Tenzer 2012:1).

Founded first in Java, his *Taman Siswa* system was exported to Bali in the early 1930s. Perlman (2004) and Sumarsam (1995) outline Dewantara's efforts to inaugurate a *téori* of the arts based upon scientific methods (Perlman 2004:122). The nationalist attempt to democratize the arts through *theori* had at its heart a paradox in which Western epistemologies were adopted as a means to reject Western colonization.

Sumarsam (1995) describes the production of a *téori* of *karawitan* through the interactions between Javanese and colonial music scholars prior to independence. The comparable sophistication of Javanese models colluded with the Javanese hegemonic position within the independence government to render the Balinese second-class *téori*-ticians. Javanese models were emulated even when they occasionally contradicted Balinese practice or when Balinese models of analysis were already available. Beginning in the 1950s and 1960s a string of Balinese theorists, including Rembang, Griya, Beratha, and Kaler, studied and taught at ASKI (*Akademi Seni Karawitan Indonesia*, Indonesian Music Academy) in Solo. They returned with Javanese theories of mode (*pathet*), rhythm (*irama*), and structure to KOKAR Bali where they sought to demonstrate their traditions as a theoretically consistent analog of Javanese practice.[2] In 1960 Rembang, Griya, Kaler, and Semadi published their *Titilaras Dingdong*, an ambitious effort to document and stabilize extant Balinese repertoire through a form of modernized notation that combined Balinese *aksara*-pitch markings with Javanese *kepatihan* notation conventions.

Prior to the incorporation of Javanese terminology most Balinese tunings were categorized as *saih*, a term representing the characteristic tuning of a type of *gamelan*. *Gender wayang*, for example, was described as *saih gender wayang* rather than being associated with the broader theoretical term *slendro*, as it is today. Almost all Balinese ensembles (including *jegog*) are now classified as being either in *slendro* or *pélog*.[3] The subsumption of the regional variety of Balinese *saih* into these theoretical models apparently followed both Western and Javanese scholarship. Writing in 1934, the Balinese author Balyson states: "Purportedly our music is *pélog*" (1934:164). As evidence of this, Balyson refers the reader to Kunst.[4]

While Javanese *pathet* was a highly theorized concept by the mid-twentieth century, similar Balinese conceptions, described variously as *patutan* or *tetekep*, were less explicit, stable, and widespread.[5] Rembang's theories of Balinese mode were heavily

---

[2] In his theoretical text on composition Nyoman Rembang attempted to stabilize Balinese rhythmic theory by identifying eight levels of *laya*, blending Javanese concepts of hierarchical rhythmic densities (called *irama*) and the swelling *ombak* of Balinese *gamelan* repertoires (Rembang 1986). The influence of such concepts seems evident in at least one of Rembang's compositions (with Sinti), *Wilet Mayura* (1982).

[3] Wayan Beratha and Asnawa identified what they called a *jegog* scale on the seven-tone *saih pitu* and *semara dana* ensembles. Although the typical pitch structure of *jegog* is impossible to accurately represent in standard seven-tone *pélog*, Beratha theoretically captures it within the larger system by identifying it as an example of *pélog miring*.

[4] "*Konon musiek kita pélog: lihat kitabnya Kunst.*" See also Wakeling (2010:90).

[5] Sukerta reports that until today the *gambuh* repertoire as performed outside of the villages of Batuan and Peduganare not associated with any modal naming system, but that each piece is associated with a unique *saih* not necessarily conceived of having a theoretical connection to a seven-tone *pélog* system (p.c. July 2003).

influenced by his experience playing *gambuh* and by theories of *pathet* he encountered in Java. The Balinese conservatory's interest in revitalizing seven-tone ensembles, including *semar pegulingan, slonding, gambang,* and *luang* led to the expansion of theories of *pathet*. During the New Order, Balinese theories of mode expanded from the recognition of approximately five classical modes derived from *gambuh* to ten modes identified by Beratha on the *gamelan semara dana*.

New Order *téori* was as much a mode of analysis as a means of managing compositional development by providing sanctioned templates. However, if *téori* was sometimes felt as an arbitrary set of rules constraining composers' freedom, it also provided cultural cachet through a specialized, modern cant that fused progressive, Western-sounding neologisms with esoteric Balinese Hindu concepts previously the reserve of high-caste philosopher-priests.

A series of New Order theoretical texts, the most influential being Wayan Aryasa's 1976 *Perkembangan Seni Karawitan Bali* (The Development of Balinese Music) and Madé Bandem's 1983 *Ensiklopedi Gamelan Bali* (Encyclopedia of Balinese *Gamelan*) presented a plethora of tuning charts aligning Western, Javanese, and Balinese tunings, tables of instrument ranges, glossaries, and organologies alongside definitions and musical examples meant to stabilize the practice, form, and terminology that often varied widely by region. The consolidation of conservatory *téori* during the New Order coincided with the decrease in regional *gamelan* festivals and contests following the establishment of the centralized island-wide *kebyar* contest in 1968. Conservatory faculty and *listibiya* bureaucrats, equipped with a newly developed body of *téori*, became the core arbiters of island-wide musical developments through their central, almost exclusive, position on festival jury committees. Authorized by institutional *téori*, administrators and faculty could evaluate performances in ways that reinforced regional hierarchies. Denpasar and Gianyar, respectively the seat of government and the psychic center of Balinese Hindu tradition, consistently won the annual contests. Their expressions served as *téori*'s exemplars.

Beginning with the Old Order, conservatory faculty began to reify through *téori* the tripartite *tri-angga* form to describe many repertoires designated as *klasik*. During the early and mid-New Order, Wayan Beratha, the conservatory's leading composition faculty, expanded upon the *tri-angga* by pioneering a four-part form for the *tabuh kreasi* featured in the annual island-wide *kebyar* contests.[6] New *and* old compositions appeared as either continuous with or deviations from these normative theoretical models. While *téori* sometimes appeared as a set of consolidated facts, it was only ever an unruly consensus. Even during the New Order, conservatory formalism never reached the severity of Reimmanian functional harmony or Schenkerian structural analysis. Instead, compositional possibility was more directly constrained by vague appeals to beauty such as those embodied in the institutions' texts on aesthetics, described below.

---

[6] Consisting of *gineman, gegenderan, bapang,* and *pengecet* sections. See Sandino (2008) and Wakeling (2010) for a discussion of the emergence and dissolution of this form.

RESISTING *TÉORI*

Ketut Suanda described *musik kontemporer* as signifying the end of composers' being "hypnotized" by *téori* in favor of a return to the folk, unbounded aesthetics of *pangus* (B), personalized feeling, or sense of fit (p.c. July 2010).[7] Arsawijaya and Yudane often complained that the *tri-angga* form was treated as a mold into which melodic material should be poured rather than as a shape that sometimes emerged from the tendency of earlier compositions. When asked to describe the form of classic *kebyar* works, Gede Arsana, normally circumspect when it came to criticizing institutional *téori*, admitted: "to describe any of these works as really *tri-angga* feels like lying" (p.c. February 2002). In his 1993 recital work, *Laya*, Yudane pioneered the deconstruction of a number of *téori*'s favored hierarchies. Because *téori*'s *gong* forms delimited melodic possibilities, Yudane composed asymmetric melodies around which *gong* forms were stretched. Because traditional *gong* forms often implied specific melodic elaboration, drumming, and dynamic structures, to be liberated from them broke open a range of new compositional possibilities, recalling the cubists' exploration of open forms in unframed space. It is crucial to recognize, however, that resistance to the restrictive tendencies of institutional *téori* emerged from within the institution itself. Writing in 1986, Sadra, a faculty member at STSI Solo, critiqued the idea that prescribed *gong* forms and structures, rather than the unique gestures of individual composers, gave rise to compositions (1986:109). Although writing from the different academic and aesthetic climate of Solo, Sadra's colleagues in Bali, principally Arnawa, would later voice similarly self-reflexive critiques from within the Balinese conservatory [Track BV-5/1].

If *téori* imagined the *gamelan* to resemble an idealized community following prescribed ethical norms, Yudane inverted its orchestration: low *jegogan* instruments now played fast interlocking melodies while high pitched *gangsa* proceeded slowly, as in his 1995 *Lebur Seketi* (B), Broken Form. Arsawijaya elaborated on deconstructing *téori*'s ethical model of orchestration:

> To say that the *jegogan* has to play only a supporting role and that the *suling* can only decorate the melody is like saying that you should be happy with your lot in life and not to question it. It is when we remove this ethical dimension that music can become *kontemporer*! I first realized this when I saw Americans compose for *gamelan*. They don't worry about the traditional roles of the instruments, but only use it as a *media*. This is what we should do, and who can predict the result?! (p.c. July 2008) [Track BV-5/2]

---

[7] During this era rerelease of historical recordings made possible the reintroduction of lost colonial-era compositions. Most influential were the Rykodisc's (1995) rerelease of the Fahnestock expedition of 1941 and Arbiter's rerelease of late-1920s Odeon discs (2001, 2011), brilliantly annotated by Edward Herbst. As early *kebyar* works re-entered the repertoire, composers noticed how they sometimes resisted the categories of institutional *téori*. The ways in which these compositions broke the rules (before such rules had been formalized) became further evidence for the disjunction between *téori* and practice and emboldened composers to forge idiosyncratic approaches.

Several composers argued for the need to develop compositions based upon explicit, verbal concepts (I: *konsep*) of musical structure as opposed to the vague themes (I: *tema*) historically favored at the conservatory and in contest settings. The theoretical *konsep* distinguished the true *kontemporer komposer* from the institutional focus upon *tema* and *téori*. Yudane frequently argued that concepts could only be developed within a climate that fostered meaningful criticism and critical thought. The Balinese, he maintained, too often conflated criticism with spiteful denigration. Yudane suggested that many traditional-minded Balinese regarded talking and discussion as a self-indulgent waste of time: "*koh ngomong*, just talking, we say. But you need to talk to be smart. We don't have this tradition of healthy conversation that you need in order to develop your concepts. All the while, the Javanese are talking" (p.c. September 2001) [Track BV-5/3].

THE *PRAKEMPA*

July 2008. Madé Arnawa animatedly described his compositional experiments at a roundtable discussion on musik kontemporer *hosted by Wayan Dibia at his GEOKS arts foundation. Hailing from the countryside of Tabanan, he accepted a position in ISI's music department shortly after graduation and quickly became a favorite among the young composers for his patient and committed advising. In 2003 Arnawa completed a master's degree in composition in Solo, studying under Sadra and Sjukur, returning with a particular enthusiasm for* musik kontemporer. *By 2008 he found himself allied with the* sanggar *movement and students who protested ISI's corruption and conservatism. Speaking at Dibia's foundation alongside other composers with ambivalent, if not hostile, relationships to institutional administration, Arnawa described a set of compositional processes that appeared to sidestep ISI's core* téori *while maintaining a distinctive Balinese identity.*

In a series of compositions begun in Bali and continued in Solo, Arnawa transferred the numerological possibilities of Balinese Hindu cosmological concepts, primarily the pangider buana, *to rhythmic and melodic structures. He described a process of mapping this complex cosmological compass, which links eleven orientation points (eight cardinal directions plus center, up, and down) to deities, pitches, and colors, to a maze of complex musical possibilities:*

> I was only doing tradisi *until 1999, but then, I don't know why, I felt an urge to step outside. I needed to find a new form. In* tradisi, *we always play together: one* polos, *one* sangsih; *the* jegogan, calung, *and* pemadé *always playing together.*[8] *But what if we took the numbers from the* pangider buana, *giving this person a five-beat pattern, that one seven, another nine, another eight, what would happen? I couldn't imagine it in my head! This is new but ancient all at once!*

Like many of his students, Arnawa explored ways in which musical patterns might be arranged that did not appear fully determined or controlled, giving complex

---

[8] *Polos* and *sangsih* refer to the interlocking pairs of Balinese *kotekan*.

responsibility to instruments previously assigned only simple, supporting roles. The results appeared polyphonic, if not purposefully somewhat chaotic. By appealing to esoteric Balinese religious concepts that appeared to predate even colonial contact, composers forged works that allegorically recalled the social transformations of their moment.

As a concept appropriate to new musical composition, the *pangider buana* emerged following the conservatory's publication in 1986 of an ostensibly ancient *lontar* palm-leaf manuscript entitled the *Prakempa*. The conservatory edition included an Indonesian translation alongside the original Kawi (middle Balinese), extensive graphs, photographs, and a commentary by Dr. Madé Bandem, the institution's then rector. Through its status as a required conservatory text, the *Prakempa* quickly became an authoritative source of *téori*. Bandem's introduction suggests a precolonial origin for the original manuscript. The absence of reference to colonial-era forms such as *gong kebyar* evokes a musical life prior to the dissolution of the courts and the advent of tourism and modernity in Bali.[9] With its focus upon the mystical and theoretical unification of *pélog* and *slendro* and the discussion of extant and ostensibly extinct seven-tone ensembles, the *Prakempa* aligned with the conservatory's interest in the revitalization of *gambuh* and seven-tone repertoires. Coinciding with the publication of the *Prakempa*, Wayan Beratha invented the seven-tone *genta pinara pitu*, a predecessor to the modern *gamelan semara dana*, based upon ancient seven-tone ensembles described in the text.

The *Prakempa* maps the tones of *slendro* and *pélog* upon diagrams of the *pangider buana*.[10] Rather than a static diagram, the *pangider buana* (B: *revolving world*) suggests a churning helix. The overlapping of asymmetric rhythms in *kontemporer* works drawing upon these patterns suggested a similar processual unfolding in musical form. Arnawa's compositions *Gong* (2003), *Pendro* (2004), and earlier recital works drew upon the *pangider buana* to develop both rhythmic and melodic patterns.[11] Invoking the *Prakempa* allowed composers to demonstrate academic credentials while simultaneously authorizing radical experiments through affiliation with the ancient cultural signs described in the text.

The *Prakempa* revels in mystical taxonomy without ever explicating the exact relation between theory and practice. Music is presented as an aspect of the divine or an expression of its agency; gods express unique aesthetic preferences and are associated with specific ensembles and tunings. Syllables associated with pitches are imagined to be

---

[9] In this the *Prakempa* is similar to two prior *lontar* dealing with music, the *Aji Gurnita* and the *Gong Wesi*.

[10] Kadek Suardana suggested this mapping was a relatively new concept. Otherwise, he argued, it would be a part of the symbology of the Balinese *mecaru* ceremony. Contrastingly, the renowned Balinese artist Nyoman Gunarsa treats the concept as an ancient aspect of Balinese cosmology and has represented it in his abstract paintings (cf. Jenkins 2010:20).

[11] Several of Arnawa's advisees at ISI developed similar *kontemporer* recital works based upon information found in the *Prakempa*. See for instance Wakeling's discussion of Mariyana's (2007) *Tawur* (Wakeling 2010:203). The prevalence of groupings of eleven within *kontemporer* structures suggests the diffusion of the *pangider buana* as a musical virus during the *reformasi*. Consider Ketut Dewa Alit's preference for beat structures in eleven in his *Mecaru* (2003) and Widnyana's use of an eleven-tone scale in his *Trimbat*.

intrinsically rather than arbitrarily related to their meanings. The text ends with the poet identifying himself as Gottama addressing his students. The conflation of ancient poetic style, the absence of reference to modern expressive forms, and the appeal to the ancient Buddhist (over Saivite Hindu) Gottama satisfies a contemporary Balinese tendency, practically an axiom, to value anything perceived as old.

Several composers privately questioned the pedigree and provenance of the source upon which the conservatory's edition was based. In interviews, Bandem suggested that the *Prakempa* is much younger than its predecessor, the *Aji Gurnita*. As the latter *lontar* does not appear in Van der Tuuk's colonial catalogues, it likely emerged after 1890, postdating Dutch colonization (Wakeling 2010:114, Vickers 1985:146). This would place the *Prakempa* as a pre-independence (1945) colonial text at the earliest. Bandem suggested that the original *lontar* was discovered and given to the conservatory by the composer and faculty member Gusti Putu Madé Geria (or Griya 1906–83) who had passed away shortly before the work's publication (Bandem 1986:1). The deference and respect with which he was paid is indicated by Bandem's directly associating him with the putative Gottama of the *Prakempa*.

While a fact-fiction approach to Balinese historiography is generally inappropriate (Schulte Nordholt 1992), that some composers treated the *Prakempa* as a forgery, while for others its pedigree was simply not an issue, suggested transformations in the Balinese understanding of history itself. In either case, the *Prakempa as history,* like any history, represented a reworking of the past for present concerns. The author(s) sought to establish certain aspects of Balinese music as true by linking them to an ostensibly ancient origin, thereby attempting to prefigure the future of Balinese music. The text's focus upon seven-tone musics, for instance, all but ensured their preservation and development in the future, recalling Habermas's notion of "future-oriented memories" (1979:69). In interviews, Bandem glossed the meaning of *Prakempa* as "guiding rules" (I: *pakem-pakem*): "It is a set of basic rules that can be further developed in accordance with the current situation in the artistic field. The author's intention was clearly to leave open possibility through ambiguity" (p.c. Madé Bandem, July 2001).

The conservatory's edition of the *Prakempa* was as much about contemporary preoccupations with *tradisi*, preservation, and development as it was a representation of historical practice. The text's repeated description of music's ability to instill calmness and order in the people (I: *masyarakat*) through idealized images of the relations between ruler and ruled is consonant with New Order governmentality (Bandem 1986:97). The work fed the conservatory taxonomic machine, providing cladistic trees with *nekara* (bronze drums) at the top and *kebyar* at the bottom (ibid. 18), demonstrating the classic New Order periodization of the past in which formal types are neatly and unproblematically delineated from one another in time (literally boxed in), straightforwardly and without rupture linking origin to present.[12]

---

[12] These charts invert the order of most cladistic diagrams in which older elements are figured at the bottom as roots. In the *Prakempa,* the *nekara,* a reference to the *bulan Pejeng,* is positioned at the top, closest to the gods (having fallen from heaven); *kebyar* is on the ground as it were, as the most recent, earthy and connected to the people. Interestingly, despite the inclusion of the chart in the conservatory's edition, neither the *nekara* nor *kebyar* are referenced in the Kawi text.

The *Prakempa* categorizes tuning systems as *slendro* and *pélog* (rather than *saih*), recalling Javanese *téori* rather than pre-Independence Balinese practice. The identification of three esoteric *papatutan* (modes) within both Balinese *pélog* and *slendro* strongly recalls the three *pathet* identified in Central Javanese practice.[13] Indeed, a general will-to-theory, a preoccupation with the compiling, identification, and invention of terms to describe function, technique, and playing styles, linked Geria to his contemporaries in Solo, principally Martopangrawit and Warsadiningrat.[14]

Ethnographers recognized Bali in the *Prakempa*; it satisfied the academic need for local forms of authentic taxonomy and fulfilled Western expectations of difference.[15] The text provided a convenient, if dubious, chronology that exonerated researchers from the well-nigh impossible task of actual historical fact-checking. By placing origins prior to the colonial era, it assuaged the classic ethnographic fear that we may be, in part, studying our own engagement in a hybrid culture. Investing in Indonesian *tradisi* as a sign of difference and cultural plurality, the American Ford Foundation underwrote the publication of the conservatory's edition. The resulting work, positing recovered origins, was promptly taken up by Western scholars looking for local taxonomies to feed their own Theory. Completing the intellectual loop, local scholars could then further concretize the truth claims of the *Prakempa* by citing Western scholars' citation of it.

AESTHETICS

Both through their compositions and rhetoric, many composers engaged in *musik kontemporer* during the *reformasi* challenged institutional aesthetics—the often implicit normative values that guided *téori*—that had defined artistic validity during the New Order. Refiguring pre-existing metaphors and returning to variegated village aesthetics, these composers sought an alternative aesthetic sensibility more compatible with the heterogeneous materials which populated their works. In this section I consider the Balinese notion of *estetika* (I), aesthetics, and its relationship to Western aesthetics.

Aesthetics is that field of knowledge that allows, or compels, us to recognize art and what pertains to it. As Ranciere (2009) suggests, aesthetics is not the only epistemology available for evaluating an image, object, or sound. Ranciere calls an "ethical regime" that mode of knowledge that identifies the intrinsic truth of a representation as measured by

---

[13] The text identifies three *papatutan* in *pélog: demung (tembung), selisir,* and *sundari (sunaren),* recalling Javanese *pathet lima, nem,* and *barang* respectively. In *slendro* we find: *pudak sategal, sekar menoning, asep Cina,* recalling (although ambiguously) Javanese *pathet sanga, manyura,* and *nem.*

[14] The publication of STSI Denpasar's critical edition of the *Prakempa* interestingly mirrors the earlier STSI Solo publication of a similar Javanese musical treatise, the *Weda Pradangga,* edited by then STSI rector Sri Hastanto. The *Weda Pradangga* was created by a known author (Warsadiningrat) in the early twentieth century and contains more practical and historical information (such as composers' names) than does the *Prakempa*. However the *Weda Pradanga,* like the *Prakempa,* also recounts the mystical origins of *gamelan* ensembles and ancient repertoires.

[15] The text is a central source in several important recent works on Bali, including Basset (1995), Tenzer (2000), Gold (2006), Hood (2011), Harnish (2006), Jenkins (2010), and Herbst (1997).

the impact it has upon ways of being. In Bali this might be Ganesha as a shrine or temple music as an offering. Ranciere's "representative regime" evaluates technique and form over truth. In Bali this could be Ganesha's form as a particular style or the stylistic veracity of a temple composition. In what Ranciere describes as the "aesthetic regime," art (for now it is properly art) does not become such through conformity to a canon of representation or style but from a mode of being. An aesthetic regime can adjudicate anything (even urinals) as art. In this case aesthetic refers to sensibility and inheres more in reception than form.

As represented in the conservatory's texts, Balinese *estetika* appears as a combination of Ranciere's distinct epistemologies; it remains as much about doing as being through its fusion of the pedagogical and evaluative. In Bali the same works undergo different evaluations depending upon their place, time, and context (B: *desa, kala, patra*) of performance. Performed at a temple ceremony, music may be principally evaluated through an ethical regime while at the conservatory it is evaluated through a representative regime. *Musik kontemporer* composers interpreted works primarily through an aesthetic regime. The ability to hear any sound as music, even the grinding of a *gong*, depended more upon reception and attributing artfulness as a mode of being rather than through conformity to a canon of representation.

At the conservatory, *estetika* was a discourse intended to engage interpreters in a historical community through the formation of a shared aesthetic mind as distinct from the more subjective experience of *rasa* (I), feeling. Institutional *estetika* provided neophytes with a shared criteria for judging artworks. Both subjective evaluations and *estetika* placed a high value upon a rather vague and culturally contingent notion of the beautiful. The Balinese term *ramé* (I: *ramai*), derived from the Sanskrit *ramya*, meaning beautiful (Becker 1979:234), suggests a particular kind of busyness or baroque that can refer both to the bustle of people in a temple ceremony or the arabesques of *kotekan* interlocking. More generalized notions of beauty are encapsulated in the Balinese *kelangen*, from the Old Javanese *lango*, meaning both enraptured and enrapturing (Zoetmulder and Robson 1982)[16] and the Indonesian *indah*, the closest to the English "beauty." The latter is primarily reserved for the visual realm and is less commonly applied to sound. The particular ideals of musical beauty enshrined in *estetika* appealed principally to the *madya* forms of precolonial expressions, that is, *semar pegulingan, gambuh*, and *pelegongan*, in which a shift from the ostensible ethical functions of *kuno* (ancient) forms (i.e., *slonding, gambang*) are superseded by a courtly representative regime.[17]

Why should music be expected to be principally beautiful in any culture? Cook argues that sonorous beauty emerged as a quality of the exchange value that accrued to music as it became mechanically reproducible and commoditized and that in those cultures in which there is no need for beauty, there is also no open exchange of musical

---

[16] Hughes-Freeland (1997:482) critiques Zoetmulder's description of the Old Javanese *lango* (*alango*) as a courtly transformation of the aesthetic canons of classical India. She argues that *lango*, as an aesthetic theory, more likely emerged from later colonial interactions.

[17] As in Rembang's 1984 text on *lelambatan*. See also Wakeling (2010:154) for similar ideas expressed by Astita.

products as commodities (1996:31). Although this characterization seems to deny aesthetic experience prior to modernity, Cook's notion may provisionally apply to the Balinese case in which notions of beauty commensurable to Western aesthetics appear to emerge with Bali's increasing incorporation into a global tourism and sign economy. The retroactive identification of the emergence of the beautiful within precolonial *madya* expressions represents a rearguard tactic meant to establish an ancient origin for contemporary *estetika*.

Estetika locates musical beauty in a particular sense of balance (I: *keseimbangan*). In his 1984 text on ceremonial *lelambatan* repertoire, Nyoman Rembang suggests that balance is achieved in a work's spirit (I: *jiwa*) and direction (I: *tujuan*) through following appropriate rules and orders (I: *aturan, tata cara*). Balanced composition is expressed by the shape of the melody (I: *lagu*) and the arrangement of the colotomic *gong* strokes. That is, what exactly balance (and therefore beauty) is remains almost completely implicit in New Order *estetika*, leaving it to be identified by authorized arbiters.

From the late New Order through the *reformasi* the principle and required text on *estetika* for all conservatory students in Bali was A. A. Djelantik's *Estetika: Sebuah Pengantar* (I), *Aesthetics, an Introduction* (1990, updated 1999). Djelantik (1919–2007), a widely respected prince of the Karangasem court and a physician who specialized in malaria at the WHO, was also a painter and had lectured on and off at the conservatory since 1966. His text on aesthetics reads as a kind of cookbook for beauty and several of the taxa he identifies are incorporated into the recital criteria described in Chapter 3. Aspects of Western classical aesthetics are described as objective (iii) and *estetika* is explicitly linked to New Order ethics (I: *etika*) (5) through the linking of *estetika* to social upgrading and its characterization as a way to protect the Balinese from outside influence (14). Djelantik argues that the work of art should inspire calmness and not shock the audience through excess or experimentation (50). The text ends upon a rather negative evaluation of abstract expressionism with no mention of either the avant-garde or postmodernism despite an exhaustive review of classical Western aesthetics from Plato to Dickie.[18]

Institutional *estetika* preferred arborescent models symbolizing musical and social structure. According to KOKAR faculty member Asnawa:

> If you make music without a sense of, or background in, tradition your creations will be malnourished and die. If you make something new, don't forget the traditional music. If you cut the roots the tree will die. The roots must be there even if the branch goes in a different direction. (p.c. Ketut Gede Asnawa, August 2001)

Traditional music was often idealized by faculty as the nourishing roots of a tree, whereas new music was, by implication, the ephemeral leaves, whose existence is

---

[18] See Wright (1994) for a discussion of the adoption in the New Order conservatory of depoliticized modes of individual expression associated with "universal" (i.e., Western) aesthetic movements.

contingent upon the roots. They may fall and be brushed aside, while the roots persist. The firebrand Yudane rejected this image:

> I will make new trees with a strange fruit. One tree cannot contain us. Where is *kebyar* from? Everyone says it's from a different place: the north, the west, and also the south. And all these places, even today, have their own unique style. These were different trees competing for nourishment. That is, audiences. (p.c. Wayan Yudane, September 2001)

ANTI-*ESTETIKA*

WY:(B) Don't follow *estetika* à la ISI. Much less its ethics; it is all myth.
PC: (I) That's right! *Estetika* and ethics are only a foil to dampen the creative potential of young artists.
SA:(I) Maybe these folks [ISI] need a reminder that *estetika* can be more than the beautiful.
WY:(I) There is beauty, but it can only be felt, seen, or heard individually. Beauty that is framed by an institution is false. Indonesian, and especially Balinese, art has been turned into this by the traditionalists, who all still wallow in the mud of "beauty."
PC:(I,B) Yes! Let those who "know nothing" and stand outside of ISI and are ignorant of the institutions be our guides.
 –Facebook conversation between Balinese *musik kontemporer* composers. Posted August 7, 2010.

Many composers involved with *musik kontemporer* appealed to a subjective aesthetics and tended to idealize folk terminology in response to institutional *estetika*. Recapitulating colonial anthropological romances, *musik kontemporer* composers saw in the villages a more authentic aesthetic system putatively informed by an integrated praxis (see Gombloh 2003:10). The composer Ketut Suanda stressed the notion of *pangus*, a Balinese term referring to appropriateness or fit and which, for many composers, subsumed all other aesthetic concepts, including *rasa* (p.c. Suanda, Windha, Arsawijaya, Arsana, July 2010). According to Suanda: "Older generations knew, and the villagers today still know *pangus;* they had it, but they were also *bodoh* (I), ignorant, in terms of compositional techniques. Today, some of us educated composers are no longer *bodoh*, but we've lost a sense of *pangus*" (ibid.). Arsana and Arsawijaya described *pangus* through water metaphors as a flow that could carry listeners along. Other evaluative adjectives outside the *estetika* discourse included those related to food, as in *luwung* meaning good or ripened or *lebeng* meaning well cooked. The over-ripened composition of a composer pulling out all the tricks to impress an audience might be *kempuh*, spoiled [Track BV-5/4].

Rasa, from the Sanskrit meaning flavor or essence, suggested a complex interaction of feeling, understanding, being, emotional meaning, and metaphors of scent and taste.[19] *Rasa* was also part of the language of institutional *estetika* but, being at base an aspect of individual perception and understanding, it was not, or could not be, tightly codified into an ideology. The character types embodied in musical topics and described as aspects of *rasa* in Benamou's (2010) study of Javanese music were often differentiated as *karakter* (I), character, by Balinese composers.[20]

While Vickers describes emotions such as happiness adhering in the meters of classical *malat* poetry (2005:175), musicians I interviewed suggested that music was a representation of emotion, rather than its direct embodiment. Although *rasa* was not a completely private way of knowing music—it had aspects of a social semiotics—one could not be wrong in one's evaluation of *rasa*. The term appeared more restricted to the description of certain elements of composition, especially dynamics and timing, and was more often an evaluation of a particular interpretation or performance than compositional structure. Musical improvisation and the process of fine-tuning a *gamelan* was directed by the implicit nature of one's own, individualized *rasa*.[21] Gusti Sudarta suggested that one's unique *rasa* could be inherited between subsequent incarnations, which may explain certain young composers' uncanny ability to create new works that sounded old. Nevertheless, the *rasa* which one either felt or expressed was primarily the manifestation of one's particular place, time, and context (p.c. July 2008). *Rasa* was most vibrant in those areas of musicality in which institutional theory was most ineffectual; it was an expression of one's unique identity.

The *Komposer*: New Identities

> The musicians are an integral part of the social group, fitting in among ironsmiths and goldsmiths, architects and scribes, dancers and actors, as constituents of each village complex. Modest and unassuming, they nevertheless take great pride in their art, an art which, however, is so impersonal that the composer himself has lost his identity. (McPhee 1935:163)

Throughout the New Order and the *reformasi*, the Balinese *komposer* was an emergent figure distinguished partly through his/her relationship to the theoretical concepts

---

[19] *Rasa* suggests a riot of meaning both through its Indian etymology and its historical usage in Balinese, Javanese, and Indonesian; see Benamou 2010.

[20] The stately refinement of a king as expressed through the *selisir* mode in *gambuh* represents such a topic and may be described as a refined (B: *alus*), *rasa*. Nyoman Windha differentiated *karakter* such as stately (B: *agung*), mature, profound, (B: *wayah*), *alus*, and *keras* (B), rough, from the proper *rasa* of sad (I: *sedih*), and sweet (I: *manis*) (p.c. July 2010).

[21] For an example that neatly demonstrates the confrontation of explicit (religious and mathematical) logics against the idiosyncrasies of personalized *rasa*, see Wakeling's (2010) discussion of Wayan Sinti's process tuning his *manikasanti* ensemble.

discussed in the first half of this chapter. Equally important were the relationships to new forms of subjectivity, changing notions of authorship, and new interactions with audiences.

How should we think of identity in Bali? How is it articulated through *musik kontemporer*? In the West, modernity precipitated theories of subjectivity as fragmented. Proust's narrator describes himself as not one man only "but the steady advance hour after hour of an army in close formation, in which there appeared, according to the moment, impassioned men, indifferent men, jealous men." In his study of time and being Heidegger (2008 [1962]) suggests that we are never identical with ourselves but always in a state of becoming through time. We are never finished. For de Certeau (1984), subjectivity is the art of the tightrope walker, making constant adjustments to maintain equilibrium in the present. Subjects living in multicultural and globalized contexts are increasingly theorized as hybrid through their ability to multitask serially among a community of inner selves (Reuter 2006). These images resonate with notions of contemporary Balinese subjectivity as expressed by the statements of many Balinese composers.

In Bali, as in America, identity is understood as both innate and constructed. It is simultaneously the inalienable essence of blood and biology and a form of voluntaristic self-fashioning expressed through acts of consumption and expression. Identity is the irreducible tension between ascription and choice. Through the ethnographic lens, Balinese identity has often disappeared through a communal washout. Mead, Bateson, Belo, and Geertz portray Balinese identity as a type, a rather nameless cog within the communal machine. Geertz (1977) doesn't deny the Balinese individual identities, but foregrounds their characteristics as types over their idiosyncrasies as tokens. Individuals appear as tokens of timeless types through teknonymy; one is a Wayan, a first born of a particular caste, before one is an identifiable individual. Vickers (2005:211) similarly focuses on the universal features of Balinese subjectivity as divided between the manifest person and its mystical siblings (B: *kanda mpat*). The subject is the incarnation of a specific, transcendental soul that has, nevertheless, gained a particular karmic identity through prior life experiences as an ancestor.[22] Agency in the anthropologically conceived Balinese subject is a complex result of divine, karmic, and manifest causes and forces.

Although the Balinese subjects I encountered did not appear as cogs, many did focus on the perceived qualities of inborn traits, usually referred to as *watak*. As in America, being the first or second (or third, etc.) born brought with it specific expectations that many individuals conformed to. One's birth date potentially influenced one's character; Yudane and his community often linked his sometimes hot headed or rebellious nature to his being born under the "bad sign" of *tumpek wayang*, a kind of Balinese Friday the thirteenth. *Watak* characterized one's own developing personality as well, and these personality types were sometimes associated with the characters of *wayang*

---

[22] Balinese souls are typically all in the family.

plays. Flirtatious men might be associated with Arjuna, a link that might even encourage, explain, or excuse womanizing.

The obsession among cultural commentators concerning what modernization (I: *moderenisasi*) and globalization (I: *globalisasi*) were doing to the Balinese character was an omnipresent and, for some composers, suffocating and regressive discourse (see Burhanuddin 2008:9). Many in the middle class, and especially composers engaged with *musik kontemporer*, instrumentalized the very forces of modernization and globalization to infuse lives with possibility as opposed to forms of identity overdetermined by caste, class, or karma. Musicians increasingly spoke of styles (I: *cara*) of behavior. Faced with a dispute over performance fees following an intercultural *kontemporer* project, Gusti Komin Darta wondered if he should approach the issue *cara Bali* (in a Balinese manner, i.e., through innuendo) or *cara Barat* (in a Western manner, i.e., directly) (p.c. February 2011). That there appeared to even be an option suggested the possibility of multitasking identities.

While the classic anthropological image focused upon the Balinese person, as constituted externally by the obligations, rights, roles, and structure of society, my experience with composers highlighted Balinese selves—the idiosyncratic, interior qualities developed through subjective experience and expressed through a unique artistic voice. Many composers described a tension between the interests of their self versus the expectations society and the tourist gaze placed upon their person. Economic pressures, social stress, alienation (and its opposite, social smothering) sometimes threatened to split the self from the person. As Arsawijaya explained, "not having a regular job can drive you a bit crazy, as can living with your mother-in-law" (p.c. July 2008). Music was often a refuge of the self; composition was a practice that brought balance back to the subject.

Thus far I have sometimes referred to *musik kontemporer* composers as if we could neatly distinguish between them and composers engaged primarily with *kreasi* or *tradisi* forms. This is rarely the case. However, *tradisi* and *kreasi* forms were often figured as expressions of the Balinese person as a communal being. According to Bandem: "There is nothing Bali is more proud of than her arts, and music and dance are the most expressive of these. Through them, Westerners will know the Balinese mind, soul, and personality" (in Tenzer 2011:132). Here Balinese culture is the expression of a communal ethos over individual minds, a representation that plays into the suspicion that composers may not really exist in Bali, as suggested by McPhee (see also Feliciano 1983:1).

In response to this image, many composers have sought to express the self by delimiting older forms of composition as a form of craft as opposed to the individualistic art of the *komposer*. This represents a continuation of the national conservatory's tendency to define and normalize the divisions between musicians, composers, theorists, and listeners, as well as between professionals and amateurs, which had previously remained comparatively undifferentiated. For Yudane, those involved in *musik kontemporer* were "real composers" as opposed to the craftsmen (I: *tukang*) who cobbled together pieces largely through the collage of pre-existing materials (p.c. July

2008). To become a true *komposer*, as opposed to the *penata tabuh* (I), music arranger, associated with *kebyar* and *tradisi* forms, entailed facing challenges and misunderstandings from one's community (Bing 2003:18-19). *Kontemporer* works during the *reformasi* increasingly circumscribed community by highlighting individualistic or even solo performance.[23] However, the paradoxical tensions between communalism and individualism in contemporary Bali was foremost in many composers' minds. Although Widnyana, for instance, cultivated his identity as a modern *komposer*, he worried about what this might implicate for the future of Balinese communal expressions and traditions [Track BV-5/5].

Engagement with *musik kontemporer* expressed a cosmopolitan identity through its links with expressive forms, aesthetic networks, and lifestyles from beyond Bali. This sometimes manifested in voracious desires—to eat all foods, to visit all places, to fornicate with all women—but was in reality a kind of "grounded cosmopolitanism" (Appiah 2006); rarely able to leave Bali, to the extent that they could, composers experienced the world's diversity at home as it came to them through the Internet and seasonal waves of tourists, artists, and academics. Socializing, performing, and creating within a cosmopolitan milieu, many imagined themselves to belong to a community among communities, sharing a language of aesthetic and moral value. After graduating, Arsawijaya described *Geräusch* as an example of global art (p.c. July 2007). By 2008 many students at the conservatory cited performances of world musics on YouTube and experience performing with foreign students as being more influential in their compositional process than their experience at the conservatory itself [Track BV-5/6].

TRICKSTERS

June 2003. Suanda danced onto the stage in nothing but a thong, the sort worn by Balinese farmers in bygone days, shifting his exposed buttocks right to left in rhythm to a rustic tune chanted by his musicians. Sitting next to me, the normally restrained composer Nyoman Windha laughed so hard his eyes welled with tears. He yelled teasingly to the performers as if we were at a village odalan performance rather than at the elite, air-conditioned Ksirarnawa hall: "This isn't funny! (B: tengal) Go home!" Carrying a small traditional wicker basket containing a puppy, Suanda sat down at a set of Sundanese (West Javanese) drums and broke into a blazing solo, punctuating the final cadence by striking the puppy. When it yelped loudly in time with the music the Balinese, rather infamously indifferent to animal rights, burst into hysterics as the several European and Japanese audience members stared in disbelieving shock. Suanda continued his solo, playing the puppy as an instrument, beating it in time to punctuate phrases with its miserable cry. The work concluded with Suanda throwing a ball at a large gong hung at the back of the stage, an otherwise highly irreverent and offensive

---

[23] Yudane's solo performance at the *Musik Masa Kini* festival, Subandi's and Suanda's appearances as soloists in their various *kontemporer* works presented at the Bali Arts Festival, and Teja's 2007 recital composition, the first solo recital work presented at the conservatory, provide examples.

act which, performed in this context, seemed to bother no one. Suanda was, after all, a clown [Track BV-5/7].

Wayan Sadra often spoke of the need for *kontemporer* composers to be naughty (I: *nakal*), for it was a sign of intelligence (Gombloh 2001:8). The Sumatran *kontemporer* composer Ben Pasaribu similarly encouraged young composers to be both *nakal* and outright transgressive (I: *kurang ajar*) (Gombloh 2000b:6). *Musik kontemporer* was a tricky artistic practice and composers sometimes adopted the mantle of the trickster. In Balinese traditional culture the trickster appears in *topeng* dance as the *panasar*, in *wayang* as a host of recusant figures, and in regional tales as a character named Bungkling.[24] Bungkling pops up in tales solely for the purpose of pissing off otherwise sympathetic characters by grilling them endlessly and annoyingly about Balinese tradition; he arrives to undermine our commitment to the values we have settled into. Strolling uninvited into a cremation ceremony, he asks why small mirrors are placed on the corpse's eyes and when told that this will ensure beautiful, clear eyes in the next life, he sarcastically asks his interlocutor, who suffers from cataracts, if maybe her mirrors were just a bit cracked in her previous life. Like his global avatars Hermes, Rabbit, Legba, and the Signifying Monkey, Bungkling and the composers who channel him are often bawdy and revel in inverting sacred hierarchies. They encourage social cohesion through communal laughter but through confusion can catalyze social change in stagnant times [Track BV-5/8].

The trickster paints in grotesqueries. Embodied in excess, filth, and the macabre, the Balinese grotesque is a rich symbolic field that links the spiritually powerful (B: *tenget, sakti*), unmanifest, *niskala* world with aesthetic transgression. Bakhtin's grotesque realism and its focus upon gaps, mixed categories, orifices, and filth figured in decentered and eccentric arrangements recalls the deconstructed forms and heterogeneous topics of some *musik kontemporer*, the choreographies in mud by the dancers Sardono and Erawan, and the inversion of cultural symbols as in Arsawijaya's *Geräusch*. In the hands of composers such as Sadra, Yudane, and Arsawijaya, the *kontemporer* arts sometimes resembled the carnival—a temporary suspension of prevailing authority through excess, hybridity, and defilement.

In 2006 Wayan Dibia commissioned Agus Teja to produce a *kontemporer* work for a festival of new music hosted at his GEOKS arts space. Teja's *Senggama*, meaning intercourse, calls for inverted *gong*, African mbira, water drums, cymbal, voice, tuned glasses, and flutes. The performance involved interlocking rhythms spanked out on buttocks, rude sloshing and slurping sounds played on pans filled with water, and musicians simulating orgasms. Above this sexual soundscape Teja improvised on tuned glasses and a Balinese flute modified to sound like an Indian *bansuri*. At the work's climax a musician called out a Western woman's name: ohhh Susie! In an otherwise stuffy academic event, Teja's composition stood out. Observing its enthusiastic reception by a

---

[24] This figure was better known around Denpasar; some musicians in Ubud had never heard of him.

multigenerational audience including local villagers and academics made me wish that my own avant-garde took itself a bit less seriously [Track MK-5/1].

COMMUNITY?

At the 1998 Young Composers' Week (PKM) held in Jakarta, government officials implored artists to "develop modern music in Indonesia as a creative community" (Dewan 1998). However, *musik kontemporer* composers have historically displayed only a low level of group solidarity or shared identity. The efficacy of the New Order state in managing culture lay in its ability to unambiguously identify people as representatives of groups and order them as such. Sadra described the tendency, beginning in the mid-1980s, for innovative composers to reject attempts at aesthetic centralization (Sadra 2002). To appear as a radical singularity, an individual—an artist—without a comprehensible identity was something the state could not come to terms with. As Dewa Ketut Alit suggested, he would rather be "many things than some thing" (p.c. July 2007). For some, being *kontemporer* was to resist prescribed notions of identity and the pat boxes one could be placed within.

Kontemporer-ness was only a vaguely articulated communal symbol, one associated loosely with an upwardly mobile middle class of artists who shared a commitment to aesthetic innovation. A subcategory of *kontemporer* composers spoke a shared idiolect that aligned radical expression with overt political critique. Sadra's article for the inaugural issue of *Gong* in 1999 appeared to some to be a kind of manifesto for this community. Following on the heels of Suharto's ouster, Sadra envisioned a performance piece that involved the fiery destruction of twelve Javanese bronze *gongs*.[25] To this small grouping of composers, *kontemporer*-ness represented a kind of subculture, a mode of being in the world with its own aesthetic principles, social hierarchies, ideologies, and symbolic meanings.

AUTHORSHIP AND THE *KOMPOSER*

Mead and Bateson described the production of Balinese art as an assembly line (1942:4); Covarrubias claimed that artistic property cannot exist in the communal Balinese culture and that Balinese artistic production is "the anonymous...expression of collective thought" (2008 [1937]:138). These images are persistent in the ethnographic and touristic image and are often encouraged by Balinese elites. Tradition is a more valuable commodity than innovation in Bali; attributing representations to the anonymity of tradition adds to their depth.

Tradisi's tendency to disaggregate compositional voice has long appealed to Western observers.[26] McPhee characterized the Balinese process of composing as radically

---

[25] This work foretold Arsawijaya's *Geräusch,* although the younger composer denied any connection.
[26] However, many works are attributed to both *tradisi* and named composers. Lotring's works are standards of *tradisi* but are still regarded as examples of his particular genius. None of the composers with whom I worked could name composers prior to the early decades of the twentieth century.

different from Western composition; Balinese processes were a form of craftsmanship, "so impersonal that the composer himself has lost his identity" (1935:163), representing an idealized form of nonexpression. Although earlier practice did tend towards attributing creation to a diffuse community, by the New Order new works were often attributed to a singular author even if they emerged through collaborations, borrowings, transformations, and theft.[27]

Many Balinese highlight their traditional creative process as communal while Western society tends to celebrate the singular genius of the lone author. Both images deny basic commonalities. It takes a rather obsessive belief in the ideology of individualism to attribute Beethoven's works, for instance, to him alone rather than recognizing the widely distributed field of creation that gave birth to them and made them intelligible to audiences. Rather than an example of absolute alterity or self-containedness, Beethoven moved around pre-existing materials much more than we like to admit. It takes a similarly romantic investment in the ideology of communalism to deny particular artistic genius to historic Balinese composers.

As Western theorists announced the disaggregation of meaning, intention, and authority in the 1960s—embodied in Barthe's *Death of the Author* (1967)—Balinese artists were simultaneously celebrating its birth. This is not to say that clearly delineated, singular expressive voices did not exist in Indonesia prior to the New Order—we could produce a long list of earlier composers: Madé Regog, Wayan Lotring, Gede Manik, Pan Wandres, and others—but that the author came to increasingly resemble his or her idealized form in Western culture, particularly in terms of expectations of originality, voice, and ownership. The *komposer* of *kontemporer* works became more visible as a singular author than creators in otherwise *tradisi* contexts through the perceived need to explain creations in relation to society and for the new perceptual demands the works made upon audiences' interpretive habits. Writing in 1986, Sadra described *komposisi* as a mode through which the *komposer* expressed an "individual character and originality," in contrast to the characterization of a more communal status for the Southeast Asian composer, as proposed by Jose Maceda (1986). As differentiated from *tradisi* contexts, the *komposer* needed to make statements—in interviews, in programs, and through synopses—that served as the exegesis of one's process and intent.

The discursive shift to the singular artist's voice in the New Order and *reformasi* suggests transformations in the ways in which subjectivity itself is imagined. The concept of expressive voice presupposes a subject as separated from the group, as a monad with a discrete interior through which intents, emotions, and meanings are thought to diffuse into the work. Whether or not this is an actual, historical shift versus simply a discursive transformation is unclear. Composers increasingly talked of their own and others' works as embodying specific personalities, intentions, and meanings; they were the expression of a persona.

---

[27] See Tenzer (2005) and Ornstein (2006) for a discussion of Wayan Gandera's relationship to the compositions *Hujan Mas* and *Gambang Suling,* often attributed to him, but which apparently emerged earlier in the northern village of Kedis Kaja.

Kontemporer composers spoke of their process using the neologism *berkompos* (I), to compose, or as *bikin komposisi* (I), make a composition. Older terms evoked the creative process in more traditional settings. *Ngolah* referred to everyday acts of creation; its root *olah* suggested the physical transformation of materials and connoted the face-to-face labor of creation in rehearsal rather than the kind of intellectual unfolding of a composition in a singular mind, prior to rehearsal, associated with *berkompos*. On the backs of the ubiquitous *gamelan* cassettes sold at roadside stalls, *kreasi baru* composers were listed as *penata tabuh* (I), music arrangers. *Menata*, from the root *tata* (I), order, system, was not a term considered appropriate to *musik kontemporer* for which expectations of originality were apparently higher.

During the *reformasi*, transformations of authorship and ownership often pivoted upon the relationship between work and performance. Balinese composers have long distinguished between a work's melody (I: *lagu*) and its elaboration.[28] In reference to *tradisi* and *kreasi baru* forms, Nyoman Windha suggested that significant changes in melody, which he referred to as a composition's basis (I: *basik-nya*), fundamentally transform a work's identity. For Windha, elaboration, tempo, dynamics, and drumming patterns, which he referred to as the "feeling embodied in a particular performance," could be changed—but only to a very subjective point—without a work losing its core identity (p.c. July 2010). Contrastingly, for composers including Arsawijaya and Alit the core identity of a *musik kontemporer* work could lie in elaborating (i.e. interlocking) patterns, without there necessarily even being an identifiable melody (p.c. July 2010). The flexible dialectic between work and interpretation that defined *kreasi baru* and *tradisi* forms seemed not to apply to *musik kontemporer*. Composers engaged with *musik kontemporer* appeared to increasingly adopt the Western notion of *werktreue*: "the objectivist's belief that a work is fixed in meaning before interpretation takes place" (Goehr 1992:276). *Kontemporer* works generally received only single performances, almost always in the presence or under the direction of the composer, forestalling the potential for the performative transformations evident in *tradisi* and many *kreasi baru* works. While *tradisi* and *kreasi baru* works were never really finished, endlessly refigured from village to village and through time, *kontemporer* composers more often appealed to a sense of accomplished closure. These composers seemed to understand that works must be conceived as being finished in order to be copyrighted and to fully realize their exchange value [Track BV-5/9].

In 2010 several younger composers excitedly pointed out to me, in hushed voices, the striking similarities between Wayan Beratha's *kreasi baru* works *Palgunawarsa* and *Penyembrama* to the earlier works *Manik Amutus* and *Sekar Jepun* from Jagaraga in northern Bali, suggesting that the maestro had stolen those materials to claim as his own. However, there had long been dynamic, mutually influential interactions between the north and south and it is highly unlikely that musicians and composers would not have noticed the similarities between Beratha's compositions and those from Jagaraga

---

[28] See Balyson's description for an early example of this distinction (1934a:164).

as the works were composed.[29] Either Beratha's powerful status muted any critique or, more likely, such transparent borrowings were not considered theft, as they are sometimes today by a generation of composers and musicians whose notions of authorship, ownership, and originality are increasingly conditioned by the concept of copyright [Track BV-5/1].

Copyright

December 2001. Aware that I was living at the home of a conservatory instructor and recital jury member, a group of students passed me a cassette of Japanese new age music by Kitaro, cryptically suggesting I give it a listen before the upcoming recitals. For his final recital Ari Hendrawan arranged several kendang *in stands, playing them in the manner of* taiko *while a keyboardist performed melodies strongly reminiscent of the Kitaro recording. Despite the fact that several jury members were aware of the strong resemblance between Hendrawan's music and Kitaro's, he graduated with high marks. This outraged several of his rivals and articles were published in the* Bali Post *(January, 2002) accusing Hendrawan of violating copyright (I:* hak cipta*). Then rector Wayan Dibia defended the jury's evaluation by suggesting that Hendrawan had created a sufficiently original* kontemporer *work and that, although materials were borrowed from other sources, they were used in creative ways. In interviews Dibia suggested that the Balinese arts directly benefited from the lack of enforceable, Western-styled copyright. If every composer was expected to develop an idiosyncratic compositional language, Dibia argued, Balinese audiences would quickly become overwhelmed, confused, and alienated. Dibia suggested that copyright in Bali would "kill creativity" (I:* mematikan kreativitas*) and further the "modern negative trend towards individualism" (ibid.).*

In July, 2010 Yudane angrily approached the organizers of the Kodya regency *gong kebyar* committee after discovering that they intended to restage his 1992 *Murdaning Seketi* for the 2010 *gong kebyar* festival. If Kodya continued without his permission, he argued, Yudane would sue to protect his creative rights. Organizers eventually arranged a financial settlement and agreed that any transformation to the work should be approved by Yudane.[30] In 2007, frustrated that his compositions were to be performed and recorded by the Cudamani ensemble following his break with the group, Dewa Ketut Alit demanded that his copyright be respected and he argued that the works should not be performed, recorded, or transformed without his permission. The ensemble continued to perform them anyway, arguing that the compositions had emerged from a communal creative evolution that continued after Alit's departure.

---

[29] Sadra (1991:31, 42) describes the close personal and artistic relationship between Beratha and Gede Manik, of Jagaraga, and the earlier links between the *gamelan* at Belaluan, led by Beratha's father, Madé Regog, and ensembles from Buleleng.

[30] Originally listed in 1992 as a co-composition with the more senior composer Komang Astita, many composers suggested that Yudane was the primary, if not sole, composer, and that Astita's name was originally used to give the then young and unknown Yudane access to the festival.

Since the *reformasi*, Balinese notions of authorship, ownership, and creativity have been increasingly influenced by copyright.

Local record producers faithfully included copyright warnings on their cassettes, although I knew of no composers who had ever received royalties. Instead, all recording agreements were based upon a single, upfront fee. During the late New Order and early *reformasi*, copyright was largely treated as a running joke among Balinese composers. However, the introduction of new intellectual property and copyright laws in 2002, the heated discourse surrounding cultural patrimony, and the sudden possibility of selling recordings on the Internet energized discussions concerning copyright, ownership, and the status of the *komposer*. Although monetary returns were not yet felt, discourses surrounding intellectual property laid the conceptual groundwork for potentially far-reaching future transformations of the Balinese aesthetic economy. Many composers were aware of the painter Nyoman Gunarsa's attempt to bring a copyright suit against imitators and forgers and saw in its failure a fundamental misunderstanding by the state of the nature of innovation (Jenkins 2010). By 2010 composers, including Subandi, Sadra, Rai, Teja, Suweca, Yudane, and others, were listed with BMI or ASCAP [Track BV-5/11].

Western copyright emerged in tandem with capitalism and bourgeois ideologies of art and the artist transforming the ephemeral products of the mind into transferable properties. Veiled in a moralistic rhetoric of protection and artists' rights, copyright was created primarily to protect publishers from one another. In 1899 the concept was internationalized through the Berne convention and domesticated in Asia through colonization.[31] During the twentieth century, Western internationals and conglomerates lobbied for the extension of copyright terms and restricted fair-use rights while encouraging international organizations such as WIPO (World Intellectual Property Organization, an agency of the United Nations) and the WTO (World Trade Organization) to require developing nations such as Indonesia to become signatories of international copyright and intellectual property protocols in order to receive development loans.

During the *reformasi*, transforming notions of authorship and ownership were caught in the tension between concepts of singular copyright versus communal rights embodied in the idea of intangible cultural heritage as articulated by WIPO and UNESCO. The passage of new, sweeping regulations in 2002, which devolved ownership of intangible cultural heritage—including traditional performing arts—to the nation rather than to local communities, precipitated extended discussion between artists in Bali and among critics in the pages of *Gong*.

Western notions of intellectual property naturalize the movement of shared ideas from creative commons to ownership by named parties—individuals, communities, and governments—who have not necessarily requested such human rights and who may have historically held different conceptions of ownership and rights (Aragon

---

[31] Indonesian copyright laws were expanded and made more articulate in subsequent laws passed in 1982 (UU No. 6), 1987 (UU No. 7), 1997 (UU No. 12), and 2002 (UU No. 19).

and Leach 2008:1). The adoption and strengthening of intellectual property laws in Indonesia suggests substantial transformations in the ways in which the production of knowledge, and culture itself, are imagined to originate and belong to individuals, ethnic groups, and the nation. While the attempt to designate local expressions as national cultural property appears as a patriotic strategy intended to protect cultural expressions from predatory globalization, the identification of art as an object tied to named owners—individual, communal, or national—nevertheless allows for its later commercialization, transforming its ontological status from gift to commodity.

The communities to which WIPO's 2006 definition of Traditional Cultural Expressions (TCEs) refers are as large as entire nations. Gill has situated these developments within what he terms the 'new constitutionalism:' the attempt to "make transnational liberalism, and, if possible, liberal democratic capitalism, the sole model for future development" (Gill 2003:132). This regime increasingly favors the security of property owners and investors and through increasing surveillance mechanisms eases the flow of transnational capital. While WIPO has encouraged the privatization of intellectual property, UNESCO has, seemingly contradictorily, argued that intangible cultural heritage is irreducible to private property—individual or collective—and seeks to preserve cultural expressions for the entire human community[32] through various preservation and documentation initiatives including its Representative List of Intangible Cultural Heritage, a list tightly correlated with the geography of IMF investment.[33]

As employed by organizations including WIPO and UNESCO the term "traditional knowledge" refers to knowledges that are "generated, preserved, and transmitted in a traditional and intergenerational context" (quoted in Antons 2009:2). That is, all expressions that fall outside of the highly specific Western concept of copyright are classed as traditional knowledge and are based upon the highly subjective, dubious notions of authenticity and tradition. In practice the term appears to refer to any primarily oral/aural mode of expression, a designation that would include most Balinese *tradisi* and *kontemporer* expressions.

To the extent that they believed they might benefit from preservation programs initiated by the state or UNESCO, Balinese composers and *sanggar* highlighted the continuity of their expressions with *tradisi* and the compositional commons. To the extent that they believed that Western-styled copyright structures might lead to royalties or control, composers highlighted their works' idiosyncrasies. In the first context

---

[32] See UNESCO's *Convention for the Safeguarding of Intangible Cultural Heritage* (2003).

[33] The Indonesian government has co-opted this effort as a proxy for its continued confrontation with Malaysia, touting its successful inclusion of *angklung*, *batik*, and the Balinese *subak* traditional irrigation system as a score against Malaysia (www.indonesianewyork.org, accessed May 2012). This conflict reached a boiling point following Indonesia's (misplaced) accusation of Malaysia's "theft" of the Balinese *pendet* offering dance in 2009. See articles in: *Rakyat Merdeka* (August 22, 2009), *Suara Karya* (September 7, 2009), and *Bisnis Bali* (December 16, 2009). Earlier and highly visible cases included the Malaysian government's use of the song *"Rasa Sayang"* in its 2007 tourism campaign which led members of the Indonesian government to pursue unspecified legal actions (Antons 2009:54).

creators face the demands of a potentially oppressive authenticity; in the second they are obliged to downplay intertextual linkages, if not *tradisi* itself, through concepts of authorship that many artists viewed as dangerous forms of Westernization (*Tim Redaksi Gong*, 2010). When brainstorming ways to raise further funds for his *Ceraken* organization, Subandi suggested that his use of the ancient *gambang* ensemble might make him eligible for UNESCO intangible cultural heritage funding, while his experimental works for that very ensemble might be copyrighted through ASCAP and potentially enable applications for funding for innovative projects through the Ford-funded *Kelola* foundation.

Many composers engaged with *musik kontemporer* simultaneously eschewed classically Balinese notions of communal ownership and authorship *and* straightforward Western notions of singular, total copyright. The former discourse encouraged the notion of identity as communal and stressed a subject's personhood; the latter discourse focused upon the self as a more singular, idiosyncratic voice. Some composers eyed copyright suspiciously as yet another conduit through which aspects of their culture (increasingly perceived as property) might be siphoned away.[34] Simultaneously, the appeal to the communal production and ownership of all intangible expressions appeared to many as a retrogressive move that recapitulated the anthropological romance of the Balinese.

AUDIENCES

Besides new relationships to theory, authorship, and ownership, composers engaged with *musik kontemporer* were characterized by new relationships to audiences and new technologies for communicating to them. During the *reformasi*, audiences underwent significant transformations, becoming more heterogeneous and anonymous in new types of performance spaces. How do Balinese audiences come to understand new compositions? How has the relationship between audiences and composers changed over time? How have new venues transformed audience behavior and compositional styles?

Balinese audiences are famously vocal, even rowdy, and many have compared them to the sometimes ornery audiences at Western sporting events.[35] Audience members, especially those at popular *gong kebyar* performances, jeer mistakes and applaud virtuosity. They often talk throughout a concert, resembling eighteenth-century Italian

---

[34] The unlicensed recording and sale (and apparently arbitrary renaming) of several traditional and contemporary Balinese works by the American-German label Sonoton only reinforced that impression among many composers. Mislabeled, unattributed works by Wayan Beratha, Nyoman Windha, and others have appeared on several releases on Sonoton's "Authentic" series, most recently their 2010 *Original Music from Bali*.

[35] "I don't know if it is because of overcrowding or the thunderous yelling, but the performances are like soccer matches. I sometimes can't handle it, watching these friends of mine who have rehearsed for up to six months, and then the audience goes so crazy you can't even hear the music. They sometimes even throw things onto the stage!" (p.c. Wayan Sinti, December 2002).

opera house audiences more than new music concerts in the West where silence and immobility are considered signs of appreciation and courtesy. Balinese audiences generally applaud what they find familiar and virtuosic and sometimes have little patience for the pretensions of *musik kontemporer*. Wayan Suweca recounted a performance of his *kontemporer* work *Fajar Menyingsing* in the mid-1980s in which performers improvised on experimental and found instruments (in black concert dress) while the audience continuously jeered, eventually shouting in unison: Stop! [Track BV-5/12].

Musik kontemporer lacked *kebyar*'s large audience base: an overwhelmingly young and male crowd that sometimes displayed the kind of mob mentality that recalled the testosterone-laden political rallies held prior to the violent emergence of the New Order (Ida Bagus 2006). Unruly audience behavior was a major concern of cultural elites and organizers of the Bali Arts Festival; internal reports during the New Order suggested that while the performances are sufficiently good, the manners of the audiences need to be upgraded through guidance and education (PKB 1989:38). By 2010, MCs at the popular *kebyar* performances on the Ardha Chandra stage bade audience members to turn off their cell phones, to not speak during the performances, and to applaud only at the end of works. Although many spectators giggled at such requests, audiences have become markedly tamer, a change Wayan Dibia described as more civilized (I: *beradab*) and which Arsawijaya attributed to progress (I: *kemajuan*). In the spaces in which *musik kontemporer* was often performed—at Dibia's GEOKS foundation, the indoor Ksirarnawa hall at the Bali Arts Festival, the conservatory proscenium stage, and various other sites—audiences often behaved in ways that approached, but never conformed with, Western expectations of seated, immobile silence. Many composers associated their audience's comparative stoicism with *musik kontemporer*'s perceived social prestige.

Older composers celebrated what they understood was a robust relationship between the performing arts and the general Balinese audience, especially as compared to perceived audience alienation in both the West and in Java.

> We're a collective—all under one roof [I: *wantilan*]. Balinese composers still care about the audience. In Java it's sometimes different. Composers there have ventured out on their own. We take only short steps so that the audience can keep up with us. The Javanese have partially lost their traditional arts because they weren't careful about maintaining that relationship. (p.c. Ketut Gede Asnawa, August 2001)

Evoking the structure of the *wantilan*, the traditional Indonesian open-air structure, Asnawa suggested that Balinese composers and their audiences interact as in a communal market. While Asnawa's appeal to the *wantilan* evokes a blurred division between performer and audience as a metaphor for cultural integration and communal values, the proscenium stage may better symbolize *musik kontemporer*'s status. Fixed seats, program booklets, and a clear division between audience and performer, often separated by a gulf of several meters, stood as a metaphor for the comparative independence between *kontemporer* composers and their audiences and their sometimes divergent aesthetics.

Composers began to compose specifically for new acoustic spaces in the late New Order. In traditional performance contexts *gamelan* is often performed in *wantilan* or in the open yard along a temple wall. These acoustic spaces favor low frequencies and can accommodate the rich inharmonic spectra of *gamelan*. The performance of large traditional *gamelan* ensembles upon the proscenium stage presents certain acoustic problems; compositions that appear clear in the *wantilan* may sound cluttered on a proscenium stage such as the Ksirarnawa hall at the Bali Arts Festival. Alternately, small or solo ensembles cannot saturate the open acoustic space of the temple courtyard or *wantilan* as they can the proscenium stage. Dewa Ketut Alit's *Salju* opens with a quiet, almost imperceptible striking of the highest key, the logical opposite of the loud, tutti *kebyar*. For the work's premiere at the Bali Arts Festival, a sudden venue change from the indoor Ksirarnawa proscenium stage to an outdoor courtyard had, in Alit's words, "ruined the piece." After all, he had composed it for the indoor theater (p.c. July 2008).

While indoor spaces were often reserved for elite and foreign performing groups and were important venues for the upwardly mobile to be seen, the large Ardha Chandra amphitheater accommodated all levels of Balinese society. Social strata manifested literally in its space; government officials, jury members, ticket holders, and tourists sat in padded seats closest to the stage. They entered through a central door manned by both police and Balinese *pecalang* guards. As seats ascended away and up from the stage, working-class crowds milled, talked, and ate, half-listening on concrete benches as if at a temple ceremony. In a kind of inversion of traditional caste priorities, the highest seats were left for the lowest of society.

Kontemporer performances were distinguished by their existing outside of competition contexts and for eschewing the flamboyant *gaya*—choreographed poses—that have become increasingly popular among *kebyar* ensembles performing *kreasi baru* on large stages such as Ardha Chandra. Recognition of the familiar against the grain of the mildly new was the essence of *kreasi baru* in which broadly shared aesthetic experiences linked the individual to the group. Although *musik kontemporer* did not draw primarily from the same compositional commons, its composers did not wish to throw their works, like messages in a bottle, out to an uncaring sea. Most wanted to be understood and appreciated but often found themselves composing for heterogeneous audiences of listeners who did not always share interpretive schema. When composing *kreasi baru* the same composers could easily manipulate the shared tastes of Balinese lay audiences; when composing *kontemporer* they were not so parochial, but by reaching beyond their own group sometimes entered murky semiotic waters.

Electronic Mediations

Musik kontemporer emerged alongside transformations in listening precipitated by the widespread use of electronic media. The interiorization of musical experiences through headphone technology appeared nearly simultaneously with the expansive exteriorization of sound made possible through large PA systems. The ability to either interiorize or exteriorize sound was a sign of class distinction and transformations in sonic space were complexly entangled with changes in social space.

Radio Republic Indonesia (RRI) began broadcasting in Singaraja and Denpasar in 1950 but it was not until the 1970s that most Balinese could afford cheap radios and tape players. In the late 1960s local recording companies established a dynamic cassette culture dominated by recordings of local *gamelan* ensembles. By 2010 the major local labels Bali Stereo, Maharani, and Aneka sold a combined catalogue of over 2,500 local releases. If electronically mediated sound was previously a more social affair—listening in groups to the communal radio in the *banjar*—by the middle of the New Order listening had become a more private practice. Listeners tuned in to RRI's daily 6:30 a.m. *Acara Karawitan* (I: *karawitan* broadcast) which popularized Wayan Beratha's *kreasi baru* after the introduction of the island-wide *kebyar* festivals in 1968 (Tenzer 2000:106).[36] Festival *kreasi baru* and *tabuh lelambatan* have been mainstays of the station's broadcasts along with traditional music and theater forms, primarily *arja*. Independent stations emerged during the New Order and flourished under the *reformasi*, streaming online to make themselves available outside of their broadcast area. New music enthusiasts tuned in (or logged on) to Sapto Raharjo's weekly program of *kontemporer* music on Radio Geronimo, Yogyakarta. The *kontemporer* generation was the first to have access to digital networks connecting them to a "global sonorous space" (Nancy 2007) through which, it appeared, musics from all places and all times were available.

Amplification became increasingly prevalent throughout the New Order and *reformasi*. Composers chuckled resignedly as their complex interlocking patterns that ensembles worked so hard to perfect were distorted through imbalanced amplification. Most composers complained about poor mic-ing schemes and distorted sound systems.[37] While amplification during the New Order was primarily a display of social prestige irrespective of fidelity, during the *reformasi* poor amplification began to emerge as a sign of backwardness as contrasted to the more cosmopolitan sounds of sophisticated (I: *canggih*) sound reinforcement. During the 2008 premier of his *Salju* at the Bali Arts Festival, Dewa Ketut Alit hung his head in despair as the sound system continuously fed back: "Aduh, seperti zaman dulu" (I), "God, it's like the old times" (p.c. July 2008). Access to the brute power of amplification conveyed the social status of elites in the New Order; knowing how to use it belonged to the cosmopolitans of the *reformasi*.

In the late New Order recordings had become a potential source of (albeit minor) income for composers; recordings of annual festival compositions were the most lucrative. In the early 1990s commissions rose to two million *rupiah* per cassette (approximately $400); by 2002 Nyoman Windha was receiving up to ten million *rupiah* (approximately $1,000) for his adventurous *kreasi baru*. Funds derived from recording commissions were divided among players, composers, and others involved in the management of the ensemble,

---

[36] Certain composers, including Sadra, maintained that applause tracks were frequently inserted into radio broadcast recordings of Beratha's and KOKAR's *gong kebyar* recordings of the 1970s as a way to increase their popularity. Inserted into the pauses in opening *kebyar* phrases, the manufactured applause was meant to suggest that the recordings were live broadcasts received with wild enthusiasm. I was not able to corroborate this controversial claim. RRI suggests that these early recordings have been lost, and Beratha and those closest to him deny such claims. See also Sadra 1991:74–75.

[37] Compare this to Sutton's identification of distortion as aesthetically appropriate in otherwise traditional Javanese settings (1996).

PLATE 5.1 Gus Teja listens to the playback of his *Bara Dwaja*. Photo by the author.

with the composer taking the highest percentage.[38] Recording technology also appeared to impact processes of composition: "When I know that my work will be heard more often on a machine with a rewind button than in live performance, I feel obliged to put more into the composition; I don't want to bore listeners" (p.c. Arsawijaya, June 2008). By 2003, older artists began to complain of the overfullness of new *kreasi* composed for the festivals, sometimes describing them as too *kontemporer*.[39]

Composers such as Yudane and Sadra sold self-produced studio recordings at local cassette shops and circulated them through digital networks of *kontemporer* composers and connoisseurs.[40] While local cassette companies recorded *kebyar* ensembles using a stereo track mobile field studio, *kontemporer* composers increasingly patronized private studios in Denpasar, Sanur, and Kuta, sometimes recording multitrack works. Gus Teja, pictured in Plate 5.1, recorded his self-described *kontemporer world musik* CD *Rhythm in Paradise* in 2010 with a pop engineer in Denpasar (p.c. Gus Teja, July 2010). Saving funds earned from tourist performances, Teja underwrote the production himself, uploading the music for digital download. Teja distributed free copies to the many spas in Ubud and the airport in Denpasar. Within a month his music appeared to be the veritable soundtrack of the tourist industry and Teja was bemoaning the absence of strong copyright enforcement in Indonesia.

---

[38] This was a single fee, however, and did not entail royalties.
[39] Wayan Dibia, Ketut Gede Asnawa, and Wayan Beratha often expressed such sentiments.
[40] Some of these recordings, such as Yudane's 1992 *Laughing Water*, met with some success selling in shops catering to tourists in Ubud.

6 The Materials and Technologies of *Musik Kontemporer*

JULY 2008. WHILE *many of his peers saved their funds to build contemporary homes, some raising mixed families with foreign wives, Arsawijaya settled with his college sweetheart in her family's compound in a densely populated neighborhood in southern Denpasar. I found him sitting in a balé pavilion, his infant daughter on one knee, his laptop on the other. Wearing headphones, he was busy composing a new gamelan work using a sequencing program. Sealed off from the bustling sounds of the family around him, he sang along loudly in Balinese solfege syllables to the playback, prompting giggles from a group of old women sewing together palm leaf offerings.*

By 2006 the computer had become an essential tool in Arsawijaya's compositional process. Since the beginning of the reformasi, a small group of musik kontemporer *composers, including Arsawijaya, Hendrawan, Yudane, and Suardana, traded pirated music software programs. They were bewitched by the ability to compose and record multitrack works by oneself, independent of the complex social and economic logistics of extensive live rehearsal. Only Arsawijaya regularly used these programs to compose works for large* gamelan *ensembles. His favored program, Fruity Loops, allowed him to arrange music using an intuitive box-unit interface, avoiding Western notation altogether. The program made possible the almost instantaneous construction of complex forms that would require hours of rehearsal if working with live musicians.*

Like many urbanized Balinese, Arsawijaya presented offerings each morning to his electronic devices. But the computer received more elaborate offerings and a favored place on a high shelf. He fretted when it got "sick" (with viruses), and seemed genuinely saddened when his first machine "died." We joked about how other valuable objects such as gamelan and keris (I), swords, were treated as humans: given names, birthdays, and offerings and were seen to have distinctive personalities and to host spirits. Why not, he asked, a computer?

Musik kontemporer emerged through the confluence of new technologies and new materials. The first half of this chapter considers the technologies of *musik kontemporer.* Forms of notation—Balinese, Western, and digital—were increasingly adopted as part of composers' tool-kits. The *kontemporer* generation was the first to have access to computers and Internet technology, bringing an unprecedented variety of musics to Balinese ears. During the New Order and *reformasi* new instrumental technologies and approaches towards tuning and intonation emerged. *Gamelan* intonations and orchestra types intersect with social groupings and hierarchies. The instruments and

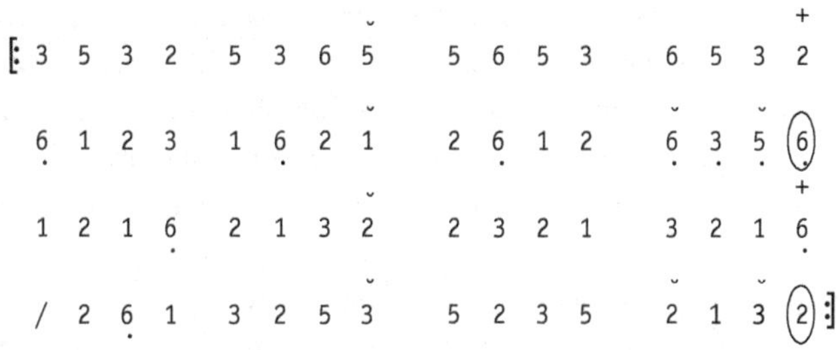

```
⁝: 3  5  3  2    5  3  6̆  5     5  6  5  3     6  5  3  2⁺

   6  1  2  3    1  6̣  2  1̣     2  6̆  1  2     6̣  3  5  ⑥
                                                          ̣⁺
   1  2  1  6̣   2  1  3  2      2  3̆  2  1      3  2  1  6̣

   /  2  6̣  1   3  2  5̆  3      5  2  3  5      2  1  3  ②:]
```

FIGURE 6.1. Cipher notation for the *pengawak* of *Rejang Dewa*.

intonations composers favored represented an ideological stance indicative of a specific aesthetic, community, and personhood.

The second half of this chapter concerns the materials of *musik kontemporer*—the musical ideas that composers developed within their works. Here I draw upon the linguistic concept of markedness to discuss stylistic change in *musik kontemporer*. Related to markedness, I analyze various musical topics—short musical passages that trigger clear associations with styles, genres, and expressive meanings (Hatten 2004a:2)— within *musik kontemporer*. I identify three classes of topics in *musik kontemporer: tradisi*, foreign, and *etnik*. Many composers engaged with *musik kontemporer* drew upon topics, which they often referred to as viruses, from *klasik* and *tradisi* repertoires but were primarily interested in foreign and *etnik* topics. These materials were conspicuously displayed within their compositions and functioned as a sonic representation of composers' spatial imagination, placing their others alongside themselves. I conclude with a consideration of the role that markedness and new topics play in catalyzing stylistic change.

Notation

Although *lontar* palm-leaf manuscripts have historically included highly schematic mnemonic notations of liturgical vocal melodies, it was not until Djirne and Ruma's *Taman Sari* collection of 1939, which combined traditional Balinese *aksara* pitch indications with Javanese *kepatihan* cipher conventions, that widespread collections of notation emerged.[1] The 1960 *Titilaras* collection produced by Griya, Rembang, Kaler, and Semadi further developed the technology by including novel indications for drum and *gong* strokes. Like Javanese *kepatihan*, Balinese notation is end-weighted with each four-beat bar indicated by an extended space between the fourth and subsequent first pulse. As in the Javanese form, rhythmic indications are adapted from the Western system of beaming and colotomic points are indicated by symbols above the pitches as seen in Figure 6.1. While institutional publications typically use Arabic numerals, Balinese composers more often sketch out compositions using Balinese *aksara*.

---

[1] See Hood (2011:91) for a discussion of rare *gong gede* palm-leaf notations.

Most Balinese notations are monophonic, mnemonic, and define only *pokok*, or core melodies, similar to Javanese *balungan*. However, while *balungan* could be used as a starting point for the improvisations (J: *cengkok*) that enliven Javanese *karawitan*, Balinese *pokok* do not necessarily indicate the types of elaborations (I: *payasan*, i.e., *kotekan*) that represent some of the most technically challenging aspects of a Balinese work. Like *balungan*, the *pokok* is not the mental map upon which a composition is based, but its post hoc abstraction. That is, the flowing, semi-improvised melody (I: *lagu*, B: *neliti*) as performed on the *ugal* or *trompong* is often identified as the core of a work's identity, from which the *pokok*, generally performed at the half-note level on the single octave *calung*, is derived. While the *pokok* neatly fits the economical technology of Balinese notation, to imagine it as a prescriptive form of notation is to reverse performance practice and composition itself.

By the early 1960s composers and faculty at KOKAR, including Wayan Beratha, were regularly using notation in both teaching and composition. But by the late 1980s Beratha seemed to have developed a wariness of the technology, viewing it as an aid to meet the state conservatory's increased expectations of compositional productivity, rather than quality (cf. Sadra 1991:54). The habitual inclusion of notation in student theses at the conservatory beginning in the late New Order functioned more as a demonstration of the successful assimilation of institutional *téori* than as meaningful forms of analysis or as artifacts of the composition process. However, most composers engaged in *musik kontemporer* during the *reformasi* adopted forms of notation as part of their process. Arsawijaya produced multi-staff scores (Example 6.1) transcribed from music-sequencing programs. Apparently as an artifact of the software display, these scores often combined Balinese end-weighted and Western front-weighted phrasing. Through this process Arsawijaya developed novel double *gong* forms punctuated by *gong* both at their beginnings and endings, functionally integrating Balinese *gongan* and Western meter (Example 6.2) [Track BV-6/1].[2]

Arsawijaya has spoken of the ways in which the intuitive time-box-unit notation system in the Fruity Loops sequencing program (pictured in Illustration 6.1), encourages users to compose visually as well as sonically.

EXAMPLE 6.1 Sang Nyoman Arsawijaya's prescriptive, multi-staff notation for a dance accompaniment (2010). Note front-weighted *gong* phrasing. Transcribed by Arsawijaya from composition sequenced in Fruity Loops.

---

[2] Yudane, Widnyana, and Alit began to explore similar structural concepts almost simultaneously.

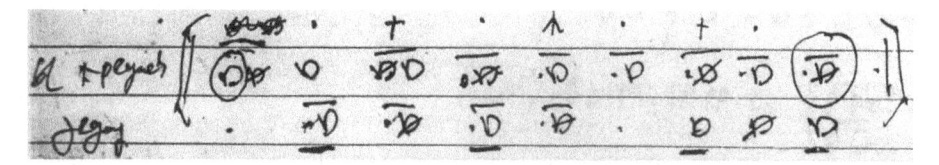

EXAMPLE 6.2 Sang Nyoman Arsawijaya's notation of a double *gong* structure for a dance accompaniment (2010). *Gongs* symbolized by circles.

Sometimes I create patterns as shapes in the notation box. It's easy to orchestrate this way and to create structures like sequences and canons. Of course, I quickly found that, without the limitations of human abilities, I could compose anything I could imagine. That sometimes becomes a problem. In composing my very *kontemporer kreasi baru Pinara Tunggah* for the 2009 PKB, I found I was trying to force the musicians to do some difficult, unnatural things that ended up taking up far too much rehearsal time and we had to cut them. (p.c. July 2010)

The problems Arsawijaya encountered are immediately obvious when comparing the sequenced and final live versions of the work. In the sequenced version, the complex opening passage that incorporates elements of canon as it descends from the high *kantil* through the *pemadé* was forbiddingly difficult for the musicians and is replaced in the live version by simpler material recycled from Arsawijaya's prior compositions. We

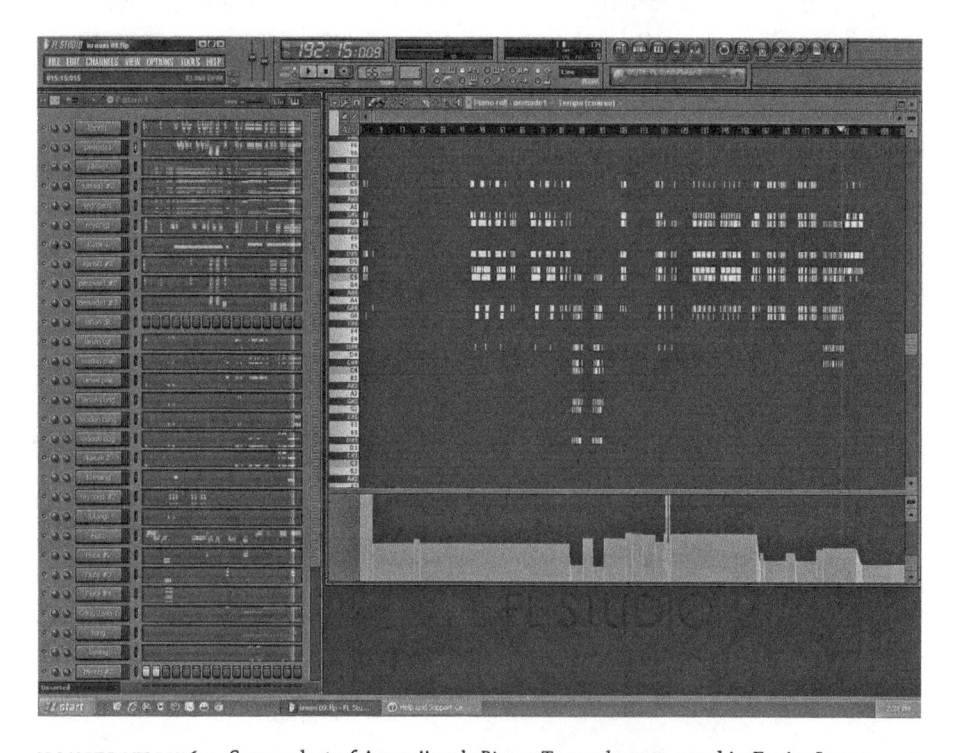

ILLUSTRATION 6.1 Screenshot of Arsawijaya's *Pinara Tunggah,* sequenced in Fruity Loops.

might also wonder what compositional consequences may arise from the combination of *gamelan* samples and equal-tempered flute and percussion patches used in the program [Tracks MK-6/1 and 6/2].

Notation encouraged the development of musical forms that might otherwise be difficult to imagine in a purely oral tradition. In their *musik kontemporer*, composers often eschewed the complex temporal and dynamic waves (I: *ombak*) characteristic of forms such as *gong kebyar* and which are highly difficult to represent in both Western and Balinese forms of notation. The prescriptive use of notation appears to have in some cases encouraged the development of complex, polyphonic, and polyrhythmic patterns. While composing his *kontemporer gender wayang* work *Aptiningulun* (2009), Gusti Komin Darta relied heavily on notation:

> I had ideas in my head that, at first, I couldn't play, so I wrote them down. And then I saw that there were gaps and structures in the notation that I didn't anticipate and that I began to develop and fill in. But then it became very complex and I had to study my own notation just to be able to play it! (p.c. March 2012)

As illustrated in Example 6.3, the beginning of the work immediately announces its *kontemporer* attributes. Rather than the open, sustained tone that marks the beginning of many overture works (B: *tabuh petegak*) of the *tradisi gender wayang* repertoire, *Aptiningulun* opens with a choked note followed by rhythmic phrases primarily, but not consistently, in a 7/8 (2+2+3) meter uncharacteristic of the *tradisi* repertoire [Track MK-6/3].

Ida Bagus Widnyana used notation to sketch out highly complex polyrhythmic forms for his *Trimbat* (2004). *Trimbat* is a conflation of the Balinese *tri* (three) and *embat* (tuning, or range). For this work Widnyana combined *gamelan* instruments from three differently tuned ensembles, producing eleven pitches per octave (see Table 6.1). For the work's final motif Widnyana developed a complex theme by cycling through all of the available pitches, producing a series of ascending chromatic (I: *kromatis*), cells. Using a multiple staff form of cipher notation, Widnyana was able to develop this pattern further. Inspired by the *pangider buana*, he assigned each instrument the eleven-note pattern: 11122233555 (666...) This 3-3-2-3 grouping pattern is then cycled throughout the five-note ambitus of each *gamelan* instrument with each cycle starting

EXAMPLE 6.3 Gusti Komin Darta. *Aptiningulun*, excerpt.

EX. 6.4 Ida Bagus Gede Widnyana. Trimbat, polyrhythm excerpt. (11:40). See Example 6.10 (measure 1) for the same pattern in Western notation.

Beat	*		*		*		*		*		*		*		*		*		*		*		*
calung 1		1		1		2		2		2	3		3		3	5		5	6		6		6	1		1
calung 2	1		1		1		2		2	3		3		3	5		5		5	6		6	1		1
calung 3	1		1		1		2		2		2	3		3	5		5		5	6		6		6	1
jeg. 1	1				2				3				5				6				1			
jeg. 2		1			2				3				5				6				1			
jeg. 3		1				2				3				5				6				1		

at a different place in the pattern. Given that the lowest common denominator of five and eleven is fifty-five, the pattern for a single set of instruments is long and complex:

[: 11122233555666111222333555666112223335556611122233355666 :]

Widnyana, pictured in Plate 6.1, then assigned this pattern to each of the differently tuned *gamelan* in a three (*gamelan*) against four (pulses per beat) phrasing. The melodic/rhythmic polyrhythm then becomes 3:4:11. Here the 4:3 counter-rhythm is highlighted by the *jegogan* playing dissonant clusters at the half-note level, thus expanding the polyrhythm to 165 *calung* tones against forty tones of the *jegogan* pattern. The phrase is not performed to its logical conclusion.[3] The result is a wall of sound, an incredibly complex form that through the sheer virtuosity and energy of the young players, is still exciting and listenable. Example 6.4 reproduces a fragment of Widnyana's prescriptive notation for the pattern [Track MK-6/4].

Although several Balinese composers—including Nyoman Windha, Ketut Gede Asnawa, Komang Astita, and Desak Madé Suarti Laksmi—had some facility with standard Western notation, only Yudane used it regularly to compose both new works for *gamelan* and works for Western contemporary ensembles. Mentored by the composer Jack Body while studying in New Zealand, Yudane has emerged as the first Balinese composer trained in *gamelan* traditions to have developed an oeuvre of modernist compositions for Western ensembles. Although Yudane occasionally transforms Balinese materials within these works, they are at times indistinguishable from those that might emerge from modernist composers anywhere. As seen in Example 6.5, passages from the second movement of his *Entering the Stream* (2010) for piano trio evoke the motor rhythms of *kotekan*, the intervalic structure of the *pélog* tuning system, and the reductive bouncing often heard in *gender wayang* repertoire, indicated in measure 151 as increasingly dense rhythmic patterns on the violin. Since returning to Bali from New Zealand in 2009 Yudane has worked closely with Alit and Arsawijaya through the

---

[3] Considering the highly complex polyrhythms involved, Widnyana discovered that it would take nearly three minutes, or a fourth of the total work, to realize a single iteration of the pattern.

144 | Radical Traditions

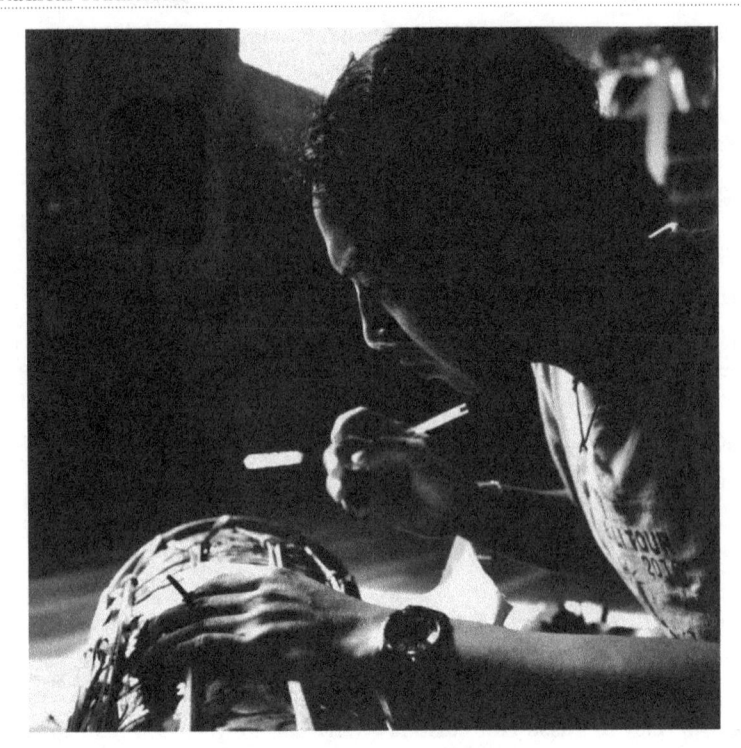

PLATE 6.1 Ida Bagus Gede Widnyana. Photo by Evan Gilman.

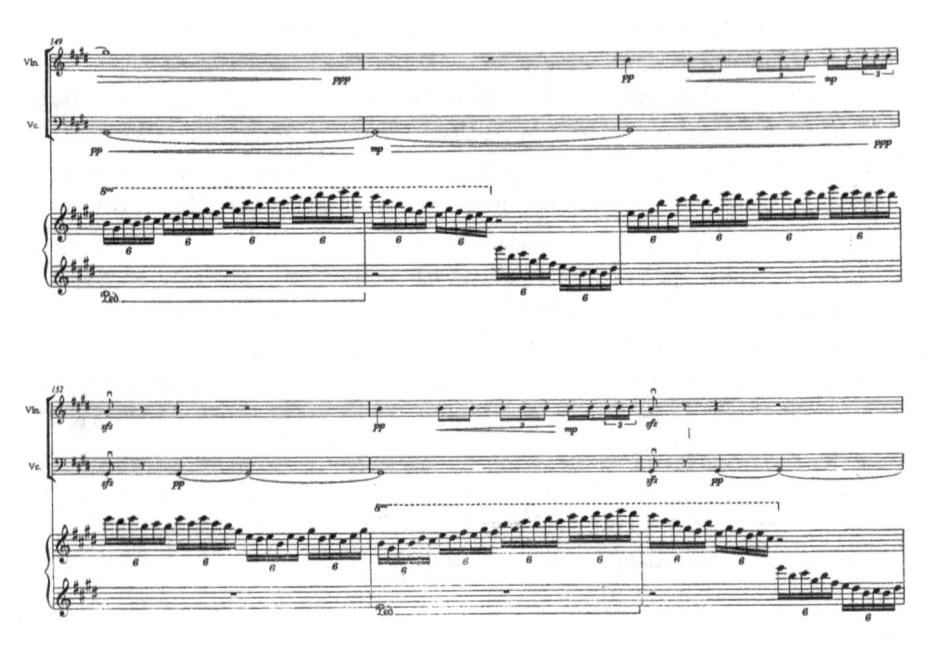

EXAMPLE 6.5 Wayan Gede Yudane. *Entering the Stream*, excerpt. Reprinted by permission of the publisher.

Wrdhi Swaram ensemble in Denpasar, a *sanggar* that grew out of the student ensemble Arsawijaya assembled to perform his *Geräusch*. Under Yudane's mentorship, several musicians in the ensemble have learned to read the Western notations he uses to compose, teach, and perform his new *gamelan* works [Track MK-6/5].

Ideologies of Intonation

The contemporary Balinese soundscape reverberates with a polyphony of differing tuning schemes. Aesthetic transformation can be read in the palimpsest of tuning scratches (B: *nyurutin*) left underneath *gamelan* keys. Like rings in a tree stump, these scorings reveal the life of a *gamelan* as it was tuned a few cents up, then back, then up again, adjusting to shifting tastes. The very material of *gamelan* (bronze, iron, bamboo, and wood), their various qualities, and the specific intonations they sound, intersect with social groupings and hierarchies. The instruments with which Balinese composers worked were indicative of a specific kind of community and personhood.

Like singers, each *gamelan* has a unique *embat* or tuning/timbrel quality. Even if a gongsmith refers to an older prototype when forging a new set, over time and successive retunings a *gamelan* will ideally develop a unique *embat* and personality, mirroring a human's increasing individualization from infant to adult. A *gamelan's embat* comes to represent an aural watermark for a community. *Gamelan* outline an auditory and social space corresponding to particular notions of territory primarily concerned with mutual acquaintance. Everyone knows what it sounds like to be home.

Gamelan tunings are not immutable, although they appear so, forged into solid, heavy metal slabs. They are an icon of a community and thus change with that community and its tastes. Poor-sounding instruments are humiliating to the collective and can cause shame. While old metal is often valued partly because it has previously been consecrated and stands as an integration of the past and present, instruments perceived as out of tune might be retuned or even melted down to be forged again, a process that often involves substantial intonational transformations.

Western discourses of intonation have represented a somewhat consistent tension between naturalists—those who would attempt to find a universal scale based on the harmonic partials of musical tones—and rationalists who slice the scale into mathematical subdivisions, tempering their system to accommodate the idiosyncrasies of human audition. Balinese ideologies of intonation are by and large not concerned with either approach, instead representing a much more contingent, variable, and individualistic paradigm. Whereas the highly abstract slicing of sound achieved by equal temperament is a totalizing ideology appealing to universality, Balinese *gamelan* has never followed a universal pitch standard; regional variety is valued even if certain tunings, such as Wayan Beratha's interpretation of *gamelan gong kebyar*, are hegemonic.

NOMENCLATURE

Some Balinese theorists suggest that seven-tone *pélog* and five-tone *slendro* are extracted from a prototypical, ancient scale-type lost to history. These theorists (primarily Sinti, Rembang, and Geriya) describe this system as encompassing seven, nine, or ten pitches.[4] An ancient unification of the two may be supported by the playful ambiguity between the two systems in Balinese *tembang* singing (Herbst 1997:37).[5] This contrasts with most Javanese theories which hold that the two systems are altogether different from one another, having distinct histories. Some Western theorists have suggested that the two scale types entered Indonesia at different historical periods (e.g., Hood 1988) and the distinction between *slendro* and *pélog* are sometimes compared to the two *diêu* of Vietnamese music, linking an origin for *slendro* and *pélog* to the prehistorical flow of Austronesian populations from mainland to insular Southeast Asia (Powers et al.). Widdess (1993) proposes a possible historical connection between South Indian *jatis* and the structure of *pathet* in Java; both incorporate contrasting pentatonic types drawn from a larger gamut. Most Western theorists followed Kunst's presumption that Balinese intonations should be linked to Java via Majapahit migrations and the presumed shared heritage of *gambuh*. Wallis, however, problematizes *gambuh*'s pedigree as Javanese (1980:43).

As expressed in pitch-mysticism illustrated in the *Prakempa*, a combined *pélog-slendro* ur-scale represents an indigenous platonic ideal. The theoretical unification of *pélog* and *slendro* is a mystical/theoretical desideratum, one that iconically recalls the ancient Balinese Hindu concept of *rwa bhineda*, or the principle of oppositions, in which the interaction of converse powers and attributes (e.g., male/female, heaven/earth, etc.) is believed to imbue the universe with life and dynamism. Within the *Prakempa*, *pélog* is characterized as male and *slendro* as female. The hybrid, ten-tone *slendro-pélog* system suggested in the *Prakempa* may represent a Balinese effort to localize Javanese intonational *téori* by imbuing these originally Javanese terms with arithmetic and mystical attributes resonant with Balinese Hinduism.[6] The continued theorization of the origins of extant tuning systems has encouraged intonational experiments in Balinese contemporary music since the late New Order.

---

[4] The seven-tone version of this prototypical scale is sometimes, as in the *Prakempa*, referred to as *genta pinara pitu*. How such a prototypical scale-type would differ, if it does, from contemporary seven-tone *pélog* is not clear.

[5] Richter (1992) strongly asserts that the association by foreign and Balinese theorists of the *gambuh* repertoire with the seven-tone *pélog* system is incorrect and that it should instead be conceptualized as a scale-type of ten notes potentially conceived as combining five-tone *slendro* with a five-tone *pélog*.

[6] However, questions abound: Is the archaic Balinese *pelok* described in the *Prakempa* and *Aji Gurnita* a five-tone system, and do modern Balinese seven-tone systems represent the combination of this ancient *pelok* with two borrowed *salendro* tones? If most Balinese theorists agree that the modern usage of the terms *slendro* and *pélog* are recent imports from Java, then what accounts for the reference to *salendro-pelok* in the *lontar* but not, apparently, in oral traditions? How old, in fact, are these two *lontar*? Why is it that Balinese composers and *gong* makers have expanded their conceptions of *pélog* to contain versions of *slendro*, but not the other way around, as is the case for contemporary Sundanese musicians? Weintraub describes the expansion of the *slendro gamelan* to a ten-tone system out of which various *pélog* subsets can be identified (2004:131).

INTROSPECTIVE INNOVATIONS: 1983–

By "introspective innovations" I refer to the development of new *gamelan*, new tunings, and new ways of talking about tunings that are self-consciously connected to prior repertoires and are imagined to represent an unbroken extension of *tradisi*. Gamelan makers and musicians have likely always experimented with new instrumental, orchestral, and intonational possibilities, but these experiments seem to have intensified after independence in 1945 and again during the New Order's development of the national arts infrastructure from the 1970s to 1990s. The most influential innovation of the past century was the development of the *gong kebyar* in the first decades of the twentieth century. Balinese composers' contentment with the five-tone *kebyar* system persisted for decades before seven-tone music captured their attention once again.

Balinese intonational innovations in the mid-1980s coincided with similar developments in Central Javanese and Sundanese *gamelan* traditions, and begin with Wayan Beratha's invention of the *gamelan genta pinara pitu* in 1983 and the *gamelan semara dana* in 1987, the latter encompassing the range of the seven-tone *semar pegulingan* and the five-tone *gong kebyar*. The effort to create a novel all-in-one *gamelan* appear to have first been proposed by the theorist, teacher, and composer Wayan Sinti in a *Bali Post* article published in 1981 in which he suggested that the government should underwrite the creation of a *gong gede saih pitu*. Although Sinti's concept was rooted in fears of cultural loss and an interest in preservation, Beratha seems to have adopted and transformed his proposal—through his invention of the *gamelan semara dana*—primarily to accompany new theatrical forms such as *sendratari*. Sinti eventually realized his goals in the creation of his *gamelan manikasanti* in 1994.

While Sinti and Beratha sought the unification of historical intonations and repertoires on a single hybrid ensemble, embodying the centralizing ethos of the New Order itself, other composers have developed new tunings and orchestras based upon the opposite impulse. Avoiding the creation of a universal scale-type or orchestra, they instead seek to create novel tunings inspired only loosely by historical models and directly guided by their personal *rasa*. For these composers the heart of Balinese intonational aesthetics does not lie in a prototypical scale-type but in contributing to the riot of intonational variety that Bali has historically enjoyed. Ida Bagus Granoka, a Brahman philosopher from Karangasem, founded the Bajra Sandhi ensemble in 1991 after moving to Denpasar. According to Granoka:

> When young Balinese composers talk of wanting to break free of rules (I: *pakem*) they are really referring to the aesthetics espoused at ISI. It is not as if ISI invented the idea of rules; they always existed in every village. But historically every village had their own *pakem*, their own aesthetic and way of doing things, including tuning *gamelan*. Today this individuality has to a large extent been replaced by the singular set of *pakem* developed in the conservatory that represents a combination of various village aesthetics that have been centralized, formalized, and ossified by ISI. One of the most obvious manifestations of this

has been the erasure of local unique tunings to be replaced by Beratha's interpretation of five-tone *kebyar*. (p.c. July 2009)

Granoka sought to create a unique seven-tone intonation that he referred to as *saih pitu* rather than *pélog*. By sidestepping modern, Javanese-derived *téori*, Granoka can imbue his *gamelan* with local authority and justify unique intervals divergent from officially sanctioned versions of the *pélog* scale-type. Rather than claiming to find a prototypical Balinese ur-scale through the reunification of extant ancient tunings, Granoka claims rights to the essence of Balinese tuning aesthetics by forging an idiosyncratic tuning based upon his own *rasa*.

Similar to Granoka's experiment, Dewa Ketut Alit's *gamelan salukat*, invented in 2007, is primarily intended as a medium for *musik kontemporer* works, but takes historical Balinese intonations, primarily *luang* and *slonding*, as its principle referent. Like Sinti's *manikasanti*, the *salukat* ensemble incorporates an extended seven-note gamut in all of its octaves and includes historical and modern instrument types, such as rare bamboo *caruk* instruments. Alit's compositional approach, however, is generally intended to "kill the seven-note polemic" (p.c. June 2009) by eschewing traditional five-tone modal structures and conceiving the gamut as a seven-tone palette rather than a scale with its attendant notions of pitch hierarchy.

The expansion of orchestras and scales in Bali is resonant with an aesthetic regime in which most things—offerings, ceremonies, dance costumes, homes—are imagined to be better the bigger they are to unambiguously express wealth, power, and authority.[7] By extending the intonation and range of their *gamelan*, composers can claim authority and control over a vast collection of ancient seven-tone repertoires. The extension into seven-tone (and beyond) scale-types must also be understood as a (sometimes implicit) reaction to the increasing encroachment of Western equal temperament.[8]

EXTROSPECTIVE EXPERIMENTS

By extrospective experiments I mean innovations that facilitate intercultural interaction through the incorporation of foreign intonations.[9] In the late 1990s the Balinese guitarist Wayan Balawan retuned several of his *gamelan* instruments to an

---

[7] Weintraub (2004) suggests the same concerning the expansion of Sundanese instruments in the late 1980s. The enormous *gamelan gong gede* created by the Balinese musician and actor Ketut Suanda represents an extreme case. Flush with cash from a successful career as a clown, Suanda commissioned a *gamelan* so comically oversized and heavy that many musicians refused to play it, knowing that they would be called upon to move it for performances. When asked why he no longer joined Suanda's ensemble, the composer Madé Subandi cited health reasons: "My back can't take it!" (p.c. July 2009).

[8] Alit discussed his intention to retune the paired tuning in the *gamelan salukat* from an interval of 8hz to roughly 15hz. The effect would produce a fast beating effect, and the pitches would be theoretically far enough apart to be used as distinct rather than paired pitches, thus producing a fourteen-tone scale and "outdoing" the Western-tempered chromatic scale (p.c. July 2010).

[9] Sumarsam describes earlier colonial-era combinations of Western instruments and *gamelan* in Surakarta (Sumarsam 1995:63-83).

equal-tempered B-flat major scale, eschewing paired tuning. According to Balawan, tuning *gamelan* instruments to Western standards, in the "easy key" of B flat, facilitates interaction with Western instruments and instrumentalists. Within the political economy of the Balinese performing arts this invests Balawan with cultural authority through fluency with global and Western musical systems and increases the potential for lucrative collaborations, record deals, and performance tours abroad. The same impulse inspired Gus Teja's 2006 creation of a set of chromatic bamboo and iron instruments, pictured in Plate 6.2.

In 2009 the Arti Foundation in Denpasar, directed by the composer and director Kadek Suardana, created a set of nine-tone *diatonis slonding*.[10] Suardana's instruments adhere to equal temperament in their lower octave only while the second octave display the stretching typical of Balinese traditional intonations.[11] Through the combination of stretched octaves, the maintenance of paired tuning, and the combination of *diatonis* instruments with both Western instruments and traditionally tuned *gamelan* instruments in the same ensemble, Suardana's experiment represents a complex intonational negotiation between Balinese and Western aesthetics and serves as an example of the mutation of the diatonic "virus" into the Balinese *diatonis* tuning system.

Since 2005 the composer and gongsmith Wayan Widia has created or retuned several *semara dana* sets to a *diatonis* tuning, one that approaches, but does not completely adhere to, a D major diatonic scale while retaining stretched octaves and paired tuning. In 2008 Nyoman Windha retuned his seven-tone *semar pegulingan* to closely adhere to a B major equal-tempered scale. His set, tuned using an electronic tuner rather than traditional aural techniques, eschews stretched octaves and closely adheres to Western tunings in all octaves.[12] Retuning facilitated a collaboration in 2009 with a symphony orchestra in Jakarta directed by the composer Dwiki Dharmawan. Navigating the intonational negotiations that must be performed when combining Western equal-tempered instruments with traditional *gamelan* tunings often requires extensive face-to-face rehearsal and extended performance techniques. Windha's collaboration with Dharmawan—entitled *Soul of Indonesia*—included only one rehearsal, preceded by extensive file-sharing and correspondence through e-mail. Both Windha and Dharmawan felt that the collaboration would have only been possible with a *gamelan* that adhered to Western tunings [Track MK-6/6].

In 2005, while teaching in Seattle, Wayan Sinti built a *gamelan* similarly intended to facilitate cultural interaction but that eschewed Western tunings altogether. Instead, Sinti developed an idiosyncratic nine-tone system he termed *gamelan siwa nada*. Like *manikasanti*, this system could approximate all known Balinese repertoires but also, he claimed, allow for the performance of various world art musics (*Bali Post*, July 8, 2007).

---

[10] The *saron* were tuned to: d, e-, e, f, g, a, b-, b, c, encompassing a two-octave range.
[11] Interestingly, neither Suardana nor the tuner was aware of this; both thought the tuning faithfully adhered to equal temperament.
[12] While exhibiting paired tuning the ensemble incorporates a beating rate slower than would be expected of a modern *gong kebyar* or *semara dana*.

PLATE 6.2 Gus Teja's *kromatis tingklik*. Photo by the author.

In the *siwa nada* ensemble the expansionist ideology represented by earlier innovations reaches its ultimate logical (although not yet practical) realization; while *gamelan* such as the *semara dana* and *manikasanti* can represent all known Balinese repertoires, the *gamelan siwa nada*, Sinti maintains, can approximate all known musics. In a 2008 Bali Arts Festival performance featuring his American students, Sinti arranged various Balinese, American, and Japanese musics for the *siwa nada*, including themes from Dvorak's *New World Symphony*. It is somewhat ironic, but certainly purposeful, that the iconoclastic intonation of the *gamelan siwa nada* prohibits any straightforward combination with Western equally tempered instruments. While the ensemble can incorporate a wide range of foreign material, it will nevertheless always *appear* completely traditional.[13]

HOMOGENIZATION?

Beyond awareness of the first partial—often the octave—*gamelan* tuners do not recognize, have a terminology for, or attempt to tune the partials of *gamelan* instruments.

---

[13] See Wakeling (2010:199) for a detailed discussion of Sinti's process and philosophy in tuning *gamelan siwa nada*.

That bronze *gamelan* keys and chimes produce inharmonic partials is likely one reason why traditional Balinese tuners and theorists never developed or appealed to a concept of universal intonation based upon simple ratios related to harmonic partials, as did their Western counterparts. However, while the rational subdivisions of equal temperament have come to represent the alienating aspects of civilization for some Western composers, many Balinese composers have come to value the striated space of equal temperament for its predictability and transferability, symbolizing to many upward social mobility, progress, complexity, and cosmopolitanism.

Over the past decade, Balinese notions of in-tune-ness also appear to have converged upon a Western model. Some composers have attempted to narrow the pitch tolerances of *gamelan* intonations especially in terms of non-fixed-pitch instruments such as *suling* and *rebab*. The young *musik kontemporer* composer Ari Hendrawan was adamant in his defense of Western intonations, often referring to Balinese tunings as *palsu* or *fales* (I), false or out of tune. According to Hendrawan:

> I work with many *suling* players, but few of them understand issues of tuning. I push my *suling* and *rebab* players to be able to completely control the intonation on their instruments, and I don't allow them to switch instruments, as they are not made to any standard in Bali. (p.c. Hendrawan, June 2009)

Hendrawan has constructed flutes tuned to Western standards and intensely rehearses his musicians, disciplining them to manipulate their embouchure and employ half-fingerings so that they can match pitch within Western tolerances [Track BV-6/2].

Changing intonational ideologies are a metaphor for and a manifestation of cross-cultural encounters brought about through processes of globalization. Within this encounter, intonational knowledge represents a special power, one that requires guarding lest it be lost. The power to interface authoritatively with Western cultural codes is profound; it must be forged, controlled, and sometimes hidden. A renowned young composer and *suling* maker often provided slightly out of tune *diatonis* instruments to colleagues engaged in intercultural projects, hiding accurately tuned instruments at home for use in his own collaborations.

The Materials of *Musik Kontemporer*: Markedness, Topics, and Musical Change

Changing technologies—new forms of notation, computer-based composition, new instruments and intonations—facilitated the incorporation and development of new materials in *musik kontemporer*. These new materials marked the form as a site of rapid change in Balinese expressive culture. In this section I borrow concepts of *markedness* and *topic* from linguistics (via Western musicology), arguing that while *musik kontemporer* exhibits transformative processes similar to those found in other Balinese forms, it incorporates its materials from a much broader palette of possibilities. I suggest that the heteroglossic play of heterogeneous topics in *musik kontemporer* is a sonic cartography through which composers express novel spatial and temporal imaginations.

MARKEDNESS

Form opens up the possibility of transgression. (Luhmann 2000:28)

Following the linguists Greimas and Shapiro, Hatten describes musical markedness as the "valuation given to difference" (2004a:34). Differentiation produces an asymmetrical signifying system in which one element of a pair is marked and serves as a figure to the ground of an unmarked term which occupies a narrower, more specific expressive range. In English, cow is unmarked as referring to any animal of the species; bull, referring narrowly to the male, is marked. In the Western classical style the more common major scale, capable of a wider field of expression (ibid.), was unmarked against minor.

Markedness leads to stylistic change. Asymmetry allows at each new branching a niche for new entities, creating a slot for unstable novelties. Marked tokens that function as anomalies from a type can eventually converge to forge a new type in which previously variant features become invariant. This may lead to the development of new stylistic resources within a genre, the creation of new genres, or even the emergence of new kinds of music.

As an example, Hatten discusses the Picardy third in which the marked use of the major third on the tonic of a minor key eventually became stylistically viable enough to allow its substitution in later Beethoven by chords of further remove. Komang Astita's (1979) composition *Gema Eka Dasa Rudra* provides a similar example of stylistic expansion through markedness. In twentieth-century Bali, the *kebyar* ensemble became unmarked through its ubiquity, effectively censoring older seven-tone repertoires through repletion. As a consequence, the five-tone *selisir* mode associated with the ensemble—and mono-modal works generally—became unmarked. Astita's works followed on the heels of the resuscitation of *gambuh* through its transference at the conservatory to *gamelan semar pegulingan*. As illustrated in Example 6.6 below, Astita combined multiple five-tone modes borrowed from the *gambuh* repertoire. The languorous *pengawak* section alternates from *tembung* (mm. 5-13) to *selisir* (mm. 14-16). This once-rare technique has since become commonplace.

The aesthetic hegemony of the conservatory gradually functioned to render as unmarked the tunings, *gong* forms, elaboration techniques and performance styles practiced at the institution. Composers could take as their starting point for experimentation the unmarked pair of any of these categories. The *kebyar* proper, the a-metrical, unison display of virtuosity that hailed the emergence of the form, developed in the beginning of the twentieth century as a hypermarked intrusion upon the kinds of musical temporality of earlier styles. By the *reformasi*, the *kebyar* technique was unmarked and it had become a sign of *kontemporer*-ness to begin a piece with metrical periodicities.

TOPICS

By ignoring semantic meaning, formalist analysis may provide an incomplete perspective of a musical event. Newcomb's (1984) analysis of Schumann's second symphony

EXAMPLE 6.6 Komang Astita. *Gema Eka Dasa Rudra, pengawak.*

demonstrated that standard formalist analysis may suggest structural incoherence while a semantic reading, such as a narrative interpretation, may better demonstrate the way a work is put together. A formalist analysis of *musik kontemporer* compositions such as Asnawa's *Kosong,* Astita's *Gema Eka Dasa Rudra,* and more recent works including Madé Suanda's *Boreh* (2001) makes little sense without recourse to a temporal, narrative interpretation that recognizes the deeply theatrical character of such works. The musical topic, as analyzed by Ratner (1980), Agawu (1991), and Tenzer (2000) is a similarly semantic approach, one that recognizes and values the extramusical meanings attached to specific musical motifs, be it the fanfare and march of the classic style or the reference to *gambangan* in *gong kebyar.*

The topic is typically a short musical passage that triggers clear associations with styles, genres, and expressive meanings (Hatten 2004a:2); it is a musical figure associated with extramusical experience determined by cultural convention. Musical indices of ceremony can be present in otherwise secular forms such as *gong kebyar* through the presence of topics referencing sacred forms. While topics may appear with dense

EXAMPLE 6.7 *Leluangan* topic.

richness in expressions such as *gong kebyar* and *musik kontemporer,* they can never amount to a lexicon and do not coalesce into coherent syntagms as do the words of sentences. The identification of topics cannot amount to a musical syntax but helps us understand the deep meaning and layers of richness informed listeners derive from performances.

Tradisi Topics

Gong kebyar composers drew extensively upon topics from older forms, such as *gambang, luang, batel,* and *gilak,* daringly juxtaposing them in an assemblage in which topical materials were pulled from the totality of their original contexts to evoke new meanings. For instance, as deployed in *gong kebyar,* informed listeners might hear in the *leluangan* topic (Example 6.7) a resonance of the sacred, esoteric *luang* ensemble of Singapadu village and its attendant affect of sadness (p.c. Sudirana, October 2010). For younger listeners, unfamiliar with *luang* as a distinct, borrowed topic, such affective resonance may be weaker. For novices, including most Western listeners, the *leluangan* topic would likely register simply as *kebyar,* its original reference having been completely laundered. For them its later incorporation into *musik kontemporer* might even suggest *kebyar*-ness rather than *luang*-ness. To more informed listeners it might suggest the complex resonances of *luang* through the filter of *kebyar* potentially to be ironically commented upon again within *musik kontemporer*. While Tenzer (2000) describes the presence of topics in *kebyar* as a kind of intertextuality reaching out to the prior meanings that adhere in the genres they suggest, we may also wonder to what extent *kreasi baru* and *musik kontemporer* work to strip these topics of their distinct meanings into a freer play of signs, especially for younger generations.

In some *kreasi baru* and *musik kontemporer* contexts, topics borrowed from older *tradisi* and *klasik* repertoire can function as sonic skeuomorphs, making the new feel reassuringly familiar. As exemplified in graphical user interfaces by the realistically textured buttons that audibly click when you press them, the skeuomorph demonstrates the ways in which the social and psychological disruption of innovation can be ameliorated by replication. According to Hayles: "the skeuomorph looks to the past and the future, simultaneously reinforcing and undermining both. It calls into play a psychodynamic that finds the new more acceptable when it recalls the old that it is in the process of displacing and finds the traditional more comfortable when it is presented in a context that reminds us we can escape from it into the new" (1998:17). Subandi suggested the same in discussing the relative balance of new and topical elements from *tradisi* repertoire in his *kreasi baru:* "I often want to be very *kontemporer* in my *kreasi baru* for the PKB, but sometimes the local organizers complain and so I might include some patterns from *gender wayang* or *klasik kebyar*, for example, and that makes them feel more comfortable" (p.c. July 2010). Sonic skeuomorphs function as the regulation valves of stylistic change, allowing composers to fine-tune their relationship to audiences and patrons. Although they can make a composition appear more user-friendly, sonic skeuomorphs in innovative works may have radically different meanings from their original contexts.

Foreign Topics

Alongside the rich topical repertoire inherited from *kebyar*, of which all appeared indigenous, composers engaged in *musik kontemporer* identified a second class of new topics understood as foreign imports.[14] The incorporation of non-Balinese topics, those imagined to be borrowed from and to evoke specific foreign peoples and places, arose alongside a discourse of multiculturalism and demographic transformations that included more tourists, expatriates, and internal migrants. Such borrowings are present in earlier compositions—as in Beratha's transformation of Sulawesian Akkarena drumming in his *Gesuri*—but might have been purposefully concealed or heavily laundered through elaboration.[15] In contrast, foreign topics in *reformasi*-era *musik kontemporer* and *kreasi baru* often attracted attention to their very foreignness.[16]

Composers often referred to foreign topics as a *virus*. To me this seemed a perfectly appropriate term to describe relatively self-contained bits of musical style easily detached from original contexts and mutated through the semiosis of musical interculturalism. Unlike otherwise *tradisi* material, which was often perceived automatically and unconsciously, foreign viruses made themselves known to consciousness; their novelty demanded attention. Some foreign viruses had a kind of phylogenetic inertia; they were more likely to persist, making appearances in numerous compositions over time. The diminutions of Carnatic rhythmic patterns, the compound patterns of djembe drumming, Western contrapuntal forms, and so on, flowed into *musik kontemporer*, sometimes retaining enough of their original structure to make them recognizable to listeners from their original contexts. Some topics manifested not as literal forms of quotation but as more general idiomatic resemblances, a vague sound character, recalling Heile's concept of "perceptual representations" (2004:74). Here foreignness is represented positively through the aesthetic interaction of the Balinese and their others; foreignness is domesticated and contained by Balinese aesthetic systems, providing salutary contributions without overrunning the composition—an

---

[14] McPhee described Balinese music, specifically referencing *kebyar*, as completely indigenous: "While Balinese pictorial art has been sentimentally nursed and corrupted by romantic Westerners, Balinese music is still something created for a Balinese audience alone, uncontaminated by foreign suggestion" (1949: 277). I remain skeptical, however. Foreign materials likely entered as topics that later became laundered through the *kebyar* machine.

[15] See Sadra (1991:62-63, 105) for a discussion of Beratha's borrowing materials from West Java, Sulawesi, Lombok, and other areas.

[16] For examples of laundered foreign materials, consider the use during the New Order of Javanese *gerong* melodies by Nyoman Windha and the incorporation of Western vocal music and Japanese popular music (*enka*) in the *gender wayang* repertoire of Sukawati (Heimarck 2003).

idealized representation of cultural tourism in which groups arrive to stimulate local economies without overwhelming the cultural or ecological landscape.

Named foreign topics included: *India*, *ngejaz* (I), in a jazz style; *minimalis* (I), minimalism; *ngerok* (I), in a rock style; *Afrika* (I), Africa; *kanon* (I), cannon; *taiko* (Japanese drumming); *konterpoin* (I), counterpoint; *orkes* (I), orchestra, referring to *suling* arrangements imagined to imitate Western wind ensembles; *diatonis* (I), diatonic tuning or seven-tone scales; *harmonis* (I), three part harmony; *kromatis* (I), chromaticism. The topic *Tenzer* (Michael Tenzer) referred to the subdivision of the pulse into five, rather than the normal four, subdivisions, a technique evident in Tenzer's *Banyuari* (1992) for *gamelan gong kebyar*.

Arsawijaya referred to the *virus improvisasi* (I), improvisation, as a form of complete freedom that appealed to Western forms of non-idiomatic improvisation as opposed to the highly restricted forms of improvisation performed by the *suling* in *tradisi* contexts (p.c. Arsawijaya, July 2010).[17] In his score for *Geräusch* (excerpted in Example 6.8), Arsawijaya uses an abstract symbol to indicate passages of free improvisation (*improvisasi bebas*) to be performed on the *gong*, using a metal grinder.

The topic *konterpoin*, as in Arsawijaya's *Pinara Tunggah* (2009), represented varying degrees of independence between multiple melodic lines—an approach that might

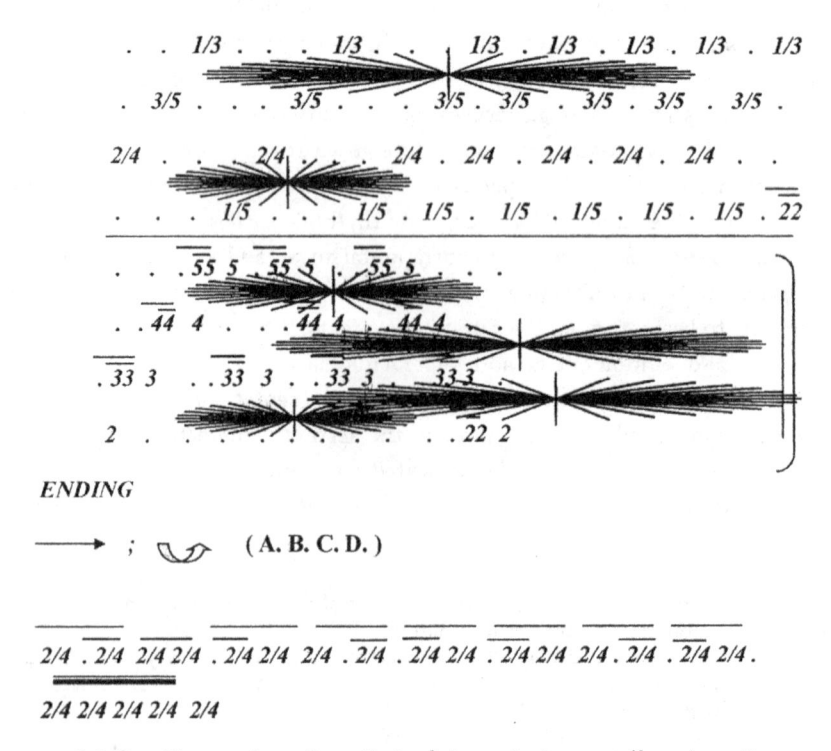

EXAMPLE 6.8 Sang Nyoman Arsawijaya. *Geräusch*, *improvisasi* excerpt (from Arsawijaya 2005).

---

[17] See Gray (2011) for a discussion of improvisation in *tradisi* styles, primarily in *gamelan gender wayang*.

not be recognized as strict counterpoint by Western composers. As illustrated in Example 6.9, this manifests primarily in repeated cells performed on the *suling* flutes in triple meter, followed by a phrase in 4/4 performed on the *jublag*. This texture orients attention horizontally and allows Arsawijaya to disregard the *empat* harmonies (approximating the Western fifth) favored in *tradisi* repertoire. The exact harmonic relationship between lines is, according to Arsawijaya, not tightly controlled as in

EXAMPLE 6.9A–C Sang Nyoman Arsawijaya. *Pinara Tunggah*, konterpoin excerpt. (*Continued*)

EXAMPLE 6.9 continued. [Track MK-6/2]

Western counterpoint but is a happenstance (I: *kebetulan*) consequence of the layering of different melodies.

The topic *kromatis* referred to the construction of intonationally dense works rather than equal-tempered chromaticism, impossible on the *gamelan*. Widnyana's *Trimbat* combines instruments from three differently tuned five-tone *selisir pélog gamelan*: the lowest set a *gong gede* from the village of Tulikup in Eastern Gianyar; the middle set from a *gong kebyar* from *Pengosekan,* and the highest set of instruments from a *pelegongan* ensemble from Ubud. Widnyana used only the *jegogan* and *calung* pairs from each of the *gamelan* with the addition of three *gongs*, for a total of fifteen instruments and thirteen players. The distance between the bottom pitches of the lowest and highest *jegogan* was roughly a minor third; from this Widnyana was able to produce eleven pitches per octave.[18] Figure 6.1 illustrates the closest Western equivalent pitches. As seen in Example 6.10, Widnyana takes advantage of this expanded gamut to create complex patterns of alternating cells (first staff), expanded melodic patterns (second staff), and dense harmonies (third staff).

Foreign topics flowed within a local field of meaning that had little to do with their ostensible origins. Similar to the representation of ethnic others in the Hollywood soundtrack, such references sometimes reduced entire groups, nations, or continents to stereotyped musical passages. These topics were not faithful reproductions of the groups or traditions from which they were imagined to be borrowed but were 'representations as' (Wakeling 2010:184 after Goodman 1968:27–31), shaping reality for particular audiences, in particular contexts, and for particular reasons. Composers such

---

[18] Because the instruments included *ngumbang-ngisep* pairs Widnyana actually had access to twenty-two pitches per octave; however, he maintained the traditional Balinese practice of always playing paired pitches together.

FIGURE 6.1 Three *gamelan* used in Widnyana's *Trimbat*.

Key Number	Closest Western Pitch
1	D#
2	E
3	F#
4	A#
5	B

Key Number	Closest Western Pitch
1	D
2	E-Flat
3	F
4	A
5	B-Flat

Key Number	Closest Western Pitch
1	B
2	C#
3	E-Flat
4	F#
5	G

Saih Cenik. Highest *Gamelan - Pelegongan* Ubud.
Saih Madya. Middle *Gamelan - Gong Kebyar* Pengosekan.
Saih Gede. Lowest *Gamelan – Gong Gede* Tulikup.

as Yudane, Alit, and Arsawijaya often discussed the incorporation of *kanon, konterpoin,* and *kromatis* as signs of compositional maturity and cosmopolitanism. *Ngejaz,* favored by Nyoman Windha after his experiences studying at Mills College (2002–04), evoked a Jakartan kind of cosmopolitanism, suggesting the cultural preoccupations of the national elite. Imitating Japanese *taiko* drumming by placing large *kendang* in vertical stands, as in Suanda's *Boreh* (2001) and Hendrawan's recital composition (2001), displayed composers' upwardly mobile social and aesthetic links to Japanese culture and artists.

Topics inspired by Indian classical music were the most popular during my research. They recalled a history of colonial-era intercultural interactions between Indian and Indies artists of which contemporary composers seemed unaware. Subandi often incorporated the rhythmic diminutions characteristic of Carnatic compositions (termed *mora*), which Subandi and his cohort referred to as *pohon* (I), tree, and the call-and-response patterns of *jugalbandi*. Example 6.11 illustrates alternating, reductive call-and-response patterns performed between *pélog* and *slendro gender* in Subandi's *Gender Romantis* (2009), which Subandi referred to as *jugalbandi*. In several

EXAMPLE 6.10 Ida Bagus Gede Widnyana. *Trimbat, kromatis* excerpt. [Track MK-6/4]

EXAMPLE 6.11 Madé Subandi. *Gender Romantis, jugalbandi* and *pohon* excerpt. Left hand only. [Track MK-6/7]

EXAMPLE 6.12 Agus Teja. *Senggama*, excerpt. [Track MK-5/1]

of Teja's works Indian topics manifested as imitations on the *suling* of the ornamentations and slides performed on the *bansuri* flute and the use of odd metrical cycles as in his *Senggama* (2006), illustrated in Example 6.12.[19] Sudarta idolized the vocal style of the famous Pakistani qawwali singer Nusrat Fateh Ali Khan and incorporated and transformed elements of the style in his *Kidung Mpu Tantular* (2008), illustrated in Example 6.13. In this work Sudarta combined lyrics in Sanskrit with a vocal style associated with Islamic cultures to symbolize a philosophy of cultural and religious tolerance. Younger composers sometimes included more obvious borrowings, as in Kadek Astawa's incorporation of *solkattu* drumming syllables in his *Keta* (2010) [Track BV-6/3].

Etnik Topics

A third class of topics, related to those described above, represent regional and national groups described in *reformasi* Bali as *etnik* (I), ethnic. These include the musics of marginalized groups such as the Aga and its *slonding* ensemble; local Muslim populations symbolized by the *terompet* shawm, *rebana* frame drum, and Sasak melodies; Chinese populations symbolized by plucked zithers, the *gong beri* ensemble, and *erhu* fiddle; and peripheral populations such as those in the far west of the island represented by the massive bamboo *jegog* ensemble. Composers who incorporated *etnik* topics were rarely native performers of these musics but may

---

[19] This material was later transformed and recycled in his 2007 festival *kreasi baru Bara Dwaja*.

EXAMPLE 6.13 Gusti Putu Sudarta, *Kidung Mpu Tantular*, qawwali excerpt. [Track MK-4/3]

have developed rudimentary ability in them through their experience of the conservatory's multicultural curriculum. Through topical representation, groups such as the Aga, whose cultural expressions were previously marginalized as rustic in comparison to the high cultures of the central plains Majapahit Balinese, were incorporated into a pluralistic notion of Balinese society that recapitulated the New Order's aestheticized celebration of ethnicity.

Sadra contrasted the democratic, grass roots, and explorative incorporation of *etnik* materials during the *reformasi* against the centralized and exploitative incorporation of regional expressions during the New Order, exemplified in genres such as *musik nusantara* and the forced combinations that sometimes appeared at the PKM (p.c. September 2003). *Kontemporer* compositional approaches that embodied the former, explorative aspects—what Sadra dubbed *transmedium* composition—would incorporate and transform *etnik* materials in ways that fostered egalitarian sonic and social interactions across perceived boundaries. Such interactions were vital, Sadra believed, in the formulation of a new post-totalitarian civil society in which new collectivities needed to be forged within multicultural (and often urban) spaces to ensure successful democratic reform and resist ethnonational conflict (see McGraw 2013a) [Track BV-6/4].[20]

Sadra's *transmedium* concept is exemplified in both Arsana's *Moha* and Windha's *Lekesan*. In *Moha* Arsana incorporated a topic he referred to as *Cina* to represent the Sino-Indonesian minority attacked during the dissolution of the New Order. This topic is represented through pentatonic melodies that he referred to as a "Chinese-esque *slendro*" (*slendro ke-Cina-an*) performed on a keyboard using a zither

---

[20] The intersection of *etnik* and *kontemporer* arts is considered extensively in *Gong* 28, 2001.

EXAMPLE 6.14 Wayan Gede Arsana. *Moha, Cina* excerpt. [Track MK-4/1]

EXAMPLE 6.15 Nyoman Windha. *Lekesan,* Sasak melody excerpt. [Track MK-4/4]

patch (Example 6.14). In Windha's *Lekesan*, a topic he called *Sasak* (referring to Islamic communities from Lombok) is intended to represent the musical cultures of various Muslim populations in multicultural Denpasar (Example 6.15).

MUSICAL CHANGE

By 2004 several senior faculty members at the conservatory, principally Wayan Dibia, Wayan Beratha, and Wayan Sinti, heard much *kreasi baru* and *musik kontemporer* as a farraginous mixture. They complained that these forms, as demonstrated by student recitals and Bali Arts Festival performances, had become overloaded with materials and were losing any sense of compositional cohesion or performative nuance through a frantic attempt to engage with, it seemed, everything.[21] Critiques by elders recalled colonial-era analyses by both Western and Balinese critics of *gong kebyar*—that form that Dibia, Beratha, and Sinti upheld as the ideal against which *musik kontemporer* appeared to them as a deterioration. A generation earlier, McPhee similarly disdained *kebyar* as simply a potpourri of the classics, illogically put together (1942:4), while the Balinese author Balyson lamented the flagging use of *gong gede* for *kebyar,* characterizing the latter as faddish and capricious (1934) [Track BV-6/5].

What critics of both *kebyar* and *musik kontemporer* appeared to be reacting against was a proliferation of *meaning* as much as materials—a complex heteroglossic play of topics seemingly out of coordination with previous life experience. If the bringing

---

[21] Dibia complained that "everything is overfull and too difficult; composition has become narcissistic" (p.c. September 2001). Beratha despaired that the new works were beyond his ability to hear (p.c. October 2001). Sinti suggested that new works did not display unity but were merely a random combination of ingredients (p.c. September 2002). Their comments bear an uncanny similarity to Zhdanov's social realist critique of the modernist avant-garde (see Attali 1985:8).

together of diverse topics in *musik kontemporer* appeared as information overload or poor composition to older observers, to younger composers such topics combined as a way to come to terms with the increasingly dominant discourse and experiences of *globalisasi* (I), globalization. The fusion, or collision, of topical referents, for example, *slonding* alongside *kanon* (as in Arsawijaya's *Chanda Klang*, 2007), formed tropes in which new, unpredictable meanings could emerge.

For many composers and listeners, *musik kontemporer* mapped Bali's geographic placement in a global aesthetic network and evoked a sense of temporal simultaneity. It brought together topics (if not actual instruments) deemed ancient (B: *kuno*, e.g., *slonding*), classic (B: *madya*, e.g., *semar pegulingan*) and *moderen* (e.g., *kebyar*) and placed local, regional, and foreign topics side by side. *Musik kontemporer* represented the spatial imaginations of Balinese composers during the *reformasi* era—a musical cartography in which composers placed their others and their forebears alongside themselves.

7 Ombak

TIME, ENERGY, AND HOMOLOGY IN THE ANALYSIS OF BALINESE MUSIC

JULY 2009. DEWA *Ketut Alit and I sat in plush new seats in the air-conditioned Ksirarnawa hall at the Bali Arts Festival watching a Japanese* gamelan *ensemble perform* kebyar *classics. Invited dignitaries, conservatory administrators, and elderly maestros sat in front of us while a more rambunctious audience of Balinese families filled the seats in back. The Japanese performed challenging works with a speed and precision that exceeded the skill of any foreign ensemble either of us had previously seen. I was hatching a tour to Bali with the* gamelan *from New York City, but this performance left me feeling defeated. Surely we could not apply the same level of discipline to achieve such exacting standards. Could Alit, if he closed his eyes, even tell that this was a foreign ensemble? "Immediately," he answered without pause. "We can always tell which groups are really Balinese, even if the repertoire is simple. Balinese groups have* bayu *(B), energy, and perform with* ombak *(I/B), waves. Foreign groups are best at playing the aspects of the music that they can write down. But when it comes to sounding Balinese,* kotekan bukan esensi gambelan" *(I), interlocking is not the essence of* gamelan. *I realized I had been listening to, teaching, and composing* gamelan *too often as if from a Western transcription, prioritizing the discrete striation of "the notes" over the smoothness of temporal and dynamic flows. But it was also clear from Alit's own work that time and energy were transforming in* musik kontemporer. *The ethnomusicologist in me wondered what this implied about transformations in Balinese society more broadly.*

In this chapter I shift temporarily from ethnographic to formal analysis to consider some of the structural features that distinguish *musik kontemporer* from other forms. Here I am interested in music as a process—a movement in time—rather than as a thing in space, I am not concerned with the formalist notion that music's most profound meanings lie hidden in the deepest depths of musical structure. I do not seek to reveal the structure of composition (often the score or transcription) over the flux performance. Such a divide makes little sense within the context of Balinese music, which remains a primarily oral tradition. In this chapter I will simply slide a few of many possible filters before your eyes/ears to draw out important points difficult to express in standard Western notation.[1]

After dealing with the problems of Western notation and the ways in which it tends to distort or erase important aspects of Balinese music, I introduce the Balinese aesthetic and theoretical concept of *ombak* (I), wave, as the primary analytical frame of the chapter. Referring to both temporal and dynamic flux, these waves produce a temporal narrative that is not accounted for in analyses that characterize Balinese music as cyclical. I analyze the ways in which the unique temporal and dynamic profiles of *tradisi* forms do not align with prior theorizations of musical time generally and I argue that *musik kontemporer* is differentiated from *tradisi* forms by a tendency towards more restrained temporal profiles. This is partly due to composers' focus upon instrumental works and their eschewing the temporal logic of traditional colotomy. I then compare an analysis of dynamics in Balinese music with theoretical models developed for the Western repertoire. In traditional repertoires, colotomy, temporality, and dynamics function as an interwoven ribbon (Repp 1998) that only occasionally unravels. In many *tradisi* genres, this ribbon tightens under the gravitational pull of the *gong* but is comparatively slack in much *musik kontemporer* repertoire, occasionally unraveling altogether when traditional colotomy is absent.

I conclude this chapter with a consideration of ethnomusicology's historic tendency to identify homological relationships between music and extra-musical phenomena. The description of Balinese music as iconic of cyclical cosmological beliefs and a static society has served as a classic example of such a model. But too often homologies are more salient for the ethnographer than the informant. I argue that the case of *ombak* offers a limited heuristic model for understanding the relationship between the musical and the extramusical.

Problems with Notation

Many Balinese musicians commented that their greatest pedagogical challenge was to help foreign students develop a sense of the fluid, flexible nature of Balinese musical time. The differences between Balinese and Euro-American musical time have partially blinded Western theorists to the shape, function, and significance of Balinese temporalities. In his magnum opus, *Music in Bali* (1966), Colin McPhee describes a performance that particularly delighted him:

> With no rhythmic support of any kind, the players must follow the leading *gangsa*, partly by watching, partly by ear. They must all feel in the same way the

---

[1] The persistent appeal to the surface and depth model is, I think, ultimately of little use; none of the Balinese musicians and composers I encountered appealed to the metaphor. See Levinson (1997), Small (1998:163), Meyer (1991:241), and Cook and Everist (1999:256) for critiques of musical depths and surfaces. Koskoff (in Cook 1999) deals with the intercultural confusions that arise between Western and Balinese musicians concerning incommensurable notions of depth, surface, performance, and composition.

flexible, rubato nature of the passage. The charm of this episode, as played by the *gamelan* at Jagaraga in 1938, was irresistible. It lay partly in the melody itself, sounding thinly chiming octaves and stressed at intervals by the vibrant tones of the *jublags* and *jegogans*. But perhaps most enchanting of all was the lovely pliancy of the passage, and the perfect accord of all the players. (1966:350)

The temporal and gestural flexibility that McPhee found so irresistible is obscured once captured within Western staff notation and so is largely absent in his analysis. McPhee's tempo indications, using the vague and relative terms of Western notation, suggest only the outlines of the gestural flexibility of Balinese *gamelan* music and do not indicate the relationship between fluctuations in tempo and colotomy or the stylized interruptions known as *angsel*. McPhee's analytical lens was calibrated to bring into sharp focus those elements most easily represented in standard Western notation—melodic and rhythmic passages seen from the resolution of the standard Western 4/4 bar—but not the micro-timing nuances of groove or piece-length temporal narratives. Since McPhee, Western ethnomusicologists have favored for analysis those elements of Balinese music which are more easily represented in Western staff notation and for which they already have a systemized vocabulary and ready-made methods of analysis.[2] Tenzer deals in greater depth than his predecessors with the issue of time and tempo in his meticulous *Gong Kebyar* (2000: 345–54) although he focuses primarily upon elements of melodic contour because, according to him, timing, tempo, and dynamics are problematic in Balinese music as they are potentially more open to change in rehearsal and performance than are the notes. Why has the Western approach to Balinese music been primarily focused upon pitches and rhythms (considered the "actual" music) (2000: 345), while other important elements such as tempo and dynamics are comparatively ignored?

Elements such as dynamics and tempo can be difficult to write about because they display a wide range of variety and are not as discrete as pitches, which are perceived to coalesce into larger hierarchical structures such as modes and contours. Western staff notation is designed to favor discrete elements; continuous information such as tempo and dynamics are not as easily represented or scannable in a score. In *gamelan*, pitch information is digitial; tempo and dynamics are analog.[3] Western pedagogy reflects this bias; most music students take classes in melodic analysis and ear training, but how many of us have had seminars in dynamics, tempo, or temporality? The relative paucity

---

[2] Since McPhee, Western ethnomusicologists have consistently employed standard Western staff notation for representing and analyzing Balinese music (see Tenzer 2000, Vitale 1990, Herbst 1997, Gold 1998, Bakan 1999, McGraw 2005). In certain respects Western notation is better equipped than other forms (such as the adapted Javanese cipher system used by the Balinese) to represent the intricacies of the hallmark interlocking of Balinese music but is ill-equipped (as are cipher systems) to represent tempo, dynamics, and the complex phrasing of a-metrical, tutti *kebyar* passages. Certain authors have successfully experimented with modified forms of Western notation, such as Tenzer's end-weighted phrasing combined with Balinese solfege (2000) and Herbst's stretched staff lines (1997).

[3] This is the case regarding the fixed pitch instruments of the *gamelan*, but not of flutes (I: *suling*), fiddles (I: *rebab*), or voice.

of articles concerning large-scale tempo transformations in non-Western music suggests that temporality's status as part of an implicit, oral tradition in Western music has partially blinded theoreticians to its significance in other traditions. Those musical elements that are more neatly represented in Western notation have preoccupied us.

Ombak

Ombak is a key aesthetic and theoretical category for many Balinese musicians and listeners. Literally meaning wave (in Indonesian and Balinese), the term refers to fluctuations in temporal and dynamic flows in Balinese *gamelan* repertoire generally. These waves are iconic of ocean waves, dance motions, musicians' movements, and their breath. *Ombak*, or its synonym *gelombang*, is interchangeable with a variety of other terms, some more specific. The renowned theorist Nyoman Rembang borrowed the Sanskrit-Javanese term *laya* to describe the same musical features. According to Yudane, Rembang likened such musical flows to surfing at Kuta, suggesting that melodies (in *gamelan*) are carried like a surfer on swelling and ebbing waves (p.c. Yudane, August 2001).

Bayu, Balinese for energy, refers to the same musical elements but sometimes also to the overall spirit and feeling of a group or performance. *Pengumbang-pengisep*, more often used to refer to the paired tuning system characteristic of most Balinese *gamelan* ensembles, is sometimes used to refer to temporality and dynamics by suggesting the rise and fall of inhalation and exhalation. *Ngucab* and *ngeseh* refer to sudden increases in volume (and often tempo); when pushed suddenly by the *kendang* this is termed *nongsok*. *Ngisep* indicates a sudden dynamic drop [Track BV-7/1].

Tempo and dynamics are tightly correlated in traditional repertoires. Young male musicians sometimes playfully referred to temporal and dynamic surges as *lempung* (B), swollen, or *kenyang* (B), erect, as contrasted to the more "flaccid" (I: *lembek*) feeling of languorous tempos and softer dynamics. In this chapter I retain *ombak* over other terms for simplicity and for its iconicity with my methods of analysis and representation. It is easier to represent a wave than a breath; it is a risky business to attempt to represent musical erections. Nevertheless, we should not allow this single term from Balinese ethnotheory (Agawu 2003, Perlman 2004) to suggest that there is a singular, culturally homogenous way of speaking about and perceiving temporal and dynamic profiles in *gamelan*. Modes of speaking about *gamelan* music were as numerous as the conversations I had.

In this chapter I treat *ombak* as a gesture, a musical signification that refers to a physical event as its object. As theorized by Coker (1972), Hatten (2004b), and Lidov (2005, following Clynes), musical gestures may be arranged hierarchically; small gestures may coalesce into larger gestures. *Ombak* represent both endosomatic gesture—the world as felt through our bodies (Lidov 2005:151)—and exosomatic gesture, as part of the external world we see, as in ocean waves. Here I am inspired by Imberty's (2000) notion of "dynamic vectors" in music. This notion suggests that musical parameters create virtual environments with forces that act upon their objects. As demonstrated below, the *ombak* of musical time and energy are pulled by the gravitational forces of moon-like *gongs*. *Ombak*, however, are not automatically perceived by listeners regardless of their background; they make themselves known to consciousness when the listening body has been honed, through culture, to hear/feel them as such.[4]

TEMPORALITY

The analysis of pulse in most Balinese *gamelan* music is comparatively transparent as it is consistently and unambiguously performed on the *kajar*, a small timekeeping horizontal *gong*-chime. That is, unlike most Western music (and Javanese music, see Miller 2001), the pulse in Balinese music is phenomenal; all listeners and musicians are in agreement as to where it lies; they can literally point to it. Similarly, larger-scale metrical structures are also phenomenal and unambiguous in Balinese music, unlike meter in Western music where it is primarily conceptual, or in West African music in which it can be ambiguous or variously interpreted. In Balinese music there is little room for what Locke (1998:22) calls the "gestalt flip" potential in the experience of listening to and performing Ghanaian Ewe drumming.

Pulse in Balinese music is punctual rather than durational; the *kajar* is damped by the left hand while being struck by a mallet held in the right, producing a staccato "tuk" sound. In most contexts the *kajar* performs every four notes relative to the fastest, densest rhythmic layer of the *gamelan* most often played by the *gangsa* metallophones. Western theorists typically notate the *kajar* at the level of the quarter note. However, in certain textures, such as the slow sections (*pengawak*) of *pelegongan*, *semar pegulingan*, and *gong kebyar* repertoire, the *kajar* plays once every eight *gangsa* notes. This invites the only point of potential pulse ambiguity; American students (and some Balinese beginners) often continue to feel the salient pulse at the level of every four *gangsa* notes in these contexts. In slow sections the *kajar* maintains its density relationship with the punctuating large *gongs* while the *gangsa* double in density.[5] Tempo transformations in Balinese music have the effect of pushing attention towards new salient tempos; at certain thresholds the salient tempo can burst into a higher or lower level while the melodic content remains the same. While this might seem to be simple repetition when presented in Western notation, melodic forms perceived from the lens of different salient tempos can seem altogether novel.[6]

---

[4] While once observing a mixed audience of Balinese and Western musicians enjoying a concert of *kebyar* music at the conservatory, I was struck by how the Balinese musicians' heads and torsos bobbed up and down in sympathy with the musical waves, as if their bodies were actually floating upon water, while the Western musicians sat rigid.

[5] In the *pengawak* of certain repertoires such as *pelegongan*, the *kajar* marks long-term metrical divisions by playing an *angsel kajar* or *ngerutuk*, a sudden out-of-time, additive bouncing. The genius and charm of marking important time points by playing something completely unrelated to the tactus of the musical texture adds to the temporal richness of Balinese music.

[6] Several Balinese examples resemble the well-documented Javanese concept of *irama* change, the transformation of melodic forms through various rhythmic densities. However, as Tenzer (2000) points out, no traditional Balinese example exactly matches the Javanese approach. The accompaniment for the *pendet* offering dance as performed in Denpasar provides an interesting example of this. The opening *kawitan* section is essentially a compressed version of the more expanded, slow *pengawak* section. While

The temporality of Balinese music is intricately connected to melodic qualities. Tenzer describes melodic quality using the Balinese terms *majalan*, a verb meaning to move forward (from *jalan*, to walk) and *ngubeng*, an adjective suggesting stasis or to spin one's wheels (Tenzer 2000:178). *Ngubeng* and *majalan* are applied to the kinetic quality of melodies, which typically exhibit both *majalan* and *ngubeng* characteristics; these qualities can coexist at different levels of orchestral and rhythmic texture simultaneously. Important metrical points exert a kind of gravitational force on melodic quality; melodies tend to be more *majalan* as they approach important moments such as *gong*. The more important the metric point (the more it coincides with other pulse streams) the more force (change) is exerted upon the melody. If we apply these terms to the kinetic quality of Balinese tempos (although the Balinese themselves do not) we find a similar effect, analyzed below, in which Balinese tempos become more *majalan* (changeable) when approaching an important metric or gestural point (*angsel*) and more *ngubeng*, or static, with distance. Cognitive research suggests that perceived duration expands with increased information, as would be the case in *majalan* textures. Tempos often perceptively dip when approaching *gong*, suggesting that in Balinese music *majalan* melodic and *majalan* temporal qualities cooperate to heighten a sense of anticipation and temporal expansion towards important metric moments.

In the following charts temporal fluctuations are represented as a series of onset timings along a horizontal axis (clock time); relative speed is charted along the vertical axis in beats per minute (BPM). When viewing these charts most Balinese informants described them as iconic of *ombak*. However, it is important to remember that these abstractions are perforce reductions; any map is simpler than its territory (Lefebvre 1991) and represents as much its translation rules as its object. Furthermore, such charts tend to suggest a sense of homogenous time—that every second is in some way perceptually identical—and thus these representations remain inadequate for capturing the *experience* of musical time, a term that may be, after all, a catachresis.

In Figure 7.1, in which the salient pulse appears as a scatter of smaller dots and *gong* placement is indicated by larger squares on the 80 BPM axis, the *gong* is seen to exert a kind of gravitational force upon tempo.[7] Considering their shared powers, mythical importance, and shapes, we might think of the *gong* as a kind of moon. The temporal gravity exerted by the *gong* mimics the melodic structure of end-weighted phrasing common

---

not conforming exactly to Javanese *irama* shift rules, this structure neatly illustrates how almost identical sections can, according to Balinese musicians, *feel* quite distinct at different tempi. This informal ethnographic evidence seems to corroborate Honing's (2003) study which suggests that "listeners often do not recognize proportionally scaled rhythms as being identical" and that "rhythms are timed differently at different tempi" (2006:780). The idea of salient tempo as expressed here overlaps to a certain extent with London's concept of tempo-metric-types (2004:7).

[7] Summarizing from a larger data set (McGraw 2008) we also observe that the power of the *gong*'s gravitational pull is frequently inversely proportional to tempo; the faster the tempo the less temporal changeability around the *gong*.

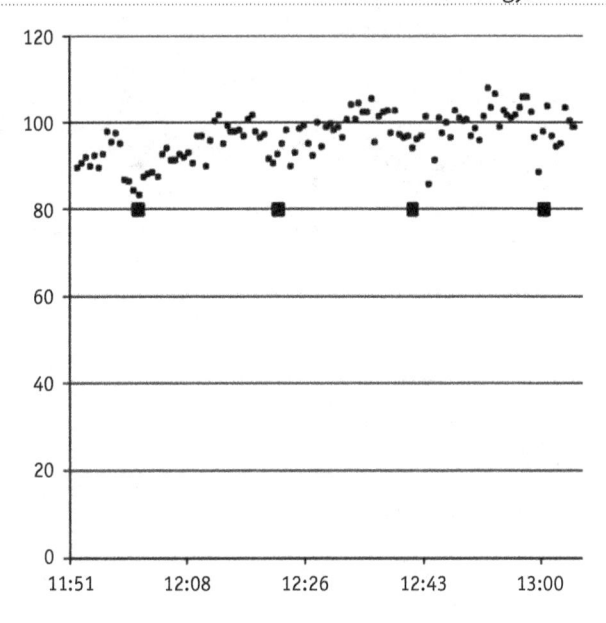

FIGURE 7.1 *Gong's* Gravity. Pulse in the *pengecet* of the traditional *semar pegulingan* work *Tabuh Gari*. [Track MK-7/1]

in most *gamelan* music. Here the ends of melodic phrases, marked by the *gong* on the last beat, are given more time and appear literally end-weighted.[8]

The intra-*gongan* temporal profiles common in medium and up-tempos of *tradisi* genres often coalesce into larger-scale inter-*gongan* waves that could be described as sawtooth patterns as seen in Figure 7.2.[9] That is, the ascent-descent temporal profile exhibited within single *gongan* is often replicated within an entire section including several *gongan*, leading to a sawtooth pattern for the section as a whole in which the first *gongan* of the section receives the most weight (time) and the final *gongan* is the lightest (shortest, fastest). While the same melodic material may be repeated in each *gongan*, literal repetition is avoided through a non-cyclical temporal narrative that continuously heightens the energy level throughout a section. While Balinese informants used the term *ombak* to describe the general flexibility of tempos, they had no terminology for this specific, and common, sawtooth form.

Looking at overall temporal profiles in *tradisi*, *kebyar*, and *kreasi baru* styles reveals active *ombak* waves: constantly undulating ripples of musical time, as seen in Figure 7.3. The *kajar* rarely finds itself at a metronomic point of stasis, instead reacting constantly to the push and pull of colotomy and *angsel* and is, as the following discussion will show, tightly linked with dynamic profiles.

---

[8] The charts presented in this chapter were produced using two different methods. For some a contact microphone was placed on the *kajar* during recordings of full ensemble performances and the inter-onset timings of the attack points were determined in sound-editing software (Audacity), exported to and then graphed in an Excel spreadsheet. For others, I charted tempos of commercial recordings using the program Sonic Visualizer, in which the data points were also visualized.

[9] A *gongan* is a full statement of a gong form.

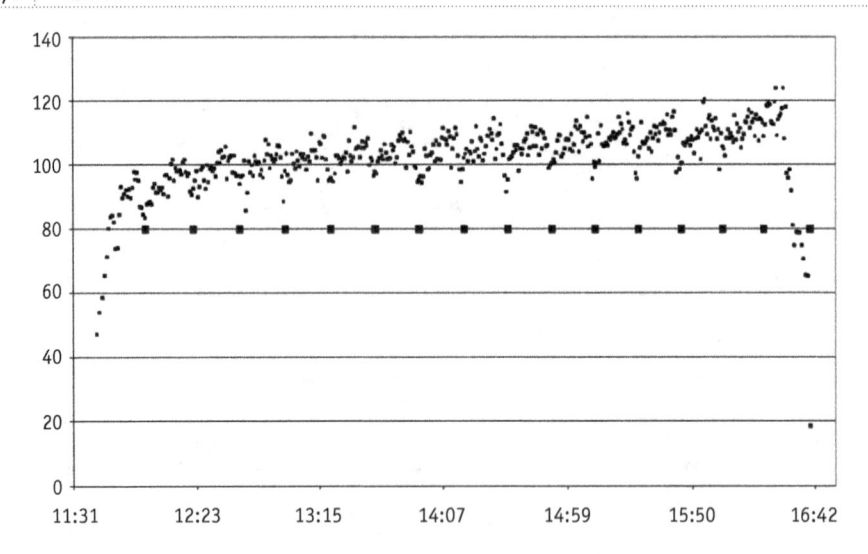

FIGURE 7.2 Sawtooth pattern in the full *pengecet* of *Tabuh Gari*.

Epstein (1985, 1995) theorized that in musical works that incorporate multiple tempos, the most common and aesthetically pleasing tempo relationships are those related by low-order proportions (e.g., 1:2, 2:1, 3:4). Arguing that this phenomenon was crosscultural and rooted in biology, Epstein suggested that tempo relations of an order of complexity beyond 3:4 may be felt as unmusical or as an unsuccessful performance. The tempos of Balinese *tradisi* and *kreasi baru* forms rarely adhere to Epstein's suggested proportions, instead exhibiting complex ratios, or apparently low-order ratios stretched beyond the perceptual boundaries of simple ratios (McGraw 2008). These stretched proportions could be conceived as a temporal analogue of the famous Balinese paired tuning system in which pairs of instruments are purposefully de-tuned to create a shimmering destructive interference effect. Here, the predictable

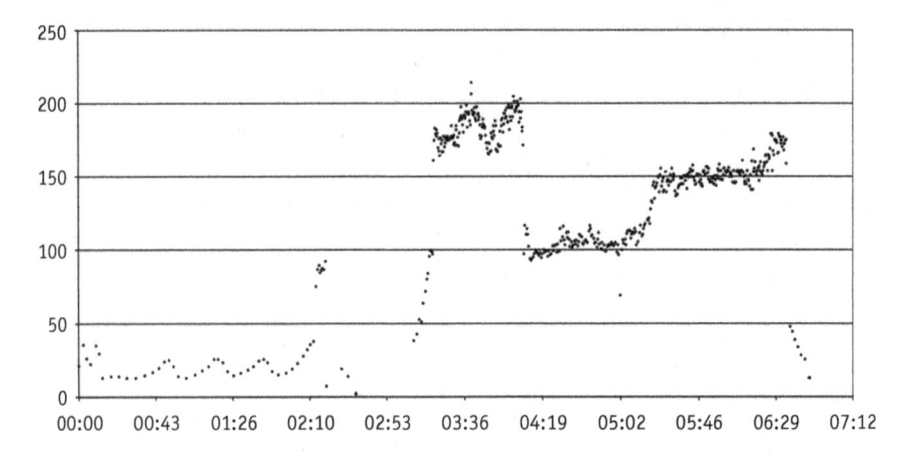

FIGURE 7.3 Long-scale waves in *Kebyar Duduk*, 1925 Nyoman Mario (Vital Records VR 401).

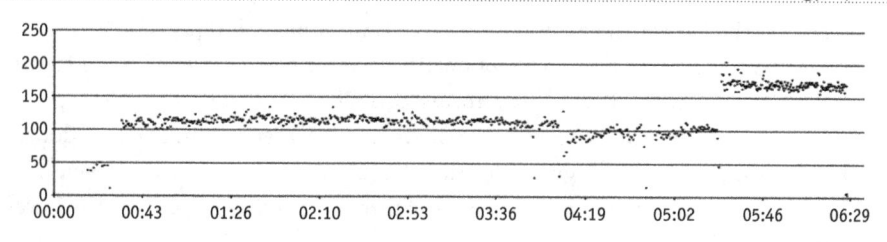

FIGURE 7.4 Long-scale temporal profile in Ketut Gede Asnawa's *musik kontemporer* work *Kosong* (1986), charting implied *kajar* tactus. [Track MK-3/1]

squareness of simple ratios is stretched just enough to be noticeable, imbuing music with a complex humanness.

Temporality in *Musik Kontemporer*

When asked what—besides obvious differences of context and orchestration—might differentiate *musik kontemporer* from *kreasi baru*, many composers appealed to a vague difference of feeling (I: *rasa*). According to Widnyana: "I don't know what the difference is, but I can always feel it" (p.c. Widnyana, June 2007). Temporality often resides within an implicit realm of feeling in both Balinese and Western musical understanding. When we analyze tempos of works described by their creators as *musik kontemporer*, as illustrated in Figures 7.4 and 7.5, we find that they frequently demonstrate more metronomic temporal profiles, low-order proportional tempos, sudden shifts into stable tempos rather than continuous transitions, and odd meters and phrasing, as seen in the examples below.

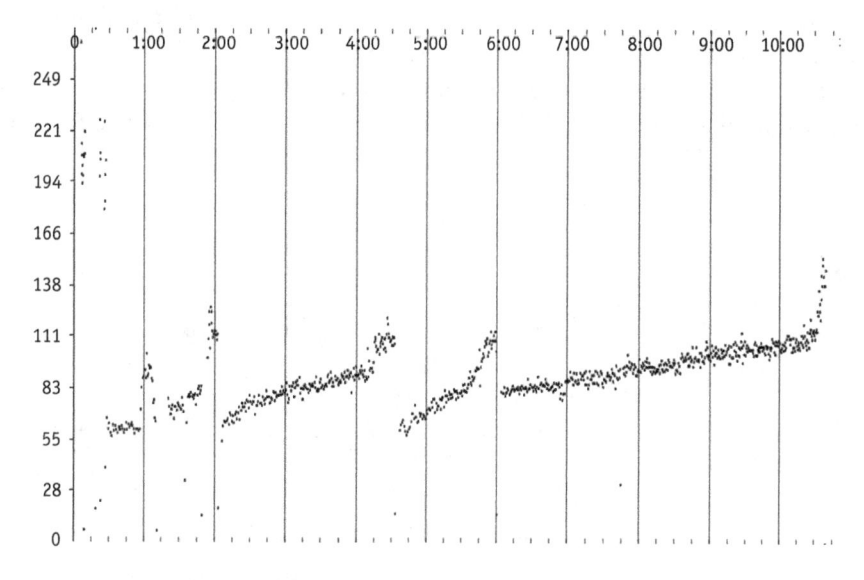

FIGURE 7.5 Long-scale temporal profile in Sang Nyoman Arsawijaya's *musik kontemporer* work *Pamoksa* (2007), charting implied *kajar* tactus. [Track MK-7/2]

Often detached from the temporal logic of traditional colotomy, *musik kontemporer* works are typically more metronomic than either *tradisi* or *kreasi baru* forms. Freeing oneself from traditional *gong* forms also allows composers to develop odd pulse phrasing, as in Alit's example below where odd meter manifests as double bands of time. As seen in Figure 7.6, Alit incorporates a continuous eleven-beat (2+2+2+2+3) *kajar* pattern in which the longer three-note pulse appears as the lower point in the band.

Composers using sequencing programs tended to focus on the aspects of music for which such programs are designed, primarily the manipulations of melodic formulae and the construction of complex polyrhythm. The tempos of works created in such programs generally remained comparatively static, as in Arsawijaya's *musik kontemporer* work *Pamoksa* (2007) shown in the Fruity Loops screenshot provided in Illustration 7.1. Temporal profiles in older repertoires such as *kebyar* and *pelegongan* recall the topography of Balinese footpaths, tracing up and down deep gorges between villages. The temporal profiles of *musik kontemporer* were more reminiscent of the smooth, paved asphalt straightaways and bridges of the late New Order and *reformasi*.

Comparing instrumental with dance works over several decades, we find that the former tend to display less variable temporal profiles than the latter. However, considered over the long term, it appears that instrumental works have become temporally restrained over time. Madé Regog's *Kebyar Ding* (Figure 7.7), first recorded in 1928 and rereleased by Arbiter in 2009, displays highly fluid tempos and extended a-metrical periodicities through lengthy *kebyar* sections—appearing as empty passages within the temporal profiles—both at the beginning and within the body of the work. Wayan Lotring's *Liyar Samas* (Figure 7.8), composed in the 1920s, is an instrumental work in the *pelegongan* style that channels the topics of the *legong* dance and, while highly fluid, appears less variable than *Kebyar Ding*. Wayan Beratha's *Kosalia Arini* (1969) (Figure 7.9), a classic of the early New Order *kreasi baru* contest style, devotes less time than many earlier *gong kebyar* works to a-metrical *kebyar* passages to focus on

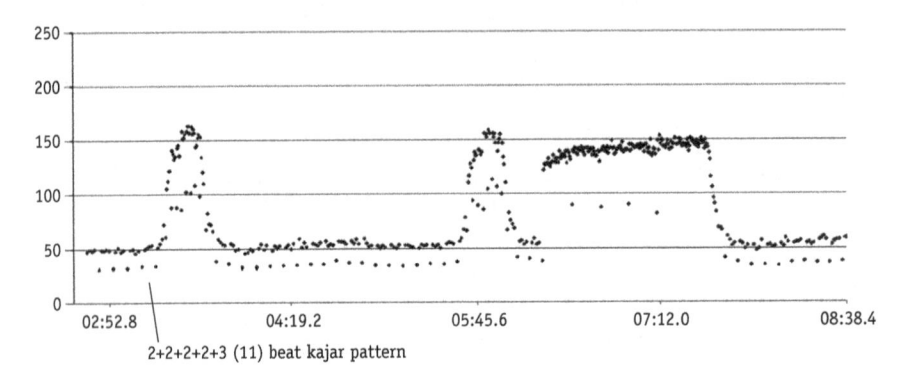

FIGURE 7.6 Long-scale temporal profile in Dewa Ketut Alit's *musik kontemporer* work *Mecaru* (2003), charting *kajar* tactus. [Track MK-7/3]

Ombak: Time, Energy, and Homology | 175

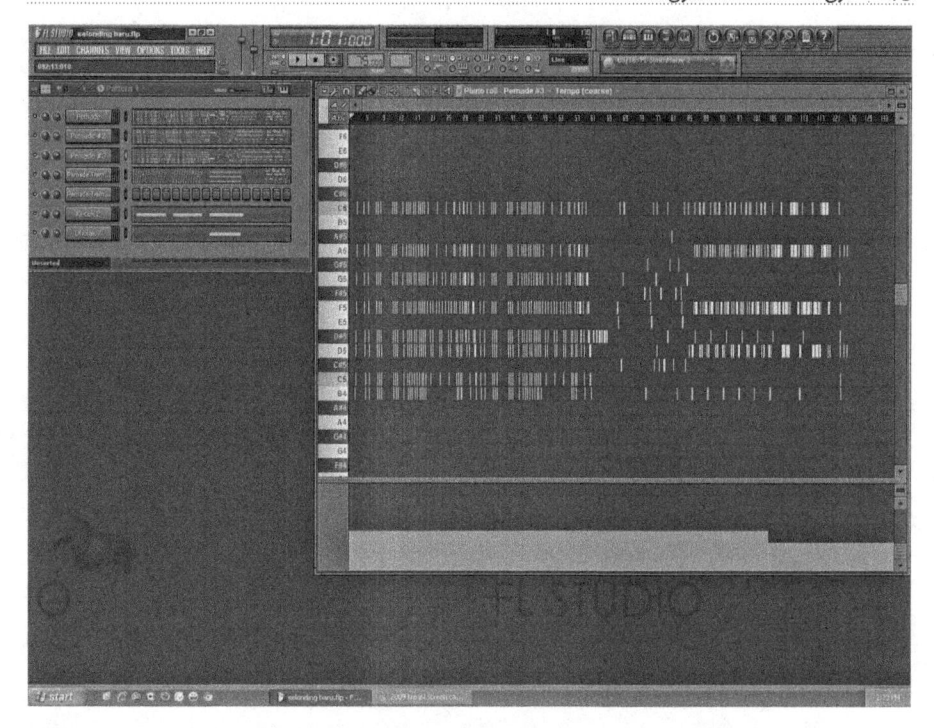

ILLUSTRATION 7.1 Screen shot of Sang Nyoman Arsawijaya's *Pamoksa* (2007), composed in Fruity Loops. Note metronomic tempo profile in bottom right half of the image.

innovations in elaboration and orchestration built upon extended passages of more stable time. Nyoman Windha's *Jagra Parwata* (Figure 7.10), an award-winning *kreasi baru* work of the late New Order, displays a comparatively restricted temporal range. A-metrical *kebyar* passages, in which the entire ensemble must perform tightly

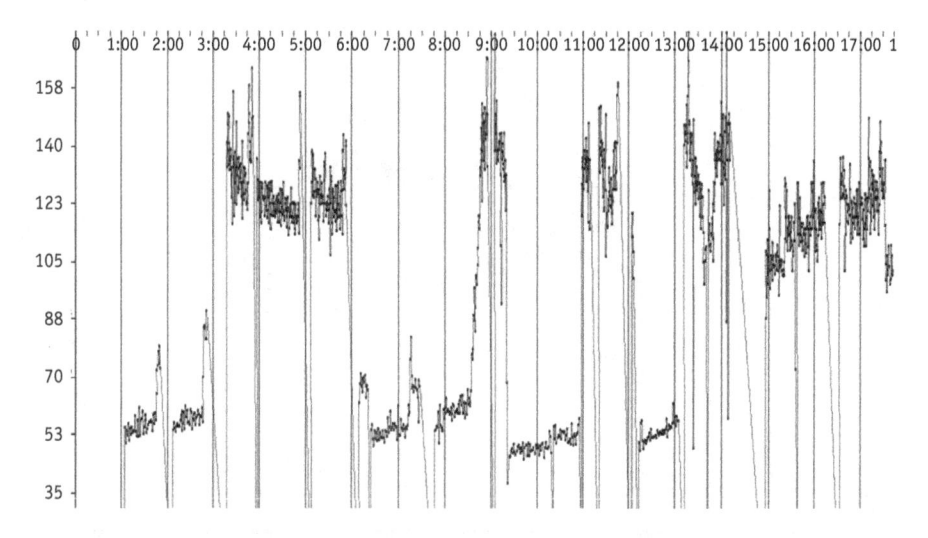

FIGURE 7.7 Long-scale temporal profile in *Kebyar Ding* (1928), charting *kajar* tactus.

176　Radical Traditions

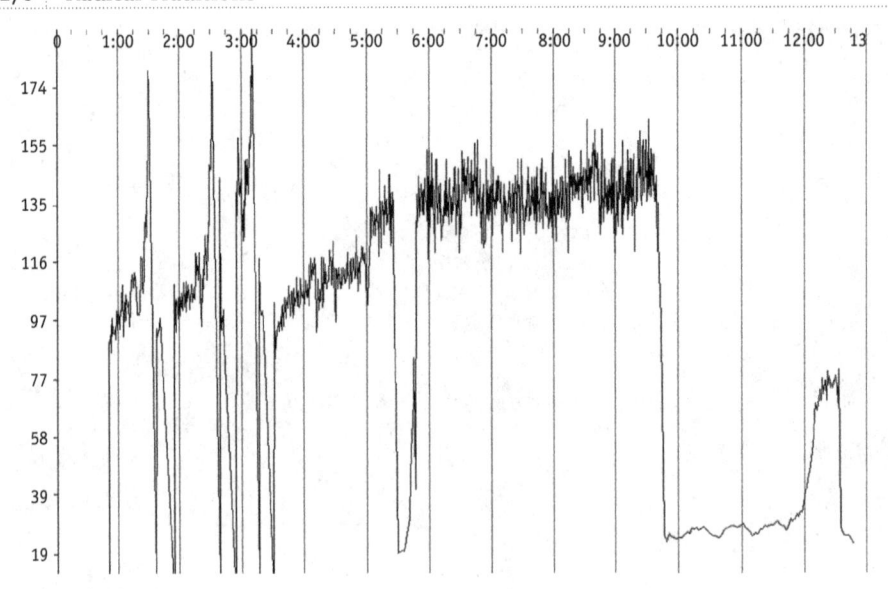

FIGURE 7.8　Long-scale temporal profile in Wayan Lotring's *Liyar Samas* (*Layar Samah*) (192?), charting *kajar* tactus.

coordinated tutti passages, are restricted to short phrases in the beginning, while the bulk of the composition is devoted to melodic development upon a comparatively stable frame. While four works hardly represent a scientific sample, that many composers cited these very compositions against which to contrast the different "feeling" of their own works is indicative of the affective transformations they felt their compositions embodied.

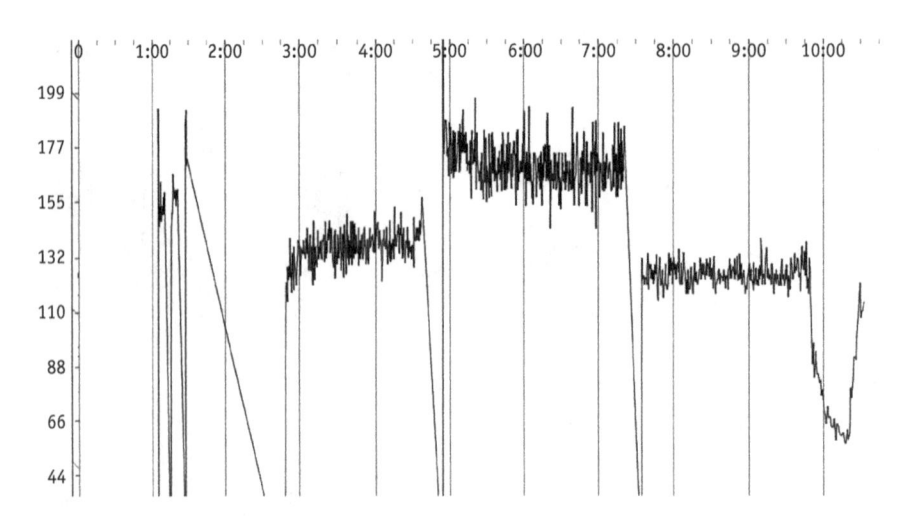

FIGURE 7.9　Long-scale temporal profile in Wayan Beratha's *Kosalia Arini* (1969), charting *kajar* tactus.

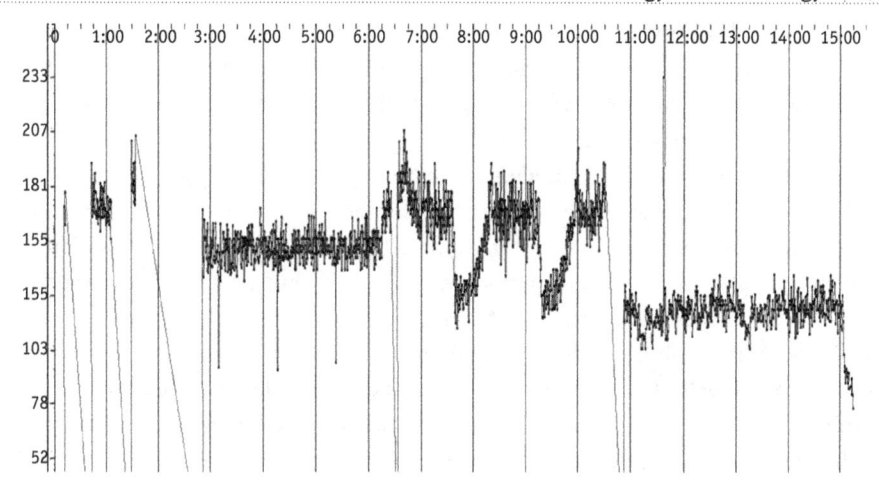

FIGURE 7.10 Long-scale temporal profile in Nyoman Windha's *Jagra Parwata* (1991), charting *kajar* tactus.

DYNAMICS

As a musical category, dynamics has received comparatively little analytical attention. Prior work has dealt almost exclusively with Western classical music and has been concerned primarily with: 1) describing general contours prescribed in scores (Huron 1991); 2) the seemingly universal tendency for increases in tempo to be linked to increases in loudness (Todd 1992); 3) detailed studies comparing variations between performances; and 4) the potential connections between dynamics and expressive timing (rubato) (Repp 1998). The term "dynamics" encapsulates a complex of overlapping phenomena and terminology including: loudness, a culturally dependent and hermeneutic term; amplitude, an apparently more empirical category; and volume, referring often to embodied experiences of pleasure and pain.[10]

As is the case with both long- and short-scale temporality, Balinese musicians typically learn about dynamics implicitly through performance rather than through explicit instruction. In Balinese traditional repertoires dynamic contours are generated automatically, as it were, as they are tightly linked to temporal and colotomic strata. That is, dynamics are rarely consciously composed into traditional or neo-traditional works in genres such as *pelegongan*, *gong gede*, and *semar pegulingan*, but are a part of stylistic norms and ensemble virtuosity. In *gong kebyar*, and especially contemporary *kreasi baru*, dynamics are sometimes an independent profile, one that is more often explicitly composed and rehearsed either by the work's composer or by the performing

---

[10] The study of dynamics in performance practice is complicated by the nature of their representations within audio signals. Microphone placement can distort performers' intention and audiences' experience of dynamic variation. Software applications cannot accurately gauge the absolute air pressure/loudness of an actual performance as each recording has inevitably undergone microphone level setting, compression, and normalization, making accurate, objective comparisons between performances difficult. To generate an accurate representation of *perceived* loudness, dynamic contours often need to be combined with a signal's spectrogram in a single image.

ensemble. As described below, the dynamic profile in *musik kontemporer* is often dissociated from other profiles, including temporality, inviting comparisons to the independence between dynamics and timing in both Western-styled popular music *and* ancient Balinese sacred ensembles.

Previous analyses of Balinese music have rarely dealt directly with the problem of dynamics.[11] Tenzer identifies the relationship between timing and dynamics and their occasional independence in *gong kebyar*, suggesting that dynamics contribute to structure in important, although not always explicitly composed ways: "dynamics are *systematically* shaped, however, only at cyclic, metacyclic, and noncyclic levels of structure" (2000:347 emphasis in the original), by which he means that dynamic profiles are only consciously structured within *gongan* and sectional (multi-*gongan*) levels and within a-metrical *kebyar* sections but not (one assumes) at the micro level of groove or the macro level of piece-length narratives. Importantly, Tenzer reveals the crucial relationship between colotomic and dynamic structure, namely that diminuendos are often employed nearing *gong* and other important structural markers.

The interwoven ribbon of colotomy, tempo, and dynamics varies in tightness. In most traditional repertoires the dynamic profile dips suddenly to get out of the way of the comparatively quiet colotomic *gong* markers. This is often linked to a slowing or stretching tempo. In Figure 7.11, the opening *kawitan* section of the *semar pegulingan*

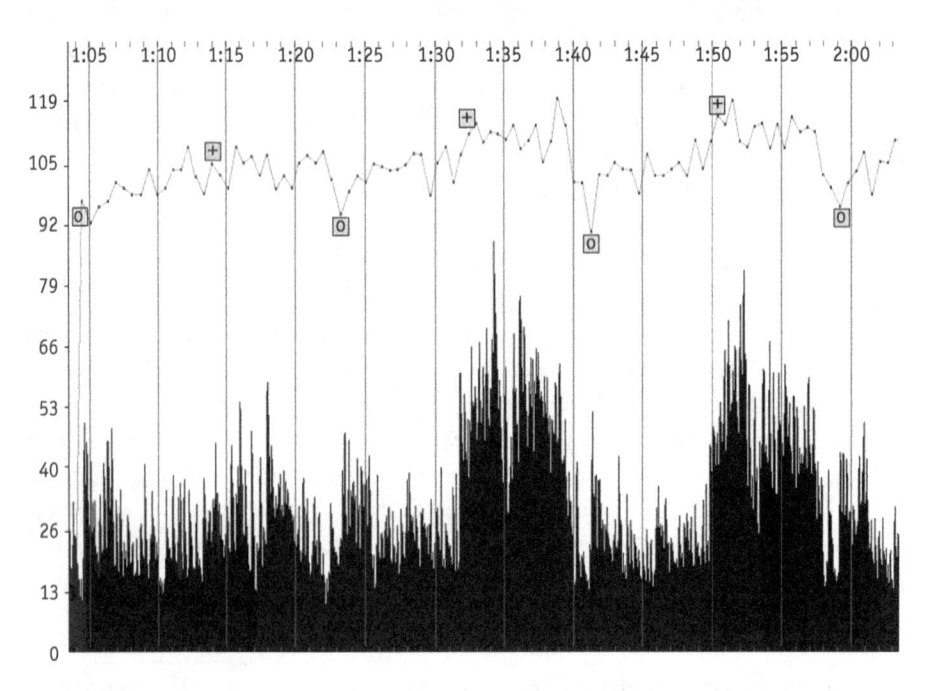

FIGURE 7.11 Interaction of temporal, colotomic, and dynamic strata in *Lengker* charting *calung* tactus. [Track MK-7/4]

---

[11] McPhee provides only one detailed example of dynamics, using Western notation, in his transcription of Lotring's *Gending Angklung* (1966:326).

work *Lengker* displays dramatic dips in both dynamic profile and tempo at the moment of *gong* (O), in both unmarked *gongan* (preceding the second *gong*) and *gongan* incorporating *angsel* (preceding *gongs* three and four). Within these charts the dynamic profile can almost be read inversely, in which we could scan for the deepest troughs to determine important colotomic points. Interestingly, this structure contradicts theories of Western music proposing that dynamics are independent of, and often contradict, meter. Todd (1992) suggests that at points of metric coincidence in Western music, dynamic and temporal threads unravel to allow performers greater interpretative leeway as a sign of personal expression. Contrastingly, within Balinese traditional genres points of structural stress (the *gong*) represent the most tightly wound points on the temporal-colotomic-dynamic ribbon.

But changes in dynamics are not always linked to changes in tempo in Balinese traditional repertoires. In the *lelambatan* style, the ends of melodic lines (B: *palet*) are marked by *kempur* (medium-sized *gong*) strokes; these points rarely receive perceivable temporal stretching, but are dynamically highly marked by the sudden disappearance of the loud *ceng-ceng kopyak* (hand cymbals), as seen in Figure 7.12 at points 9:48 and 10:28 (*kempur* represented by U). Even the *gong* (O at 8:51) is given little temporal weight, instead followed by suddenly faster drumming. In some traditional genres, such as *lelambatan,* a change in the dynamic profile is enough to announce colotomic points without the assistance of changes in the temporal profile. While the dynamic profile may not always have the power to sway tempo, the reverse is rarely true; tempo changes are almost always marked by dynamic shifts. The restrained temporal profile of classical *lelambatan*, maintaining a comparatively metronomic profile in the face of dynamic flux, may contribute to the genre's purported affect of stateliness and repose.

However, the kinds of independence between tempo and dynamics displayed above are atypical when contrasted with the greater body of traditional repertoire performed in Bali over the past century. The tight, almost perfect alignment of

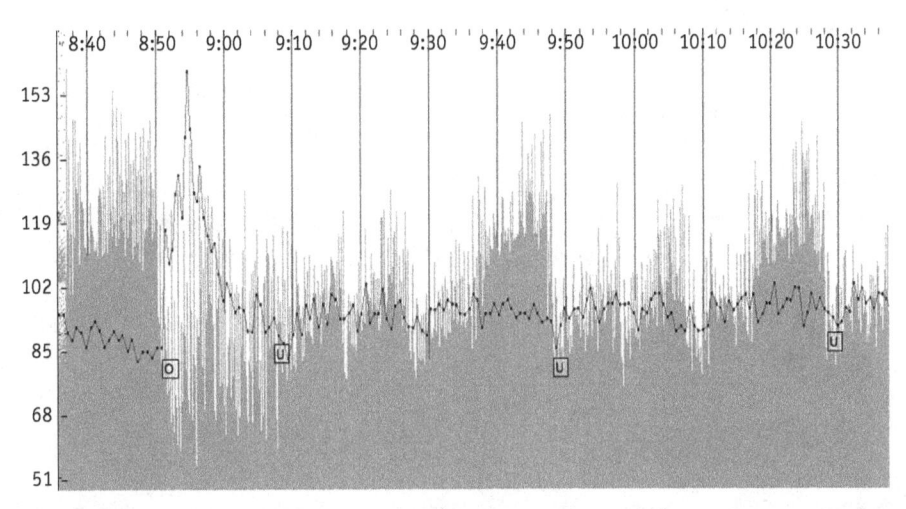

FIGURE 7.12 Interaction of temporal, colotomic, and dynamic strata in *Tabuh Pat Jagul* charting *penyacah* tactus. [Track MK-7/5]

temporal and dynamic profiles demonstrated in Dewa Ketut Alit's *Pengastung Kara* (2001) (Figure 7.13) combines the close interrelationship of dynamics and temporality typical of *pelegongan* and *kreasi baru* dance compositions.

In a 1998 study Huron compared the dynamic markings included in 435 scores of fourteen Western composers, summarizing his observations in his "ramp archetype" of dynamics. This model suggests that it is far more likely for music to gradually build and then quickly dissipate than vice versa. While suggesting that these conclusions should not be considered to be universal, Huron argues that the ramp archetype is consistent with behavioral and neurological evidence of passive auditory attention, effectively appealing to biological, and ostensibly universal, support for his theory. This claim suggests that a stimulus cannot be sustained (capture listeners' attention) indefinitely—all stimuli eventually feel static over time, even increasing loudness—and so attention must be captured once again by sudden decreases in dynamics, at which point the auditory attention cycle can begin anew.

A comparison of fifty recordings of Balinese *lelambatan*, *semar pegulingan*, *pelegongan*, *kebyar*, and *musik kontemporer* works reveals a different set of dynamic tendencies from that proposed by Huron. In these genres ramps are indeed common, but more often slope down, rather than up. Ramping up (gradual crescendos followed by short diminuendos) do exist, but are more rare and are often reserved to foreshadow transitions into new sections and new melodic/colotomic textures. Two typical examples of ramping up are provided in Figures 7.14 and 7.15. Each example follows the transition from a slower, longer melodic form to a faster, shorter form. In traditional genres, an upward sloping ramp is almost always coupled with a temporal profile in parallel motion; tempo and dynamics both dramatically increase, announcing the transition to a new section, after which the dynamic profile quickly descends while the tempo sustains a plateau at a higher level of energy.

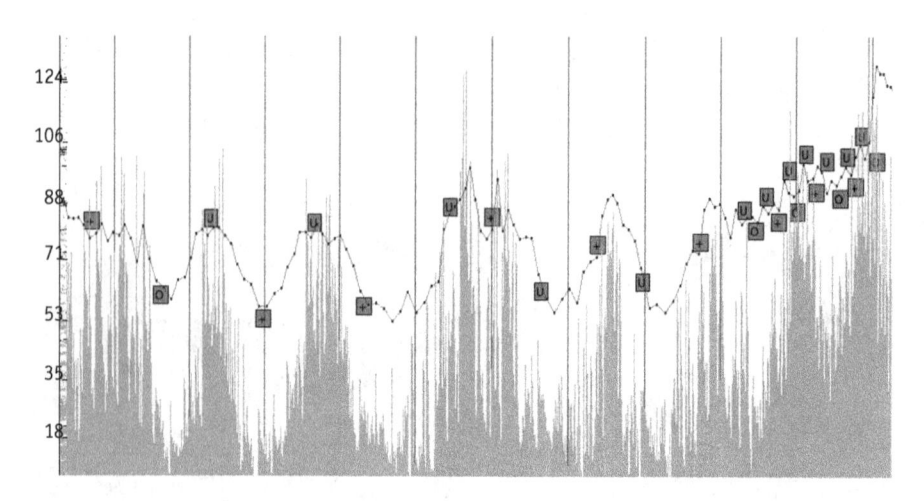

FIGURE 7.13 Close interaction of temporal and dynamic strata in *Pengastung Kara* charting *neliti* tactus (1:30–3:14). [Track MK-7/6]

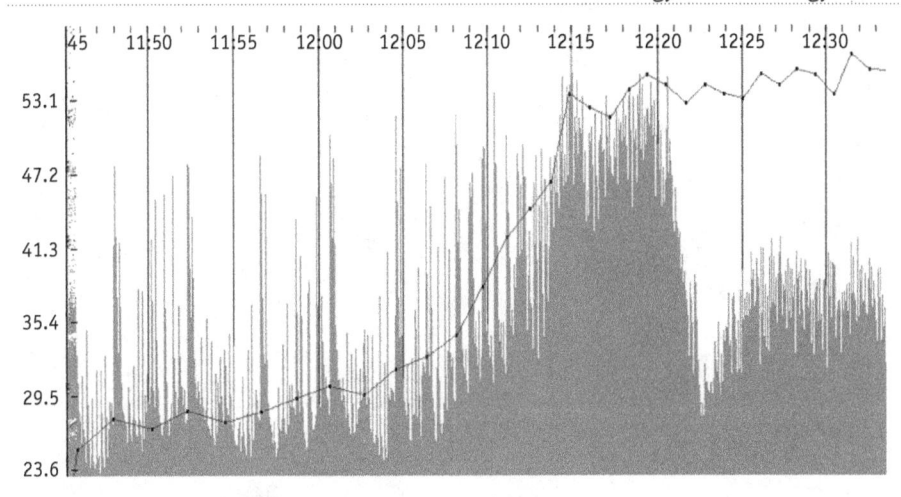

FIGURE 7.14. *Tabuh Pat Jagul*. Ramp up from *pengawak* to *gilak* charting *kempli* tactus. [Track MK-7/7]

However, downward-sloping dynamic ramps are more common in Balinese repertoires as they are often used as variations within *gongan* and multi-*gongan* sections. As seen in Figures 7.16 and 7.17, unlike the close connection between temporal and dynamic profiles in ramping-up structures, the temporal profile is more independent of dynamics in ramping-down profiles, which are often connected to dance motions or dance topics. Rather than ramps, these formations more closely resemble waves; they

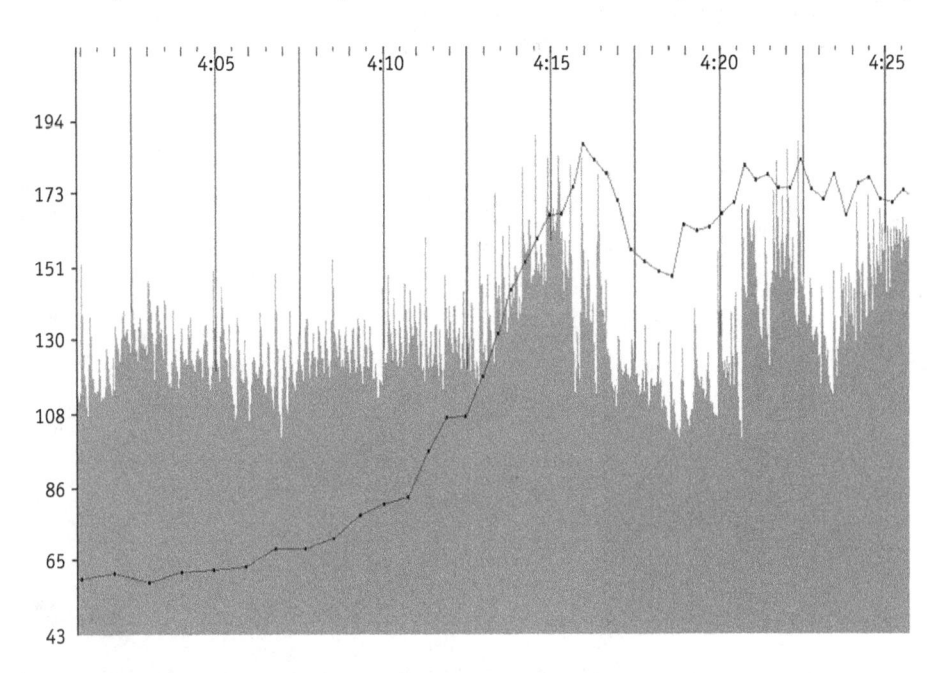

FIGURE 7.15 *Legong Keraton*. Ramp up from *pengecet* to *bapang* charting *neliti* tactus. [Track MK-7/8]

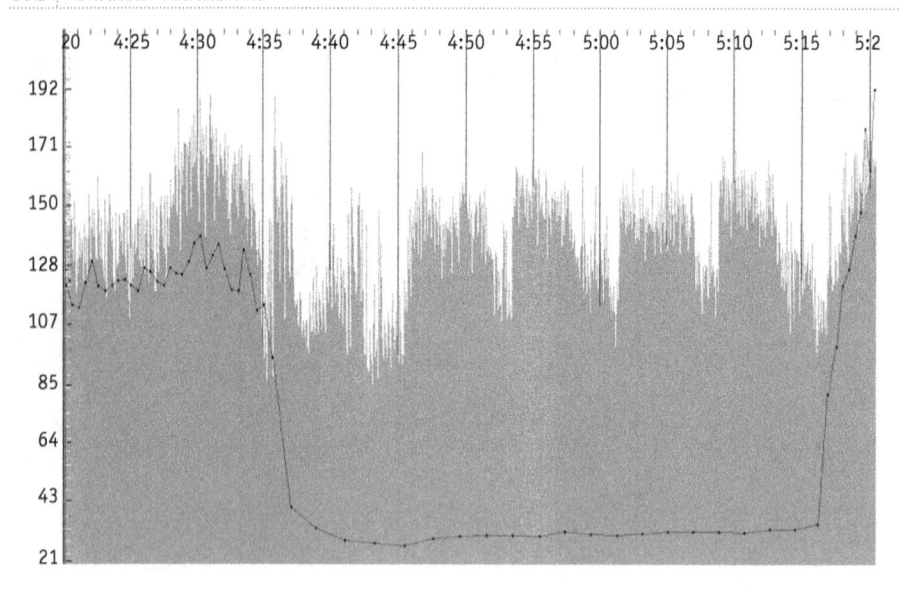

FIGURE 7.16 *Teruna Jaya*, Gede Manik (1914). Ramping down charting *kajar* tactus (Vital Records VR 401).

impact with full force at the crest, washing over in a gradual diminuendo. It is probably not a coincidence that these forms also mirror the natural strong attack and slow decay of the *gamelan* instruments themselves.

The profiles above illustrate the ways in which the interrelationship between colotomic, temporal, and dynamic profile interact with structure. As we approach new

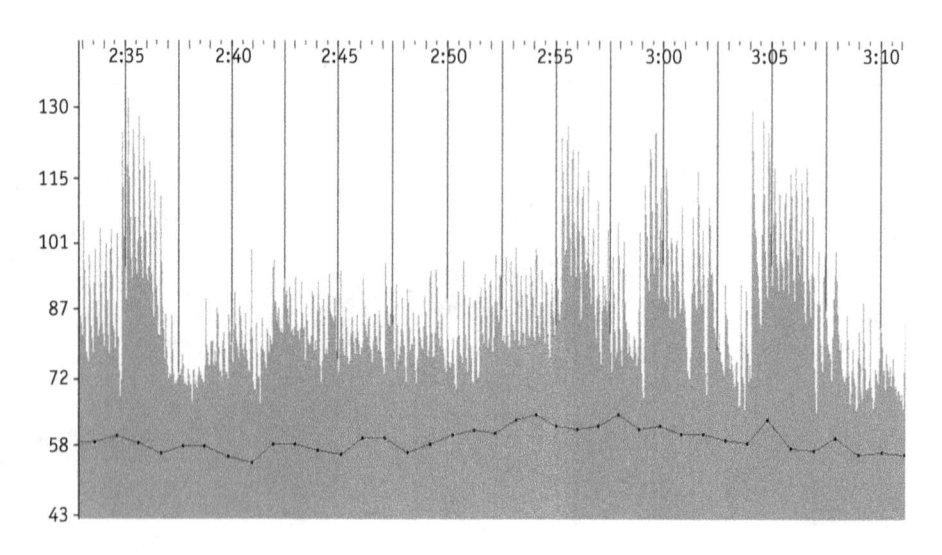

FIGURE 7.17 *Legong Keraton*. Ramping down within a medium-tempo *pengecet* charting *neliti* tactus. [Track MK-7/9]

structural material the normally tightly wound threads of this ribbon often tend to relax. In Figure 7.18 we trace the interrelationship between dynamics, colotomy, and tempo in the *pengecet* of the classic *kebyar* dance work *Kebyar Duduk*. While the tempo is comparatively stable, the dynamics are closely linked to colotomy; the dynamic profile descends prior to *gong* in regular unmarked cycles, allowing it to sound through (up to 6:06). The dynamic profile rises following the *kemong* (+). At the final iteration of the form, beginning around 6:18, dynamics and colotomy become dissociated; dynamics rise up, obscuring *gong* tones, thus cueing to musicians, dancer, and audience the impending end of the section at 6:30.

Dynamics in *Musik Kontemporer*

Dynamic and temporal profiles become increasingly dissociated in *musik kontemporer*, accelerating a trend begun decades earlier in *kreasi baru*. This is especially the case in instrumental works in which dance *angsels* and topics are not utilized. Many composers suggested that instrumental works in all genres involved considerably fewer *ombak* than do dance works. As one composer put it: "instrumental music has fewer 'curves.'" His double entendre, referring to both shapely *ombak* waves and the curves of a female dancer's body, generated giggles and approving nods among other musicians many of whom suggested that, while the flowing dynamics and tempos of dance music were appropriate for accompanying bodies (especially female bodies) in motion, the affect of sensuousness suggested by *ombak* could be eschewed in *musik kontemporer* to focus upon more "serious" compositional problems (p.c. Sudirana, June 2008). As is the case with temporality in *musik kontemporer*, there are fewer universal tendencies in dynamic profiles in this genre as compositions become increasingly idiosyncratic.

In *musik kontemporer*, dynamics appear less variable than other more explicitly composed musical elements; as in *kebyar* and *tradisi* forms, faster tempos are often

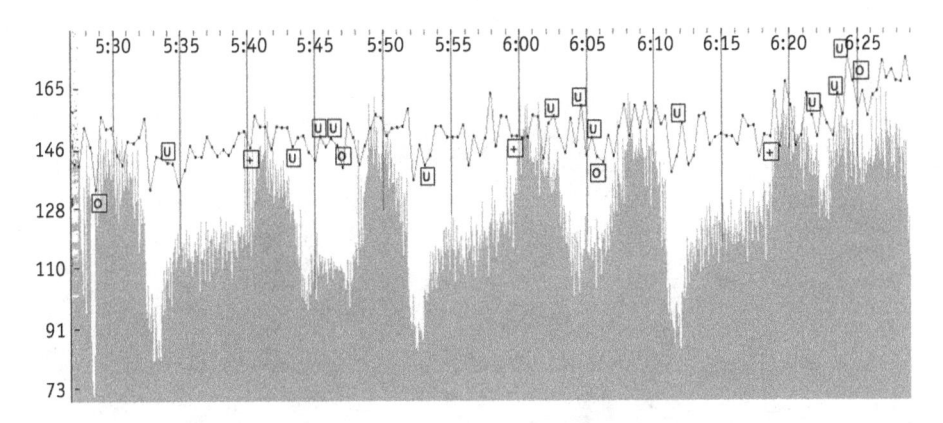

FIGURE 7.18 Rampless transition in the final iteration of the *pengecet* of *Kebyar Duduk* charting *kajar* tactus. [Track MK-7/10]

184 Radical Traditions

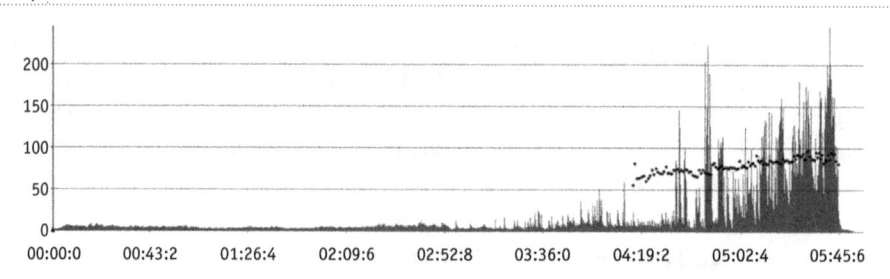

FIGURE 7.19 Dynamic and temporal strata in Dewa Ketut Alit's *Salju* (fourth movement) charting implied *kajar* tactus. 2007. [Track MK-7/11]

linked to louder dynamics. But the frequent removal of traditional colotomy and pulse-keeping *kajar* can have profound implications for dynamic profiles in *musik kontemporer*. Some works display strikingly unique overall dynamic narratives. The fourth movement of Ketut Dewa Alit's 2007 *Salju* (Snow) (Figure 7.19) appears as a direct response to Tenzer's characterization of dynamic narrative in twentieth century *kebyar*: "there are no *gending* that, for example, build large-scale trajectories toward a single dynamic peak or nadir (as the Hindustani alap-jor-jhala form does)" (Tenzer 2000:347).

As seen in Arsawijaya's 2003 *Ambisi* (Figure 7.20) and the first movement of Alit's 2007 *Salju* (Figure 7.21) stable tempos are comparatively independent of dynamic profiles. Balinese musicians often characterized temporal and dynamic profiles as embodying music's feeling (I: *rasa*) or soul (I: *jiwa*). Changes in these musical elements would seem to suggest subtle but profound transformations in the musical sensibility of a culture. Both Widnyana and Arsawijaya described these changes as subconscious (I: *dibawah sadar*) (p.c. July 2009). Looking at these graphs, it is tempting to characterize such changes as a transformation towards rational, totalizing, striated Western temporal logics and away from the smooth and fluid (Deleuze and Guatarri 1987) shapes of the figurative *ombak*. This transformation appears mirrored in the tendency towards the

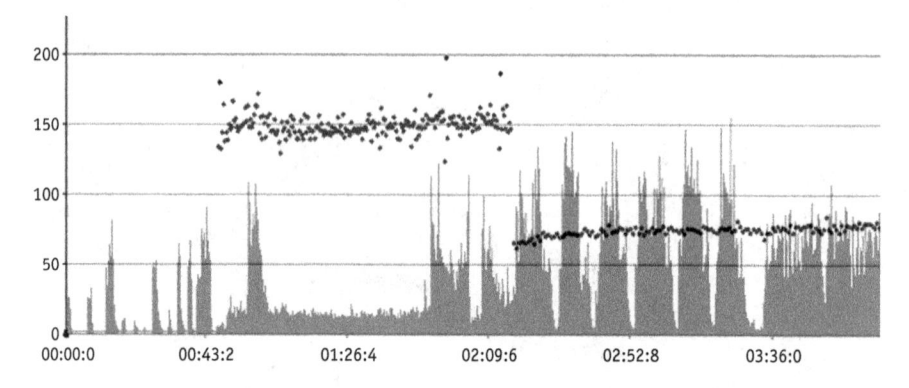

FIGURE 7.20 Dynamic and temporal strata in Sang Nyoman Arsawijaya's *Ambisi* (Ambition), charting implied *kajar* tactus. 2003. [Track MK-7/12]

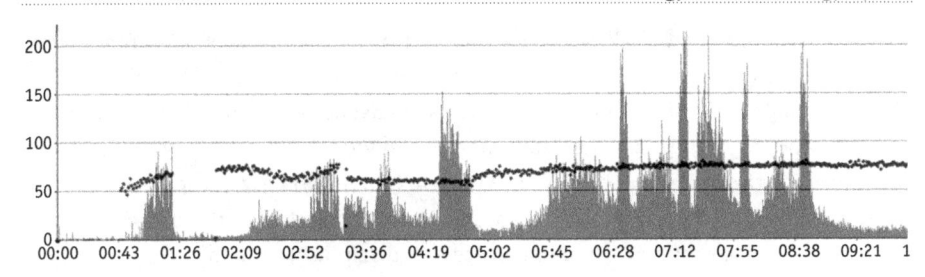

FIGURE 7.21 Dynamic and temporal strata in Dewa Ketut Alit's *Salju* (first movement.) charting implied *kajar* tactus. 2007. [Track MK-7/13]

rational, standardized, and tempered slicing of the spectrum in Balinese *diatonis* tunings as opposed to the stretched octaves and idiosyncracy of traditional tunings. In the next section I consider the implications of linking such musical structures to an understanding of Balinese society.

Homology

Seebass (1996) reflects upon the temporality of *kebyar* as the aesthetic expression of psychic disruption brought about through colonization and modernity. The shift from traditional Balinese to colonial/European modes of social organization, labor, and government, Seebass suggests, generated new modes of temporal organization (primarily condensation) in Balinese music that reminds him of European expressionism. Kramer (1988) hears in Balinese musical temporalities a communal social structure that the West has traded for rationality and progress.

In reference to *musik kontemporer*, we are tempted to identify causal or reflective connections between musical temporality and broader notions of time, the comparatively rigid temporality of much *musik kontemporer* recalling the disciplined hands of the clock marking the hours of nine to five. Increasing numbers of Balinese organize their lives around modern service economies dominated by a time regime removed from the fluid, contextual temporalities of harvests and temple ceremonies with their shifting intensities. We may identify *musik kontemporer's* tendency towards sudden ruptures rather than smooth transitions as reflective of the social conditions of the *reformasi* and we may interpret the comparative absence of periodic *gongan* as a sign of the erosion of the Hindu faith with its focus on cyclic time.

Composers' descriptions of the sensuous and fluid *ombak* of dance repertoire recalls the West's own wave metaphor with its connotations of fluidity and excess that have been associated with female bodies throughout Western history and philosophy (Rodgers 2011:68). "Within the science of acoustics, developed during the eighteenth and nineteenth centuries, to analyze and control sound meant to experience the pleasure and danger of unruly waves... to seek their control from a distanced perspective, and thus to further the consolidation of archetypal white, Western, male subjectivity" (ibid.). Restraining *ombak* allowed *kontemporer* composers to focus upon more "serious" problems of composition. The synchrony required during a complex group tempo shift, as in Balinese *ombak*, requires high levels of ensemble coordination. The order of stable tempos may facilitate the expression of individualistic creativity—a level surface on which the individual can riff in reference to his own beat, rather than through continuous temporal realignment with the group. Does the flattening of Balinese *ombak* represent a subtle neo-imperial process of disciplining sound?

Identifying homological relations between sound and society is one of musicology's historic preoccupations.[12] Through this musicologists mapped Marx's greatest achievement, "the unmasking of *things* in order to reveal (social) relationships" (Lefebvre 1991:81), to sound itself. Characterizations of aesthetic production as reflective of social structure have been most common. These appear in Hegelian, Marxian, Weberian, and Adornian versions (see Born 2010a), and by Bourdieu in his linking the consumption of art to social reproduction (Bourdieu 1984). Adorno maps the shift from mere reflection to the generative powers of music to the emergence of European musical modernity (i.e., Beethoven).[13] Attali extends this notion to suggest that music is prophetic of future social dynamics and structures—if not directly generative, then at least reflective of the future: "Our music foretells our future. Let us lend it an ear" (1985:11). While many of these models have been critiqued as deterministic and mechanical (see Born and Hesmondhalgh 2000), more recent homological models have suggested that music plays a crucial role in the formation of sociocultural identities and engendering communities or scenes.

In ethnomusicology, Feld's work (1981, 1988, 1990) has been the most influential in extending homological models by establishing logical coherences between sound and social structures, partly as a response to Lomax's use of statistical correlations to suggest the same through the controversial Cantometrics project (Lomax 1976). Many ethnomusicologists have suggested implicit connections between sound and society—often apparently unconscious to their informants; others focus upon explicit notions talked about in everyday music making.[14]

Too often homologies are more salient for the ethnographer than the informant; our identification of structures of time, society, and the cosmos (etc.) in music may stand as icons *for the ethnographer only* if not supported by explicit corroborating statements. Even when informants proffer homological relations explicitly, these are sometimes examples of esoterica—the Indian *naada* and Chinese *lu* may fall into

---

[12] Homological relationships are often described as iconic. Iconicity suggests a putative likeness to some other object through mimesis or convention (Eco 1976). Musical iconicity does not require a causal relationship between a sign and its object—an icon is not an index—but may simply suggest that certain characteristics of an object (concrete or conceptual) may be heard in music. Musical homology often suggests a cross-domain mapping from the sonic to the visual. The resonance of sound is swapped for a diagram of the cosmos, a chart of social relations, the structure of religious sites, and so on.

[13] See Jameson's discussion of Adorno in Attali (1985:x).

[14] See Becker (1981), Becker and Becker (1981), Seeger (1987), Gottlieb (1981), Turino (2008), Small (1998), Martinez (2001), Bar-Yosef (2001), Lansing (1983), Monson (1999), Roeder and Tenzer (2011). See Born (2010b) for a virtuosoic analysis of homological models in music studies.

this category—and may not be part of the everyday conceptual framework of musicians, composers, and listeners. This is what Bourdieu (1993:4) called the "odd philosophy of action," a methodological approach that reduced the individual to a bearer of unconscious expression of the culture itself. Bourdieu rejected theories which suggest homological relationships (either reflective or generative) between the structures of expressions and social structure itself (as in Lukacs and Goldman) and which portrayed the author as an unconscious spokesman for society at large. Bourdieu negatively associated this with the Romantic myth of the poet-*vates* in which the author simply becomes a medium for the group whose worldview, in complete correlation with the artist's expression, is imagined as completely homogenous. Such homological approaches neglect both the autonomy of the artistic field and the artist. Writing in 1986, Wayan Sadra similarly argued for the idiosyncratic independence of the artist and rejected the tendency to "always correlate *karawitan* with extra-musical thought, such as philosophical ideas about the micro and macro cosmos" (Sadra 1986:2).

To suggest that *musik kontemporer* necessarily represents incursions of Western temporal regimes into the Balinese psyche would be to confuse correlation with causation and ignore the aesthetic heterogeneity between individuals. Such determinative models would suggest facile connections to which we can find numerous counterexamples, as in the sinuous *ombak* of time and energy in *kontemporer* works including Widnyana's *Trimbat* (Figure 7.22).

Western-styled popular music, as much or more than *gamelan*, is the stuff of the contemporary Balinese soundscape, heard in stores, on car radios and home television sets and while hanging out in the *banjar*. We can hypothesize that the constant exposure to this music, with its more static temporal and dynamic profiles, has influenced the aesthetics of contemporary *gamelan* composers. This may be the case. However, many composers appeal to ancient forms to ratify their *kontemporer* works, often borrowing instruments and musical topics from sacred forms such as *slonding*, *luang*

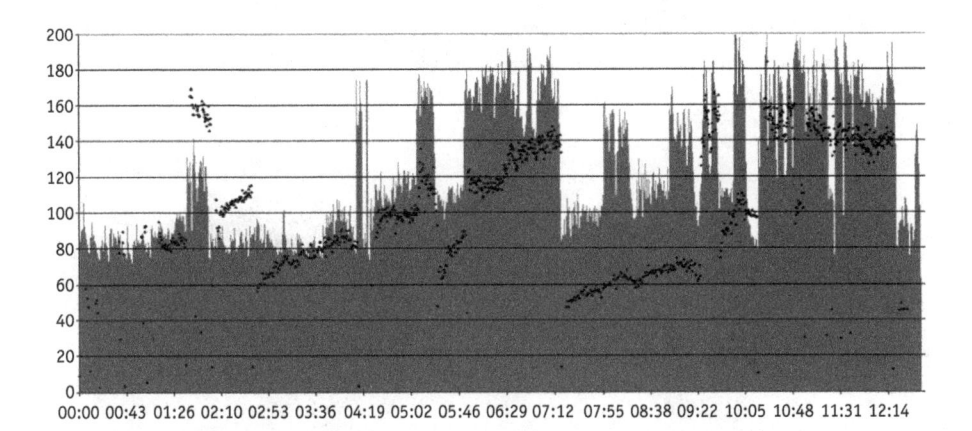

FIGURE 7.22 Dynamic and temporal strata in Ida Bagus Gede Widnyana's *Trimbat*, charting implied *kajar* tactus 2003. [Track MK-6/4]

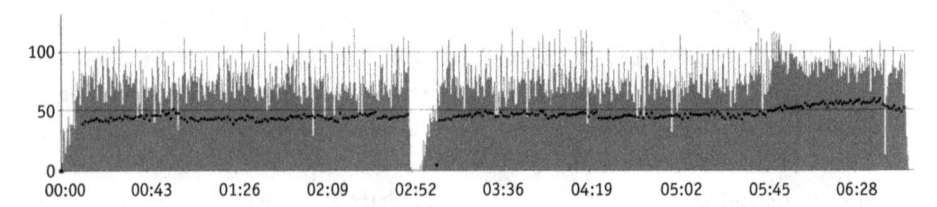

FIGURE 7.23 Dynamic and temporal strata in traditional *luang,* charting *neliti* tactus (personal recording). [Track MK-7/14]

(Figure 7.23), *gender wayang,* and *gambang* (Figure 7.24). The repertoires of each of these older forms appear dynamically and temporally restrained as compared to the music of *klasik* ensembles such as *pelegongan* and *kebyar.* These similarities problematize any tendency to imagine an intruding West flattening (with the false implication of impoverishing) Balinese musical temporalities.

CYCLICITY: AN OVERDETERMINED HOMOLOGY

> I am inclined to believe there is no such thing as repetition. And really how can there be? (Gertrude Stein 1998:292)

The persistent thematization of Balinese music as cyclic, a trope practically engineered to generate difference, presents an example of an overdetermined homological model in ethnomusicology. Certain music theorists and ethnomusicologists have suggested that Balinese music is primarily repetitive, cyclical, and isoperiodic, finding that it represents nonlinear cultural attitudes and styles (Kramer 1988:24), that it has no climax,[15] and so is similar to several other forms of Southeast Asian music in that in it stasis has become a musical form in itself (Maceda 1986).

It is possibly due to romantic anthropological notions of Balinese culture as existing somehow out of time that theorists including Kramer would be inspired to suggest that Balinese music is made up of rhythmic cycles which repeat seemingly without end and that it is thus not surprising that Balinese musical performances simply start

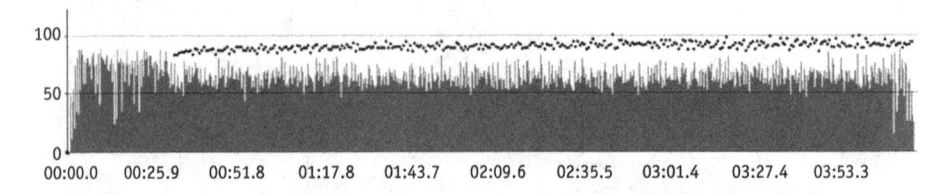

FIGURE 7.24 Dynamic and temporal strata in traditional *gambang,* charting implied *kajar* tactus. [Track MK-7/15]

---

[15] The lineage of this thought seems to have flowed thus: Kramer (1988), quoting Geertz (1973b) referencing McPhee (1966).

and stop but have neither beginning gestures nor ultimate final end (Kramer 1988).[16] Such statements, besides being patently wrong, play too transparently into colonial tropes of timeless Oriental life and of Asian culture as nonprocessive and, by extension, European culture and thought as progress-based and teleological.

We might trace this idea back to Marx's notion of the Asian Mode of Production, which Anderson describes as a political history that was "essentially cyclical: it contained no dynamic of cumulative development. The result was the...inertia and immutability of Asia" (Anderson 1974:483). This image reappears in both Bateson's theorization of the steady state and later characterizations of the Southeast Asian state as a static recapitulation of cosmological beliefs in which the *negara* produces a magical correspondence between the universe and the world of men "acquiring a power with which to dominate space, time and social relations" (Heine-Geldern 1956:1).

It is seductive to think of Balinese music in terms that accord with assumed Balinese worldview and concepts of time-in-general. Becker suggests that the most prominent feature of iconic power in Javanese or Balinese music is coincidence—small coincidings and large coincidings of recurring sounds, all iconic with the cycles of calendars and cosmos and thus, for the Javanese (and, one assumes, Balinese), appearing completely "natural" (Becker 1981:207). Similarly, many scholars have connected Indian concepts of *tal* with the Hindu cosmological notion of *kalpa*, or world cycles. In classical Indian cosmology the *kalpa* repeat, but not in detail, just as do *tala* cycles. However, as Clayton points out: "Musical time is no more a circle, or a wheel...than it is a rule or tape measure...or indeed a helix or a wave" (Clayton 2000:19).[17] In Balinese music the cycle is similar to the linguistic notion of the signifier. As demonstrated by the complex temporal structures of *gongan* described above, approaching it more closely, cyclicity seems to dissolve as you notice the narrative aspects of temporal profiles.

As two-dimensional representations, the charts above highlight the linear over the cyclical; *gongan*, when they are employed, are not always evident within them. One way to mediate between the cyclical and linear aspects of highly periodic musics is to represent onset timings along a three-dimensional helix in which a full turn through

---

[16] The understanding of Balinese music as principally cyclical may be due to what cognitive theorists term categorical perception, the condensation and accumulation of similarities and differences between objects and events (Hoopen 2006). Some Western theorists might conceive of Balinese music as cyclical not only because Western notation flattens out many of its narrative aspects, but for reasons of perceptual economy; there are so many other novel, exciting, and distracting elements to the music (orchestration, interlocking, tuning, etc.) that its temporality is quantized to fit a manageable Western category, that is, the cycle.

[17] The circular-linear opposition and the identification (as by Gurvich) of so-called relativistic time have been roundly critiqued in anthropology (see Munn 1992, Gell 1992). To a great extent, conversations about temporality in music have retreaded this ground. When it comes to music, the problem is not as bad as we make it sound. Our differences lie between the tension between concepts of objective (linear, forward-moving) time and the conception of return (of agrarian, ceremonial, natural, musical form, clock, calendar) time. For humans, time is *like* a wheel; events *seem* to recur. But for the passage of time to be perceived, the (cyclic) wheel's rubber meets the road of (linear) time at a single point we never pass over again.

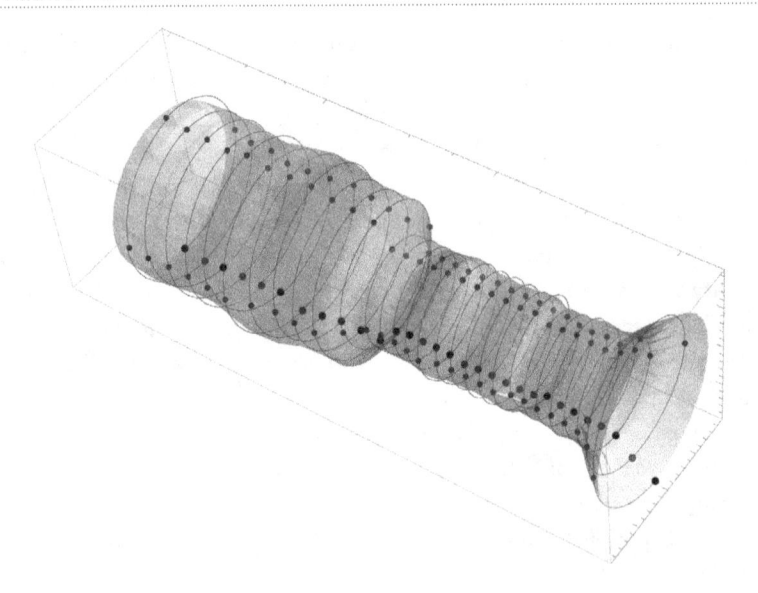

FIGURE 7.25 Helical representation of *gongan* in *Bapang Selisir*, Pinda village.

the helix equals a full cycle, or *gongan*. In this model, represented in (Figure 7.25[18]), the z axis (here moving left to right) represents absolute track timing. The x/y axes represent beats per minute; helical compression indicates a faster tempo, helical expansion a slower tempo. When represented thusly even the simplest and most highly periodic examples of traditional Balinese repertoire appear anything but static or literally cyclic.

Identifying homologies is a highly abstract process; when we describe homological relationships between cyclical or static music and cosmological beliefs or cultural constructions of time, we are identifying homologies between *ethnographic representations* of culture with *conceptions* of music, not the music itself. Iconic relationships suggest shared structural forms. But our idea of structural form in music is always already metaphorical and culturally mediated. When we say that melodic dips in Kaluli music are iconic of waterfalls, we have to remember that the idea of music dipping (it doesn't really) is already a metaphor; the same could be said of *ombak*. We are speaking of iconic relationships between metaphors, but not of the thing itself. Possibly one reason there are so many citations of the Kaluli metaphor, why it resonates among Western ethnomusicologists, is that it appears that the Kaluli think of melody along a vertical axis the way Western musicians do. The homological relationships identified in ethnomusicology often represent iconic relationships between the ethnographer's culturally mediated metaphoric representations of foreign music with his or her culturally mediated metaphoric conceptions of things like time, social structure, and so forth.[19]

---

[18] This image maps *calung* onset tones from a recording made by the author in Pinda village in March, 2012. *Gong* strokes are indicated along the bottom of the helix by larger points.

[19] Bar-Yosef suggests the same: "Analogies can mislead. An analogy between two cultural domains that may seem to evolve from a shared property may actually stem from the terminology we use; it may

Overdetermined homological models are rarely stated with clarity in ethnomusicology. At worst, they are anti-guides that make it possible to do away with the individual, living actors because the model tells us what they think (and feel) anyway. To suggest that the homological relationship may in fact be subconscious is to endow the ethnographer with godlike powers over and above the informant. There may be truth to the claim that Western harmonic progression represents a Western cultural focus upon progress and change or that Balinese *gongan* are connected to beliefs in reincarnation, but what we need to ask is if such homological relations are important in the creation of musical meaning as experienced by individual composers, performers, and listeners.

OMBAK AS A LIMITED MODEL

Many Balinese musicians do enjoy metaphorical, homological play. They liken domiciles to crocodiles (Boon 1990), drums to women (and men), interlocking to intercourse, intonations to inhalations, and tempos to the ocean's waves. The act of composition *is* an act of mediation connecting the practical experience of everyday life with realms of memory, feeling, historical consciousness, and philosophy, but we are on more solid methodological ground when we identify homologies explicitly named and used in the everyday by musicians, composers, and listeners rather than positing those homologies ourselves. Balinese musicians I encountered spoke of their music as waves, not as circles or cycles, not as stasis or as a calendar or as symbolic of reincarnation. Rather than risk selling the reader theoretical lemons, we should limn the scope of homology by starting with the demotic.

For instance, during my research Balinese musicians increasingly spoke of the spiritual resonances of paired *ngumbang-ngisep* tuning as a direct manifestation of the Balinese Hindu philosophy of *rwa bhineda,* or dualistic balance. Paired tuning causes the famous shimmering effect, also called *ombak,* which became an increasingly important compositional concern of composers including Asnawa, Alit, Widnyana and others.[20] As described in Chapter 5, the *pangider buana,* the Balinese cosmological compass, became another trope for explicitly linking musical form and religious belief. Explicit discourse such as this *can be* generative of musical structure and we may take its terms as a heuristic for understanding.

The heuristic connects two phenomena not by way of causation (because) or through iconicity (isomorphism) but as a way of offering an expanded thinking of one through the other; the heuristic is allegorical. This is a very general proposal; if you hold the concept of *ombak* to your ears, Balinese music comes alive in specific ways. Once we shift from the heuristic to causal mediation we enter the realm of making claims about the shaping of individual subjectivity. This suggests a logical chain of priority; society

---

refer to minor features that do not represent the main cultural characteristics we are looking for, and it may also result from the fortuitous co-appearance of features that are prevalent across many cultures and cultural domains, such as hierarchical relationships, or binariness, not indicating a unique cultural pattern" (2001:425).

[20] See also Wakeling 2010.

(economy, power, etc.) is the actor that acts upon the object of music that in turn acts upon individual subjectivity. This is part of ideology's caboodle and is a relation that can only be talked about in terms of determination. Instead, limited, explicit heuristics such as the *ombak* allow us to consider music through the idea of a specific type of physical motion. Through its very generality the heuristic allows for an expanded thinking of music as opposed to overdetermined homologies that may restrict listening imaginations.[21]

---

[21] I am indebted to the music scholar Joshua Clover for expanding my thinking on these topics.

8   The Semiotics of *Musik Kontemporer*

IN 2003, PRIOR *to founding his* Ceraken *arts club, Madé Subandi suggested we collaborate on a work with the musicians in his* banjar *in Batuyang, Gianyar. Responding to Subandi's demand for something "different," I composed a fast section in 12/8 inspired by my experience playing West African music. I transformed the iconic Ewe-Ghanaian* gankokue *bell rhythm into an interlocking* kotekan *pattern to elaborate a melody I borrowed from my Javanese teacher Harjito, who in turn intended it to suggest "Balinese-ness" in a* kontemporer *composition of his own.*[1] *Subandi's musicians teasingly named the work* Cara Landa, *meaning roughly "White Guy Style," and for a season Balinese composers traded similar compound patterns throughout their compositions, referring to them generically as the virus "*cara landa.*"*[2] *Materials borrowed from West Africa and Java had come to signify "whiteness" in Bali.*

The work proved extremely difficult for the musicians to learn and perform correctly. The gangsa *players constantly rushed, attempting to fit the regular four, rather than the intended three, notes within a single beat. If the* gangsa *players got it right, the beat player would begin to drag, similarly fighting the compound pulse. Although they eventually learned it, the groove didn't seem to lock in convincingly; it might have been considered "wrong" back home. I wondered if my attempts to perform Balinese music sounded similarly skewed to my teachers.*

Several months later Subandi incorporated and transformed my 12/8 section in an instrumental work entitled Nrtta Dewi *composed for Gus Teja's arts club in Ubud. Although many of the elaborating interlocking patterns were retained, the supporting* calung *often played every two, rather than three, notes, and the beat-keeping* kajar *seemed to occupy a separate temporal stream, sometimes aligning with the* gangsa *every three notes, sometimes phasing against it. Ironically, the exact alignment of the beat to every three notes which occupied so much of our time learning* Cara Landa *seemed an afterthought in the new work.*

In 2008 I traveled to Accra to continue my studies of Ewe drumming, focusing on the Agbadze dance that incorporated the same bell pattern I had used in *Cara Landa*. As

---

[1] Harjito's work, entitled *Cuplikan* (I), Quotation, was itself an arrangement of materials borrowed from his teacher, Martopangrawit.

[2] Although *landa*, a retention from the colonial-era term *Hollander*, can be rather derogatory; whitey or cracker might be closer to the mark.

my teacher and I listened to music on my computer after a long lesson, *Cara Landa* and *Nrtta Dewi* came up on the playlist. I asked: "Does any of this sound familiar? Do these patterns make sense to you?" Francois answered: "Nah, chale, this is just static to me!"

In this chapter I consider the interaction between listening and meaning. Are there cultural modes of listening? What happens to the meaning associated with musical signs when they move between Bali and America, for instance? Why, the first time I heard the Balinese work *Mesem* when watching the Balinese shadow play, did it bring the grandfather sitting next to me to tears, while it breezed past me, stirring no emotional tension? Why does it now choke me up? Beyond semantic meaning, I am concerned with the *means of production* of meaning. That is, I am interested not only in what but in how music means.

Below I present a semiotic model of listening intended to, in part, demonstrate the mechanisms that catalyze the mutation of representations at the level of individual perception and which, when scaled up, appear as stylistic and cultural change. Following my informants, I accept that music has meaning, although its status is ambiguous and not rigorously semantic.[3] Each of the examples discussed below emerged from a concrete ethnographic event in which I asked informants, simply: What does this music mean to you? Responses were consistently immediate and rich; no one questioned the presumption that music should have meaning.

The model I outline combines formalist, semantic, and pragmatic concerns and borrows from both Peirce and Sperber's notion of a tripartite model of semiosis. The most important element of this model is the *interpretant*, which we can think of most generally as a habit of interpretation. I identify three classes of musical interpretant. The *interstylistic interpretant* describes the habits of interpretation shared between related styles; these may appear biological or universal but are primarily conventional and learned. The more specific *stylistic interpretant* evokes primarily structural expectations and affects and appear as explicitly named styles. Most listeners hold a wide repertoire of stylistic interpretants. *Topical interpretants* are forms of intertextuality suggesting other styles and their associated references. Most experiences of music involve a complex interaction of multiple interpretant types.

I argue that the interpretants both individuals and groups hold change over time, allowing contagious musical viruses to take hold within styles. Interpretants are not rigidly contained within bounded cultures, suggesting that both culture and style are not stabilized things but force fields of consensus that can only be approached without finally being met. Listening through differing interpretive frames, across the perceived boundaries of culture, may produce the effect of musical homonyms, although some listeners may develop forms of interinterpretive bimusicality, allowing them to

---

[3] Kivy (2002) argues that meaning should refer only to linguistic reference, and so to describe music as having meaning is a category error similar to asking whether a rock is dead (Patel 2008). Nattiez, on the other hand, sees meaning in any signification, implying that meaning needs an interpreter and does not inhere in music itself. Despite the vigorous and rich project of musical semiotics, there is hardly a consensus on whether or not music has meaning and if so what kind of meaning it might be.

hear musical signs as this or as that. In intercultural contexts performers may play together, but hear differently, using disparate sets of interpretants. As demonstrated by a Balinese recomposition of an American Christmas tune, hearing representations through interpretants for which they were not designed can inspire their mutation. Although these might be thought of as misunderstandings, they are the mechanics of semiosis that help to catalyze change.

Semiotics

Saussure defined semiotics generally as the "science of the life of signs in society" (1974 [1916]:16). Semantics, often considered a subfield of semiotics, is traditionally concerned with the signification of the sign—its meaning—rather than the abstract rules that may guide the relationship between signs, often referred to as syntax. Pragmatics recognizes that speakers communicate more than they say (Moeschler 2004:59), and focuses upon the relationship between communicated meaning and social context. The emerging field of intercultural pragmatics examines the ways in which non-shared knowledge impacts the retrieval of intended meaning.

Structural-formalist musical analysis tends towards the syntactic; the hermeneutic exegesis of new musicology tends towards the semantic. Championed first in the nineteenth century by the Viennese critic Eduard Hanslick, formalist analysis—a form of musical determinism—banished emotions and extra-musical meaning to focus upon the pure and disinterested experience of contentless form. Re-energized by developments in linguistics, musical semioticians, led by Nattiez, developed rigorous paradigmatic analyses in the 1970s that explored a more constructivist approach suggesting that musical meanings could be extrinsically developed by discourse or context. Semantic studies of music have concerned both narrative structure and topical references pointing to extra-musical objects.[4] The semantic aspects of music, its ability to stand as a conventionalized (non-mimetic) symbol of something outside it, do not exist without acculturated interpreters. Musical pragmatics considers the interpretive slack between different listeners, composers, and performers considering the same sign.

Semiotic analysis mediates the tension between, on the one hand, the perception of meaning as inhering in a work, as a voice being expressed through it, and as a conduit and producer of new information and, on the other, the perception of meaning as if projected onto the work by an interpreter. The former is concerned more with the author, intention, and structure, the latter upon the viewer, listener, or reader. It is hard to remember, and our intuition and aesthetic reflexes rebel against it, that meaning is not necessarily intrinsic in sounds but are also given meaning by an interpreter. It is especially hard, in the split-second decisions and valuations we perform when listening or improvising music with others, to remember that the meaning we feel we

---

4 This is what Coker referred to as the "extrageneric contents" of music (1972). For analysts such as Tarasti (1994), musical themes and motifs function as actors or actants operating within a narrative structure.

receive is as much a reflection. If the reader detects a constructivist tendency in the discussion below, this is in part to provide an additional perspective to Tenzer's more formalist analysis of Balinese music.

Viral Mutations

As digital networks facilitate the increasing flow of information between peoples, we might pause to consider what is involved in this process; what is transferred, lost, invented? We might ask why certain representations are more contagious than others. Here we are reminded of Sperber's notion of the "epidemiology of representations" (1996) introduced in Chapter 1. Although, as Sperber admits, comparing ideas with diseases is in many ways old hat, his notion introduces several novel concepts useful for the present study. First, epidemiological models are bottom up, beginning with semiosis at the level of the individual. Phenomena at the level of style or culture are then the cumulative effect of individual-level processes, events, and experiences, not a structure that encages the individual from the top down and tells him or her how to interpret a representation. Some representations are held by an individual for only a few seconds, others are held by groups over generations; these are what we tend to think of as culture although there is no firm threshold between individual and cultural representations (1996:58). Whereas mutation is the exception in the case of biological viruses, which are often replicated literally, the opposite is the case for representations in human culture. It is this mutation at the level of individual representations that, when scaled up, appears as cultural change. For Sperber, a representation involves: "a relationship between three terms: an object is a representation *of* something *for* some information-processing device [a person]" (1996:61). This tripartite structure of semiosis is adapted from Peirce and informs the music-semiotic model provided below.

A Listening Model

> To be listening is to be inclined toward the opening of meaning. (Nancy 2007)

In the late-nineteenth century the American polymath C. S. Peirce, working independently and prior to Saussure, developed a highly nuanced semiotic model most basically outlined in the triadic relationship of the Sign, Object, and Interpretant. These three categories were further refined into various classes. My use of this basic model differs from previous applications in both linguistics and musical semiotics through a focus upon a specific class of interpretant and an object field rather than the interaction of designata/designatum (as in Boiles 1982).

In the model I illustrate below the sign is music itself existing in the real world—an acoustic phenomena as heard: not a score, or memory of music. Most generally, the sign is something that stands for something else for an interpreter. Music is not a sign until it is interpreted by a listener in a specific space and time. The interpretant is a person's habit of interpretation, discoverable through ethnographic methods. The interpreter may have more than one interpretant for interpreting a sign. That is, a listener may apply different cognitive modes or listening habits to the same musical passage. Different interpreters/listeners may or may not share an interpretant or repertoire of interpretants for the same musical sign, resulting in sometimes highly divergent readings.

In Peirce's model the object is something to signify, the subject matter of the sign—its referent. But music is not language; it is not capable of propositional meaning, nor can it ask questions or make meta-linguistic statements; its semantic specificity is highly limited. Because of this, it makes little sense to imagine musical semiosis in a binary Saussurean model. Music's object is a complex field of affect, iconicity, semantic implication, and indexicality.

Peirce's notion of the interpretant as a habit of interpretation shares characteristics with later theories of language, including Ingarden's concept of schemata, the pre-understandings a reader brings to any work in order to construct a coherent meaning.[5] Gadamer's notion that readers approach all works with prejudices based upon their experience similarly recalls the interpretant, as does Geertz's concept of webs of significance, DeNora's preparatory sets (2003), and Feld's interpretive moves (1984). Like these concepts, the interpretant is helpful for freeing us of the structuralist picture theory of language in which each word would be unproblematically attached to an item in the world or a metaphysical essence or archetype. Instead, both Peirce and later the deconstructionists suggest that a unique set of interpretants appear for each signifying event. The meaning of a sign (a word, a musical passage) is then contingent upon context and enters the territory of pragmatics.

In the present model I identify three classes of musical interpretant. I call the *interstylistic interpretant* (I_{IS}) the habits of interpretation shared between related styles. Interstylistic interpretants may appear biological or universal but they are primarily conventional and learned. Ethnomusicologists might refer to these as cultural modes of listening although this is misleading for reasons detailed below. Western Tonal Harmony is an interstylistic interpretant; from Baroque music to contemporary pop, most of us typically expect V to resolve to I. The referents of signs interpreted through the interstylistic interpretant are generally conceptual, conventionalized structural expectations and affects. Interstylistic interpretants may also produce gestural objects such as a descending or sighing melodic line. While they may feel universal, these referents emerge as the products of interpretants developed through a listener's experience of conventionalized forms of inter-domain mapping. A melody that may appear iconic of a physical descent to a listener familiar with Western classical music may appear to be getting larger to a listener more familiar with Balinese traditions. Interstylistic interpretants are rarely named or conceived consciously by listeners; they are a part of implicit musical common sense.

---

[5] Huron has similarly explored a theory of musical schemas as applied to crosscultural musical experiences (2006:218).

Stylistic interpretants (I_S) are more specific than interstylistic interpretants and evoke a range of referents, primarily expectations and affects, more highly conventionalized than those of the interstylistic interpretant. Stylistic interpretants are explicitly named—romanticism, reggae, *semar pegulingan*, and *slonding*—and most listeners hold a wide repertoire of stylistic interpretants through which they can choose to hear a given musical sign. Sonata form evokes a specific object field of formal expectations and affective suggestions to those equipped with the stylistic interpretant of the Western Classical Style. Similar musical signs may evoke different objects if heard through differing stylistic interpretants.[6]

Topical interpretants (I_T) interpret forms of intertextuality that reach beyond the stylistic conventions of a work (but often remain within interstylistic conventions) to suggest other styles and their associated object fields. Topical interpretants may suggest more strongly the social conditions of the styles they evoke than the structural conventions of those styles themselves. For instance, a composer may include references to the *gamelan slonding* within a new work for the *gamelan gong kebyar*. For those holding the relevant stylistic interpretant, this momentary passage may reach beyond the stylistic conventions of the *kebyar* genre to suggest the musical conventions of *slonding*. However, the social conditions of *slonding* within Balinese culture may be the more salient objects produced within this context. These objects may be, for instance, Aga villages such as Tenganan, notions of *tradisi*, the *etnik*, the sacred, and the ancient. While interstylistic and stylistic interpretants continuously scan the surface of the musical sign, topical interpretants may appear as more occasional, discrete moments: blips of intertextuality on the semiotic radar.

It should be remembered that the referents that appear in the object field are signs as well. The object field represents an endless chain of signification; an essential *slonding*-ness, for example, could never be identified or stabilized. As described by both Eco (1976) and Derrida (1985), signification is an endless process of deferral; there can be no predefined limits binding the potential meaning of any representation (Cumming 2001:294). You can endlessly describe a sign within the object field beyond the intentions attributable to its author or original cultural context. But the more widely shared between listeners referents in the object field are, the more social salience they have.

During my research, many composers spoke of using different glasses or lenses (I: *kaca mata*) when listening to music; others spoke of maps and guides (I: *pedoman*). According to Pande Madé Sukerta: "I have many pairs of glasses. To avoid getting confused when working in or listening to *tradisi* forms, you need to use your *tradisi* glasses, but when you enter the field of *musik kontemporer*, you have to switch, otherwise you cannot see the relevant structures" (p.c. July 2003). These visual metaphors are resonant with Peirce's model and inspire the diagrams I provide below in which musical semiosis is represented as a filmic projection. Sounds entering our ear are, through

---

[6] In Peirce's taxonomy stylistic and interstylistic interpretants would also be signs, in this case a *legisign*, a set of conventions rather than a specific instance in the world.

top-down processes of audition, quantized into the qualities we identify as "music" or "noise." Sounds identified as music pass through an interpretive lens projecting a field of conventionalized meaning onto the screen of consciousness. In Peircian terms the lens is the interpretant, the musical signal is the sign (or a constellation of signs), and the projection presents the object field. Switching lenses produces a differently hued field of meaning.[7] In contrast to the simplistic "transmission" model of musical communication, these diagrams focus upon the listener's constructive processes in creating meaning.

Examples

The *bapang gong* form is a binary colotomic structure outlined by a low *gong* stroke and a high-pitched small *gong* (*kemong*) stroke. The *bapang* appears throughout several styles of Balinese *gamelan* music.[8] The I_{IS}(Balinese *gamelan*) produces various conceptions, expectations, and understandings of this sign: we expect the *bapang* to repeat and for it not to be rigidly metronomic but to fluctuate under the direction of specific drumming patterns; we understand that the *gong* lands on the last beat of the pattern which is bisected by the *kemong*; we hear melodies beginning after, rather than on the *gong*. Heard through the I_{IS}(Balinese *gamelan*), the *bapang* may also evoke objects such as the kinds of refined, often feminine, dance motions typically performed to *bapang* in several Balinese styles. This referent might thus initiate a further chain of semiosis if a listener chooses to consider Balinese meanings of femininity (Figure 8.1).

In the context of the *gamelan gambuh* the *bapang gede* melody is performed in the *tembung* mode to accompany the dance of the *patih* (king or prime minister) in the *gambuh* dance drama. As heard through the stylistic interpretant of *gambuh*, both the character and, by extension, its musical accompaniment (the most important elements of which would include mode, melody, form, and drumming patterns) is considered by many Balinese listeners to evoke a strong and heroic affect (B: *agung, gagah*). The sign produces these referents for those listeners applying the I_S(*gambuh*) independent of the social context of an actual *gambuh* performance (as when hearing a recording). Within the context of a *gambuh* performance, the *bapang gede* melody often anticipates the dancer's actual arrival, producing these referents prior to their direct association with the *patih* character (Figure 8.2).

---

[7] The visual mode was not the only way in which Balinese composers spoke of meaning in music. Many discussed meaning in terms of other sensory modes, such as smell and feel. When speaking in Indonesian, many composers spoke of the particular *suasana* a work might evoke. Although *suasana* literally means atmosphere, within the context of music it suggests a certain feeling or mood. When speaking Balinese most composers used the term *bo* (*ba*), similar to the Indonesian *bau*, literally meaning smell. Compositions have certain types of aroma, which may evoke other repertoires or affects, as in *bo-ne cara angklung*, meaning it sounds like (literally "smells like") *angklung*. The term *rasa*, meaning feeling or taste, may stand in for *bo*, but was typically used by conservatory-trained musicians when speaking in Indonesian, although the term is known in Balinese.

[8] The form may include medium-sized *gong* (*kempur*) strokes on beats 2 and 6 in *kebyar* styles.

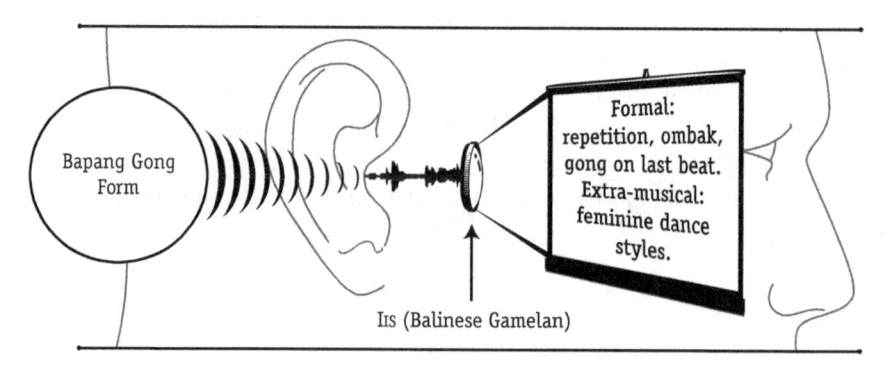

FIGURE 8.1 Interstylistic Interpretant.

Topical interpretants guide the listener beyond the stylistic conventions of the immediate musical texture to produce meaning from intertextual references. Wayan Sadra's *musik kontemporer* work, *Beringin Kurung* (excerpted in Example 8.1), was composed for the instruments of the classic *keroncong* ensemble: violin, flute, light percussion, ukulele, and guitar. Much of the work represents an extension and deconstruction of *keroncong* textures, but the beginning presents a syncopated motor rhythm that, for some Balinese listeners, evoked the music of the *slonding* ensemble. None of the Javanese listeners interviewed made this association; some instead heard references to heavy metal. Sadra admitted to pilfering the *slonding* style in this section of the work. For him, this passage evoked the "ancient sounds of Aga tradition" and brought to mind the "rural, rustic" image of pre-Hindu Balinese village life. The effect of refracting premodern *slonding* through the sound of *keroncong*—a form that evokes for many Indonesians a nostalgia for Independence-era modernity—produced for Sadra a host of unstable and emergent meanings, (illustrated in Figure 8.3), which he described as a "culturally improbable sound" (p.c. September 2003).

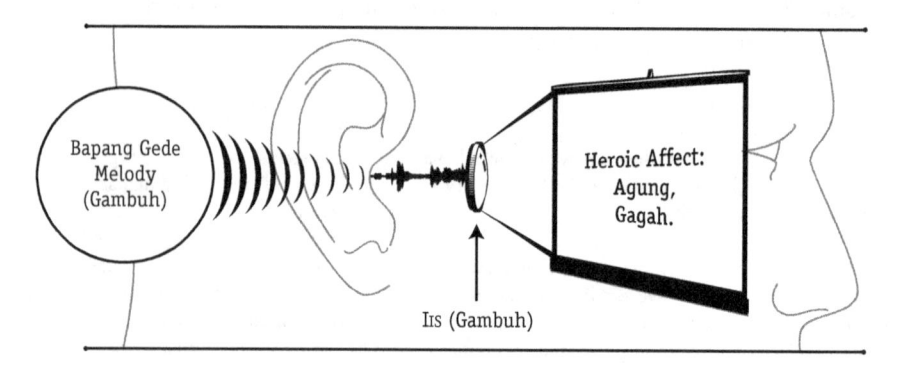

FIGURE 8.2 Stylistic Interpretant.

violin, guitar, erhu, mandolin ♩=178

EXAMPLE 8.1 Wayan Sadra. *Beringin Kurung*, introduction. [Track MK-2/1]

For most of us, the experience of listening to a musical composition is a flowering of almost innumerable signs, each producing a rich field of objects only some of which reside within the spectrum of named, explicit emotions or meanings (Bharucha et al. 2012:144). This is illustrated in Figure 8.4 below. Depending on our particular repertoire of interpretants, we may experience each moment differently, sometimes applying multiple interpretants simultaneously. We may attend to a topical reference to the *gender wayang* repertoire in *gong kebyar* contexts (as in Gusti Putu Madé Geriya's 1969 *Jaya Warsa*) through the I_T(*gender wayang*), evoking specific scenes, moods, or character types from the shadow-play repertoire. We may simultaneously consider, through the I_S(*gong kebyar*), its structural implications in relation to the stylistic conventions of *gong kebyar*. Asymmetric *gong* patterns, stretched to fit the sometimes uneven phrases of *gender wayang*, take on a special prominence and novelty within *gong kebyar* in which *gong* patterns are overwhelmingly binary.

Musik kontemporer exists in the spaces between the routinized interpretive habits of many Balinese listeners. The bowing of percussion instruments began to appear in

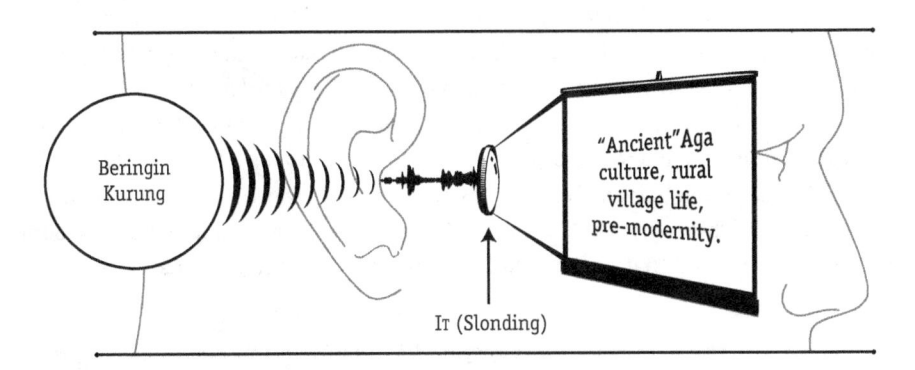

FIGURE 8.3 Topical Interpretant.

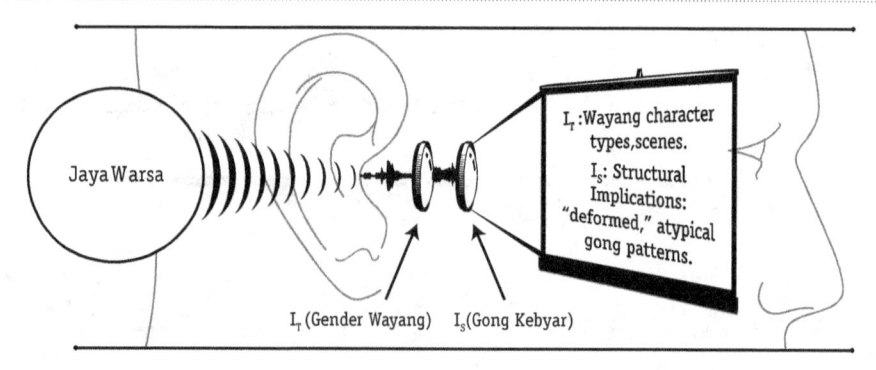

FIGURE 8.4. Interaction of interpretant types.

musik kontemporer in Bali during the *reformasi* and was used extensively in the fourth movement of Dewa Ketut Alit's *Salju* (2007). Asked to respond to the passage, an eminent elderly composer seemed bewildered: "It has no meaning; I cannot *hear* it." Using all of the interpretants at his disposal, the composer claimed it did not produce any objects but was instead a kind of null sign.[9]

A similar semiotic phenomenon can be identified in Yudane's incorporation of innovative *gong* structures, first developed in smaller *kontemporer* contexts, into several of his *kreasi baru* and *musik kontemporer* compositions of the early 1990s. Rather than using the typical binary structures outlined by the large *gong* and in which melodic forms should conform, Yudane fit *gong* forms around asymmetrical melodies, performed syncopated accents on colotomic instruments, and aligned melodic cadences away from *gong* points. Although prefigured by works such as Geriya's *Jaya Warsa*—which included *gong* patterns stretched to fit *gender wayang* phrasing—and Wayan Beratha's 1968 *Palgunawarsa*—which included five-beat *gong* phrases—Yudane took the concept much further, most clearly illustrated in his 1994 *Yudhaskanda Sargah*. Yudane referred to this technique as "breaking the *gong*" (I: *merusak gong*). When first developed, this technique confused and sometimes alienated listeners, including many older composers. For these listeners, the stylistic interpretant for *kreasi baru* rendered only noise as the object for the broken *gong* sign. Indeed, many suggested it was simply a null sign; it produced no meaning. Not only was Yudane's approach generally unintelligible through the expected stylistic interpretant of *kreasi baru*, it appeared to make little sense from the interstylistic perspective of Balinese *gamelan*.

Eventually, however, Yudane's works began earning top prizes at the annual *kebyar* contests and several composers began copying the broken *gong* technique. By 2010 the approach was commonplace. That is, the same sign had, over time, come to produce a different, and richer, object field for many listeners, as illustrated in Figure 8.5. Some composers suggested that the dissolution of formalistic *gong* patterns represented a

---

[9] Based upon similar reactions by other older composers, my hunch is that the passage did in fact signify to this listener. However, rather than producing musical referents (structural expectations) it likely suggested concepts such as youth, foreignness, and rebelliousness.

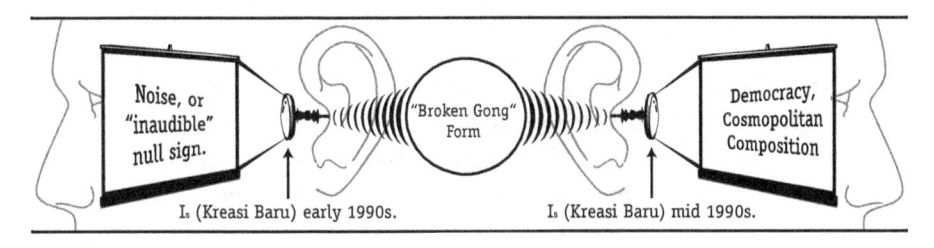

FIGURE 8.5 Single I_s, Changing social context, across time. [Track MK-8/1]

new ethical model of interaction in the *gamelan* and an allegorical reference to democracy.[10] Yudane himself discounted such accounts, suggesting that listeners came to accept these structures simply out of the "herd mentality" of typical Balinese audiences. He argues that few contemporary listeners can actually hear or understand them (p.c. March 2012) [Track BV-8/1].

Example 8.2, taken from Yudane's 1995 *Lebur Seketi*, illustrates, in a more simplified form than his *Yudhaskanda Sargah*, the ways in which he pushed and pulled the 16-beat *bapang gong* form—gong (O), *kempur* (U), *kemong* (+), *kempur* (U)—that had become a standard, fast tempo section incorporated into the second half of many New Order *kreasi baru*. Besides adding beats (as in mm. 12), Yudane also shifts the alignment of melodic beginnings away from the *gong* (as in mm. 7), further unsettling any sense of even meter or phrase.

EXAMPLE 8.2 Wayan Gede Yudane. *Lebur Seketi*, broken *gong* excerpt.

---

[10] For some older listeners, still employing the I_s(*kreasi baru*) of the New Order, the broken *gong* sign remained unintelligible during the *reformasi*. The inability to hear new musics recalls Asaf'yev's concept of the intonational crisis: "New people, a new ideational direction, a different 'emotional attitude', all call forth different intonations, or the re-evaluation of familiar ones. Woe to the composers who do not hear these changes! People will not listen to them, for they do not hear the idea of their music" (quoted in Till 1976:715).

MODE AND AFFECT

Conservatory theorists I interviewed (primarily Asnawa, Sinti, Beratha, and Rai) suggested a tight correlation between the modes (*pathet*) derived from *gambuh*—which they mapped onto seven-tone bronze ensembles such as *semar pegulingan* and *semara dana*—and specific affects. As performed on metal ensembles, the *tembung* mode, it was suggested, continued to evoke a sense of strength and grandeur through its historic association with the *patih* character from the *gambuh* dance drama. *Selisir*, associated with refined characters in *gambuh*, evoked sweetness. These theorists argued that because of their historical uses each mode evoked a bounded semantic field shared among Balinese listeners (cf. Rai 1996).

But when playing recorded examples of works in various modes for younger, conservatory-trained composers, almost none identified the affects that conservatory taxonomy suggested they should. Possibly because they had not encountered either *gambuh* or other seven-tone ensembles prior to entering the conservatory, the meanings of various modes was for them highly labile. Ida Bagus Gede Widnyana's response was typical of his peers:

> When I was taught this taxonomy at ISI I did feel, well, confused. I didn't hear what they were talking about. I can't say they are "wrong" but even within one culture, one era, we disagree and argue! In fact, we can create all moods in *slendro,* or with the five-tone *selisir* on the *gong kebyar.* On a *semar pegulingan* we can use the *tembung* mode to make something sad, profound, sweet, or romantic. There are many factors here: the sound of a particular set of instruments, the melodic form, the tempo, the drumming style, *and* the mode. The same melody played at different tempos can suggest very different moods. We're not even talking yet about the situation of a particular performance, which can deeply inflect how a piece feels, independent of the musical structures. (p.c. March 2012) [Track BV-8/2]

The affects suggested by the conservatory taxonomy appeared to many composers during the *reformasi* as effaced when heard through topical interpretants and very weak, for many nonexistent, when heard through interstylistic interpretants. That is, while the *tembung* mode sometimes stood as a sign for heroic and strong affects in *gambuh* for those trained in the conservatory taxonomy, this association was far from guaranteed as a referent in interstylistic contexts. At most, it may only retain a vague, implicit affective resonance as male or strong. By the *reformasi* era, composers including Dewa Ketut Alit were composing accompaniments for refined female dances in the *tembung* mode on the *gamelan semara dana* (e.g., *Pengastung Kara*) as if to purposefully disaggregate the institutionalized referents of the sign.

The conservatory taxonomy assumes, first, that Balinese listeners have a well-developed sense of mode and, second, that listeners should hear pitches as members of a specific mode from the get-go when it is in fact the gradual unfolding of melody that allows listeners to *infer* a sense of mode (when they can). Localized variations in tuning, terminology, and meanings work against the potential for universal associations between mode and affect in Bali. Conservatory theorists have attempted to police meaning by tying affect to specific exemplars drawn from a particular style of *gambuh*. Most composers, however, appear to have developed a repertoire of interpretants based upon the abstraction of information from a range of prototypes, among which structures such as drumming, tempo, melody, and colotomic form seem to have more coherence than mode or intonation.

The conservatory's "taxonomy fever" (p.c. Suardana, March 2012) appears as a response to the apparent fixity and rationality of both Western and Javanese aesthetic systems. Many Western listeners associate minor modes with sadness and major modes with happiness. Although this is a generalization, it is nevertheless the case that Western keys are considerably more semantically determined and shared among listeners than Balinese modes, probably because of a long history in the West of a universal tuning standard and widespread exposure to the association between specific keys and specific moods (primarily through film). This situation produces interesting consequences when we consider listening crossculturally.

INTERCULTURAL OR INTERINTERPRETIVE MEANING?

The smell of wintergreen is pleasantly reminiscent of chewing gum to most Americans while it reminds most British of old-fashioned medical ointments.[11] As the self-same representation passes between interpretive frames, one cannot consider that one is dealing in each case with the same discursive event (Foucault 1972:143). Foucault described such signs as "enunciatively different." But what, exactly, makes them different? To attribute this difference to an abstract culture is to reify difference itself—to posit an essential, homogenous otherness. The expansion of Europe's geography during the age of exploration introduced the persistent model of cultures as territories bounded by lines that can, or cannot, be crossed. We hear of closed and open cultures. However, no essential American-ness or Balinese-ness, for example, could ever be identified; no absolute cognitive commonalities bind members of a so-called culture. When artists, governments, funding organizations, and theorists speak of "intercultural collaboration," they are being vaguely metaphorical. Cultures do not interact or communicate with each other, people do.

To describe Balinese or American cultural ways of hearing seems to forestall the possibility that Balinese can hear a string quartet in ways similar to their European counterparts or that Americans could ever hope to hear *gamelan* in ways similar to Balinese composers. Rather than intercultural listening—a notion predicated upon a concept of culture as a bounded space of inside and outside—it may be better to refer to acts of *interinterpretive* listening.[12] Such a frame recognizes the possibility that listeners, from

---

[11] I'm grateful to the scholar of scent James McHugh for this.
[12] In Chapter 9 I retain "intercultural" for those projects in which culture is an explicit and fundamental category of thought by artists, audiences, and patrons.

whatever cultural context, have the ability to develop interpretants commonly associated with their others. Neither culture nor style are stabilized things but are force fields that one can approach without ever finally meeting. The interinterpretive does not necessarily imply a hybrid identity or creolism, but recognizes interaction between differentiated groups of people. The interinterpretive holds the potential for revealing the contingent nature of all cultural practice. As John Cage insisted, new modes of listening, as through interinterpretive frames, are just as important as new musics (1961:10).

Listeners sometimes come into contact with sounds for which they may not share the basic stylistic or interstylistic interpretants used by those closer to the center of a style's force field. Sometimes this leads to incomprehension, as when my teacher in Ghana heard Balinese *gamelan*. But listeners often doggedly produce meaning. Our habit of producing meaning suggests that a musical sign is never exhausted by the intentions of its author or the implications of its original style. This is not to say that there as many Fifth Symphonies or *Taruna Jaya*'s as there are listeners; as we approach the center of a stylistic force field, listeners' interpretants begin to overlap, leading to increasingly, but never completely, shared experiences.

I could make little sense of Balinese *gamelan* when I first encountered it in a world music class in America in 1995. Listening through my available interpretive repertoire, *Taruna Jaya*—now one of my favorite works—seemed to signify only vague notions of Asia and evoked a sense of strangeness and the exotic. Listening to works for which our habits of interpretation were not designed, new music can seem to be a rather undifferentiated experience for the novice, a gestalt in which the entire work is undercoded, signifying in rather limited ways. Upon first hearing *Taruna Jaya*, I may have formed a broad category for otherness to which new sounds were indiscriminately assigned, grouping individual representations into broad categories. A similar process of categorical perception leads us to perceive the continuously varying series of individuals as discretely bounded cultures, for example, the Balinese. This is a kind of listening as if through a colonial census; as the conquistadors saw only *hidalgos* in the Americas, the Dutch looked to Asia and, at first, saw an endless series of *chinezen* (Anderson 1991).

However, rather than a completely undifferentiated gestalt, first encounters can be semiotically rich, albeit in ways that differ from the experience of expert listeners. The interstylistic interpretant of Western music can evoke in non-Balinese listeners certain expectations of repetitions and interruptions. It may produce the object of sweetness by rendering the *selisir* mode as A-major pentatonic (as it still often does for me, to my distress) or lead them to interpret melodies as gesturally iconic of rising or descending motions. While it is likely that a listener equipped with I_{IS}(Balinese gamelan) has a more highly differentiated experience through being more conversant with stylistic conventions and topical references, the novice's experience may be just as meaningful and rich as the expert's. Indeed, when the expert can understand everything through an ability to completely parse music's signs, he or she might find it dull. The overlaps between different interstylistic interpretants and the ability for interpretants associated with one tradition to make meanings (even if they are culturally inappropriate) out of expressions of other cultures lies at the heart of the possibilities of interinterpretive communication and inspires the mutation of representations that drive innovation and stylistic change.

MUSICAL HOMONYMS

Homonyms are words that share pronunciation but differ in meaning. As seen in Figure 8.6, similar phenomena can be identified in interinterpretive musical semiosis. While Balinese informants often described the music of the *gamelan angklung* as sad due to its association with the Balinese *ngaben* cremation ceremony, many American listeners, listening through the interstylistic interpretant of Western Tonal Harmony, hear it as joyful and carefree, likely to due to the structural similarities between the *angklung* tuning and the Western major scale. This kind of implicit, top-down cognition can make it extremely difficult to develop new interpretants and is a form of categorical perception, one in which the complex, particular intonation of *gamelan angklung*, which often diverges considerably from the equally tempered major scale, is quantized, as it were, into the closest equivalent Western schema. A similar phenomena occurs when Western listeners hear the *tembung* mode, which has structural similarities to the equal-tempered minor scale. However, this is not a straightforward case of musical homonyms; while *tembung* often produces strong, unambiguous affects of sadness and pathos for me, it may produce no *specific* affects for Balinese listeners independent of other musical information such as form and tempo.

Reilly (1987) provides a convenient visual illustration of these cognitive processes. Having just learned his letters, a child or a non-native reader may interpret Illustration 8.1 as it is: the cht. Readers using interpretants developed through contextualized experiences of written English will derive the intended meaning: the cat.[13]

In 2007 I collaborated with the composers Ida Bagus Widnyana and Wayan Sudirana on a work for the *gamelan semara dana* entitled *DyDeDi*. In his contribution to the work Widnyana developed an ambitious exploration of each of the Balinese five-tone *pathet* modes.[14] After establishing each mode horizontally through melodic passages,

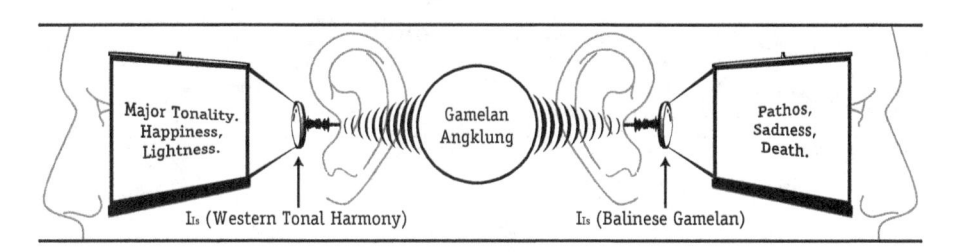

FIGURE 8.6 Interinterpretive meaning. Musical Homonyms.

---

[13] Working among the Inuit, Boas similarly discovered that "linguistic transcriptions were strongly influenced by sounds expected and misperceived by fieldworkers on the basis of their European cultural conditioning" (Myers 1992:118).

[14] Traditional works are typically restricted to single modes and many *kontemporer* seven-tone works often employ only two or three modes.

THE CAT

ILLUSTRATION 8.1 Categorical Perception. From Reilly (1987); reprinted by permission of the author.

Widnyana then stacked them vertically in a sequence of clusters, that is, *selisir*: 12356, *tembung*: 12456, and so forth. Listening through the I_{IS}(Balinese *gamelan*), Widnyana reported that he could continue to hear the modal identity of each cluster. I, however, tended to hear the passage through the I_{IS}(Western Tonal Harmony) such that each cluster appeared as a chord within a key, producing referents that suggested the structural logics of Western common practice harmony and the affective attributions of each chord, that is, I = major, tonic; iv = minor, and so on. Widnyana and I experienced the same musical sign in very different ways, as illustrated in Figure 8.7. The Balinese composer Ari Hendrawan claimed to be able to hear the passage in either way. Trained in both *gamelan* and Western harmony and theory as a guitarist, Hendrawan frequently composed *musik kontemporer* that combined Western and Balinese musical systems and instruments. Beyond simply developing a performative bi-musicality, as many American students of *gamelan* have, Hendrawan had developed a sophisticated interinterpretive ability; he could hear musics through multiple interstylistic interpretants.[15]

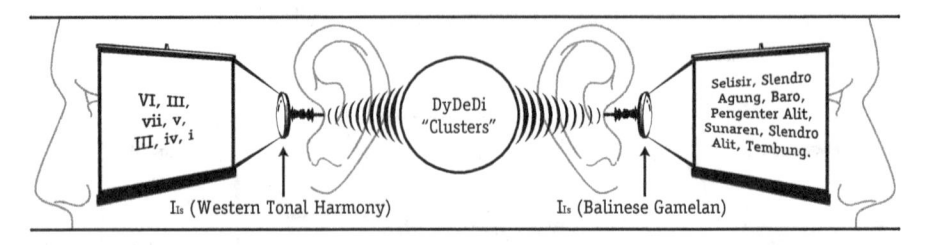

FIGURE 8.7 Interinterpretive Listening. *DyDeDi*. [Track MK-8/2]

---

[15] In his exploration of crosscultural musical schema Huron (2006:218) asks the fascinating question: "How do existing listening schemas interfere with or prevent the development of other listening schemas?" If we provisionally conflate the notion of the schema and the interpretant, Hendrawan's comment seems to suggest that they do not. However, no matter how hard I tried, I found myself unable to completely rid myself of a sense of tonal harmony, despite over a decade of experience with Balinese music.

HEARING AS

Listeners such as Hendrawan can hear music as this or as that much in the way our perception shifts from seeing the rabbit or the duck in Wittgenstein's famous *trompe l'oeil*.[16] We may choose to hear many West African rhythms in either compound or binary time and while the structure of the music itself does not change, our perception and experience does.[17] When we are truly interinterpretive listeners, as Hendrawan was, we can choose to hear music through this or that interstylistic interpretant. When we encounter texts that challenge us to develop new interpretive habits we face what Gadamer called the "horizon of our own prejudice." As Gadamer suggested, these prejudices—habits of interpreting—are our very condition of being in the world; to change them is to change ourselves. After several years spent studying in the West, Wayan Sudirana felt that the transformation of his interpretive modes was indicative (or generative) of a more profound mutation:

> When it comes to listening, I think I now have an alter ego, a second Sudirana, that is more like you than the old me. I can't use my old knowledge to listen to new music, or non-Balinese music. I don't know if I am using eye-glasses or a map anymore; or if it is a second self. I'm not consciously changing glasses. Maybe I can now ignore my background, to strip that all away and just have nothing in me in order to try to listen objectively. And now I can hear Balinese music in a different way. Before I came [to Canada] I never thought about those aspects of the music that I thought were normal. Now that I can listen to them as a Westerner, I wonder about them all the time. (p.c. May 2012)

Traditional Balinese paintings do not differentiate between foreground and background, but compress all elements into a single plane. Viewing these images through the interpretant of Western perspective, we may become frustrated and miss their play of temporality and narrative. Listening to *musik kontemporer* through the interpretants (or, as Sukerta phrased it, glasses) developed for *gong kebyar* can be a similarly frustrating experience for older Balinese listeners. The trend towards increasingly homogenous temporal and dynamic profiles in *musik kontemporer* pressured listeners to develop interpretive habits divergent from those used for *gong kebyar* and *kreasi baru* in order to attend more directly upon novel features. *Musik kontemporer* has emerged in tandem with the apparent expansion of young Balinese listeners' repertoire of interpretants—their increasing ability to hear sound as *gamelan* or *musik*.

---

[16] Wittgenstein's concept of "seeing as" was later applied by Hester to describe poetic metaphor and by Scruton to music (Spitzer 2004).

[17] Whether or not we can see the rabbit *and* the duck, or hear West African rhythms in compound and duple feels simultaneously, or if we simply transition rapidly between the two perspectives, is a matter of debate (see Friedson 2009:219).

In July 2009 Gusti Putu Sudarta invited the Javanese performer Tri Hartono and me to participate in a free improvisation (I: *improvisasi bebas*) at the Bali Arts Festival. The improvisation involved Sudarta playing an African *udu* idiophone, Hartono on Javanese *rebab* and *gender,* and me on a Javanese *kenong gong* chime. At a certain point in the improvisation Sudarta played references to the music of Banyuwangi which I at first mistook for a reference to hip-hop. The improvisation continued for some time before I realized my mistake, based upon subsequent patterns played by Sudarta.

Only at the moment of this mistake did I consider what must have been numerous other missed encounters in this improvisation and in other intercultural musical contexts. To what extent were we hearing the same music? To what extent did the audience, likely sharing many of Sudarta's interpretants, realize what I was missing? In the intercultural musical encounter we tend to respond to recognizable sounds, repeating them, as in the encounter between two speakers of mutually unintelligible languages. But what we perform back to the other may only be understood as a proto-gesture, a kind of phoneme rather than a recognizable musical unit. Caught between interpretive frames, we perform sounds in-between.[18]

In 2007 a Japanese producer arrived at the Cudamani compound with the concept of arranging American Christmas tunes on *gamelan* for release as a holiday novelty album in Japan. The producer provided several Cudamani composers with midi recordings of Christmas tunes and invited them to arrange the melodies as they saw fit. Many composers referred to the resulting compositions as *musik kontemporer*. Although the source materials seemed hardly experimental to me, the new arrangements displayed complex musical and interpretive negotiations and transformations common to *musik kontemporer* more generally. Ida Bagus Widnyana's arrangement of *Santa Claus is Coming to Town* for the *gamelan semara dana* provides an example.

Listeners using the interstylistic interpretant of Western meter understand the first note of the tune as an anacrusis, a pick up note, and that the agogic stress should be felt on the second note we hear, the first note of the form. Widnyana appears to have heard the tune through the interstylistic interpretant of Balinese *gongan* and in his arrangement has placed the agogic stress (here signified by the placement of the *gong* note [O] and the supporting *calung* notes [C] at the half-note level) as *beginning* with the anacrusis and continuing along what would be the Western beats two and four. The result is a rather radical rhythmic re-contextualization of the tune. Reaching the end of the melody, Widnyana seems to have realized that things don't match up and breaks a rule of Balinese *gongan* form by adding an extra *gong* and *calung* note, without pause, upon the last melody note. As if realizing the formal problems involved, here the arrangement momentarily halts, without beat or sense of pulse, to allow the *gong* to fade before repeating the form. Whereas the Western

---

[18] I borrow this term from Carter's (1992) fascinating study of intercultural encounter and (mis)communication.

arrangement could literally repeat, Widnyana faces a formal problem in which the *gong* is forced to both begin *and* end the melody. Western listeners might hear this as a misunderstanding, but for Balinese listeners this may suggest an experimental form that challenges many of their fundamental interpretive habits through alloying aspects of both Western meter and Balinese *gongan*.[19] This example, illustrated in Figure 8.8, neatly demonstrates the mechanics of Sperber's notion of mutation in the epidemiology of representations. Heard through interpretants for which it was not designed, the representation *Santa Claus is Coming to Town* re-appears transformed, a novel representation to both its original and host cultures, feeding the constant flow of cultural change.

Misunderstanding?

I was baffled by the way a piece ended always unexpectedly, as if in mid-phrase, still in mid-air. (Coast 1953:7)

Do such mutations emerge through misunderstanding? Did the musicians of Peliatan with whom Coast worked understand their compositions as ending in odd places? As half-finished? Misunderstandings are theorized in spoken language but rarely in music. This is probably because music in the West is often celebrated as a universal language while intercultural musicking is hailed as a means of symbolizing global utopias. Misunderstanding assumes that there can be understanding in the first place; but understanding itself can never really be assumed or proven. Aesthetic understanding is, like culture or style, a force field that can be approached without ever being encountered definitely. Framing semiotic processes as misunderstanding risks fetishizing difference while simultaneously helping us avoid the dangers of overdetermined ethnography. Ethnographers dwell on what they understood rather than misunderstood in the field, often presenting a heroic overcoming of the lightness of

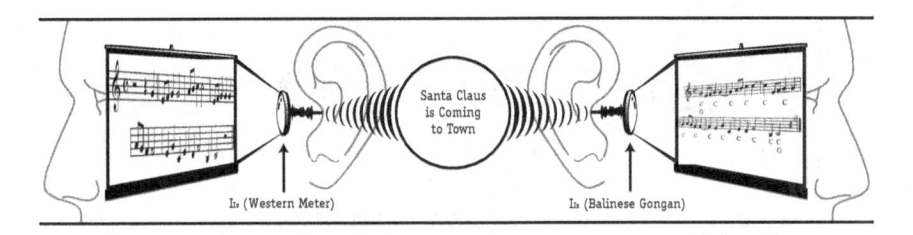

FIGURE 8.8 Interinterpretive Mutation. [Tracks BV-8/3 and MK-8/3]

---

[19] Widnyana's arrangement coincided with the development of double *gong* structures by both Arsawijaya and Dewa Ketut Alit, discussed in Chapter 6.

understanding over the shadows of confusion. When playing bop with Javanese musicians in Yogyakarta, and noticing that they occasionally got it wrong, or in observing how both myself and fellow Balinese students fell short in our efforts to play Javanese music (and wondering how and why we rarely made the same kinds of mistakes), the significance of misunderstandings in shaping new musical expressions and catalyzing stylistic change became apparent.

Ultimately, many of the misunderstandings we might identify in *musik kontemporer* are willful (mis)representations. In a *kontemporer* work entitled *Ambisi* (I), ambition, composed in 2003, Arsawijaya created what he described as *kanon* (I), canon, patterns for a small ensemble of five-tone *gong gede saron* instruments. Poring over English-language music theory textbooks for inspiration, Arsawijaya became attracted to baroque canon and fugue. Not able to read Western notation nor fluent in English, he gleaned what he could of the Western concepts, inventing idiosyncratic material to fill in gaps of understanding. To me, these patterns did not appear as true canon, but as a kind of musical misunderstanding. Arsawijaya's *kanon* rarely entailed literal repetition, as in the classical Western canon because, with only five notes, "parts have to be varied, otherwise it quickly becomes boring" (p.c. July 2003).

Example 8.3 illustrates a short example of *kanon* from Arsawijaya's *Ambisi*. The first statement of the twenty-five-note theme occurs on the first *saron* followed by entrances on the second *saron* and *kantilan*. However, the second *saron* begins on the seventeenth note of the pattern, *foreshadowing* the first *saron*. The *kantilan* then enters on the sixteenth note of the pattern. This complex splicing disorients any simple sense of melodic beginnings or endings, or a straightforward sense of Western canon. Although Arsawijaya managed the harmonic relations such that close harmonies are avoided, there are several examples of parallel fifths and fourths, typically

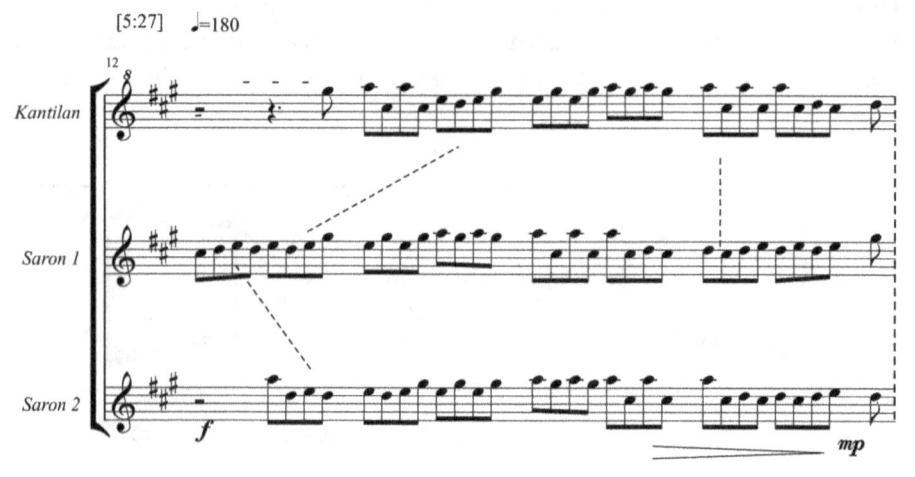

EXAMPLE 8.3 Sang Nyoman Arsawijaya. *Ambisi*, excerpt. [Track MK-7/12]

avoided in Western canon, but standard within the traditional Balinese practice of *empat* harmony.

While the control of vertical harmony is an essential element of Western canon, it was sometimes inessential to Arsawijaya, for whom such control would have sounded too Western. He wondered: "How can we make a kind of 'harmony' that is not purposeful; that is 'half-Western'? (I: *setengah barat)*" (ibid.). In this way Arsawijaya's *kanon* appeared as much a misunderstanding of its Western precursor as a kind of Saidian contrapuntal writing. If musical signs have onion-like layers of significance, Arsawijaya peeled off only the first layer of the canon, chucking the rest. Like Western tonal harmony of the late seventeenth century, the freedom allowed in Balinese *kreasi baru* of the late twentieth century was primarily the freedom to express oneself through its established rules (Attali 1985:64). Arsawijaya's example illustrates the freedoms opened up when the rules of the game aren't fully known. Divorced from its cultural history—associations with European liturgy, sense of the ancient, virtuosic improvisation, and so on—Arsawijaya's *kanon* appears to resemble Baudrillard's concept of the floating signifier, creating a simulacra by pointing only to itself. But in the apparent referential vacuum of the *kanon* a new object field emerged; following Arsawijaya's experiment several composers adopted and transformed the topic and it became a highly contagious virus in both *musik kontemporer* and *kreasi baru*. For them the *kanon* suggested the *moderen* and associated notions of education, cosmopolitanism, and class [Track BV-8/4].

While Arsawijaya's transformation of the canon into the *kanon* was a primarily conscious process, other examples suggest something more like linguistic misunderstanding conceived as an involuntary and unconscious process of reception. This may more accurately describe both my mishearing Sudarta in the improvisation and Widnyana's approach towards arranging the Christmas tune. In the case of the improvisation, misunderstanding was resolved through new information in a face-to-face interaction similar to a spoken dialogue. We might describe such misunderstandings as *proximal*; they could be interactionally corrected through pragmatic and incoming information. In the case of the Christmas tune, a new representation was forged from the web of partial mutualities shared among different interstylistic interpretants. In developing the arrangement, Widnyana was not in direct interaction with anyone equipped with the interpretants associated with Western tradition.[20] We might call such a process *distal* misunderstanding; working only with his own constructive cognitive processes, no new pragmatic information was available to Widnyana. And even if it was, I highly doubt Widnyana would have cared. This example recalls the experimentation with purposefully bad translation in Southeast Asian experimental theater during the *reformasi* in which the staging of misunderstanding becomes

---

[20] We are reminded here of Ambros's harmonic arrangements of South Asian melodies during the nineteenth century (Tarasti 1994:33).

a metaphor for a critique of cultural identity and communication (Lindsay 2006).[21] Widnyana's example demonstrates the ways in which new representations (and new selves) emerge by encountering the other across an interpretive gap. The literary theorist Harold Bloom described as misprision the unconscious misreading of a text; for him this was no pejorative term but a process that was to be celebrated as a form of creativity: poets become strong by mis-taking all texts anterior to them (1982:117); Widnyana expanded his personal compositional style by mis-taking American Christmas tunes.

Framing any representation that crosses lines of power as misunderstanding is a highly charged proposition. But the sometimes confusing products of interinterpretive semiosis are invaluable for providing the shock of seeing one's own signs from different angles, providing an awareness (if only momentarily) of the arbitrariness of one's modes of interpretation. Borrowing and transforming foreign materials and addressing heterogeneous audiences, composers engaged with *musik kontemporer* often spoke with forked tongues in the argot of the in-between. Productive misunderstandings emerged as a jam to hold open the door of the future as a space where understanding across perceived cultural boundaries might eventually be approached.

---

[21] In intercultural theater, Pradier's concept of "productive misinterpretation" (1989:174) similarly aims to transform misunderstanding into sense-producing energy.

9 *Musik Kontemporer* and Intercultural Performance

JULY 2009. INTERVIEWS with Dewa Ketut Alit (Plate 9.1) were intense. Conversations with other composers converged slowly upon research questions only after meandering chitchat. Alit spoke quickly and to the point with a multilingual vocabulary that had me scrambling for dictionaries. He felt his words intensely and if a point was particularly meaningful he might begin to twitch or vibrate, ticks I found myself reproducing during our conversations. Everything discussed was vital. There was no point wasting time. I learned not to schedule lessons following our meetings, knowing that I would be intellectually exhausted afterward.

I parked my motorbike alongside Alit's jeep and walked up to his newly built home in Pengosekan. He sat in the half-finished rehearsal space where young members of his Salukat ensemble worked through a tricky passage of Salju (I), snow, a composition inspired by Alit's experiences teaching gamelan in Boston the previous winter. The musicians performed

PLATE 9.1 Dewa Ketut Alit. Photo by Jeanny Tsai.

overlapping interlocking patterns atop complexly asymmetric descending melodies. It sounded like snow.

Alit stared blankly into space, his young son asleep in his lap. Just up the hill, at his brother's home, a group of visiting American students practiced the accompaniment to a traditional offering dance. "Ah!" He realized I was standing in front of him. His wife called in Japanese and the child in his lap awoke and darted up to the main house. "Why are we always your object [I: obyek]?" Our conversation seemed to have begun as a monologue prior to my arrival. Before I could respond, Alit described his recent participation in an international trade exposition in Singapore. "Japan had robots. China had farming equipment. Korea and Taiwan had computers. Singapore had cell phones. What did Indonesia have at its stand? Balinese gamelan *and tourist pamphlets. The best Indonesia could do was 'culture.' We are exported and imported as objects.*"

Not sure where Alit was going, I asked him how the situation he described was new. He had recently taken part in several major intercultural collaborations with American, Australian, and Japanese artists. He argued that, since 9/11, a new level of intercultural interaction between Balinese artists and their others held the potential for more equitable collaboration and for complex, novel representations. But instead, he saw projects that recapitulated the culture-as-commodity dynamic of the Singapore expo. In these projects foreign artists often determined, if delicately, the terms of the collaboration. Creative artists were reduced to their being Balinese.

"And what are you after?" he asked. Since 2002, I had taken part in and initiated several small-scale collaborative composition projects with Balinese artists. Alit asked what my motivation was, what I expected of my collaborators, did I ever hear them say "no"? As I struggled to formulate an answer, my left eyebrow began to twitch. We sat together, silently staring into space, Americans playing Gabor *in our left ears, Balinese playing* Snow *in our right.*

> Everything can be summed up in aesthetics and political economy. (Stéphane Mallarmé)

Throughout this text I have linked the evolution of *musik kontemporer* to historic interactions between the Balinese and their others; from ancient aesthetic networks to the contemporary introduction of foreign musics facilitated by digital media. *Musik kontemporer* is as much about the mutation of the representations and aesthetic philosophies of the Balinese's others as it is the product of completely indigenous aesthetic processes. I do not claim that it is simply a hybrid form—nothing but the unalloyed mélange of various local and foreign styles—nor that the genius of local composers transforming Balinese materials is somehow less a part of the *musik kontemporer* story than is interculturalism. Neither am I suggesting that cultural change only occurs through processes of intercultural interaction. But the history and evolution of indigenous materials has been the primary focus of many exhaustive and careful ethnomusicological works on Bali to date, as represented in the scholarship of McPhee, Tenzer, Gold, Ornstein, Bakan, Herbst, Hood, Harnish, Bassett, and many others. My focus on interculturalism is partially a response to the inward-looking focus of prior studies.

Interculturalism enriches and variegates the Balinese performing arts. Contemporary intercultural collaboration is a process by which the Balinese come to expand their global image, forge meaningful personal connections with their others, imagine alternatives to cultural institutions and representations they no longer find meaningful, enhance their aesthetic traditions, and supplement their income. It is a positive experience for many involved. However, as suggested by Alit's concerns in the passage above, contemporary aesthetic interculturalism, especially in the Indonesian scene, remains a site of highly asymmetrical relations. While many composers engaged with *musik kontemporer* cited the importance of the aesthetic freedoms (I: *kebebasan*) that intercultural performance provided as compared to *tradisi* contexts, embedded asymmetrical relations raise questions regarding the exact nature of this freedom and of the ethics of the intercultural project itself.

As I describe in this chapter, modern intercultural performance linking Indonesian artists with their counterparts from the Western metropole emerged in the early twentieth century and was sustained by the cultural diplomacy of the Cold War. Intercultural interactions expanded during the New Order, facilitated by increasingly inexpensive international travel and private foundational and university support. During the second half of the twentieth century the conditions enabling Western artists to collaborate with local practitioners around the globe were, and remain, underwritten by Western, primarily American, military and economic forces. This has fostered the rapid spread of *gamelan* ensembles in America, Japan, and Western Europe, a movement that has alternately awed and occasionally disturbed Indonesian observers.

The reinvestment in cultural diplomacy following 9/11 re-energized the intercultural project, bringing together artists from America and its geopolitical allies in an effort to demonstrate the acceptance of American democratic principles through the arts. During the *reformasi*, intercultural performance projects were not only instigated in the West but were enthusiastically accepted and initiated in Indonesia as a demonstration of *"go internasional"* credentials through which artists and administrators could display upwardly mobile internationalisms that aligned with the nation's continued development interests.

In the second half of this chapter I analyze the precarious entanglements of contemporary Balinese culture and geopolitics through the example of the American *gamelan* movement and recent intercultural projects. I theorize the ideological effects such projects produce through their complex systems of signification and their ambiguous relationship to appropriation and exploitation. Finally, I consider the ethics of intercultural performance as the functional equivalent in the cultural realm to calls for global human rights and the freedom that has become an increasingly abstracted sign of the post-9/11 American Empire of Liberty. My intent is to temper recent celebratory, Deleuzian interpretations of intercultural performance as the nonhierarchic, rhizomatic play of radicants.[1] Center-periphery models do indeed deserve deconstruction, but we can't as yet, in the case of most intercultural projects involving Indonesians, completely dispose of them. Many of the intercultural experiments that serve as an

---

[1] This perspective is a response to earlier critical analyses by Bharucha (2000) and Pavis (1996). See Ferrari for the rhizomatic perspective (2010).

important catalyst for contemporary Balinese *musik kontemporer,* while often appealing to a discourse of equitable interaction, reproduce relations of inequity. This is due in part to a denial of coevalness engendered through cultural relativism, an ideology that, while intended to dismantle historicist, cultural evolutionist models of cultural development, ironically produces the problematic effect of amplifying difference itself by placing interculturalists in separate moral communities.

While I believe that intercultural performance is an overwhelmingly positive project that contributes to sociocultural, individual, and aesthetic growth, I am concerned here to look beyond the celebration for a moment to consider the mechanisms that subtend the project itself. Many of the artists involved in the projects discussed here have been my own teachers with whom I have been involved in several intercultural projects. My occasional disquiet arising from those projects inspires the present discussion. I thank my colleagues and mentors for their forbearance with my sometimes critical analyses. Working in a global milieu, our works are open to public analysis and critique and are the better for it.[2]

Indonesia and Intercultural Performance

Modern intercultural performance was prefigured by Artaud's conception of Oriental Theater and his development of the Theater of Cruelty following his experience of the performance by the ensemble from Peliatan at the 1931 World Exposition in Paris. During the same era, a cadre of American and European dancers with little or no training in Indonesian traditions established careers performing imagined versions of Javanese and Balinese dance for audiences willing to accept dubious claims of authenticity.[3] Many of these artists collaborated with modernist composers inspired by *gamelan* traditions.[4] While some of these composers imagined a fictitious Javanese or Balinese musical other, others, including McPhee and Godowsky, creatively interpreted their direct experiences of *gamelan.*

Intercultural aesthetics and semiotics appear to have informed the development of Balinese forms during the same period. In the 1930s Walter Spies collaborated with

---

[2] As are my own. See Steele (2013) for a critical analysis of the author's intercultural compositions.
[3] Cléo de Merode and Matahari (Geertruida Zell) were followed by Ruth St. Denis, Takka-Takka, Raden Mas Jodjana, Ram Gopal, Mary Wingman, La Meri, and Xenia Zaria, each performing faux Javanese and Balinese works or modernist works loosely inspired by these traditions (Cohen 2007a:14). Ruth St. Denis and her husband, Ted Shawn, studied in Java and Bali in 1926. Their Denishawn dance company in Los Angeles later became a major institution in the development of American modern dance. Before moving to New York, Martha Graham studied under St. Denis from whom she developed her lifelong interest in Indonesian dance forms (ibid.). Graham later became Humardani's mentor during his residency in New York. See Cohen (2010) for a brilliant analysis of intercultural performance in interwar America and Europe.
[4] Including Henry Eicheim, Jape Kool, Colin McPhee, Leopold Godowsky, Alexander Tasman, Josef Holbrooke, Paul Seelig, Constant van de Wall, and Eva Gauthier. According to Cohen (2007a:15), Gauthier, a Canadian who collected Malay songs and had reputedly studied singing in the Solonese court, was accompanied by McPhee on piano for her North American tours in the late 1920s. Gauthier likely sparked McPhee's interest in Bali.

Balinese artists to create the now-iconic touristic *kecak* and, as Herbst notes, both *kebyar* and *janger* appear to have emerged as partial responses to Western culture. Herbst quotes elder musicians in Bungkulan who suggested that *kebyar* was influenced by the dynamism of Dutch marching band music. He links transformations in early *kebyar* performance practice to Balinese musicians' experience of Western performance and their involvement in the early tourist industry. When it first emerged, *kebyar* was performed in an inward-looking square formation, with the instruments encircling the dancer. This quickly evolved into the front-facing proscenium-style staging known today (Herbst 2009:20). Writing in the 1970s, the musician Wayan Simpen (b. 1907) linked the etymology of *kebyar* to the flash of light from a bulb, known to the Balinese through the light switches and cameras brought by the Dutch.

Foreign consumption of *kebyar* seems to have been an important engine for its early development. During the colonial era several of Bali's foremost ensembles appeared in the Bali Hotel's twice-weekly performances for tourists in Denpasar. Wayan Beratha, then a young cook at the hotel, closely observed these performances from the sidelines, noting passages that he would later incorporate into his own compositions with the *gamelan* from Belaluan, which later established regular performances at the hotel. Deprived of tourist audiences during the Second World War, the performances were halted and compositional activity fell into a slump (Sadra 1991:34).

Immediately following the war the English producer John Coast began developing a touring program in collaboration with the ensemble from Peliatan led by Anak Agung Gde Mandera, who had performed at the 1931 Paris Exposition. Coast and his Javanese wife Luce were intimately involved with the production of the program: picking pieces, dancers, repertoire, costumes, and whittling performance times down into a package "suitable for Western ears and eyes" (Coast 1953:158). The ensemble's *legong*, for instance, was compressed from nearly an hour in length to approximately ten minutes.[5] Coast removed instruments whose tone he found offensive, including the *rebab*, which he described as a "devilish two-stringed fiddle, perpetually off tone, and which I nicknamed the Cat's Voice when they used it once to see if I liked it" (ibid. 142). The now classic *kebyar* work *Oleg Tamulilingan* was composed collaboratively by Coast, the dancer Sampih, and musicians in the Peliatan ensemble, with the costume designed by Coast's wife. As described by Coast, the work was carefully crafted to satisfy both Balinese and Western tastes. He tested the program before Western tourists in Bali, enlisting the help of the visiting Broadway producer Freddie Schang. Coast's primary concerns were to tame Balinese temporality and to present the ensemble as an emblem of tradition. While auditioning dancers in the Peliatan ensemble, he complained of their failed attempts to appear modern:

---

[5] Processes of temporal compression were not only a result of intercultural interaction between Indonesian and Western artists and audiences. *Stambul* groups such as Dardanella similarly condensed and simplified repertoires from around the archipelago for consumption by modern audiences (Cohen 2010:183).

[the] group had deliberately softened their Djanger to make it finer, and they had thus devitalized it also, it had become pretentious, for the dancers first appeared boxed in on a tiny "stage" behind a singularly dirty orange-colored curtain. This, we feared, was offered as proof of their modernity. (ibid. 23)

While on tour in America, Coast disallowed a toothless, elderly musician from wearing on stage a set of dentures he had proudly received from an American friend in order that he appear appropriately primitive (ibid. 226).

During the second half of twentieth century Balinese composers increasingly understood their work to exist within an intercultural, globalizing zone of production and consumption. While performing on a cultural mission to the 1964 World's Fair in New York, Wayan Beratha composed the short instrumental work *Jayasemara*, crafted as a short "tour" of the entire *kebyar* ensemble, demonstrating to outsiders the roles and abilities of each part of the orchestra. In his biography of Beratha, Wayan Sadra notes the "popular tendencies" of Beratha's works as compared to more difficult compositions by his contemporaries (Sadra 1991:10). It is likely no coincidence that Wayan Beratha and Nyoman Windha, the two most renowned modern composers of *gong kebyar*, typically composed works within reach of foreign ensembles, facilitating the continued globalization of Balinese culture. The non-native performance of *gamelan* emerges first among Indonesia's colonizers, the Dutch (beginning in 1913) and later the Japanese (beginning in 1940), but by the late New Order was dominated by American ensembles.[6]

In response to the perceived need to forge official signs of global harmony between the West and Indonesia during the Cold War, state and educational institutions began to support self-consciously intercultural projects between Indonesians and Americans. Supported by State Department USIS funds in 1960, the American jazz clarinetist Tony Scott and the Carnegie Hall conductor Wheeler Becket both composed works in Indonesia in collaboration with local traditional musicians. Mantle Hood established an extracurricular *gamelan* study group at UCLA upon returning in 1954 from the Netherlands, where he purchased a *gamelan* and untertook practical instruction in Javanese music with the Dutch musician Bernard Ijzerdraat. Hood subsequently studied in Java with support from the Ford Foundation. By 1959, Indonesian artists supported by Rockefeller began collaborating with American students of *gamelan* at UCLA's Institute for Ethnomusicology, directed by Hood.

---

[6] In 1816 Raffles sent back two sets of Javanese instruments during British colonial rule of the East Indies. Tuned to diatonicized *pélog*, it is unclear if these sets were ever performed in Britain (Quigley 1996). Momo (2010) describes the first regular performances of non-native *gamelan* in the Netherlands, at the Hague, beginning in 1913. In 1940 Japanese artists employed Javanese instruments for a propagandistic opera rationalizing Japan's later occupation of Southeast Asia (Steele 2012). In 1941 a group of musicians in Amsterdam began forging their own *gamelan* by melting down church bells. The ensemble, named Babar Layar, performed Javanese compositions studied from recordings and with the occasional help of migrant Javanese (Sadra 2007:52).

The dissolution of the anti-imperialist Sukarno government in the mid 1960s and the introduction of the pro-Western New Order catalyzed a new generation of intercultural interactions between Indonesian and American artists. Balinese artists became regular participants at the American Society for Eastern Arts (ASEA, later the Center for World Music) in its summer classes on the American west coast beginning in 1963 where their students included minimalist composers such as Steve Reich. These developments spurred the growth of the American *gamelan* movement, both the invention of autochthonous sets of instruments by composers including Lou Harrison, and the proliferation of imported sets from Java and Bali to numerous liberal arts institutions for whom the acquisition of a large set of exotic instruments and faculty trained in esoteric traditions was (and remains) an elite status symbol.

By the late 1970s Western global dominance was signified by the spread of a postmodern avant-garde most spectacularly expressed in intercultural celebrations that vaunted a universal (but implicitly Western-centered) aesthetic. Inspired by Artaud's effort to energize avant-gardism through the expressions of the other, later exponents of intercultural performance, including Jerzy Grotowsky, Peter Brook, Arian Mnouchkine, Eugenio Barba, Richard Schechner, Robert Wilson, and Peter Sellars, conducted sustained face-to-face workshops with artists from various global traditions, a milieu in which Balinese artists were highly represented. While Artaud sought to disturb bourgeois aesthetics through the disruptions and alienating effects of Balinese material, later practitioners expressed a utopian one-world vision through the attempt to meld forms or to identify a pre-cultural or pre-expressive common ground through which one detects a self-congratulatory penance for colonization and neocolonialism.

INTERLUDE: FROM COLD WAR CULTURE TO PUBLIC POLICY

Believing its global cultural influence assured, the US government began to ramp down its significant Cold War investment in cultural diplomacy in the 1980s. Following the recommendations of the Heritage Foundation's "Agenda for Change," the Reagan administration defunded arts programs and pulled out of UNESCO in 1984 following the organization's effort to protect smaller nations from the globalization of American corporate media.[7] Reagan replaced former directors of American cultural diplomacy programs at the State Department, USIS and USIA (United States Information Agency) with advertising executives who viewed cultural diplomacy as a form of propaganda by other means. While academics predicted that future conflicts were as likely to be cultural as military, these agencies failed to argue successfully for their relevance in a post-Soviet world. By 1998 foreign affairs spending had dropped seventy-five percent from 1968 levels, representing one percent of the national budget (Arndt 2005:538). During the Clinton administration, Jesse Helms, holding Fulbright's former chair at

---

[7] The sudden loss of a quarter of its budget ($60 million, or half the cost of an F16 fighter jet) brought UNESCO to near collapse (Arndt 2005:531).

Foreign Relations, saw little meaning in cultural diplomacy; by 1999 USIS was dead. At the beginning of his administration, George W. Bush hired advertising executives to reform US public diplomacy through branding.

In response to the defunding of cultural diplomacy, universities established new scholarships and cultural exchanges. Ford continued to conduct preservation programs in Indonesia, while Rockefeller focused upon exchange programs that brought foreign artists to the United States. The nonprofit Asian Cultural Council (ACC) emerged in 1980 from the Asian Cultural Program of the John D. Rockefeller III fund. Rockefeller and ACC both focused upon individual cultural exchanges between the US and Asia in the hope that such interactions would improve international relations. By the mid-1980s the fund had developed a strategic plan with Ford to train Indonesian ethnomusicologists in America—including many Balinese—who would then, it was hoped, open local graduate programs for the study of traditional musics (p.c. Ralph Samuelson, October 2010).

INTERCULTURALISM, CONTINUED

In the 1970s, the residencies of American theater students, including Julie Taymor, John Emigh, Kathy Foley, and Larry Reed, coincided with the emergence of local experimental theater projects such as Kadek Suardana's *Sanggar Putih* in Bali in 1976 and the Javanese choreographer Suprapto Suryodarmo's *Wayang Buddha* experiments beginning in 1974.[8] Both of these projects catalyzed early *musik kontemporer*. The founding in 1979 of *Gamelan Sekar Jaya* in Berkeley and later *Gamelan Sekar Jepun* in Tokyo intensified intercultural interactions. By the mid-1990s performances by foreign *gamelan* ensembles and collaborations between Balinese and foreign artists were a regular feature of the Bali Arts Festival.[9]

In 2001 the Indonesian magazine *Gong* devoted an issue to the non-native study and performance of *gamelan*, critiquing it as a form of therapy for alienated Western moderns (Gombloh 2001b:3). The intercultural performance of *gamelan* continues in the tradition of Mead's anthropologies *for* Western Civilization.[10] *Gamelan* is often characterized as a balm to heal the wounds of alienation through providing a context for social interaction understood as free of the market and the exclusionary gender, racial, generational, and class inflections of many Western forms.[11] Non-native performers have

---

[8] On the American interculturalists see Snow (1986) and Cohen (2007b). On Suardana's theater projects see Nabeshima and Noszlopy (2006).

[9] During my research such performances had become rather cliché for Balinese audiences. By 2010 the arts festival appeared to be as much a venue for foreigners to perform their cosmopolitanism by staging intercultural collaborations as it was an arena for urbanized Balinese to socialize, shop, and catch an occasional performance. For a Balinese critique of this phenomenon see Soethama (2006:47).

[10] Margaret Mead, *Coming of Age in Samoa, A Psychological Study of Primitive Youth for Western Civilization*. (New York: Blue Ribbon Books, 1928).

[11] Nevertheless, as they are often encountered first in liberal arts institutions, the overall demographic of the American *gamelan* community is overwhelmingly white and middle class.

used the tradition in ways that sometimes dumbfound native practitioners, including the occasional performance of anachronistic repertoire and the association of *gamelan* with meditation, music therapy, elementary education, and prison programs.[12]

As is globalization, interculturalism is a simultaneously celebratory and anxious discourse in Bali. Primarily lauded as a sign of the extent to which their culture is capable of "going international" and of the ability of the Balinese to partly transform their others into themselves, interculturalism occasionally raises submerged fears of cultural inadequacy and theft. Gus Martin, reviewing the first tour in Bali of a foreign *gamelan* ensemble in 1985 for the *Bali Post*, seemed alternately awed, proud, and unsettled:

> Who didn't feel shaken up and unnerved when Gamelan Sekar Jaya from California demonstrated their skill? This group of white-skinned players were so intimate with and sensitive to a set of *gamelan* instruments. How nimble their hands were dancing above the keys of the *gamelan*. When Gamelan Sekar Jaya appeared...it was as if they were cracking a joke in front of us. No matter what, watching them meant witnessing a warning for us. We have two perspectives: from one perspective, we feel proud; from the other, we feel small. Proud because the culture which we possess has gotten the highest recognition, which is not only held in amazement, but also studied by another culture. Small, because many of us (Balinese people) can't play and don't even know how to hold a mallet. An uncomfortable feeling sometimes appears among us.... Something becomes extremely valuable if it is in the hands of Westerners. Only then, when suddenly Balinese art is performed by all of them, do we feel amazed at something that has never before amazed us. They are playing. They are dancing. And us? We've just become stupid audience members.[13]

Martin's sentiment recalls colonial-era self-loathing, raising the unsettling specter of foreign *gamelan*'s latent neocolonial potential in spite of the homage and admiration at its origin. The review recalls the cosmopolitan thinkers of the *polemik kebudayaan*, such as Alisjahbana, and the Japanese theorist Takeuchi who in the 1930s suggested that true self-consciousness could not occur in the East until it was invaded and defeated by the essence of Western modernity (Sakai 2010:442). Detached from its original place, time, and context, *gamelan*—as performed by non-Balinese—becomes further reified for the Balinese as a detachable cultural object, one that can be damaged, sold, lost, or stolen.

September 2001. I woke up sneezing, per the morning ritual, when the acrid stench of putrefied shrimp paste seized my sinuses. As Ibu stirred it into the fried rice downstairs I could

---

[12] The use of primarily Javanese ensembles in elementary school, special education and prison programs appears more prevalent in the UK. The perception that their tradition may somehow be appropriate to the socially deviant and intellectually underdeveloped has generated not always positive responses from native performers.

[13] Courtesy of and translated by Wayne Vitale.

hear her and the twins giggling between my fits. I wobbled into the kitchen, groggy after returning late from a shadow play in Gianyar. The twin six-year-old girls, Yuni and Yoni, had recently decided we were fast friends after two months of pretending I did not exist. We played our morning game; they fed me the most potent of Balinese dishes, laughing as I winced in pain. My wife called from Boston, her voice shaking: "Turn on the television." I tuned in to a loop of the towers falling over and over. I was studying gamelan on America's dime, staying in Denpasar with Ketut Asnawa's family while he was teaching gamelan in the Bay Area, funded by a combination of governmental and private foundations. As pundits suggested Middle Eastern extremists, it was difficult to resist the thought that the disproportionate attention Balinese culture had historically received from the West—there are many more gamelan than Middle Eastern maqam ensembles on American campuses—was somehow linked to its very geopolitical irrelevance.

Following 9/11 the US government scrambled to account for the failings of American public diplomacy. Agencies began to invest more heavily in the struggle for hearts and minds, often through heavy-handed forms of propaganda such as the glitzy, ineffectual Alhurra satellite station beamed to the Middle East by the State Department. Public (or "soft") diplomacy became a form of management for the contemporary neoliberal empire, a space bounded not by the Cold War notion of the free versus the communist world, but by the nebulous distribution of freedom itself (Kennedy and Lucas 2005). Following the attacks, freedom became increasingly abstract and deterritorialized until it was a signifier of American imperialism, a "harbinger of the 'empire *for* liberty' which combined the reinstantiation of the national security state with the pursuit of 'virtuous war'" (ibid. 325). Recalling the West's Cold War focus upon abstract expressionism as against Soviet realism, a vague notion of artistic freedom would again become a keyword of America's sprawling post-9/11 Enduring Freedom campaign.

During this era American arts agencies supporting intercultural performance were funded by a constellation of private and governmental agencies. The Asian Pacific Performing Arts Exchange (APPEX), directed by the Center for Intercultural Performance at UCLA, hosted a regular six-week residency between Asian and American artists during its annual summer programs (1996–2010) held both in California and Bali. APPEX combined funds from Rockefeller, Ford, ACC, the Soros Foundation, NEA, and, following 9/11, the US State Department to underwrite the unfettered free play of artists from America, Asia, and the Islamic world. During my residency with the program in 2006 at UCLA, State Department auditors occasionally observed rehearsals from the periphery. Between 2005 and 2013 the State Department's One-Beat project of its Cultural Visitors Program invited up to sixty-five young musicians a year from key countries in the "Muslim world" to the United States to perform collaborations and improvisations with local musicians in order to "enhance crosscultural understanding and demonstrate democratic values such as collaboration, cohesion, and innovation."[14]

---

[14] The program focused upon genres including but not limited to urban, hip-hop, roots, rock, electronic, and world music. (http://edocket.access.gpo.gov/2011/2011-6272.htm)

While appearing to offset the imperial, universalizing tendencies of Western modernism, such programs similarly functioned to subsume identities within a particularly American idea of a world community. Membership within this community was ratified by adopting American notions of freedom and expressed by the staging of the playful interaction between the folkloric ethnicities of America's geopolitical allies.

In composition workshops in Indonesia following 9/11, Wayan Sadra cited the difficulty of working with ineffectual and corrupt local institutions and recommended that *musik kontemporer* composers appeal directly to increasingly well-funded foreign organizations interested in supporting the arts in the world's largest "Muslim nation."[15] From 2002 to 2010 Balinese experimentalists sought sponsorship from foreign-funded NGOs including the Kelola Foundation (funded by Ford) and Arts Network Asia, supported by the (Rockefeller-funded) ACC. Following America's return to UNESCO in 2004, the foundation underwrote international artistic collaborations and activities on the island.[16] Many Indonesian artists believed that foreign funding facilitated the creation of "purer works" (Gombloh 2001), although several worried that arts panels dominated by Western or Western-trained arbiters of innovation would inevitably lead to homogenization or Westernization (p.c. Sudarta, July 2003).

Go Internasional

July 2009. The Organizing Committee of the Bali Arts Festival had scheduled an evening of "International Collaborations" in the coveted indoor, air-conditioned Ksirarnawa space without actually booking any acts for the event. Called in to help rustle up potential performers, Gusti Sudarta arranged an "improvisasi bebas" (I), free improvisation, with Tri Hartono (a Javanese faculty member at ISI), himself, and me. Without prior discussion, we walked onto the stage before a full audience of Balinese and foreign elite. A cameraman from Bali TV aimed his floodlight in our faces as a young female announcer made grand pronouncements about the inherent values of cultural bridges (I: jembatan budaya) and how the komposisi we were about to perform—for which she spontaneously improvised a title: Ambaja *(America, Bali, Java)—was a symbol of "cultural harmony" and Bali's peaceful coexistence with other nations. Civil servants and politicians, identified by their matching pea-green uniforms, sat in reserved spots in the first row. Finding a large Javanese* kenong gong-chime *placed before my spot on the floor, I upended it to pour my drinking water in. At this the audience applauded loudly, rendering Tri's delicate* rebab *introduction inaudible. Sudarta sang in a manner reminiscent of Pakistani* qawwali *music while playing an African* udu *idiophone.*

---

[15] Comments from a July 2003 workshop in Yogyakarta. Being nominally Hindu, and working with mostly nominally Muslim Javanese musicians, Sadra winked as he uttered the phrase Muslim nation (I: *negara Muslim*) to which the young audience chuckled.

[16] As evidenced by the names of funded projects—the Sacred Rhythm Festival and the Sacred Bridge Foundation—UNESCO associates Balinese culture with notions of *tradisi* and neoliberal spirituality in a manner consistent with both early ethnography and the cultural tourism industry. The island has frequently served as a meeting venue for the UN and its various organizations since the early 1950s (Coast 1953:98).

Tri responded with idiomatic passages on a Javanese gender. *Nothing seemed to connect; it reminded me of Brautigan's prose.*[17] *The improvisation oscillated between predictably intensifying rhythms followed by passages of alap-like free time, climaxing in an inevitably ejaculatory finale. Backstage we all agreed: despite knowing each other for years, the* improvisasi *seemed to go nowhere; no "bridges" were formed; it was embarrassingly foolhardy to attempt it before an audience. We agreed to get together in private to try again. Two well-respected conservatory faculty appeared backstage, and, as we braced ourselves for an upbraiding, we were surprised when they gushed. Dubious, we outlined each fault. They persisted, describing the performance as a demonstration of the ability of the Bali Arts Festival, the conservatory, and its faculty to successfully* go internasional.

After the Cold War, the New Order ushered in an era of openness (I: *keterbukaan*) marked by new development projects in which internationalism received special focus (Vickers 2003). Around this time the English term "go international," borrowed from market economics, entered the Indonesian lexicon to refer positively to anything that conveyed a sense of internationalism or cosmopolitanism. *Go internasional* was the functional opposite of *kampungan* (I), village backwardness. Local projects, expressions, and people could *go internasional*, but not those backward-looking elements of *kampung* culture. Positive evaluations of globalization during the *reformasi* period appealed to ideals of equality and freedom enshrined in the revolution but perceived as obstructed during the New Order. Following the 2002 Bali bombing and the subsequent advent of *Ajeg* fundamentalism, the older, negative discourse of globalization, figured as dangerous cultural change (i.e., Westernization), re-emerged to achieve a precarious balance with *go internasional* optimism. Artists and bureaucrats were tightrope walkers, balancing between the two positions. In 2003 the conservatory, with Ministry of Education funding, initiated a series of *go internasional* initiatives seeking to place junior faculty in Western institutions for graduate study and encourage the publication of articles within international, English-language journals. Any conservatory project with an international element was favored for institutional upgrading credit.[18] By 2010 the *Ajeg* rhetoric had cooled and intercultural projects received more sustained attention and funding from organizations such as the Bali Arts Festival. That year, the *gamelan* ensemble with which I worked in New York became the first non-Balinese ensemble invited to perform on the Ardha Chandra stage as part of the annual *gong kebyar* festival. Festival committee members suggested that our intercultural performance would demonstrate to local audiences the extent to which the Balinese performing arts could *go internasional*.[19]

---

[17] "'Good work', he said, and went out the door. What work? We never saw him before. There was no door" Brautigan (1976).

[18] During my research, the many foreign students in residence at the conservatory participated in a miniature *go internasional* economy. Faculty often engaged foreign students in intercultural projects, anticipating the institutional upgrading credits they would receive for their internationalisms. Such credits established higher status and income levels for faculty and staff.

[19] For more positive evaluations of the globalization of *gamelan* see Sadra (2007) in which he argues that *gamelan* embodies a "global culture."

Contemporary Intercultural Projects: *Odalan Bali*

Intercultural projects loomed large on the *musik kontemporer* scene during my research. Musicians eagerly vied to become attached to such projects through which they hoped to extend their aesthetic networks, secure potential touring and teaching opportunities, gain significant income (an often unrealistic expectation), and be exposed to new, foreign *viruses* to incorporate within their own works. Balinese grapevines were concerned with who was working with whom and for how much, tips on how to resolve or elide aesthetic and social confrontations, and the ways in which artists intended to use their newly gained materials for the following year's arts festivals and contests. Their collaborators evinced a kind of frisson particular to the Western interculturalist working in Bali for whom the island often appeared as an artistic paradise overflowing with pure creativity. Balinese artists seemed willing to work and rehearse with an intensity not found at home. But the intercultural project was an embodiment of differential geopolitical relations: a nexus of complex communication and miscommunication, expectations and projections.

I will now discuss *Odalan Bali,* a major intercultural project that brought together leading Balinese and American artists and producers between 2005 – 2007. The project introduced American audiences to a new generation of virtuosic performers, highlighted brilliant examples of *musik kontemporer,* and re-energized the performance of several *tradisi* forms. *Odalan Bali* represented perhaps the most significant intercultural collaboration since Spies's involvement with the modern *kecak* dance-drama and Coast's collaboration with the ensemble from Peliatan. Nevertheless, the project evoked highly divergent responses from Balinese artists, including some involved in the performance itself. My aim here is to account for these varying voices and to expand the perspective of the work beyond those published elsewhere.[20]

Founded in 1997, the Cudamani ensemble coalesced around the virtuosity and charisma of Dewa Putu Beratha and Dewa Ketut Alit, brothers from a widely respected family of musicians based in the village of Pengosekan, just south of Ubud. Growing up performing before temples and tourists, both were educated at the national conservatory, and frequently collaborated with American musicians and ensembles. Cudamani quickly became a center of innovation, attracting a core of virtuosic young performers and composers. By 2000 the ensemble had established extensive professional and familial connections to American university faculty and *gamelan* students. With Americans acting as co-managers and collaborators—principally Emiko Susilo (Beratha's wife) and Judy Mitoma—the ensemble secured funding from Ford to underwrite the study of traditional forms and began developing an innovative holistic performance package. With aid from their American contacts, Cudamani began promoting the performance to Western concert halls in 2003. Entitled *Odalan Bali,* the production toured America, Japan, Canada, and Europe in various incarnations from 2005 to 2007.

---

[20] For alternative perspectives on *Odalan Bali* see Harnish (2013) and Weiss (2013).

Eschewing the standard concert program format, *Odalan Bali* staged the devotional practices of the Balinese Hindu *odalan* temple ceremony, as practiced in Pengosekan, through daring compositional and choreographic innovations.[21] Rather than viewing a program of individual set pieces, audiences were invited behind the scenes, as it were, to experience culture-as-praxis. Despite this innovative structure, many of the old chestnuts were retained—the offering dance, *kecak, kebyar, legong,* and *barong*—but presented within the context of ceremonial practice. Cudamani's American collaborator Wayne Vitale produced a custom soundscape to subtly suffuse the hall with the sounds of the primeval Balinese jungle. Musicians, dressed as priests, offered benediction while dancers weaved between elaborate temple offerings set about the stage. The use of anachronistic dress served as a form of temporal distancing—functioning to overwrite descriptions of contemporary experimentalism in the program notes—while the improbably naturalistic soundscape encouraged a postcolonial historical amnesia (Gandhi 1998:7). Bali's acoustic ecology is marked today more by motorbikes, ringtones, and televisions than by frogs. Despite profoundly virtuosic performances and innovative musical, staging, and choreographic elements, *Odalan Bali* reinforced the canonical images produced by Covarrubias, Belo, Mead, Coast and McPhee.

Even at its most cutting edge, the performance remained for audiences a potent index of the possibility of premodern tradition. According to founding member Dewa Ketut Alit: "We formed this ensemble to oppose the image of a bygone Bali (I: *Bali masa lampau*) but in the end we wound up presenting just that" (p.c. July 2008). Kadek Dewi Aryani, a dancer and former member of the ensemble, described the production as "beautiful but staged, like Disneyland." The performers in *Odalan Bali* appear as skeuomorphic Balinese. Their appearance and behavior are reassuringly traditional—a user-friendly presentation that ameliorates (or camouflages) profound innovations.

In *Odalan Bali,* Balinese culture attains the dream of total aestheticization described by Covarrubias (1937). Quotidian activities are *performed*; cooking becomes music; ritual circumambulations become choreography; offerings become props. The field is brought to the stage for the consideration of viewers-cum-anthropologists in their plush armchairs. While *Odalan Bali* appears to affirm cultural difference through the presentation of ethnicity on the Western stage—the Balinese exercising their human right to cultural distinctiveness—the complex plurality of contemporary Balinese culture itself is absent.

Former ensemble member Gusti Komin Darta explained the subtle management of the Balinese image in the process of creating the production:

This topic of image is difficult to penetrate. We, I mean Americans *and* Balinese, often camouflage our aims. We all are thinking and politicking. But it is indirect. It is never stated like this: "look, it has to be this way. The Balinese have to be this way." (p.c. Gusti Komin Darta, March 2012)

---

[21] Coast's original staging for the 1952 tour of the Peliatan ensemble included the performance of similar ceremonies, which were ultimately eliminated to meet time constraints.

American presence on stage was limited to a single performer, Emiko Susilo, an American of mixed Japanese and Indonesian heritage who has lived for years in Bali and understands its culture with a depth unrivaled by most academic Indonesianists. Nevertheless, most audiences likely read Susilo as a Balinese, enabling interpretations of the performance as a completely indigenous expression and satisfying touristic desires for authenticity. Although all but one performer was Balinese, American management of visas, performance contracts, and production funds invested American collaborators and presenters with disproportionate creative control. Alternately adamant in their creative vision and profoundly sensitive to postcolonial power dynamics, no amount of cultural sensitivity could have returned to the Balinese their full voice. Processing visa forms and holding purse strings, power was for the Americans to disburse.

Reactions by Balinese members regarding issues of equity and control were complex. Gusti Komin Darta's comments were shared by many of his peers:

> A collaboration is like this [interlocking his fingers]. Issues of aesthetic control should be balanced. We all aimed for this, but it was sometimes unbalanced. And balance is very difficult to achieve. As members, we want a strong result, and so we try to position ourselves in the middle. Forty people trying to be in the middle, can you imagine this? If it is not peaceful, some people will leave and that is very dangerous. (ibid.)

Regardless of appeals to cultural sensitivity and efforts to achieve balance, as an international touring production designed to sell tickets to audiences interested in ethnographic representations of the Balinese, both Balinese and American collaborators were caught up within a market system and economy of representations beyond their control. Within this context Americans might have better understood the particular expectations of authenticity and tradition among Western ticket buyers. However, for at least one performance in Japan local producers requested that Emiko Susilo, as a non-Balinese, remove herself from the production to assure a purer performance. After much discussion with the group, she agreed.

The subtle elision of American and Balinese authorship in *Odalan Bali* leads us to always ask: Who is speaking? Western audience members, likely unaware of the entangled intercultural processes of the project's development, generally understood *Odalan Bali* to be a purely Balinese expression. American and Indonesian media portrayed the performance as a return to traditional roots and essences, un-ironically highlighting the ensemble's refusal to perform for tourists.[22]

Odalan Bali took the form of a didactic moral lesson. As represented in the production, Bali is not a lost Eden but an implicit criticism of contemporary (that is, Western) society, and it is here that the hand of the American collaborators is most visible. Western culture is implicitly figured as alienated in contrast to Balinese culture, in

---

[22] See for instance Supriyanto (2010).

which art and life are imagined to remain integrated, staged *as art* to inspire new, more nurturing human relationships in Western society. As Fabian (1991) reminds us, ethnic, ethnos, ethos, and ethic are etymologically related; *Odalan Bali* searches for an alternative bourgeois ethic through the ethos of the ethnic, aligning it with the historical avant-garde through an attempt to produce simultaneously a social and aesthetic effect.

As in the assimilation of the historic avant-garde into modernism, contemporary intercultural projects such as *Odalan Bali* symbolize the tendency of bourgeois culture to forestall the potential *realization* of social alternatives by relegating them to the aesthetic realm. Rather than exposing the conditions that make the intercultural encounter possible in the first place, such projects primarily feed neoliberal Western notions of spirituality, the personalized appropriation of once-localized religious beliefs and cultural practices that attempts to elide cultural boundaries by appealing to an imagined a priori unified world. The Western bourgeois listener's direct access to ethnic musics, unfettered by local doctrines, practices, and social restrictions, serves as the soundtrack to the individual quest of spirituality (Keister 2005). Any sense of solidarity within the spiritualist community is built upon a shared disavowal of ethnocentrism; a "we" that enlarges itself as an ethnos increasingly variegated with multiple ethnics brought together through the celebration of multiculturalism (Rorty 1989:192).

An irony of the spiritual quest to unify (for one's self) the world through multiculturalism is that it sometimes downplays actual cultural commonalities. The West worries that it has constructed the non-West and requires proofs to the contrary. Accordingly, the celebration of difference in *Odalan Bali* conceals our many concrete similarities. The Balinese staged in *Odalan Bali* do not wear their daily dress—that is, what we wear—and appear ignorant of technology and cultures other than their own, when in fact they are active participants in contemporary digital social and aesthetic networks.

If Western society is difficult and messy—a constant political and moral struggle among parties with vested interests—the Balinese community as staged in *Odalan Bali* often appears as a seamless, harmonious whole. Through its staged focus on sociability and the presentation of an idealized commune, *Odalan Bali* shares features of Bourriaud's (1998) notion of relational aesthetics in which the object or work of art is subordinated to the social (relational) aspect of its performance. Associated with global anticapitalist movements, relational aesthetics seeks to break divisions between audience and performer, hoping to create microtopias of interaction in which art is a form of social exchange (Martin 2007). In *Odalan Bali*, we appear to be seeing the *staging* of Bourriaud's concept. We witness a Balinese community apparently disengaged from capitalist exchange and the law of profit. Their artfulness is so intimately connected to their sociability as to not be readily distinguishable as works of art. In the program notes we are reminded that the ensemble has risen above performing for tourists. As audience members we may imagine that we share the performers' struggle to keep art integrated within the community rather than fetishized within the commodity. But then we notice the ticket stub in our hands.

Theorizing Intercultural Performance

Western interculturalists often appeal to an aesthetic common ground (as in Mitoma 2004), the implication being that contemporary intercultural performance is somehow freer than earlier modes of creation from hierarchy or core-periphery structures and thereby produce more symmetrical representations. In this context differences are represented as equivalences on a stage in which ethnic and aesthetic pluralism are stripped of the signs of actual socioeconomic pluralism, that is, inequality.

Celebratory intercultural performance is rooted in a faith in cultural relativism. Reacting against the racism of cultural evolutionism in which Western societies were placed at the top of a tree of progress, anthropologists, first led in America by Boas, proposed a relativistic universe. However, this model imposed a cognitive apartheid between cultural groups as if to say: If we cannot be superior in the same world, let each people live in its own (Sperber 1982:179). Relativism amplifies difference. If Balinese and Western cultures are related relativistically, the argument goes, then the former can (in fact should) retain its supposed timeless and cyclical qualities, proving its difference from the West and its ostensibly linear culture. By suggesting cultural flavors of categories such as time and ethics, cultural relativism implies a local encoding of precultural, natural experiences of those categories, whose interrogation is deferred to philosophy or the psychology of perception (Fabian 1983:41). At its most mundane, cultural relativism makes others' way of doing things merely pretty. At its most extreme, it produces the same effects as cultural evolutionism by denying coevalness. Habermas suggests that the Western invention of relativism led it to imagine itself as vaccinated from being relativized by other cultures, thus subtly reasserting its superiority (in Dascal 2003:490).

The cultural relativism of many intercultural performance projects resides in a particular understanding of multiculturalism, one that maintains signs of difference and circumscribes the flow of information across cultural boundaries. Cultural relativism is symbolized in the lining up, side-by-side, of ethnicities in costume without allowing them to transform into each other. We might call this a managerial as opposed to an organic multiculturalism. The former is represented by those high-profile projects funded by the state, foundations, and the market. The latter is embodied by sharing, borrowing, and stealing across cultures at the level of the individual through the practices of everyday life. Managerial multiculturalism fetishizes difference and is often complicit with global capitalism; organic multiculturalism is too viral to manage. This is not to say that the celebratory interculturalist is merely an unwitting mouthpiece for ideology; the humanist faith in diversity cannot be breezily dismissed. It is a generous spirit that sometimes mistakes an aesthetic for a material world held in common.

July 2009. Kadek Dewi Aryani and I met at an upscale café frequented by well-heeled Western expatriates living in the Ubud area. Since graduating from ISI, Dewi had become a leading kontemporer *choreographer and had participated in numerous intercultural projects. She described interculturalism generally as exploitative, arguing that such projects provided funds only slightly above local wages after total labor time was reckoned. "Balinese artists remain colonized! [I: dijajah]" She paused. Then speaking more softly, as if to convince herself more than me: "But from another perspective we still learn much from it, no?" She gave me a searching look before rolling her eyes, "Ah, that's very Balinese of me.... In reality, Westerners steal our ideas (I: ilmu), and we steal theirs. But while they can sell our ideas all we can do is* ngayah; *we can only sell our ideas to the gods! Or perform at the Bali Arts Festival for a bag of rice. Cheap Labor! It's our own fault; we've become the West's factory for the arts (I: pabrik kesenian)" [Track BV-9/1].*

APPROPRIATION, EXPLOITATION

Indonesian accusations of theft and misuse dogged *I La Galigo*, a massive intercultural performance conceived, managed, and directed by a company of Western theater producers led by the American avant-gardist Robert Wilson.[23] An experimental staging of a sacred Bugis myth, *I La Galigo* was performed by a cast of Balinese, Javanese, Sumatran, and Bugis performers in a series of tours to Europe, Asia, and America between 2004 and 2008. In defending the production, Rahayu Supanggah, faculty at ISI Solo and the production's musical director, suggested that the performance was a form of free promotion for Indonesia—one that offered a positive image to counter the corruption, lies, political violence, bombings, rapes, and economic crises for which the nation was more commonly known (2003b:13). Supanggah rationalized asymmetrical collaboration by equating cultural progress (I: *kemajuan*) with internationalization (I: *go-internasional-nya*), arguing that Javanese and Balinese performing arts cannot develop without the support of their intercultural interlocutors (ibid.). In responding to accusations of appropriation, Supanggah re-affirmed the colonial project by arguing that, although Indonesians are fine artists, Westerners, being objective and better able to judge Indonesians' faults, are better managers and producers (ibid.). By appealing to Westerners' ostensible objectivity, Supanggah appears as an apologist for the asymmetry of the encounter. This asymmetry was of great concern to the Balinese, recognizing that their economic well-being and international status is bound up in their image. The power differentials that subtend such projects not only remind individuals of old circuits of colonial power, but reproduce them as well.

The asymmetry of the intercultural encounter is determined by a complex system of geopolitical relations that works against the Balinese and gives Western interculturalists credit for, as the American composer Evan Ziporyn has said: "simply...showing up."[24] Western interculturalists can enter Indonesia with a $25 tourist visa, need not register with any governmental agencies, and can easily round up a large group of

---

[23] Henry Soelistiyo Budi, "director of the Bureau of Rights and Law in Indonesia's vice president's office, contended that Wilson had not gotten appropriate central-government permission under Indonesia's 2002 Copyright Law (Law 19, 2002)" (Aragon and Leach 2008:3).

[24] Evan Ziporyn, "Essays After an Opera," September 30, 2009, www.nothing2saybutitsok.com. Accessed August 2012.

musicians (including children), paying them low wages by Western standards. When we invert the process, Indonesian musicians must go through a lengthy visa application process (often being single young men from an Islamic nation), pay to travel far from home for a visa interview on another island, pay the $320 fee for a P-3 visa and pay another $250 fee (I: *fiskal*) simply to leave the country. Indonesian performers rarely have the means, and so these fees, and their substantial airfare, are covered by the Western partner, engendering a structure of indebtedness and sentiment of subservience.[25] To what extent do such projects represent a form of "distressed exchange" in which postcolonial interculturalists are obliged to sell their labor cheaply due to the structuring of the market? What should be the "moral limits" (Satz 2012) of global aesthetic marketplaces?

The asymmetrical relationship that marks many of the contemporary intercultural projects with which the Balinese are engaged reminds us of Said's point that the orientalist works like a ventriloquist to *make* the Orient speak rather than its speaking freely. In these contexts the Balinese appear too transparently as the self's shadow (Spivak 2010). Ziporyn's *House in Bali* (2008–10), an intercultural opera combining the Bang on a Can All-Stars and Ketut Dewa Alit's *salukat* ensemble, ruminated on these issues through a dramatization of McPhee's encounter with the Balinese. The production critically investigated the inequity of the intercultural encounter while ironically reproducing it in the processes of its own production. Although perceived by many Balinese and Western audiences as a collaboration—a similar number of American and Balinese performers share the stage—the entire score (for *gamelan* and chamber ensemble) was written by Ziporyn and the staging was managed by American producers (see McGraw 2013b).

By not engaging the Balinese as the producers of fully articulated texts within the intercultural encounter, such projects fail Spivak's requirement of "ethical responding" by which the Western interculturalist would engage agency in the other to move beyond a simple recognition of their other's otherness. In an ethical response the other is not a mere voice, or object of investigation (Ness 1997:69) but an equitable creative agent. Through their appearance on the Western stage under the direction of Western managers, lay audiences may be led to believe that the Balinese cannot yet make readable contemporary art inside global aesthetic networks without foreign direction.

THE ETHICS OF INTERCULTURALISM

Intercultural performance has for decades wound together rhetorics of civic universalism, humanism, and human rights, staging apparent demonstrations of the freedoms extended by the West while too often reproducing status quo relations of inequity. Rockefeller, the State Department, Ford, and their various subsidiaries speak about culture in the language of human rights as articulated in the 1948 Universal

---

[25] The P-3 visa, unlike educational visas, is not bound by any labor law; it enforces no minimal wage.

Declaration. If human rights are primarily imagined to protect bodies, intercultural performance is imagined to provide voice. The discourse of interculturalism appeals to an ethical process in order to achieve the expressive freedoms celebrated by the rhetorics of human rights, figured as a form of cultural welfare. As the Japanese theorist Karatani suggests, appeals to ethics in intercultural performance are entwined with a neo-orientalist form of aestheticentrism, the reification of the supposed aesthetic qualities of the other as its primary characteristic.

> This...stance goes hand-in-hand with an aesthetic worship of the very inferior Other. This worship, in turn, produces an uneradicable self-deceit: Those with an Orientalist attitude come to believe that they, unlike others, treat non-Westerners more than equally—they treat them with respect....Aestheticentrists always appear as anticolonialists. In the same way, they always appear as anti-industrial capitalists, although their aesthetic stance was produced by the advent of industrial capital. (1998:147, 153)[26]

While contemporary colloquial understandings of ethics suggest ideas of social justice, decency, and humanism, older usage refers to the ideological expressions of power. Philosophers of ethics including Ranciere (2009) and Agamben (1993) adhere to this notion, associating ethics not with a universal sense of human morality, but with a particular, historically constituted discourse. As Ranciere has suggested, human rights are the rights of those unable to exercise them without aid: victims of ethnic wars, minorities in totalitarian regimes, and the socioeconomically dispossessed of the Third World whose cultures are threatened by globalization. Following the Second World War, the West authorized itself to disburse human rights globally through forms of humanitarian aid, military intervention, and cultural diplomacy. Following 9/11 human rights became partly co-opted by America's war on terror, framed as a Western crusade to expand American notions of freedom globally.[27]

In this context, freedom—what so many *musik kontemporer* composers understood as the hallmark of their form and which appeared in many cases to be disbursed, as a kind of commodity, in the intercultural encounter—is not a timeless, universal essence, but a particular cultural, historically constituted concept, one characterized by specifically Western notions of authorship, ownership, originality, copyright, and democratic governance. If we accept that experimental music is defined by a sense of freedom, then, within the context of the current geopolitical configuration, we should critically assess the nature of this freedom for the ways in which it may circumscribe creative choices and opportunities for us all.

How is it that relations of inequity persist in projects produced by conscientious interculturalists concerned with social justice? I maintain it is because we have bought too fully into the notion of Balinese otherness, produced with such elegance in classic

---

[26] Also quoted in Wakeling 2010.
[27] Rumsfeld referred to the "war on terror" as a "war of human rights."

ethnography. Rorty rejects notions of justice, human rights, and freedom as particularly Western cultural notions that cannot serve as a basis of a universal ethics. He replaces these with an expanded notion of loyalty: "There has to be *some* sense that he or she is 'one of us' before we start being tormented by the question of whether we did the right thing..." (1998:45). Ironically, the cultural relativism that has guided modern ethnography has partly conditioned the persistently inequitable relations of intercultural performance by suggesting that our interlocutors are not truly one of us. If we allow that others are different from ourselves in profound cultural ways, then it becomes difficult to imagine them as residing in the same moral universe. The difference implicated by cultural relativism makes easier the practice of offering differential wages, creative rights, and authorial and managerial control, circumscribing the freedoms necessary for truly experimental practice.

Is interculturalism as such an act of oppression? If so, should the interculturalist close up shop? Is the better answer to compose within our own cultures and join concrete political movements urging social economic change? Can conditions be achieved in which musical otherness might appear as a less orientalizing, more purely aesthetic, form of difference? How might we make representations together more equitably, in concrete and practical ways that consider artists' political and economic situations as a whole, beyond the immediacy of interpersonal relations? Sidestepping the intensive capital investment that underwrites most intercultural projects might be possible through interactions on digital networks to which Balinese artists increasingly have equitable access. We might then forge a dialectical process in which parties have equal rights at each aesthetic fork in the road.

10 Conclusion

REIMAGINING BALINESE CULTURE

THE MUSICIANS PACKED *tightly in a ring, each playing a gong placed horizontally before him, moving their bodies in kinesthetic sympathy to the music, challenging each other with shouts and hand motions, shifting of the shoulders, turnings of the head, falling back en masse as some imagined cock with murderous spurs careened towards one side of the ring, surging forward again as it glanced off towards its rival. In their* musik kontemporer *work* Tajen (B), *cockfight, included within* Odalan Bali, *Cudamani's musicians demonstrated for their American audiences that, as much of America surfaces in a baseball game, democracy, or the war on terror, much of Bali surfaces in* musik kontemporer.[1]

In musik kontemporer, *composers attempt to create an interesting, if you will "deep," composition by expanding their music's semiotic field beyond the barriers of* tradisi. *The stakes are high in the "deep play" of such exotic compositions and it is rather irrational for artists to engage in them at all. In the deep play of intercultural, interinterpretive meaning, artists and ethnographers are in over their heads. Having come together in search of pleasure and knowledge they have entered into a relationship which may bring them net pain; opening themselves to critiques from conservatives, to misunderstanding, to exploitation by their others, they nevertheless engage in such play both passionately and often.*

A composition such as Tajen *is not a straightforward depiction of how things literally are in Balinese life, but what is almost stranger, of how, from a particular angle, they are represented as being. For it is only apparently musicians that are playing there. Actually, it is cultures. What sets a* musik kontemporer *work such as* Tajen *apart from the ordinary course of life, lifts it from the realm of everyday practical affairs, and surrounds it with an aura of enlarged importance is that it is interpretive: it is a Balinese reading of a foreign reading of Balinese experience, a story they tell themselves—and their others—about stories told about themselves. It is this kind of bringing of assorted experiences of everyday life and represented life into focus that* musik kontemporer, *set aside from that life as "only music" and reconnected to it as "more than music," accomplishes*[2] [Track MK-10/1].

---

[1] *Tajen* first emerged in 2001 as an ISI recital composition by the composer and Cudamani member Madé Karmawan, and was highly reminiscent of Asnawa's *Kosong*. The work was later expanded and included within *Odalan Bali*.

[2] This section is a free play of text from Geertz's (1973a) *Deep Play: Notes on the Balinese Cockfight*. New York: Basic Books.

Ethnography

I began this text with an apparently antagonistic reading of the ethnography of Bali. However, ethnography can be extremely *productive*, even if it might be a partial, possibly incorrect, representation. How can we recognize, and even celebrate, the cultural work ethnography performs? In what unexpected ways does ethnography contribute to the cultures that are its object? Hobart (2000) and Crapanzano (1986) cogently critiqued Geertz's famous analysis of the Balinese cockfight. But Geertz's work, as the composers of Cudamani know, persists as a privileged trope of American anthropology.[3] Many faculty, including myself, prepared their students for Cudamani's 2007 tour of *Odalan Bali* by assigning Geertz's essay, evoking an image of mirrors reflecting back into themselves in infinite regression. To extend Crapanzano's observation: *Tajen* represented the Balinese's constructed understanding of American's constructed understanding of the constructed native's constructed points of view (Crapanzano 1986:74). To complete the representational orbit, Geertz's *Cockfight* is in *Tajen* finally aestheticized upon the stage. If, as Hobart suggests, the Balinese cockfight was not quite the Balinese reading of Balinese experience Geertz interpreted it as (1973a:448), *Tajen* was; it appeared as a staged reflection upon the Balinese image. Transforming in reaction to its ethnographic image, Balinese culture requires constant reimagining. *Musik kontemporer* is one of the representational modes in which this reimagining takes place.

In *Tajen* a potent and renowned icon of Balinese *tradisi*—the cockfight—is reinterpreted through *radikal* musical techniques. Through it, *Odalan Bali*'s utopian image of a harmonious social unity is complicated by a scene of rowdy young men rooting for their side. In it, the members of Cudamani brought together the representational and the actual: the timeless image of the Balinese against the feeling of living in Bali today. As an element of the *Odalan Bali* production, performed for and co-managed by Americans, *Tajen* also embodied the intercultural aesthetics at the heart of much *musik kontemporer*.

The composer Gusti Komin Darta, who had taken part in many intercultural projects, sometimes complained to me about exploitation, control, and representation in the encounter. But as I would attempt to follow these lines of thought he would seem to reverse course, claiming disinterest in issues of power as he really only cared about the feeling (*rasa*) of a performance. His sole concern, he maintained, was to help forge moments of musical unity (I: *rasa kebersamaan*). Some of his fondest musical memories were drawn from such otherwise problematic intercultural contexts. He suggested that the imbalances of power and misunderstanding that often accompany intercultural

---

[3] I engaged in occasional discussions of Geertz's essay with the composers during the production of Karmawan's original *ujian* and the later Cudamani arrangement. Cudamani's was not the only *kontemporer* work inspired by the celebrated ethnographic status of the Balinese cockfight; in 2002 and 2006 *kontemporer* artists Kadek Suardana and Nyoman Sura independently developed multiple *kontemporer* theater projects based on the theme. References to Geertz's essays, many of which were translated into Indonesian during the *reformasi*, appeared with regularity in both the pages of the *Bali Post* and *Gong* during my research.

performance may appear to suddenly drop away when a performance clicks—when we forget, in the luxuriousness of that moment, all but the music itself and the connections to our fellow performers. That is, intercultural musicking, when it works, does exactly what Crapanzano *critiqued* Geertz's essay for doing: it blurs the relationship between the self and the other's subjectivities to approach coevalness (1986:74). It assumes, in those rare and precious instances of performative togetherness, that subjectivity can, for a moment, be shared even across the apparent boundaries of culture. It is partly in search of these moments that artists take the risk of wading in over their heads, to realize that difference in sound need not be divisive or hierarchical.

Culture

Although I have provided a historically grounded account of *musik kontemporer,* I do not mean to suggest that it, or Balinese culture more generally, can only be understood *in terms* of the past, as much prior ethnography of Bali and the Balinese would seem to suggest. While not denying the importance of a sense of cultural continuity in Balinese lives, I have represented present reality as a product of change over continuity. This approach has been inspired by local ideas such as Subandi's notions of the *ceraken* and *tradisi radikal.* These concepts acknowledge and value continuity but focus upon change, transformation, mixture, and outward relations. I have described the mechanics of change, both formal and semiotic, as a product of composers' constructive cognitive processes that encourage the mutation of materials. While change was embodied in the various forms of *musik kontemporer* itself, it may have been more profoundly expressed in the subtle transformations of subjects' temporal and spatial imaginations, a refrain that I have returned to repeatedly in these pages.

The composers I have discussed in *Radical Traditions* were engaged in a reimagining of Balinese culture, one in which a set of apparently antagonistic dichotomies—the production of locality and the achievement of coevalness, the actual and the representational, change and continuity, the native and the cosmopolitan, the past and the future—dissolved into the unity of their being. While *budaya* (I), culture, may have appeared to many composers as synonymous with *tradisi* during the New Order, in the *reformasi* many characterized it as something larger and more complex of which *tradisi* was an aspect. The laboratory model through which *polemik kebudayaan* thinkers imagined culture no longer captured the complexity of viral mutation that *budaya* now suggested to many creative individuals. There was a sense that culture was beyond control and may even be autopoetic; its mutational processes could not be managed or even fully known. Conservatory attempts to delineate proper modes of composition were forever undermined by the ubiquity of foreign representations available through digital networks. Many composers recognized that culture remained the primary means through which Bali was known to the world but, unlike many of their predecessors, few attempted to characterize it as a coherent totality. Culture *was* change, a complex contest between variously positioned social actors.

Conclusion: Reimagining Balinese Culture 239

If some critiqued the institutional mantra of continuities in change, many composers' praxis nonetheless embodied some of its principles. None (not even Yudane or Sadra) advocated or imagined a world of Khunian incommensurable paradigms or a model of distinct epistemic ruptures as suggested by Foucault. Many imagined and embodied a praxis recalling the history of cybernetics in which change involves periods of overlapping replication and transformation, regularly punctured by sudden ruptures of innovative momentum. While *Ajeg* commentators imagined maximal cultural stasis and memory, conservatory administrators imagined a modified Darwinian phyletic gradualism in which forms would morph continually but gradually (guided by official *téori*), while preserved exemplars of *tradisi* remained static and were never lost, as pictured in Figure 10.1.

As demonstrated in this text, many composers engaged with *musik kontemporer* spoke of culture in ways that combined aspects of phyletic gradualism and punctuated equilibrium—the rapid differentiation of forms preceded and followed by comparative periods of morphological stasis. Their ideas did not fit neatly into either paradigm, reminding us that human behavior cannot be easily flattened into neat biological metaphors. For them culture was always in the process of change, even (or especially) when attempts were made to protect exemplars of *tradisi* through preservation. However, many suggested that cultural memory cannot be tasked with remembering everything and some aspects of expressive culture should be allowed to go extinct. Their reimagination of culture was characterized by an interest in rapid innovation that valued the creative freedom of the individual and the incorporation and transformation of a wide range of materials. These were the sudden punctuations of cultural change, as pictured in Figure 10.2.

Finally, in *Radical Traditions* I have sought to frame my arguments in the spirit of *musik kontemporer*, especially as in the hands of I Wayan Sadra. As I write these words this pioneer, I have just learned via text message, has passed away too early and I remember here his exhortation to "write about us in the manner in which we

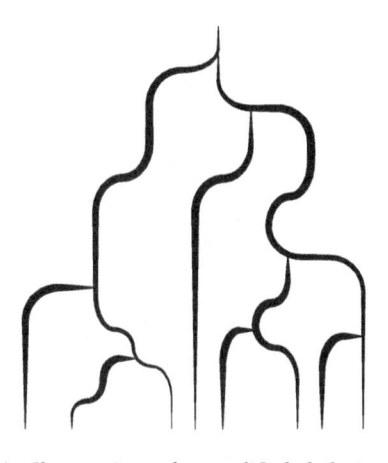

FIGURE 10.1 Continuities in Change pictured as modified phyletic gradualism.

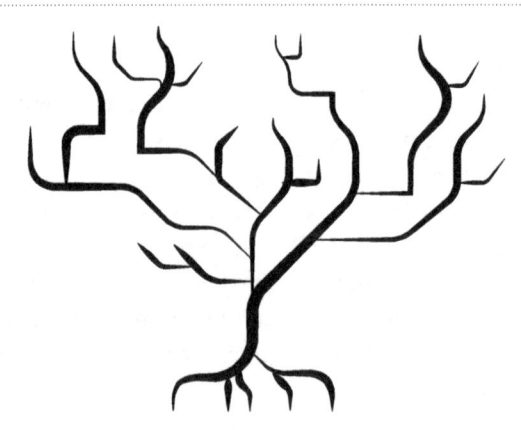

FIGURE 10.2 Radical Traditions pictured as punctuated gradualism.

compose." Sadra suggested that it was a testament to the value and strength of older practice that it could withstand the critiques posed by *musik kontemporer*. I hope this text, in its eclectic references and occasional provocations, has produced a *feeling* similar to the music itself.

Glossary

ADAT. I: Customs or traditions. Often referring to customary law rather than performing arts.
AGA. B: A designation referring to the ostensibly pre-Hindu groups of indigenous Balinese residing in a few villages on the eastern shore and the northern mountainous region of the island.
AJEG. B: Uprightness. A conservative cultural discourse emerging after the first Bali bombing in 2002.
ANGSEL. B: A dance movement and musical rhythm cued by a drumming pattern in several genres of Balinese *gamelan*.
BANJAR. B: A neighborhood ward within a larger village (*desa*); the meeting place of various organizations, such as *gamelan* ensembles, within that ward.
BARU. I: New. A conservatory designation referring to contemporary forms of *gamelan* including *gong kebyar*.
BAYU. B: Energy.
CALUNG. B: Single octave, mid-register metallophone found in several forms of Balinese *gamelan*. It typically performs melodic abstractions (*pokok*). Also called *jublag*.
CERAKEN. B: A container for spices, medicines, herbs, or the betel kit. Madé Subandi's arts foundation (*sanggar*).
CUDAMANI. A private arts foundation (*sanggar*) in Pengosekan founded by Dewa Ketut Alit and Dewa Putu Berata.
DALANG. I: Shadow puppeteer.
ESTETIKA. I: Aesthetics. More properly an institutional, ideological theory of artistic beauty espoused by the conservatory.
GAMELAN. I: Term for percussion orchestras of Bali and Java.

242 Glossary

GAMELAN GAMBUH. I: A small orchestra including deep *suling* flutes but eschewing the metallophones typical of most Balinese *gamelan*. Often described as an ancient (*kuno*) form of music and the origin of many later forms.

GAMELAN GONG GEDE. I: Large Balinese orchestra used in court and temple settings. Performs languorous *lelambatan* ritual compositions.

GAMELAN GONG KEBYAR. I: Five-tone Balinese orchestra that emerged in the beginning of the twentieth century. The most ubiquitous form of music on the island, internationally famous for its virtuosic compositions and performing techniques.

GAMELAN LUANG. I: Rare, ancient Balinese seven-tone orchestra known in only a few villages.

GAMELAN SEMARA DANA. I: Contemporary seven-tone Balinese orchestra invented in 1987 by I Wayan Beratha (1924–).

GAMELAN SEMAR PEGULINGAN. I: Five- to seven-tone Balinese orchestra traditionally associated with the courts.

GAMELAN SLONDING. I: Rare, ancient Balinese seven-tone iron orchestra associated with Aga communities.

GANGSA. B: Two-octave metallophone used to perform melodic figurations (*kotekan*) in several forms of Balinese *gamelan*.

GONG (MAGAZINE). A bi-monthly arts magazine published in Yogyakarta between 1998 and 2010.

GONGAN. I: A metrical period in Balinese *gamelan* ended by striking the large *gong*.

ISI. I: *Institut Seni Indonesia*. The Indonesian Institute of the Arts. The most recent name for the tertiary-level arts institute in Denpasar, Bali. Previous names for the institution include ASTI and STSI. Referred to herein as the conservatory.

KAJAR. B: A small, mounted *gong*-chime that marks the pulse in several forms of Balinese *gamelan*.

KARAWITAN. I: A Javanese term referring to *gamelan* music. Exported to Bali during the Old Order.

KEBYAR. B: The virtuosic, a-metrical tutti introduction to many works in the *gamelan gong kebyar* repertoire. The term may refer as well to the ensemble itself or its repertoire generally.

KENDANG. I: Barrel drums, usually found in pairs in Balinese *gamelan*. They often function as the ersatz conductor of the orchestra and coordinate the connections between music and dance.

KOKAR. I: <u>K</u>onservatori <u>K</u>arawitan. The name of the first arts institute founded in Bali IN 1959. It continues to function (under various names) today as an arts magnet high school.

KOTEKAN. B: Interlocking figuration in Balinese *gamelan* requiring the complex and virtuosic rhythmic coordination between two or more musicians.

KREASI BARU (KREASI). I: New creations. A term used since the Old Order to designate new forms of composition for *gamelan* ensembles. During the New Order and *reformasi* it was the de facto form of composition, a genre generally less adventurous than *musik kontemporer*.

KUNO. I: Old. A conservatory designation referring to ostensibly ancient forms of *gamelan* including *slonding*, *luang*, and *gambuh*.

LAGU. I: Melody. The main melody performed in a *gamelan* composition. It is abstracted at various rhythmic levels by supporting instruments including the *calung*.

LEKRA. I: <u>Le</u>mbaga <u>K</u>ebudayaan <u>Ra</u>kyat, Institute of People's Culture, the cultural arm of the Indonesian Communist Party (PKI). Outlawed in 1966 under the New Order.

LELAMBATAN. B: Literally referring to slow music; long-form compositions originally for the *gong gede* ensemble today often performed on the *gong kebyar.*

LISTIBIYA. I: *Maje<u>lis</u> Per<u>ti</u>mbangan dan Pem<u>bi</u>naan Kebuda<u>ya</u>an*, Arts Evaluation and Cultivation Board, a conservative governmental arts organization established at the beginning of the New Order focused upon the preservation and revitalization of traditional forms.

LKN. I: *Lembaga Kebudayaan Nasional*, Institute of National Culture, the cultural arm of the Indonesian National Party (PNI), generally antagonistic to the PKI and LEKRA.

MADYA. B: Middle. A conservatory designation referring to classic forms of *gamelan* associated with the Majapahit era and including *gamelan pelegongan* and *semar pegulingan*.

NELITI. B: Correct. A term used to refer to the principal melody, most often performed on the leading *ugal* metallophone in large bronze *gamelan* ensembles.

NEW ORDER. Indonesia's second authoritarian regime. Led by Suharto between 1966 and 1998.

NGAYAH. B: Ritual performance or participation within ceremonial contexts.

OLD ORDER. Indonesia's first authoritarian regime. Led by Sukarno between 1945 and 1965.

OMBAK. I: Waves. A musical term referring to fluctuations in tempo, dynamics, and the destructive interference of paired tuning in Balinese *gamelan*.

OTONOMI DAERAH. I: Regional autonomy. Laws passed during the *reformasi* era intended to devolve greater independence and authority to local counties.

PANGIDER BUANA (BHAWANA). B: The Balinese cosmological compass with eleven points: eight cardinal directions, up, down, and center. Associated with music in the traditional manuscript, the *Prakempa*.

PATHET. I: A general term for mode. Balinese terms also include *patutan, tetekep,* and *saih*.

PAYASAN. B: A Balinese term referring to melodic figurations including *kotekan* and improvisations performed on *suling* flutes, *rebab* fiddles, the *trompong gong* chime, and *ugal* metallophone.

PÉLOG. I: Originally a Javanese term exported to Bali during the Old Order to refer to forms of seven-tone tuning systems with unequal intervals and their various five-tone subsets (*patutan*).

PKB. I: *Pesta Kesenian Bali*. The Bali Arts Festival, a major annual, month-long arts festival held at the Taman Budaya Arts Center each June and July. Established in 1979.

PKI. I: *Partai Komunis Indonesia*. The Indonesian Communist Party. Outlawed in 1965.

PNI. I: *Partai Nasional Indonesia*. The Indonesian National Party opposed to the PKI.

PKM. I: *Pekan Komponis Muda*. Young Composers' Week, a festival of new music held in Jakarta from the late 1970s through early 1990s.

POKOK. I: Main thing. The abstracted form of the melody (*lagu*) in Balinese *gamelan* repertoires. Generally performed at the level of the pulse or every other pulse on the *calung* metallophone.

PRAKEMPA. A *lontar* traditional manuscript published in an academic edition by STSI (ISI) Bali in 1986 and edited by Madé Bandem.

RASA. I: Feeling, sense, flavor. A category of subjective aesthetic evaluation.

REFORMASI. I: Reformation. The era of chaotic change and reform in Indonesian politics and civil society following the end of the New Order and Suharto's ouster in 1998. A quick succession of political upheavals led by presidents Habibie, Wahid, Megawati, and Yudhoyono.

SANGGAR. I: A privately owned arts club or foundation. *Sanggar* flourished during the *reformasi* era.

SELISIR. B: A five-tone mode derived from the *gambuh* repertoire. A tonality associated with the *gamelan gong kebyar*. Herein notated as: c#, d, e, g#, a.

SLENDRO. I: Originally a Javanese term exported to Bali during the Old Order to refer to forms of five-tone tuning systems with roughly equal intervals.

SULING. I: Balinese end-blown ring flute made of bamboo.

TÉORI. I: Theory. More properly an institutional, ideological set of theoretical ideas concerning compositional form and process espoused by the conservatory.

TRI-ANGGA. B: Three sections. An aspect of Balinese music theory, especially popular at the conservatory, meant to refer to ostensibly tripartite compositional forms.

UJIAN. I: Test. Herein referring to final recital compositions performed at the conservatory.

Bibliography

Acciaioli, Gregory. 1985. Culture as Art: from Practice to Spectacle in Indonesia. *Canberra Anthropology* 8 (1): 148–71.

Adorno, Theodore. 1997. *Aesthetic Theory*. London: Athlone Press.

———. 2002. *Essays on Music. Selected with Introduction, Commentary, and Notes by Richard Leppert*. New translations by Susan H. Gillespie. Berkeley: University of California Press.

Agamben, Giorgio. 1993. *The Coming Community*. Minneapolis: University of Minnesota Press.

Agawu, Kofi. 1991. *Playing with Signs: a Semiotic Interpretation of Classic Music*. Princeton: Princeton University Press.

———. 2003. Contesting Difference: a Critique of Africanist Ethnomusicology. In *The Cultural Study of Music: A Critical Introduction*, edited by Martin Clayton. London: Routledge, pp. 227–37.

Allen, Pamela, and Carmencita Palermo. 2005. Ajeg Bali: Multiple Meanings, Diverse Agendas. *Indonesia and the Malay World* 33 (97): 239–55.

Anderson, Benedict R. O'G. 1991. *Imagined Communities: Reflections on the Origin and Spread of Nationalism*. London and New York: Verso Editions.

Anderson, Perry. 1974. *Lineages of the Absolutist State*. London: Verso Editions.

Antons, Christoph, ed. 2009. *Traditional Knowledge, Traditional Cultural Expressions and Intellectual Property Law in the Asia-Pacific Region*. New York: Wolters Kluwer.

Appadurai, Arjun. 1996. *Modernity at Large: Cultural Dimensions of Globalization*. Minneapolis: University of Minnesota Press.

Appiah, Kwame Anthony. 2006. *Cosmopolitanism: Ethics in a World of Strangers*. New York: Norton.

Aragon, Lorraine, and James Leach. 2008. Arts and Owners: Intellectual Property Law and the Politics of Scale in Indonesian Arts. *American Ethnologist* 35 (4): 607–31.

Arndt, Richard T. 2005. *The First Resort of Kings: American Cultural Diplomacy in the Twentieth Century*. Washington, D.C.: Potomac Books, Inc.

Arsawijaya, Sang Nyoman. 2005. *Geräusch, Skrip Karawitan*. Denpasar: ISI.

Aryasa, Wayan. 1976. *Perkembangan Seni Karawitan Bali*. Denpasar: Proyek Sasana Budaya Bali.

Asia Society. 2010. *Making a Difference through the Arts: Strengthening America's Links with Asian Muslim Communities*. New York: Asia Society.

Atkins, E. Taylor. 2001. *Blue Nippon: Authenticating Jazz in Japan*. Durham, NC: Duke University Press.

Attali, Jacques. 1985. *Noise: The Political Economy of Music* Translated by Brian Massumi. Minneapolis: University of Minnesota Press.

Austerlitz, Paul. 2000. Birch-Bark Horns and Jazz in the National Imagination: The Finnish Folk Music Vogue in Historical Perspective. *Ethnomusicology* 44 (2): 183–213.

Bakan, Michael B. 1999. *Music of Death and New Creation: Experiences in the World of Balinese Gamelan Beleganjur*. Chicago: University of Chicago Press.

Bakhtin, M. M. 1981. *The Dialogic Imagination: Four Essays*. Translated by Caryl Emerson and Michael Holquist. Austin: University of Texas Press.

Balabar, Etienne. 1995. *The Philosophy of Marx*. New York: Verso.

Balyson. 1934a. Gong-Gedé (Kebijar). *Bhawanagara* 3 (11): 161–66.

———. 1934b. Gong-Gedé (Kebijar). *Bhawanagara* 4 (12): 191–92.

Bandem, Madé. 1983. *Ensiklopedi Gambelan Bali*. Denpasar: STSI.

———. 1986. *Prakempa: Sebuah Lontar Gambelan Bali*. Denpasar: STSI.

Bandem, Madé, and F. deBoer. 1995. *Balinese Dance in Transition: Kaja and Kelod*. Kuala Lumpur: Oxford University Press.

Barthes, Roland. 1978. *Image-Music-Text*. New York: Hill and Wang.

Bar-Yosef, Amatzia. 2001. Musical Time Organization and Space Concept: A Model of Cross-Cultural Analogy. *Ethnomusicology* 45 (3): 423–42.

Barz, Gregory, and Timothy Cooley. 1997. *Shadows in the Field: New Perspectives for Fieldwork in Ethnomusicology*. New York: Oxford University Press.

Basset, Catherine. 1993. *Bali, l'ordre Cosmique et la Quotidienneté*. Paris: Éditions Autrement.

Bateson, Gregory. 1949. Bali: The Value System of a Steady State. In *Social Structure: Studies Presented to A. R. Radcliffe-Brown*, edited by Meyer Fortes. Oxford: Clarendon Press, pp. 35-53.

———. 2000. *Steps to an Ecology of Mind*. Chicago: University of Chicago Press.

Baudrillard, Jean. 2001. *Selected Writings*. Translated by Mark Poster. Palo Alto, CA: Stanford University Press.

Baulch, Emma. 2007. *Making Scenes: Reggae, Punk and Death Metal in 1990s Bali*. Durham, NC: Duke University Press.

Becker, A. L. 1979. Text-Building, Epistemology and Aesthetics in Javanese Shadow Theatre. In *The Imagination of Reality*, edited by A. L. Becker and A. Yengoyan. Norwood, NJ: Ablex.

Becker, Howard. 1982. *Art Worlds*. Berkeley: University of California Press.

Becker, Judith. 1980. *Traditional Music in Modern Java: Gamelan in a Changing Society*. Honolulu: University of Hawaii Press.

———. 1981. Hindu-Buddhist Time in Javanese Gamelan Music. In *The Study of Time 4*, edited by J. T. Fraser. New York: Springer-Verlag, pp. 161–72.

Becker, Judith, and Alton Becker. 1981. A Musical Icon: Power and Meaning in Javanese Gamelan Music. In *The Sign in Music and Literature*, edited by Wendy Steiner. Austin: University of Texas, pp. 169–83.

Belo, Jane. 1970. *Traditional Balinese Culture: Essays*. New York: Columbia University Press.

Benamou, Marc. 2010. *Rasa: Affect and Intuition in Javanese Musical Aesthetics*. New York: Oxford University Press.

Benjamin, Walter. 1968. *Illuminations*. Edited and with an introduction by Hannah Arendt. Translated by Harry Zohn. New York: Harcourt, Brace and World, Inc.

Bérénice, Bellina. 2003. Beads, Social Change and Interaction Between India and South-east Asia. *Antiquity* 77: 285–97.

Bernet-Kempers, August Johan. 1988. *The Kettledrums of Southeast Asia: A Bronze Age World and its Aftermath*. Brookfield, VT: Balkema.

Bharucha, Jamshed, Meagan Curtis and Kaivon Paroo. 2012. Musical Communication as Alignment of Brain States. In *Language and Music as Cognitive Systems*, edited by Patrick Rebuschat, Martin Rohmeier, John A. Hawkins and Ian Coss. New York: Oxford University Press, pp. 139–55.

Bharucha, Rustom. 2000. *The Politics of Cultural Practice: Thinking Through Theatre in an Age of Globalization*. Middletown, CT: Wesleyan University Press.

Biddle, Ian, and Vanessa Knights. 2007. *Music, National Identity and the Politics of Location*. Burlington, VT: Ashgate.

Bing, Agus. 2003. Paul Fredrick: Kemandirian Seorang Komponis Daerah. *Gong* 49: 18–19.

———. 2004. Kumpul, Kempal, Kampus. *Gong* 54: 30–31.

Bloch, Maurice. 1977. The Past and the Present in the Present. *Man* n.s. 12 (2): 278–92.

Bloom, Harold. 1982. *Agon: Towards a Theory of Revisionism*. New York: Oxford University Press.

Bohlman, Philip V. 1998. Traditional Music and Cultural Identity: Persistent Paradigm in the History of Ethnomusicology. *Yearbook for Traditional Music* 20: 26–42.

Boiles, Charles L. 1982. Processes of Musical Semiosis. *Yearbook for Traditional Music* 14: 24–44.

Boon, James A. 1977. *The Anthropological Romance of Bali 1597–1972*. New York: Cambridge University Press.

———. 1990. *Affinities and Extremes: Crisscrossing the Bittersweet Ethnology of East Indies History, Hindu-Balinese Culture, and Indo-European Allure*. Chicago: University of Chicago Press.

Born, Georgina. 1995. *Rationalizing Culture: Ircam, Boulez, and the Institutionalization of the Musical Avant-Garde*. Berkeley: University of California Press.

———. 2010a. The Social and the Aesthetic: For a Post-Bourdieuian Theory of Cultural Production. *Cultural Sociology* 4 (2): 171-208.

———. 2010b. For a Relational Musicology: Music and Interdisciplinarity, Beyond the Practice Turn. *Journal of the Royal Musical Association* 135 (2): 205-243.

Born, Georgina, and David Hesmondhalgh, eds. 2000. *Western Music and Its Others: Difference, Representation, and Appropriation in Music*. Berkeley: University of California Press.

Bourdieu, Pierre. 1984. *Distinction: A Social Critique of the Judgement of Taste*. Translated by R. Nice. London: Routledge.

———. 1993. *The Field of Cultural Production*. New York: Columbia University Press.

Bourriaud, Nicolas. 1998. *Relational Aesthetics*. Paris: Les Presses du Réel.

Brautigan, Richard. 1976. *Loading Mercury With a Pitchfork*. New York: Simon and Schuster.

Bresnan, John. 2006. *At Home Abroad: A Memoir of the Ford Foundation in Indonesia, 1953–1973*. Jakarta: Equinox.

Budiman, Arief, and Barbara Hatley. 1999. *Reformasi: Crisis and Change in Indonesia*. Clayton, Australia: Monash Asia Institute, Monash University.

Bürger, Peter. 1984. *Theory of the Avant-Garde*. Translated by Michael Shaw. Minneapolis: University of Minnesota Press.

Burhanuddin, Yudhis M. 2008. *Bali Yang Hilang: Pendatang, Islam dan Etnisitas di Bali*. Yogyakarta: Kanisius.

Burke, Kenneth. 1957. *The Philosophy of Literary Form*. New York: Random House.

Cage, John. 1961. *Silence*. Middletown, CT: Wesleyan University Press.

Cameron, Catherine. 1990. Avant-Gardism as a Mode of Cultural Change. *Cultural Anthropology* 5 (2): 217–30.

Carroll, Michael P. 1974. The Effects of the Functionalist Paradigm Upon the Perception of Ethnographic Data. *Philosophy of the Social Sciences* 4: 65-75.

Carter, Paul. 1992. *The Sound In-Between: Voice, Space, Performance*. New South Wales: New Endeavour Press.

Clayton, Martin. 2000. *Time in Indian Music: Rhythm, Metre, and Form in North Indian Rāg Performance*. New York: Oxford University Press.

Cohen, Matthew Isaac. 2006. *The Komedie Stamboel: Popular Theater in Colonial Indonesia, 1891–1903*. Athens, OH: Ohio University Press.

———. 2007a. Dancing the Subject of "Java": International Modernism and Traditional Performance, 1899–1952. *Indonesia and the Malay World* 35 (101): 9–29.

———. 2007b. Contemporary Wayang in Global Contexts. *Asian Theatre Journal* 24 (2): 338–69.

———. 2010. *Performing Otherness: Java and Bali on International Stages, 1905-1952*. New York: Palgrave MacMillan.

Coker, Wilson. 1972. *Music and Meaning*. New York: Free Press.

Collins, John. 1993. The Problem of Oral Copyright: The Case of Ghana. In *Music and Copyright*, edited by Simon Frith. Edinburgh: Edinburgh University Press, pp. 146–58.

Comaroff, John L., and Jean Comaroff. 2009. *Ethnicity, Inc*. Chicago: University of Chicago Press.

Cook, Nick, and Mark Everist. 1999. *Rethinking Music*. New York: Oxford University Press.

Corbin, Alain. 1998. *Village Bells. Sound and Meaning in the 19th Century French Countryside*. New York: Columbia University Press.

Corona, Ignacio, and Alejandro L. Madrid, eds. 2008. *Postnational Musical Identities: Cultural Production, Distribution, and Consumption in a Globalized Scenario*. New York: Lexington Books.

Couteau, Jean. 2003. After the Kuta Bombing: In Search of the Balinese Soul. *Antropologi Indonesia* 70: 41–59.

Covarrubias, Miguel. 1937. *Island of Bali*. New York: Alfred A. Knopf.

Cowell, Henry. 1933. Towards Neo-Primitivism. *Modern Music* 10 (3): 149–53.

Crapanzano, Vincent. 1986. Hermes' Dilemma: The Masking of Subversion in Ethnographic Description. In *Writing Culture: the Poetics and Politics of Ethnography*, edited by J. Clifford and G. Marcus. London: California University Press, pp. 51–76.

Cumming, Naomi. 2001. *The Sonic Self*. Bloomington: Indiana University Press.

Dascal, Marcelo. 2003. *Interpretation and Understanding*. Philadelphia: John Benjamins Publishing.

Day, Tony. 2002. *Fluid Iron*. Honolulu: University of Hawaii Press.

De Andrade, Oswald. 1991 [1928]. Cannibalist Manifesto. Translated by Leslie Bary. *Latin American Literary Review* 19 (38): 38–47.

De Certeau, Michel. 1984. *The Practice of Everyday Life*. Berkeley: University of California Press.

De Nerval, Gérard. 1999. *Selected Writings*. New York: Penguin.

Deleuze, Gilles and Felix Gauttari. 1987. *A Thousand Plateaus*. Translated by Brian Massumi. Minneapolis: University of Minnesota Press.

Dennett, Daniel. 1991. *Consciousness Explained*. Boston: Little, Brown and Co.

DeNora, Tia. 2003. *After Adorno: Rethinking Music Sociology*. Cambridge: Cambridge University Press.

Derrida, Jacques. 1985. Difference. In *Margins of Philosophy*. Translated by Alan Bass. Chicago: University of Chicago Press, pp. 1–28.

Dewan Kesenian Jakarta. 1998. *Pekan Komponis IX Program*. Jakarta: Dewan Kesenian Jakarta.

Diamond, Jody. 1990. There Is No They There. *Musicworks* 47: 12–23.

Dibia, Wayan, and Rucina Ballinger. 2011. *Balinese Dance, Drama & Music: A Guide to the Performing Arts of Bali*. New York: Tuttle.

Djelantik, A. A. M. 1999. *Estetika: Sebuah Pengantar*. Jakarta: MSPI.

Duff-Cooper, A. 1990. *Shapes and Images: Aspects of the Aesthetics of Balinese Rice-growing and Other Studies*. Denpasar: Udayana University.

Eagleton, Terry. 2008 [1983]. *Literary Theory*. Minneapolis: University of Minnesota Press.

Eco, Umberto. 1979 [1976]. *A Theory of Semiotics*. Bloomington: Indiana University Press.

Epstein, David. 1985. Tempo Relations: A Cross-Cultural Study. *Music Theory Spectrum* 7: 34–71.

———. 1995. *Shaping Time: Music, the Brain, and Performance*. New York: Schirmer.

Escobar, Arturo. 1994. *Encountering Development: The Making and Unmaking of the Third World*. Princeton: Princeton University Press.

Euba, Akin. 1975. Criteria for the Evaluation of New African Art Music. *Transition* 49: 46–50.

Everett, Yayoi Uno, and Frederick Lau, eds. 2004. *Locating East Asia in Western Art Music*. Middletown, CT: Wesleyan University Press.

Fabian, Johannes. 1983. *Time and the Other: How Anthropology Makes Its Object*. New York: Columbia University Press.

———. 1991. *Time and the Work of Anthropology. Critical Essays: 1971–1991*. Philadelphia: Harwood Academic Publishers.

Feld, Steven. 1981. "Flow Like a Waterfall": The Metaphors of Kaluli Musical Theory. *Yearbook For Traditional Music* 13: 22–47.

———. 1988. Aesthetics as Iconicity of Style, or, "Lift-up-over-Sounding": Getting into the Kaluli Groove. *Yearbook for Traditional Music* 20: 74–113.

———. 1990. *Sound and Sentiment: Birds, Weeping, Poetics, and Song in Kaluli Expression*. Philadelphia: University of Pennsylvania Press.

Feliciano, Francisco F. 1983. *Four Asian Contemporary Composers: The Influence of Tradition in Their Works*. Quezon City: New Day Publishers.

Ferrari, Rossella. 2010. Journey(s) to the East: Travels, Trajectories, and Transnational Chinese Theatre(s). *Postcolonial Studies* 13 (4): 351–66.

Florida, Nancy. 2008. A Proliferation of Pigs: Specters of Monstrosity in Reformation Indonesia. *Public Culture* 20 (3): 497–530.

Foucault, Michel. 1972. *The Archaeology of Knowledge, and the Discourse on Language*. New York: Vintage Books.

Foulcher, Keith. 2009. Moving Pictures: Western Marxism and Vernacular Literature in Colonial Indonesia. In *Chewing Over the West: Occidental Narratives in Non-Western Readings*, edited by Doris Jedamski. New York: Rodopi, pp. 37–74.

Fox, Richard. 2002. *From Text to Television: Mediating Religion in Contemporary Bali*. PhD diss. London: University of London.

Frederick, William H. 1997. Dreams of Freedom, Moments of Despair: Armijn Pané and the Imagining of Modern Indonesian Culture. In *Imagining Indonesia: Cultural Politics and*

Political Culture, edited by J. W. Schiller and B. Martin Schiller. Akron: Ohio University Press, pp. 54–89.

Friedson, Steven M. 2009. *Remains of Ritual: Northern Gods in a Southern Land.* Chicago: University of Chicago Press.

Frith, Simon. 1989. *World Music, Politics, and Social Change: Papers from the International Association for the Study of Popular Music.* Manchester, UK: Manchester University Press.

———. 1993. Introduction and Music and Morality. In *Music and Copyright,* edited by Simon Frith, Edinburgh: Edinburgh University Press. ix–xiv and 1–21.

Gadamer, H.G. 1989. Reply to My Critics. In *The Hermeneutic Tradition: from Ast to Ricoeur,* edited by G. L. Ormiston and A. D. Schrift. New York: State University of New York Press, pp. 273-296.

Gandhi, Leela. 1998. *Postcolonial Theory: A Critical Introduction.* New York: Columbia University Press.

Gaonkar, Dilip Parameshwar. 2001. *Alternative Modernities.* Durham, NC: Duke University Press.

———. 2002. Towards New Imaginaries: An Introduction. *Public Culture* 14 (1): 1–19.

Geertz, Clifford. 1973a. *Deep Play: Notes on the Balinese Cockfight.* New York: Basic Books.

———. 1973b. *The Interpretation of Cultures: Selected Essays.* New York: Basic Books.

———. 1977. *Person, Time, and Conduct in Bali: An Essay in Cultural Analysis.* Ann Arbor: University Microfilms International.

———. 1980. *Negara: The Theatre State in Nineteenth Century Bali.* Princeton, NJ: Princeton University Press.

Geertz, Hildred. 1994. *Images of Power: Balinese Paintings Made for Gregory Bateson and Margaret Mead.* Honolulu: University of Hawaii Press.

Gell, Alfred. 1992. *The Anthropology of Time: Cultural Constructions of Temporal Maps and Images.* Oxford: Berg.

Geriya, I Wayan. 2000. *Transformasi Kebudayaan Bali Memasuki Abad XXI* Denpasar: Dikbud.

Gilbert, Elizabeth. 2007. *Eat, Pray, Love: One Woman's Search for Everything Across Italy, India and Indonesia.* New York: Penguin.

Gill, Stephen. 2003. *Power and Resistance in the New World Order.* New York: Palgrave.

Goehr, Lydia. 1992. *The Imaginary Museum of Musical Works: Essays in the Philosophy of Music.* Oxford: Clarendon Press.

Gold, Lisa Rachel. 1998. *The Gender Wayang Repertoire in Theater and Ritual: A Study of Balinese Musical Meaning.* PhD diss. Berkeley: University of California.

———. 2004. *Music in Bali: Experiencing Music, Expressing Culture.* New York: Oxford University Press.

Gombloh, Joko. 1999a. Saya Bukan Pemusik. *Gong* 4: 4–5.

———. 1999b. Makassar Art Forum. *Gong* 5: 10.

———. 2000a. Ben M. Pasaribu: Mission Impossible, Musik Nasional. *Gong* 10: 6–7.

———. 2000b. I Wayan Dibia: Biarkan Seni Tradisi Berkembang Sesuai Masyarakatnya. *Gong* 12: 6–7.

———. 2001a. I Wayan Sadra, Kita Tidak Memikirkan Kebudayaan Batin. *Gong* 17: 8–9.

———. 2001b. One World One "World Music." *Gong* 18: 3–6.

———. 2003. Sutanto: Seni Pedesaan Punya System Estetika Sendiri. *Gong* 46: 10.

Goodman, Nelson. 1968. *The Languages of Art: An Approach to and Theory of Symbols.* Indianapolis: Bobbs-Merrill.

Gottlieb, Robert. 1981. Symbolisms Underlying Improvisatory Practices in Indian Music. *Journal of the Indian Musicological Society* 12 (3/4): 22–36.

Graham, Colin. 1999. "'...maybe that's just Blarney': Irish Culture and the Persistance of Authenticity." In *Ireland and Cultural Theory: The Mechanics of Authenticity*, edited by Colin Graham and Kirkland. Basingstoke: Macmillan, pp. 7–28.

Gray, Nicholas. 2011. *Improvisation and Composition in Balinese Gender Wayang (SOAS Musicology Series)*. Farnham, UK: Ashgate.

Greenberg, Clement. 1939. Avant-Garde and Kitsch. *Partisan Review* 6 (5): 34–49.

Grimshaw, Jeremy. 2009. *The Island of Bali Is Littered with Prayers*. Charleston, SC: CreateSpace.

Habermas, Jürgen. 1979. Moral Development and Ego Identity. In *Communication and the Evolution of Society*, edited by Thomas McCarthy. London: Heinemann, pp. 69–94.

Halim, H. 1999. Arts Networks and the Struggle for Democratisation. In *Reformasi: Crisis and Change in Indonesia* by Arief Budiman and Barbara Hatley. Clayton, Australia: Monash Asia Institute, Monash University, pp. 287–98.

Harahap, Irwansyah. 2003. World Music. *Gong* 46: 11.

Hardjana, Suka. 2003. *Corat-Coret Musik Kontemporer: Dulu Dan Kini*. Jakarta: Masyarakat Seni Pertunjukan Indonesia.

———. 2004. Orientasi Penciptaan Dalam Musik Kontemporer. *Gong* 57 (6): 46.

Harney, Elizabeth. 2004. *In Senghor's Shadow: Art, Politics, and the Avant-Garde in Senegal, 1960–1995*. Durham, NC: Duke University Press.

Harnish, David. 2000. The World of Music Composition in Bali. *The Journal of Musicological Research* 20 (1): 1–40.

———. 2001. A Hermeneutical Arc in the Life of a Balinese Musician, I Madé Lebah. *World Of Music* 43 (1): 21–41.

———. 2005. Teletubbies in Paradise: Tourism, Indonesianisation and Modernisation in Balinese Music. *Yearbook for Traditional Music* 37: 103–23.

———. 2006. *Bridges to the Ancestors: Music, Myth, and Cultural Politics at an Indonesian Festival*. Honolulu: University of Hawaii Press.

———. 2013. Between Traditionalism and Postmodernism: the Balinese Performing Arts Institution, Çudamani In *Performing Arts in Postmodern Bali: Changing Interpretations, Founding Traditions*, edited by Kendra Stepputat. Aachen: Shaker Verlag, pp. 257–78.

Hatten, Robert S. 2004a. *Musical Meaning in Beethoven*. Bloomington: Indiana University Press.

———. 2004b. *Interpreting Musical Gesture, Topics, and Tropes: Mozart, Beethoven, Schubert*. Bloomington: Indiana University Press.

Hauser-Schäublin, Brigitta. 2004. Bali Aga and Islam: Ethnicity, Ritual Practice, and 'Old-Balinese' as an Anthropological Construct. *Indonesia* 77: 27–55.

Heidegger, Martin. 2008 [1962]. *Being and Time*. New York: Harper Perennial Modern Classics.

Heider, Karl. G. 1988. The Rashomon Effect: When Ethnographers Disagree. *American Anthropologist* 90 (1): 73–81.

Heile, Bjorn. 2004. "Transcending Quotation": Cross-Cultural Musical Representation in Mauricio Kagel's Die Stucke Der Windrose Fur Salonchester. *Music Analysis* 23 (1): 57–83.

Heimarck, Brita Renée. 2003. *Balinese Discourses on Music and Modernization: Village Voices and Urban Views*. New York: Routledge.

Heine-Geldern, Robert. 1956. *Conceptions of State and Kingship in Southeast Asia*. Data Paper 18, Department of Far Eastern Studies. Ithaca: Cornell University.

Hellman, Jorgen. 2003. *Performing the Nation: Cultural Politics in New Order Indonesia*. Denmark: NIAS Press.

Herbst, Edward. 1997. *Voices in Bali: Energies and Perceptions in Vocal Music and Dance Theater*. Middletown, CT: Wesleyan University Press.

———. 2009. *Bali 1928: Gamelan Gong Kebyar. Music from Belaluan, Pangkung, Busungbiu*. Essay accompanying *Bali 1928, Vol. 1*. Arbiter Records.

Heryanto, Ariel. 1995. What Does Post-modernism Do in Contemporary Indonesia? *Sojourn* 10 (1): 33–44.

———. 2010. The Bearable Lightness of Democracy. In *The Return to Constitutional Democracy in Indonesia*, edited by Thomas Reuter. Clayton, Australia: Monash Asia Institute, pp. 51–61.

Heryanto, Ariel, and Nancy Lutz. 1988. The Development of "Development." *Indonesia* 46: 1–24.

Hill, Christopher. 2006. *Survival and Change: Three Generations of Balinese Painters*. Canberra: Pandanus Books.

Hobart, Angela, Urs Ramseyer, and Albert Leemann. 1996. *The Peoples of Bali*. Cambridge: Blackwell.

Hobart, Mark. 1997. The Missing Subject: Balinese Time and the Elimination of History. *Review of Indonesian and Malaysian Affairs* 31: 123–72.

———. 2000. *After Culture: Anthropology as Radical Metaphysical Critique*. Yogyakarta: Duta Wacana Press.

Hobsbawm, E. J., and T. O. Ranger. 1983. *The Invention of Tradition*. Cambridge: Cambridge University Press.

Holt, Claire. 1967. *Art in Indonesia: Continuities and Change*. Ithaca: Cornell University Press.

Honing, Henkjan. 2006. Evidence for Tempo-Specific Timing in Music Using a Web-Based Experimental Setup. *Journal of Experimental Psychology* 32 (3): 780–786.

Hood, Madé Mantle. 2011. *Triguna: A Hindu-Balinese Philosophy for Gamelan Gong Gede Music*. Münster: LIT Verlag.

Hood, Mantle. 1984. *Legacy of the Roaring Sea: The Evolution of the Javanese Gamelan: Book 2*. Wilhelmshaven: Heinrichshofen.

———. 1988. *Paragon of the Roaring Sea*. Wilhelmshaven: Heinrichshofen.

Hoopen, Gert ten, et al. 2006. Time-Shrinking and Categorical Temporal Ratio Perception: Evidence for a 1:1 Temporal Category. *Music Perception* 24 (1): 1–22.

Hough, Brett. 2000. *The College of Indonesian Arts, Denpasar: Nation, State and the Performing Arts in Bali*. PhD diss. Melbourne: Monash University.

Howe, Leo. 1981. The Social Determination of Knowledge: Maurice Bloch and Balinese Time. *Man* 16 (2): 220–34.

Hughes-Freeland, F. 1997. Art and Politics: From Javanese Court Dance to Indonesian Art. *Journal of the Royal Anthropological Institute* 3: 473–95.

Humardani, S. D. 1981. *Masalah-Masalah Dasar Pengembangan Seni Tradisi*. Surakarta: Akademi Seni Karawitan. Indonesia Original edition originally presented at the Seminar Kesenian, Surakarta, October 2–4, 1972.

Huron, David. 1991. The Ramp Archetype: A Score-Based Study of Musical Dynamics in 14 Piano Composers. *Psychology of Music* 19: 33–45.

———. 2006. *Sweet Anticipation: Music and the Psychology of Expectation*. Cambridge: MIT Press.

Ida Bagus, Mary. 2006. Transcending Transgression with Transgression: Inheriting Forsaken Souls in Bali. In *Celebrating Transgression: Method and Politics in Anthropological Studies of Culture. A Book in Honour of Klaus Peter Kopping*, edited by Ursula Rao and John Hutnyk. New York: Berghahn Books, pp. 93–113.

Imberty, Michel. 2000. The Question of Innate Competencies in Musical Communication. In *The Origins of Music*, edited by Nils L. Wallin and Bjorn Merker. Boston: MIT Press, pp. 449–60.

Jameson, Fredric. 1991. *Postmodernism, or, the Cultural Logic of Late Capitalism*. Durham, NC: Duke University Press.
Jenkins, Ron. 2010. *Rua Bineda in Bali: Counterfeit Justice in the Trial of Nyoman Gunarsa*. Yogyakarta: ISI.
Jurriëns, Edwin. 2013. Between Utopia and Real World: Indonesia's Avant-Garde New Media Art. *Indonesia and the Malay World* 41 (119): 48–75.
Kafka, Franz. 1993 [1924]. *Collected Stories*. New York: Everyman's Library.
Kahin, George McT. 1995. *Subversion as Foreign Policy: The Secret Eisenhower and Dulles Debacle in Indonesia*. New York: The New Press.
Kant, Immanuel. 1928 [1790]. *Critique of Judgement*. Oxford: Oxford University Press.
Karatani, Kojin. 1998. Uses of Aesthetics: After Orientalism. *Boundary 2* 25(2): 145–60.
Kavanagh, James. 1995. Ideology. In *Critical Terms for Literary Theory, 2nd ed.*, edited by Frank Lentricchia and Thomas McLaughlin. Chicago: University of Chicago Press. 310.
Keister, Jay. 2005. Seeking Authentic Experience: Spirituality in the Western Appropriation of Asian Music. *The World of Music* 47 (3): 35–53.
Kennedy, Liam, and Scott Lucas. 2005. Enduring Freedom: Public Diplomacy and U.S. Foreign Policy. *American Quarterly* 57 (2): 309–33.
Kivy, Peter. 2002. *Introduction to a Philosophy of Music*. Oxford: Oxford University Press.
Koskoff, Ellen. 1999. What Do We Want to Teach When We Teach Music? One Apology, Two Short Trips, Three Ethical Dilemmas, and Eighty-Two Questions. In *Rethinking Music* edited by Nick Cook and Mark Everist. New York: Oxford University Press, pp. 545–60.
Kramer, Jonathan D. 1988. *The Time of Music: New Meanings, New Temporalities, New Listening Strategies*. New York: Schirmer Books.
Kunst, Jaap. 1973. *Music in Java. Its History, Its Theory and Its Technique*. The Hague: Nijhoff.
Kunst, Jaap, Ernst Heins, Elisabeth den Otter, Felix van Lamsweerde, and Maya Frijn. 1994. *Indonesian Music and Dance: Traditional Music and Its Interaction with the West: A Compilation of Articles (1934–1952)*. Originally published in Dutch. Amsterdam: Royal Tropical Institute Tropenmuseum, University of Amsterdam Ethnomusicology Centre.
Kurnianingsih, Ambarwati. 2008. *Simulakra Bali: Ambiguitas Tradisionalisasi Orang Bali*. Yogyakarta: INSISTPress.
Lansing, J. Stephen. 1983. *The Three Worlds of Bali*. New York: Praeger.
———. 2007. *Perfect Order: Recognizing Complexity in Bali*. Princeton, NJ: Princeton University Press.
Larasati, Rachmi Diyah. 2013. *The Dance That Makes You Vanish: Cultural Reconstruction in Post-Genocide Indonesia*. Minneapolis: Minnesota University Press.
Latour, Bruno. 2005. *Reassembling the Social: An Introduction to Actor-Network-Theory*. London: Oxford University Press.
Lechner, Ethan. 2005. Colin McPhee and the Absolute Music of Bali. Paper presented at CCSEAS Re-visioning Southeast Asia conference, Toronto.
Lefebvre, Henri. 1991 [1974]. *The Production of Space*. Translated by Donald Nicholson-Smith. Malden, MA: Blackwell Publishers.
Levine, Robert. 1997. *A Geography of Time*. New York: Basic Books.
Levinson, Jerrold. 1997. *Music in the Moment*. Ithaca: Cornell University Press.
Lévi-Strauss, Claude. 1967. *The Scope of Anthropology*. Translated by C. Jacobsen. New York: Anchor Doubleday.
Lewis, George E. 1996. Improvised Music after 1950: Afrological and Eurological Perspectives. *Black Music Research Journal* 16 (1): 91–122.

Lidov, David. 2005. *Is Language a Music?* Indiana: Indiana University Press.
Liem, Maya H. T. 2003. *The Turning Wheel of Time: Modernity and Writing in Bali 1900–1970*. PhD diss. Leiden: WSD.
Lindsay, Jennifer. 1985. *Klasik, Kitsch, or Contemporary: A Study of the Javanese Performing Arts*. PhD diss. Sydney: University of Sydney.
———. 2006. *Between Tongues: Translation and/of/in Performance in Asia*. Singapore: University of Singapore Press.
Lindsay, Jennifer, and Maya Liem. 2012. *Heirs to World Culture: Being Indonesian, 1950–1965*. Leiden: Koninklyk Instituut Voor Taal Land.
Lock, Graham. 1988. *Forces in Motion: Anthony Braxton and the Meta-Reality of Creative Music: Interviews and Tour Notes, England 1985*. London: Quartet.
Locke, David. 1998. *Drum Gahu: An Introduction to African Rhythm*. Tempe, AZ: White Cliffs Media.
Lomax, Alan. 1976. *Cantometrics: An Approach to the Anthropology of Music*. Berkeley: University of California Extension Media Center.
London, Justin. 2004. *Hearing in Time: Psychological Aspects of Musical Meter*. London: Oxford University Press.
Luhmann, Niklas. 2000. *Art as a Social System*. Stanford: Stanford University Press.
Luvaas, Brent. 2009. Dislocating Sounds: The Deterritorialization of Indonesian Indie Pop. *Cultural Anthropology* 24 (2): 246–79.
Maceda, José. 1986. A Concept of Time in a Music of Southeast Asia. *Ethnomusicology* 30 (1): 11–53.
Mack, Dieter. 2004. *Zeitgenössische Musik in Indonesien: Zwischen lokalen Traditionen, nationalen Verplichtungen und internationalen Einflüssen. Studien und Materialien zur Musikwissenschaft*, 32. Hildesheim: Georg Olms Verlag.
MacRae, Graeme. 2003. Art and Peace in the Safest Place in the World: the Culture of Apoliticism in Bali. In *Inequality, Crisis and Social Change in Indonesia*, edited by Thomas Reuter. New York: Routledge, pp. 31–45.
Martin, Stewart. 2007. Critique of Relational Aesthetics. *Third Text* 21 (4): 369–86.
Martinez, Jose Luiz. 2001. *Semiosis in Indian Music*. Delhi: Motilal Banarsidass.
McCluhan, Marshall, and Quentin Fiore. 1967. *The Medium is the Massage*. New York: Bantam.
McDermott, Vincent. 1986. Gamelans and New Music. *The Musical Quarterly* 72 (1): 16–27.
McGraw, Andrew. 2000. The Development of the Gamelan Semara Dana and the Expansion of the Modal System in Bali, Indonesia. *Asian Music* 31 (1): 63–94.
———. 2005. *Musik Kontemporer: New Music by Balinese Composers*. PhD diss. Middletown, CT: Wesleyan University.
———. 2008. Different Temporalities: The Time of Balinese Music. *Yearbook for Traditional Music* 41: 136–62.
———. 2009. The Political Economy of the Performing Arts in Contemporary Bali. *Indonesia and the Malay World* 37 (109): 299–325.
———. 2013a. The Ethical Aesthetics of I Wayan Sadra. In *Performing Arts in Postmodern Bali: Changing Interpretations, Founding Traditions*, edited by Kendra Stepputat. Aachen: Shaker Verlag, pp. 335–62.
———. 2013b. Balinese Experimentalism and the Intercultural Project. In *What is Experimental Music*, edited by Benjamin Piekut. Ann Arbor: University of Michigan Press.
———. 2013c. The Ambivalent Freedoms of Indonesian Jazz. *Jazz Perspectives* 6 (3): 1–38.

McQuire, Scott, and Nikos Papastergiadis. 2006. *Empires, Ruins and Networks: The Transcultural Agenda in Art.* Chicago: Oram.

McPhee, Colin. 1935. The Absolute Music of Bali. *Modern Music* 12: 163–69.

———. 1939. The Decline of the East. *Modern Music* 16: 160–67.

———. 1942. The Technique of Balinese Music. *Bulletin of the American Musicological Society* 6: 2–4.

———. 1966. *Music in Bali: A Study in Form and Instrumental Organization.* New Haven, CT: Yale University Press.

Mead, Margaret. 1928. *Coming of Age in Samoa, A Psychological Study of Primitive Youth for Western Civilization.* New York: Blue Ribbon Books.

Mead, Margaret, and Gregory Bateson. 1942. *Balinese Character: A Photographic Analysis.* New York: New York Academy of Sciences.

Meyer, Leonard B. 1991. A Pride of Prejudices; or, a Delight in Diversity. *Music Theory Spectrum* 13 (2): 241–51.

Miller, Christopher J. 2001. *As Time Is Stretched . . . : Theoretical and Compositional Investigations of Rhythm and Form in Javanese Gamelan Music.* Master's thesis. Middletown, CT: Wesleyan University.

———. 2011. *Becoming Cosmopolitan, Going Nativist: Contemporary Art Music in Indonesia.* PhD diss., draft. Middletown, CT: Wesleyan University.

Mills, Sherylle. 1996. Indigenous Music and the Law: An Analysis of National and International Legislation. *Yearbook of Traditional Music* 28: 57–86.

Mistortoify, Zoel. 2002. Arah Perkembangan Musik Tradisi. *Gong* 33: 11.

Mitoma, Judy. 2004. *Narrative/Performance: Cross-Cultural Encounters at APPEX.* Los Angeles: UCLA Center for Intercultural Performance, Asia Pacific Performance Exchange.

Mitter, Partha. 2007. *The Triumph of Modernism. India's Artists and the Avant-Garde, 1922–1947.* London: Reaktion.

Moerdowo, R. M. 1977. *Reflections on Balinese Traditional and Modern Arts.* Denpasar: Udayana University.

Moeschler, Jacques. 2004. Intercultural Pragmatics: A Cognitive Approach. *Intercultural Pragmatics* 1 (1): 49–70.

Momo, R. M. 2010. Jejak Seni Kontemporer Indonesia. *Gong* 119: 11.

Monson, Ingrid T. 1999. Riffs, Repetition, and Theories of Globalization. *Ethnomusicology* 43 (1): 31–65.

Munn, Nancy D. 1992. The Cultural Anthropology of Time: A Critical Essay. *Annual Review of Anthropology* 21: 93–123.

Myers, Helen, ed. 1992. *Ethnomusicology: An Introduction.* New York: W. W. Norton.

Nabeshima, M., and Noszlopy, L. 2006. Kadek Suardana: An Independent Artist in Urban Bali. *Seleh Notes* 13 (2): 14–16.

Nancy, Jean-Luc. 2007. *Listening.* New York: Fordham University Press.

Nandy, Ashis. 1983. *The Intimate Enemy: Loss and Recovery of Self under Colonialism.* Delhi: Oxford University Press.

Ness, Sally A. 1997. Originality in the Postcolony: Choreographing the Neoethnic Body of Philippine Ballet. *Cultural Anthropology* 12 (1): 64–108.

Neto, Luiz Costa Lima. 2000. The Experimental Music of Hermeto Paschoal e Grupo (1981–93): A Musical System in the Making. *British Journal of Ethnomusicology* 9 (1): 119–42.

Newcomb, Anthony. 1984. Once More "Between Absolute and Program Music": Schumann's Second Symphony. *Nineteenth Century Music* 7 (3): 233–50.

Nicolas, Arsenio. 2009. Gongs, Bells, and Cymbals: The Archeological Record in Maritime Asia from the Ninth to the Seventeenth Centuries. *Yearbook for Traditional Music* 41: 62–93.

Noszlopy, Laura. 2007. Freelancers: Independent Professional Performers of Bali. *Indonesia and the Malay World* 35 (101): 141–52.

Notosudirdjo, Franki Suryadarma (Franki Raden). 2001. *Music, Politics, and the Problems of National Identity in Indonesia*. PhD diss. Madison: University of Wisconsin.

Oja, Carol J. 1990. *Colin McPhee: Composer in Two Worlds*. Washington: Smithsonian Institution Press.

Ornstein, Ruby. 1971. "The Gamelan Gong Kebyar: The Development of a Balinese Musical Tradition." PhD diss. Los Angeles: University of California.

———. 2006. Wayan Gandera Redux. *Asian Music* 37 (2): 141–46.

———. 2010. *From Kuno to Kebyar: Balinese Gamelan Angklung* (liner notes). Smithsonian Folkways SFW50411. Washington, DC: Center for Folklife and Cultural Heritage, Smithsonian Institution.

Pandhuagie. 2006. UUHC: Author Right Atawa Copyright. *Gong* 80 (8): 6–13.

Pasaribu, Amir. 1986. *Analisis Musik Indonesia*. Jakarta: PT Pantja Simpati.

Pasaribu, Ben Marajohan. 1990. *Between East and West: A Collection of Compositions*. Unpublished MA Thesis. Middletown, CT: Wesleyan University.

Patel, Aniruddh D. 2008. *Music, Language and the Brain*. New York: Oxford University Press.

Pavis, Patrice. 1996. *The Intercultural Performance Reader*. London and New York: Routledge.

Pemberton, John. 1994. *On the Subject of Java*. Ithaca: Cornell University Press.

Perlman, Marc. 1994. American Gamelan in the Garden of Eden: Intonation in a Cross-Cultural Encounter. *The Musical Quarterly* 78 (3): 510–56.

———. 2004. *Unplayed Melodies*. Berkeley: University of California Press.

Picard, Michel. 1996. *Bali: Cultural Tourism and Touristic Culture*. Translated by D. Darling. Singapore: Archipelago Press.

———. 1999. The Discourse of Kebalian. In *Staying Local in the Global Village: Bali in the Twentieth Century*, edited by Raechelle Rubinstein and Linda H. Connor. Honolulu: University of Hawaii Press, pp. 15–50.

———. 2003. Touristification and Balinisation in a Time of Reformasi. *Indonesia and the Malay World* 31 (89): 108–18.

Pickvance, Richard. 2005. *A Gamelan Manual: A Player's Guide to the Central Javanese Gamelan*. London: Jaman Mas.

PKB. 1989. *Evaluasi Pesta Kesenian Bali*. Denpasar: STSI.

Pollack, Sheldon. 2000. Cosmopolitan and Vernacular in History. *Public Culture* 12 (3): 591–625.

Pollmann, Tessel. 1992. Margaret Mead's Balinese: The Fitting Symbols of the American Dream. *Indonesia* 49: 1–35.

Powers, Harold S., et al. Mode. *Grove Music Online*. *Oxford Music Online*. Accessed Aug. 22, 2009.

Pradier, Jean-Marie. 1989. Towards a Biological Theory of the Body in Performance. *New Theatre Quarterly* 6: 86–98.

Price, Sally and Richard Price. 1980. *Afro-American Arts of the Suriname Rain Forest*. Berkeley: University of California Press.

Putra, I Nyoman Darma. 2003. Reflections on Literature and Politics in Bali: The Development of Lekra 1950–1966. In *Inequality, Crisis and Social Change in Indonesia*, edited by Thomas Reuter. New York: RoutledgeCurzon, pp. 55–86.

———. 2008. *Bali Dalam Kuasa Politik*. Denpasar: Arti.

Quigley, Sam. 1996. The Raffles Gamelan at Claydon House. *Journal of the American Musical Instrument Society* 22: 5–41.

Raffles, Thomas Stamford. 1817. *The History of Java, Volume 1*. London: John Murray.

Rai, I. Wayan. 1996. *Balinese Gamelan Semar Pagulingan Saih Pitu: The Modal System*. PhD diss. Baltimore: University of Maryland.

Ramseyer, Urs. 2002 [1977]. *The Art and Culture of Bali*. Basel: Museum der Kulturen.

Ramstedt, Martin. 1991. Revitalization of Balinese Classical Dance and Music. In *Music in the Dialogue of Cultures: Traditional Music and Cultural Policy*, edited by Max Peter Baumann. Wilhelmshaven: Florian Noetzel Verlag, pp. 108–20.

———. 2012. The Entanglements of National and Transnational Buddhist Networks in Bali. Paper presented at the Bali and Global Asia Conference, Denpasar.

Ranciere, Jacques. 2009. *Aesthetics and Its Discontents*. Translated by Steven Corcoran. Malden, MA: Polity.

Ratner, Leonard. 1980. *Classic Music: Expression, Form, and Style*. New York: Schirmer.

Ray, Gene. 2007. Avant-Gardes as Anti-Capitalist Vector. *Third Text* 21 (3): 241–55.

Reilly, Ronan G., ed. 1987. *Communication Failure in Dialogue and Discourse: Detection and Repair Processes*. Dublin: Educational Research Centre, St. Patrick's College.

Rembang, Nyoman. 1984/1985. *Hasil Pendokumentasian Notasi Gending-Gending Lelambatan Klasik Pegongan Daerah Bali*. Denpasar: ASTI.

———. 1986. *Laya*. Denpasar: ASTI.

———, et al. 1960. *Titilaras Dingdong*. Denpasar: KOKAR.

Repp, B. H. 1998. A Microcosm of Musical Expression: Quantitative Analysis of Pianists' Timing in the Initial Measures of Chopin's Étude in E major. *Journal of the Acoustical Society of America* 104: 1085–1100.

Reuter, Thomas, ed. 2003. *Inequality, Crisis and Social Change in Indonesia: The Muted Worlds of Bali*. New York: RoutledgeCurzon.

———. 2006. Running Out of Tricks: The Experience of Ethnography and the Politics of Culturalism. In *Celebrating Transgression: Method and Politics in Anthropological Studies of Culture. A Book in Honour of Klaus Peter Kopping*, edited by Ursula Rao and John Hutnyk. New York: Berghahn Books, pp. 71–90.

———. 2009. Globalisation and Local Identities: The Rise of New Ethnic and Religious Movements in Post-Suharto Indonesia. *Asian Journal of Social Science* 37 (9): 857–71.

Richter, Karl. 1992. Remarks on the Gambuh Tone System. In *Balinese Music in Context: A Sixty-Fifth Birthday Tribute to Hans Oesch*, edited by D. Schaareman. Winterthur: Amadeus-Verlag, pp. 195–220.

Robinson, Geoffrey. 1998. *The Dark Side of Paradise: Political Violence in Bali*. Ithaca: Cornell University Press.

Rodgers, Tara. 2011. *Synthesizing Sound: Metaphor in Audio-Technical Discourse and Synthesis History*. PhD diss. Montreal: McGill University.

Roeder, John, and Michael Tenzer. 2012. Identity and Genre in Gamelan Gong Kebyar: An Analytical Study of *Gabor*. *Music Theory Spectrum* 34 (1): 78–122.

Rohner, Ronald P., Billie R. Dewalt, and Robert C. Ness. 1973. Ethnographic Bias in Cross-Cultural Research: An Empirical Study. *Behavior Science Notes* 8 (4): 275–317.

Roosa, John. 2006. *Pretext for Mass Murder: The September 30th Movement and Suharto's Coup d'etat in Indonesia*. Madison: University of Wisconsin Press.

Rorty, Richard. 1989. *Contingency, Irony, Solidarity*. New York: Cambridge University Press.

———. 1998. Justice as a Larger Loyalty. In *Cosmopolitics: Thinking and Feeling Beyond the Nation*, edited by Pheng Cheah and Bruce Robbins. Minneapolis: University of Minnesota Press, pp. 45–58.

Roth, Alec R. 1986. *New Composition for Javanese Gamelan*. PhD diss. Durham, UK: University of Durham.

Ruma, Wayan, and Wayan Djirne. 1939. *Taman Sari: Kumpulan Gending-Gending Bali I & II*. Denpasar: Cempaka No. 1.

Rustopo. 1990. *Gendhon Humardani (1923–1983) Arsitek Dan Pelaksana Pembangunan Kehidupan Seni Tradisi Jawa Modern Mengindonesia: Suatu Biografi*. Tesis Sarjana S2 (MA thesis). Yogyakarta: Universitas Gajah Mada.

———. 1991. *Gamelan Kontemporer di Surakarta. Pembentukan Dan Perkembangannya (1970–1990)*. Surakarta: STSI.

Ryle, Gilbert. 1945. Knowing How and Knowing That. *Proceedings of the Aristotelian Society* 46: 1–16.

Sadra, I Wayan. 1986. *Tinjauan Karya-karya Baru*. Surakarta: ASKI.

———. 1991. *I Wayan Berata* [sic]: *Proses Perjalanannya Menjadi Empu Karawitan, Laporan Penelitian*. Surakarta: STSI.

———. 1999. Gong Dalam Kultur Lamunan. *Gong* 1 (1): 12–13.

———. 2002. Musik Dialektis: Sebuah Pilihan Musik Kontemporer Indonesia. *Gong* 41: 34–35.

———. 2007. International Gamelan Festival Amsterdam 2007. Menegakkan Identitas Global Gamelan. *Gong* 92 (7): 52–53.

Said, Edward. 1993. *Culture and Imperialism*. New York: Knopf.

Sakai, Naoki. 2010. Theory and Asian Humanity, On the Question of Humanitas and Anthropos. *Postcolonial Studies: Culture, Politics, Economy* 13 (4): 441–64.

Sandino, Joseph. 2008. *Recent Structural Developments in Tabuh Kreasi Gong Kebyar*. Unpublished MA Thesis. Vancouver: University of British Columbia.

Santikarma, Degung. 2010. Gong-gong Theater State. *Gong* 119: 11.

Satz, Debra. 2012. *Why Some Things Should Not be for Sale: The Moral Limits of Markets*. New York: Oxford University Press.

Saussure, Ferdinand de. 2011 [1916]. *Course in General Linguistics*, edited by Perry Meisel and Haun Saussy. Translated by Wade Baskin. New York: Columbia University Press.

Sayuti, Suminto. 2002. Seni, Pendidikan, dan Perspektif Global. *Gong* 42: 17–19.

Schefold, Reimar. 1998. The Domestication of Culture: Nation-Building and Ethnic Diversity in Indonesia. *Bijdragen tot de Taal-, Land- en Volkenkunde* 154 (2): 259–80.

Schulte Nordholt, Henk. 1992. Origin, Descent, and Destruction: Text and Context in Balinese Representations of the Past. *Indonesia* 54: 27–58.

———. 1994. The Making of Traditional Bali: Colonial Ethnography and Bureaucratic Reproduction. *History and Anthropology* 8: 89–127.

———. 2000. Localizing Modernity in Colonial Bali During the 1930s. *Journal of Southeast Asian Studies* 31 (1): 101–14.

———. 2002. A Genealogy of Violence. In *Roots of Violence in Indonesia*, edited by F. Colombijn and Th. Lindblad. Leiden: KITLV Press, pp 33–61.

Schulte Nordholt, Henk, and Willem van Schendel, eds. 2001. *Time Matters: Global and Local Time in Asian Societies*. Amsterdam: VU University Press.

Seebass, Tilman. 1996. Change in Balinese Musical Life: "Kebiar" in the 1920s and 1930s. In *Being Modern in Bali: Image and Change*, edited by Adrian Vickers. New Haven: Yale, Southeast Asia Studies, Monograph 43, pp. 71–91.

Seeger, Anthony. 1987. *Why Suya Sing: A Musical Anthropology of an Amazonian People*. New York: Cambridge University Press.

Seramasara, I. G. N. 1997. *Sekularisasi Seni Pertunjukan di Bali Pada Tahun 1920–1974*. Yogyakarta: Gadjah Mada University.

Shadeg, N. 2007. *Balinese-English Dictionary*. Singapore: Tuttle.

Shapiro, Michael. 1991 [1983]. *The Sense of Change: Language as History*. Indianapolis: Indiana University Press.

Siagian, Esther L. 2005. *Gong: Buku Pelejaran Kesenian Nusantara*. Jakarta: LSPN.

Slobin, Mark. 1992. Micromusics of the West: A Comparative Approach. *Ethnomusicology* 36: 1–87.

Small, Christopher. 1998. *Musicking: The Meanings of Performing and Listening*. Hanover: University Press of New England.

Snow, Stephen. 1986. Intercultural Performance: The Balinese-American Model. *Asian Theater Journal* 3 (2): 204–32.

Soethama, Gde Aryantha. 2006. *Bolak Balik Bali*. Denpasar: Arti.

Sperber, Dan. 1982. Apparently Irrational Beliefs. In *Rationality and Relativism*, edited by Martin Hollis and Steven Lukes. Oxford: Basil Blackwell.

———. 1996. *Explaining Culture: A Naturalistic Approach*. Cambridge: Blackwell.

Spiller, Henry. 2008. *Gamelan Music of Indonesia*. New York: Routledge.

Spitzer, Michael. 2004. *Metaphor and Musical Thought*. Chicago: University of Chicago.

Spivak, Gayatri. 2010. Can the Subaltern Speak? In *Reflections on the History of an Idea: Can the Subaltern Speak*, edited by Rosalind C. Morris. New York: Columbia University Press.

Steele, Peter. 2012. Memorializing Colonialism: Images of the Japanese Occupation of Indonesia in Japanese Popular Theatre. *Asian Theatre Journal* 29 (2): 528–549.

———. 2013. *Balinese Hybridities: Balinese Music as Global Phenomena* PhD diss. Middletown, CT: Wesleyan University.

Stein, Gertrude. 1998. "Portraits and Repetitions." In *Gertrude Stein: Writings 1932–1946*, edited by Catharine R. Stimpson and Harriet Chessman. New York: Library of America.

Stephen, Michele. 2005. *Desire, Divine and Demonic: Balinese Mysticism in the Paintings of I Ketut Budiana and I Gusti Nyoman Mirdiana*. Honolulu: University of Hawaii Press.

Stepputat, Kendra, ed. 2013. *Performing Arts in Postmodern Bali: Changing Interpretations, Founding Traditions*. Aachen: Shaker Verlag.

Suharyanto. 2004. Melintas dari Ke'sufi'an Bunyi ke Ke'duniawi'an. *Gong* 56 (6): 32–33.

Sukerta, Pande Madé, and Sugeng Nugroho. 2009. *Gong Kebyar Buleleng*. Surakarta: Program Pascasarjana ISI Surakarta.

Sulistyawati, Made. 2008. *Integrasi Budaya Tionghoa Ke Dalam Budaya Bali: Sebuah Bunga Rampai*. Denpasar: Universitas Udayana.

Sumarsam. 1995. *Gamelan: Cultural Interaction and Musical Development in Central Java*. Chicago: University of Chicago Press.

Supanggah, Rahayu. 2003a. Campur Sari, A Reflection. *Asian Music* 34 (2): 1–20.

———. 2003b. La Galigo: Sawerigading ke Barat: Kebangkitan Atau Kecolongan? *Gong* 43: 12–13.

Supriyanto, Eko. 2010. "Odalan Bali" di Los Angeles. *Gong* 119: 10.

Suryani, Luh Ketut, and Gordon Jensen. 1992. *The Balinese People: A Reinvestigation of Character*. New York: Oxford University Press.

Sutanto, Mendut. 2002. *Kosmologi Gendhing Gendhing*. Magelang: IndonesiaTera.

Sutton, R. Anderson. 1991. *Traditions of Gamelan Music in Java: Musical Pluralism and Regional Identity*. Cambridge: Cambridge University Press.
———. 1996. Interpreting Electronic Sound Technology in the Contemporary Javanese Soundscape. *Ethnomusicology* 40 (2): 249–68.
———. 2004. Reform Arts? Performance Live and Mediated in Post-Soeharto Indonesia. *Ethnomusicology* 48 (2): 203–28.
———. 2006. Tradition Serving Modernity? The Musical Lives of a Makassarese Drummer. *Asian Music* 37 (1): 1–23.
Syafruddin. 1998. *Passompe*. Thesis. Denpasar: STSI.
Tarasti, Eero. 1994. *A Theory of Musical Semiotics*. Indiana: Indiana University Press.
Tarling, Nicholas, ed. 1999. *The Cambridge History of Southeast Asia 1, part 1: From Early Times to c. 1500*. London: Cambridge University Press.
Taryudin, Asep. 1996. *Musik Iringan Tari Kontemporer "Sawan Kuya."* Thesis. Denpasar: STSI.
Taylor, Jean Gelman. 2009. *The Social World of Batavia: Europeans and Eurasians in Colonial Indonesia*. 2nd edn. Madison: University of Wisconsin Press.
Taylor, Timothy. 1995. When We Think about Music and Politics: The Case of Kevin Volans. *Perspectives of New Music* 33: 504–36.
Tenzer, Michael. 2000. *Gamelan Gong Kebyar: The Art of Twentieth-Century Balinese Music*. Chicago: University of Chicago Press.
———. 2003. José Maceda and the Paradoxes of Modern Composition in Southeast Asia. *Ethnomusicology* 47 (1): 93–120.
———. 2005. Review Essay: Wayan Gandera and the Hidden History of Gamelan Gong Kebyar. *Asian Music* 36 (1): 109–22.
———. 2006. *Analytical Studies in World Music*. New York: Oxford University Press.
———. 2011. *Balinese Music*. Berkeley: Tuttle.
Till, James Robert. 1976. *B.V. Asaf'ev's Musical Form as a Process. Translation and Commentary*. PhD diss. Athens, OH: Ohio State University.
Tim Redaksi Gong. 2010. Hak Kekayaan Budaya dan Sendyakala Kesenian Tradisi. *Gong* 119: 11.
Titib, Dr. I Madé. 2005. *Dialog Ajeg Bali*. Surabaya: Paramita.
Todd, N. 1992. The Dynamics of Dynamics: A Model of Musical Expression. *Journal of the Acoustical Society of America* 31: 3540–50.
Turino, Thomas. 2008. *Music as Social Life: The Politics of Participation*. Chicago: University of Chicago Press.
Ujan, Andrew Ata, ed. 2009. *Multikulturalisme: Belejar Hidup Bersama Dalam Perbedaan*. Jakarta: PT Indeks.
UNESCO. 2003. *Convention for Safeguarding of Intangible Cultural Heritage*. http://portal.unesco.org.
Vickers, Adrian. 1985. The Realm of the Senses: Images of the Courtly Music of Pre-colonial Bali. *Imago Musicæ: International Yearbook of Musical Iconography* 2: 143–77.
———. 1989. *Bali, a Paradise Created*. Ringwood, Vic.: Penguin.
———. 1993. From Bali to Lampung on the Pasisir. *Archipel* 45 (1): 55–76.
———. 1994. *Traveling to Bali: Four Hundred Years of Journeys*. Kuala Lumpur: Oxford University Press.
———. 2005. *Journeys of Desire: A Study of the Balinese Text Malat*. Leiden: KITLV.
Vickers, Adrian, and Linda Connor. 2003. Crisis, Citizenship, and Cosmopolitanism: Living in a Local and Global Risk Society in Bali. *Indonesia* 75: 153–80.

Vitale, Wayne. 1990. Kotekan: The Technique of Interlocking Parts in Balinese Music. *Balungan* 4 (2): 2–15.

Von Eschen, Penny M. 2004. *Satchmo Blows Up the World: Jazz Ambassadors Play the Cold War.* Cambridge: Harvard University Press.

Wakeling, Katharine. 2010. *Representing Balinese Music: Practice and Theorization of Balinese Gamelan.* PhD diss. SOAS.

Wallach, Jeremy. 2008. *Modern Noise, Fluid Genre: Popular Music in Indonesia.* Madison: University of Wisconsin Press.

Wallis, Richard. 1980. *The Voice as a Mode of Cultural Expression in Bali.* PhD diss. Ann Arbor: University of Michigan.

Warren, Carol. 1998. Mediating Modernity in Bali. *International Journal of Cultural Studies* 1 (1): 83–108.

Weintraub, Andrew N. 1993. Creative Musical Practices in the Performance of Pantun Sunda. *Balungan* 5 (2): 2–7.

———. 1997. *Constructing the Popular: Superstars, Performance, and Cultural Authority in Sundanese Wayang Golek Purwa of West Java Indonesia.* PhD diss. Berkeley: University of California.

———. 2004. *Power Plays: Wayang Golek Puppet Theater of West Java.* Athens, OH: Ohio University Press.

———. 2010. *Dangdut Stories: A Social and Musical History of Indonesia's Most Popular Music.* New York: Oxford University Press.

Weiss, Sarah. 2013. Perspectives on Balinese Authenticities: Sanggar Çudamani's *Odalan Bali* In *Performing Arts in Postmodern Bali: Changing Interpretations, Founding Traditions*, edited by Kendra Stepputat. Aachen: Shaker Verlag, pp. 279–308.

Widdess, Richard. 1993. Slendro and Pelog in India? In *Performance in Java and Bali*, edited by Ben Arps. London: SOAS.

Widnyana, Ida Bagus Made. 2004. "Trimbat" Skrip Karya Karawitan. Thesis. Denpasar: ISI.

Wright, Astri 1994 *Soul, Spirit, and Mountain; Preoccupations of Contemporary Indonesian Painters.* Kuala Lumpur: Oxford University Press.

Yamashita, Shinji. 2003. *Bali and Beyond: Explorations in the Anthropology of Tourism.* Translated by J. S. Eades. New York: Berghahn.

Zemp, Hugo. 1996. The/An Ethnomusicologist and the Record Business. *Yearbook for Traditional Music* 28: 36–66.

Zoetmulder, P. J., with S. O. Robson. 1982. *Old Javanese-English Dictionary.* (2 vols.) Gravenhage: Nijhoff.

Zurbuchen, Mary. 1990. Images of Culture and National Development in Indonesia: The Cockroach Opera. *Asian Theatre Journal* 7 (2): 127–49.

Index

abstract expressionism, 31–34, 120, 224
ACC (Asian Cultural Council), 222, 224–25
ACL (Asian Composers League), 15, 29
adat, 39, 50, 68, 74, 241
Adorno, Theodore, 38, 68, 90, 186
aesthetics, xxvii, xxix, 2, 7, 15, 26–29, 33–34, 42, 48, 51, 77, 79, 81, 91, 109–10, 113–4, 118, 120–1, 134, 147–9, 187, 216, 218, 221, 230, 237, 241 (*see also* estetika)
African music, 11n8, 101, 126, 155–56, 193
Aga, 61, 74, 101–2, 161–62, 198, 200, 241
agama. See religion
Ajeg Bali, xxix, 59–60, 83, 93–6, 98–99, 102, 226, 239, 241 (*see also* fundamentalism)
Alisjahbana, 53, 223
Alit, I Dewa Ketut, xi–xiv, 24, 66, 86n4, 87, 90, 127, 129–30, 136, 140, 143, 148, 159, 165, 174, 191, 204, 211, 215–16, 227–28, 241
amplification, xxv, 30, 136
APPEX (Asian Pacific Performing Arts Exchange), 224
appropriation, 217, 230, 232–33
arak, xxviii, xxx, 66, 68
archive, 9, 72
Arnawa, I Madé, 87, 114–15

Arsana, I Wayan Gede, xi–xiii, xv, 3, 8n4, 58, 82, 92n13, 96n17, 114, 121, 152, 162–63
Arsawijaya, Sang Nyoman, xi–xv, xxv–xxviii, xxxi, 96, 102, 114, 121, 124–26, 129, 134, 137, 138, 140–41, 143, 145, 1569, 184, 211–13
art (*see also* aesthetics)
   and politics in Bali, 103–107
   as a Balinese institution, 15, 17, 18, 27, 30, 38–42, 49, 58, 68, 76–77, 87, 127
   cash economy of, xi, xii, 39, 89–91
   performance art, xxvii
   pure art (*seni murni*), xxvii, 39, 86
Artaud, Antonin, 41, 221, 218
Arti Foundation, 107, 149
Aryani, Ni Kadek Dewi, xiii, 71n22, 89, 228, 231
ASCAP, 131, 133
ASEA (American Society for Eastern Arts), 221
Asnawa, I Ketut Gede, xi, xiii, xxvii, xxviii, 8n4, 38, 47, 112n3, 120, 134, 137n39, 143, 191, 204
assemblage, 7, 83, 92, 154
Astita, I Komang, xii, xv, xxvii, xxviii, 65, 119n17, 130n30, 143, 152–53

263

Index

audiences, xiii, xxvi, 1–3, 8, 12, 17, 22n17, 25, 35, 39, 42–3, 47, 57, 63, 72, 83, 87, 90–94, 99–100, 110–11, 120–21, 123, 125, 127–28, 130, 133–5, 155, 158, 165, 169n4, 177, 183, 203, 205, 210, 214, 218–19, 222–23, 225–30, 233, 236
authenticity, 12, 14, 17, 20, 27, 45, 51, 64, 67, 76, 118, 121, 132–33, 218, 229
authorship, xii, xxx, 2, 109, 123, 127, 129–31, 133, 229, 234
avant-garde
  Western, 11–13, 15, 26, 127, 163n21, 232 (see also modernism)
  historical development of, 15, 32, 38, 221, 230
  concept of in Indonesia, xxvii, 12, 14, 22, 34, 39, 40–46, 71, 76, 79, 120

Balawan, I Wayan, 83, 89, 100, 102, 148–49
Bali Arts Festival (*Pesta Kesenian Bali*, PKB), 43, 63, 73, 89, 97, 125, 134–36, 141, 150, 154, 163, 165, 210, 222, 225–26, 232, 243
Balinization (colonial policy), 24n21, 26, 50, 59
Bandem, I Madé, xii, 20n11, 76–77, 80, 104n28, 105, 113, 116–17, 124, 243
Bateson, Gregory, xxii, 11, 16–18, 38n49, 76n28, 123, 127, 189
Baudrillard, Jean, 67–68, 213
bayu, 165, 168, 241
Belo, Jane, xxi–xxiii, 16, 21–22, 24, 38n49, 123, 228
Beratha (Berata), I Dewa, 227, 241
Beratha, I Wayan, 77, 107n33, 112–13, 116, 130n29, 133n34, 136n36, 137n39, 140, 147, 163, 204, 219–220, 242
BMI, 131
bombing, xxix, xxxin5, 84–85, 95, 96, 98–99, 102, 226, 241 (see also terrorism)
Bonnet, Rudolph, 25–26, 45
budaya. See culture
Buddhism, 19, 21, 93, 100, 117
bulan pejeng, 20–21, 117n12
Bungkling, 126
bupati, 77, 85

Cage, John, xxvii, 43, 206
canon (*kanon*), xiii, 141, 156, 159, 164, 212–13
cassette industry, 136–37

Catra, I Nyoman, 139
ceraken
  composition, xiii, 7
  sanggar, 5, 107n34, 108, 133, 193
  theorization of, xi, 6–7, 60, 93, 97, 238
Chinese
  cultural material, 21, 22, 23n19, 25, 82, 83, 108, 161–62
  population in Bali, 96, 98, 101, 103n27, 108
  investment by, 52, 64
  violence against, 82, 100, 162
CIA, 32
class, xxviii, xxix, 28, 39, 48, 50, 55, 57, 68, 70, 73–75, 77–79, 82, 85–86, 100, 101–02, 105, 107, 109, 124, 127, 135, 213, 222
Coast, John, 56, 104n28, 211, 219–20, 228
cockfight, 236 (see also *tajen*)
Cold War, 1, 15, 30–38, 58, 217, 220–22, 224, 226
colonialism, 12, 15, 41, 44–45, 55, 72, 73, 88, 223, 232
  cultural policy, 7, 9, 16–18, 23–27, 34, 37n47, 38, 49–53, 56, 59, 74–75, 101, 111, 148n9, 185 (see also Balinization)
  education under, 50, 57 (see also literacy)
  musical influences from, 25–26, 28
commercialism, 89–91, 103 (see also popular music)
communism, 32, 37, 55 (see also LEKRA, PKI, violence)
  emergence of in Bali, 57
  fears of, 84–85
community (of composers), xxii, xxvii, xxix, 43, 51, 66, 90n7, 123, 127–28, 145, 230
computer (as composition tool), xiii, 89, 138, 151 (see also sequencing, Fruity Loops)
conservatory, Indonesian
  critiques of, xxvi, xxvii, 84, 86, 107–08, 113–15, 121–22, 147
  curriculum at, xii, 4, 7, 9–10, 30, 38, 57–58, 70–79, 83, 87, 89, 91, 93, 98, 102, 110–13, 115–18, 119–21, 140, 162, 204–05, 226, 238–39
  elections at, 105–07
  history of, 1, 36, 48, 54, 56, 60, 124
  fostering *musik kontemporer*, xi, 14, 47, 62, 65, 70, 79–81, 93–94, 152
  AMI Yogyakarta, 47
  KOKAR Bali, 56, 59, 76–77, 87, 140

STSI/ISI Bali, 19n10, 59, 76–82, 87, 97, 99, 116, 147, 204, 225, 231, 236, 242
STSI Solo, xxix, 35, 76, 79n33, 80, 112, 114–15, 118, 232
contests, xxvii, 74, 78, 89, 92–93, 95, 97, 113, 115, 174, 202, 227 (*see also* Bali Arts Festival)
continuities in change, 9, 76, 239
copyright, xiii, 110, 129–33, 137, 232n23, 234
corruption, 11, 55, 85, 86, 100, 106–07, 115, 232
cosmopolitanism
  historical, 22, 32, 51
  in *polemik kebudayaan*, 48, 53–56, 223
  among contemporary composers, 3, 10, 47, 52, 66, 74, 82, 86, 90, 95n16, 103–04, 125, 136, 151, 159, 213, 226, 238
coup (failed of 1965), 32, 35n42, 36, 38, 58 (*see also* New Order, violence)
Cowell, Henry, 28
Crapanzano, Vincent, 237–38
Cudamani, 43, 66, 107, 130, 210, 227–30, 236n1, 237, 241 (*see also* Odalan Bali)
cultural diplomacy, 30–38, 217, 221–22, 224–25, 234
cultural relativism, 4, 18n8, 35, 218, 231, 235
culture (*budaya*), 3, 69, 73, 76, 88, 194, 206, 211, 225, 238
cyclicity, as musical concept, 188–92

Dadaism, 42
dalang (puppeteers), xxvii, 59, 63, 106, 241
dance (*tari*), xxiv, xxix, 4, 14, 17, 19, 25, 30, 34, 38, 57–58, 63 65n14, 67, 71n22, 104 122, 126, 183, 199, 220, 228
dangdut, 78, 92n11 (*see also* popular music)
Darta, I Gusti Komin, xi, xiii, xv, 124, 142, 228–29 237
democracy, xxvii, 55, 85, 87, 104, 203, 236
desa, kala, patra, 48, 119
development (*pembangunan*)
  history of in Indonesia, 15, 48–49, 53–54, 60–62, 64, 83–84, 86, 131–32
  discourses in the conservatory, 73–80, 111–13, 117, 147, 217, 226
Dewantara, Ki Hadjar, 27, 50, 53–55, 106, 111–12
Dibia, I Wayan, 71, 76, 87, 88n28, 105, 107n33, 115, 126, 130, 134, 137n39, 163

Djatajoe, 53, 99
Djelantik, A. A. M., 77–78, 120
Djirne, I Wayan, 139
Dungga, J. A., 29, 53–54, 87n5, 91n9
Dutch colonial government, 7, 17, 23–25, 28, 35, 37, 48–52, 55–56, 64, 68, 88, 101, 110–11, 117, 206, 219–220 (*see also* colonialism)
dynamics, 122, 129, 166–168, 176–185, 243

Eat, Pray, Love (novel), 17, 67
Eka Dasa Rudra ceremony, xii, 16, 65
estetika, 110, 241 (*see also* aesthetics)
  resistance against, 121–22
  theorization of, 118–21
ethnicity, 32, 48, 60, 66, 79, 86, 98, 162, 228
  theorization of, 100–04 (*see also* etnik)
ethnography, xxi–xxiv, xxvii, xxx, 3–4, 8, 11, 15–17, 19, 36, 38, 41, 44, 50, 64, 72, 76, 80, 98, 110, 118, 123, 127, 165–66, 170n6, 186, 190–91, 194, 197, 211, 225n16, 229, 235–38
etnik (*see also* ethnicity)
  as Balinese discourse, 84, 103, 198
  as musical topic, 101, 139, 161–63
exploitation, 58, 67, 217, 232–33, 236–37

Facebook, 10, 41, 121
Feld, Steven, 186, 197
Ferianto, Djaduk, 90, 103–04
Ford Foundation, 15, 19, 32–33, 36–38, 45, 58, 70n19, 98, 103n26, 118, 133, 220, 222, 224–25, 227, 233
freedom
  as discourse in cultural diplomacy, 32, 224–25, 234
  in intercultural performance, 217, 234–35
  in *musik kontemporer*, 85–87, 105, 113, 156, 213, 239
Fruity Loops, 138, 140–41, 174–75 (*see also* sequencing)
fundamentalism, xxix, 59, 94, 226 (*see also* Ajeg Bali)

gamelan
  angklung, 71, 92, 132n33, 199n7, 207
  arja, 58, 93n14, 136
  gambang, 65, 95, 113, 119, 133, 154, 188
  gambuh, 37–38, 56, 58, 96, 112n5, 113, 116, 119, 122n20, 146, 152, 199–200, 204–05, 242

gamelan (Cont.)
  gender wayang, 7, 39, 79, 112, 142–43, 154, 155n16, 156n17, 188, 201–02, 242
  gong beri, 161
  gong gede, 56, 110, 139n1, 147, 148n7, 158–59, 163, 177, 212, 242, 243
  gong kebyar, xxvii, 7, 9, 25, 42–43, 47, 56, 71, 74, 88–89, 91–93, 97, 103, 114, 121, 125, 130, 133–37, 142, 145, 148, 149n12, 152–56, 158–59, 165, 167, 169, 171–72, 174–77, 180, 183–85, 188, 198–204, 209, 226, 228, 241, 242
    critique of, 52, 163
    historical development of, 50n3, 52, 58–59, 113, 116–17, 147, 164, 219, 220
  jegog, 112, 161
  luang, 82–83, 95, 113, 148, 154, 187, 188, 242
  semar pegulingan, 113, 119, 147, 149, 152, 164, 169, 171, 177–78, 180, 198, 204, 242
  semara dana, xxii, 112n3, 113, 116, 147, 149–50, 204, 207, 210, 242
  slonding, xii, xiii, 7, 65, 95, 102, 113, 119, 148, 149, 161, 164, 187, 198, 200–01, 242
Gamelan Dharma Swara, 6
Gamelan Manikasanti, 122n21, 147–50
Gamelan Sekar Jaya, 222–23
Gamelan Sekar Jepun, 222
gaya, 135
Geertz, Clifford, xxii, 18n7, 24, 103, 123, 188n15, 237
geguritan, 51, 53
Gema Eka Dasa Rudra, 152–53
gender, xii, 71
genre, 11, 83, 152, 183, 198
  theorization of, 91–93
GEOKS, 87, 107n34, 115, 126, 134
gesture, 168
globalization (*globalisasi*), 12, 21, 37, 55, 62, 73, 96, 124, 132, 151, 164, 220–21, 223, 226, 234
GOLKAR (political party), 59, 95
gong
  breaking of form (*merusak gong*), xiii, 202–03
  as cultural symbol, xxvii, 22, 104–05
  magazine, 70, 101, 222, 242
Graham, Martha, xxix, 32, 35, 218n3
Granoka, Ida Bagus, 94n15, 147–48
griya, 72, 111
Griya (Geria), Gusti Putu Madé, 112, 117, 139

Hardjana, Suka, xii, 29, 47, 56, 77, 80, 91
Harrison, Lou, 221
heavy metal, 103, 200
Hendrawan, Ari, xiii, 63, 130, 138, 151, 208–09
heritage (theorization of), 40, 67–69, 74, 131–33, 221
history (Balinese conceptions of), 117 (*see also* Prakempa)
Hobart, Mark, 2, 16n3, 18–22, 76n28, 237
homogenization
  cultural, under colonialism, 50, 74
  conservatory's role in, xii, 7, 78
  of temporality, 187–88
  of tunings, 86, 150–51
homology (in ethnomusicology), 185–92
homonyms (musical), 207–08
Hood, Mantle, 20n11, 118n15, 146, 216, 220
Humardani, Gendhon, xxix, 34–36, 43, 55, 62, 71n23, 79, 88, 98
Huron, David, 177, 180, 197n5, 208n15

I La Galigo, 232
ideology (of tradition), 48, 69–73, 105
IMF, 132
improvisation, 12, 30, 80, 122, 156, 210, 213, 225–26
independence (Indonesian national), 28–29, 32–33, 50–51, 55–57, 64, 91n9, 106, 112, 147, 200
Indian music, xiii, 7, 10, 25, 126, 146, 155, 159, 161, 189
influence (theorization of), 14–16, 43–46, 111
intellectual property, 110, 131–32 (*see also* copyright)
intercultural performance
  history of, 218–25, 227–30
  theorization of, 231–35
interpretant, 194–213
intonation
  experiments in Bali, 147–50 (*see also* homogenization)
  history of in Bali, 116–18, 145–46
  mode in Bali, 112–13, 118, 146, 204, 207, 243
IRCAM, 91
ISI. *See* conservatory

Jagaraga, 23, 78n31, 129, 130n29, 167
Jakarta Arts Summit, 97
janger, 58, 219

Javanese, violence against, 99
jazz, 11, 29, 32, 83, 89, 91, 101, 156, 220

kakawin, 51
Kaler, I Nyoman, 112, 139
kali yuga, 85–86
Kalingu Kaja, xxii, xxvii–xxviii
kecak, 25, 26n24, 58, 219, 227–28
Kelola Foundation, 4, 133, 225
Kidung Mpu Tantular, xiii, 93–96, 103, 161–62
kitsch, 14, 35, 40–41, 63, 66, 90–91
KOKAR. *See* conservatory
Konolan, I Wayan, 39
Kosong, xiii, 47–48, 81, 84, 153, 173, 236n1
Kramer, Jonathan, 18, 185, 188–89
kreasi baru, xi, xxvii, xxx, xxxin4, 2–3, 7–8, 25, 42, 56, 62, 71, 78, 80–82, 87–89, 92–93, 97, 129, 135–36, 141, 154–55, 161, 163, 171–73, 177, 180, 183, 202–03, 209, 213, 242
Kridha Beksa Wirama, 52
Kussudiardjo, Bagong, 34
Kuta, xxix, 9, 84, 99, 137, 168

Laksmi, Ni Desak Madé Suarti, 71, 143
Lebur Seketi, 114, 203
Lekesan, xii, 97, 162–63
LEKRA, 33, 57–58, 83, 90, 243 (*see also* PKI, communism)
lelambatan, 25, 92, 119, 120, 136, 179–80, 242, 243
Listibiya, 59, 72, 243
literacy, 50 (*see also* colonialism)
LKN, 57–59, 76, 243
Loceng, I Wayan, 69
Lotring, I Wayan, 57n9, 92n12, 127n26, 128, 174, 176, 178n11

Maceda, José, 11n8, 29, 34, 128, 188
Majapahit, xxx, 22–24, 61, 71, 74, 98, 101–02, 146, 162, 243
Manifes Kebudayaan, 58
Manik, I Gede, 128, 130n29, 182
Manik, Liberty, 29, 53–54, 58, 87n5, 91n9
Markedness, 139, 151–52
Mas, Tjokorda Agung, 34, 36
McPhee, Colin, xxii, 16, 18, 20n11, 26, 28, 37, 52, 122, 124, 127, 155n14, 163, 166–67, 178n11, 188n15, 216, 218, 228

Mead, Margaret, xxii, 16–18, 38n49, 76n28, 123, 127, 222, 228
Megawati, Sukarnoputri, 78n30, 84–85, 95, 243
Miller, Christopher, 5
minimalism, 48, 71, 86, 97, 156, 221
misunderstanding (as creative), 211–14
mode. *See* intonation
moderen (development of), xxiii, xxiv, 3–4, 8, 17, 48–49, 51, 52, 62, 68, 69, 71, 73, 74, 76 86, 101, 108, 124, 164, 213 (*see also* tradisi)
modernism, 11–12, 15, 26–28, 32, 35, 41, 48, 51, 54, 71, 225, 230
musical (in Indonesia), 28–30
Moha, xii, 82–85, 162–63
multiculturalism, 95, 97–100, 104, 155, 230–31
musik kontemporer, critique of, xxix, 68, 163
musik nusantara, 56–57, 94, 162

New Order
cultural policy, 31, 37, 48, 58–62, 64, 68–70, 243
emergence of, 57–59 (*see also* coup, Suharto)
Ngendon, I Ketut, 26, 45
niskala, 24, 38n49, 39, 76n27, 126
notation, xxx, 4, 53, 97, 112, 138–145
critique of, 166–168

Odalan Bali, 227–230, 236–37 (*see also* Cudamani)
Old Order
cultural policy, 31, 55–57, 60, 75, 98, 100–01, 113, 243
dissolution of, 57–58 (*see also* coup, Sukarno)
ombak xiii, 97, 112n2, 142, 165–66, 168–85, 243
as heuristic, 191–92
organicism, 6–7, 60
otonomi daerah, 85, 96, 243

Pané, Armijn, 72
pangider buana, 115–16, 142, 191, 243
pangus, xii, 110, 114, 121
Pasaribu, Amir, 28–29, 42, 53, 54, 91n9
Pasaribu, Ben, 42, 80n34, 126
Pastika, Mangku, 99–100
pathet. *See* intonation
Peirce, C.S., 194, 196–97

pelestarian, 37–38, 73 (*see also* New Order, cultural policy)
pembangunan. *See* development
Penggak Men Mersi, 107n34, 108
penggalian, 69–70, 73 (*see also* New Order, cultural policy)
Pengosekan, 43, 158–59, 215, 227–28
pergerakan, 25, 53
Pinara Tunggah, 141, 156–57
PKB (*Pesta Kesenian Bali*). *See* Bali Arts Festival
PKI (*Partai Komunis Indonesia*), xi, 32, 35n42, 57–59, 243 (*see also* communism, coup)
PKM (*Pekan Komponis Muda*), xii, 65, 70, 80, 91, 97, 127, 162, 243 (*see also*, Hardjana, Suka)
PNI (*Partai Nasional Indonesia*), 58, 243
Poedjangga Baroe, 53 (*see also* polemik kebudayaan)
polemik kebudayaan, 53–56, 60, 72, 223, 238
politics (in art), 103–07
pollution, xxii, 61–62
popular / serious divide, 78, 89–91
popular music, 66, 69, 89–92n11, 100, 103, 137, 197
post traumatic stress syndrome (*see also* communism, New Order, violence), 59
postmodernism, 86, 120
Prabowo, Tony, 29
Prakempa, 109, 115–18, 146, 243
Puspayoga, A. A., 99, 108n35

qawwali music, 161–62, 225

Raden, Franki (Notosudirdjo), 2, 29, 42n55, 54
radio, xxv (*see also* RRI), 28–29, 32–33, 57, 68, 103, 136
Raharjo, Sapto, 42, 90n7
Rai, I Wayan, 105–07, 131, 204
rasa, 30, 92, 110, 119, 121–22, 147–48, 173, 184, 199n7, 237, 243
recital. *See* ujian
recording technology, xxx, 33, 63, 89, 107, 130–31, 136–38 (*see also* computer, Fruity Loops)
religion (*agama*), xii, xxx, 18n9, 21, 23–25, 30, 38, 48, 50, 54, 56, 59–60, 64, 74, 78–79, 86, 93–96, 98–99n22, 100, 102–103, 111, 116, 122n21, 161, 186n12, 191, 230 (*see also* fundamentalism)
Rembang, I Nyoman, 56n8, 76, 112, 119n17, 120, 139, 146, 168
Rendra, 104
Rockefeller, Foundation, 15, 32–37, 220, 222, 224–25, 233
Roeme (Ruma), I Wayan, 53
Roesli, Harry, 104
RRI (*Radio Republik Indonesia*), 29, 33n34, 57, 103n26, 136 (*see also* radio)
rwa bhineda, 146, 191

Sadra, I Wayan, xii-xiii, xxvii, xxix, 2–3, 8n4, 30–31, 35–36, 57n10, 73, 78n31, 79n32, 83, 86n4, 87–90, 93, 96n17, 103–05, 107n33, 111, 114–15, 126–28, 130–31, 136n36, 137, 140, 155n15, 162, 187, 200–01, 219–20, 225–26, 239, 240
Salju, 135–36, 184–95, 202, 215
sanggar, xxivn1, 4–5, 84, 87, 94n15, 104, 107–08, 115, 132, 145, 222, 241, 244
Santa Claus is Coming to Town, xiii, 210–11
Sardono, 26n24, 30n31, 36n43, 126
Sasak, 23, 97–99, 161, 163
Saussure, Ferdinand, 195–96
sekala, 24, 39, 76n27
semiotics, 23, 91, 135, 194–96, 198, 202, 211, 236, 238
sendratari, 35, 60, 147
seni. *See* art
sequencing, 138, 140, 174 (*see also* computer, Fruity Loops)
Serat Centhini, 72
Sidia, I Madé, 19, 63–64, 71n22
Singapadu, 74, 154
Sinti, I Wayan, xiii, 69, 112n2, 133n35, 146–47, 149–50, 163, 204
Sjukur, Slamet Abdul, 29, 88, 115
skeuomorph, 154–55, 228
social realism, 58, 163n21 (*see also* communism)
Sono Seni ensemble, xxix, 30, 100
space
 Balinese concepts of, 8–10, 23, 24, 26, 49, 55, 69, 71, 75–76, 86, 94
 representation of in Balinese music, 12, 15, 24, 139, 151, 164, 238
Sperber, Daniel, 15, 44–45, 194, 196, 211

Spies, Walter, 16, 25–26, 37, 218, 227
spirituality, 55, 225n16, 230
stambul, 25, 51, 53, 57, 219n5
STSI. *See* conservatory
Suanda, I Ketut, xii, 43, 107n34, 114, 121, 125–26, 148n7, 153, 159
Suardana, I Kadek, 38, 87, 102, 104, 107, 108n35, 116n10, 138, 149, 205, 222, 237n3
Subandi, I Madé, xi, xii, 3–5, 7, 9, 11, 19–20, 60, 63, 67, 71, 76, 78, 80, 96n17, 102, 107n34, 108, 125n23, 131, 133, 148n7, 154, 159–60, 193, 238, 241
subjectivity, 71, 98, 122–125, 128, 185, 191–92, 238
Sudarta, I Gusti Putu, xi, xii-xiii, 19–20, 52, 59, 62–63, 75, 78, 93–94, 96, 99, 103, 122, 161–62, 210, 213, 225
Sudirana, I Wayan, xiii, 79, 92, 93n14, 102, 154, 183, 207, 209
Suharto, xxvii, 32, 37, 57n10, 58–59, 78n30, 82–84, 86, 107, 127, 243 (*see also* New Order)
Sukarno, 32, 55–58, 104n104, 107, 221, 243 (*see also* Old Order)
Sukawati, xxv, 68n18, 69, 103, 155n16
Sukerta, Pande Madé, xi, xii, 3n1, 35–36, 43, 79n32, 92n11, 105n30, 112n5, 198, 209
Sumarsam, 27, 54, 112, 148n9
Surrealism, 42, 45
Surya Kanta, 51–53, 99

Tagore, Rabindranath (*see also* Theosophy), 25, 50
taiko, 130, 156, 159
Tajen, 236–37 (*see also* cockfight)
Taman Siswa, 50, 53, 106, 112
Tanah Lot, 95
tari. *See* dance.
Taymor, Julie, 63, 104, 222
Teja, Agus, xiii, 67, 81n36, 102, 125n23, 126,131, 137, 149–50, 161, 193
temporality
 mundane, 2, 8–9, 24–25, 64, 185–92, 209, 219
 musical, 8–9, 25, 152, 166–76
Tenzer, Michael, 2, 11n8, 29, 42n54, 75n26, 104n28, 111n1, 118n15, 124, 128n27, 136, 153–54, 156, 167, 169n6, 170, 178, 184, 186n14, 196, 216

téori
 of composition, xii, 2, 7, 109, 110–13, 116, 118, 140, 146, 148, 239
 resistance against, 109, 113–15
terrorism, xxvi, 84–85, 234, 236 (*see also* bombing)
themes (*tema*), xii, 30, 80, 109, 115
Theosophy, 48, 94 (*see also* Tagore, Rabindranath)
TIM (*Taman Ismail Marzuki*), 79–80
Tisna, Anak Agung Panji, 53
topics (musical), 153–63
tourism, xii, xxix, 8, 9, 12, 17, 40, 48, 50, 58, 61, 63–68, 70, 71, 84–86, 99, 103, 116, 120, 132n33, 156, 225n16
tradisi, xi, xii, xxiii, xxiv, xxix, xxx, 3, 8, 9, 16–17, 19, 37, 47–49, 51–52, 66, 74, 118, 127–29, 227, 238–39
 critique of, 68, 72–73, 105, 109, 133
 development of, 62, 68–72, 75–76, 78, 80, 87–88, 90, 92, 96, 117
 musical structure in, 170–72, 175–76, 178–83
 musical topics, 139, 142, 147, 154–55
 semiotics of, 198
tri-angga, 113–14, 244
Trimbat, 86, 116n11, 142–43, 158–60, 187
tuning. *See* intonation.

UCLA, 35, 220, 224
ujian (recital), xxvi, 62, 81–83, 93–94, 114, 116, 120, 125n23, 130, 159, 236n1, 237n3, 244 (*see also* conservatory)
UNESCO, 131–33, 221, 225
urbanization, 48, 73–75, 84
USIS (United States Information Service), 32, 220–222

venues (for *musik kontemporer*), 12, 64, 74, 125, 134–35, 165, 225–26 (*see also* GEOKS, Bali Arts Festival)
violence, xxvi, 58–60, 69, 84, 94, 232 (*see also* New Order, emergence of, terrorism, coup)
virus, as a musical concept, 43–44, 149, 155–56, 193, 213

Wahid, Abdurrahman, 85, 243
wayang kontemporer, 63 (*see also* Kidung Mpu Tantular)

wayang kulit, 25, 53, 94, 110, 123, 126, 222 (*see also* dalang)
Widnyana, Ida Bagus Gede, xii-xiii, 43, 86, 96n17, 125, 140n2, 142–44, 158, 160, 173, 184, 191, 207–08, 210–11, 213–14
Wijaya, Putu, 58, 104
Wilson, Robert, 221, 232
Windha, I Nyoman, xii, 74, 77, 79, 87, 89–90, 97, 99, 121–22, 125, 129, 133, 136, 143, 149, 155n16, 159, 163, 220
WIPO (World Intellectual Property Organization), 131–32
Wirjasutha, 53

world music (*world musik*)
  history of, 101
  in Indonesia, 11–12, 89, 100–01, 103, 137
Yampolsky, Philip, 37
Yudane, I Wayan Gede, xi-xiii, xxii, xxvi-xxix, 29, 66, 68, 72, 80–81, 86, 90n7, 96n17, 103, 105, 109, 114–15, 121, 123–24, 126, 130–31, 137–38, 140, 143–44, 159, 168, 202–03, 239
Yudhoyono, Bambang, 95, 243

Ziporyn, Evan, 232–233

RADICAL TRADITIONS